The GREAT PORT CITIES OF ASIA

IN HISTORY

First published in 2024 by

Talisman Publishing Pte Ltd
52 Genting Lane #06-05
Ruby Land Complex 1
Singapore 349560
talisman@apdsing.com

www.talismanpublishing.com

Publisher
Ian Pringle

Designer
Stephy Chee

Studio Manager
Janice Ng

General Editor
Zhang Ruihe

ISBN 978-981-18-8973-8

The GREAT PORT CITIES OF ASIA

IN HISTORY

KENNIE TING

TALISMAN

CONTENTS

Cauchin al Cauncinchina

I Tintosa
Sarlaon
Penin
I Ainam
Philippine

LUCO
Suday
Ilocos
Lantam
Amari
Bagarsi
Moro Hermoso
Putados
INSULAE
NIA
IN
SULA
PHILIP.
PINAE.
P.de Mantilon
Ancon triste
G. de Matilacombre
Pondam
Mondato
Parialle
del spirito santo
I de Cobos
Francisco Gomes
Ilhas del Primeiro
Suygidero
ARCI
Abo camucho Princeo

Dos Tavaquero
Pulo S. Polo
Polo Cotan
Pracel
P.de Manilha
P. de Manilha

Lantum

Pde Alau
data

Mindau
Mindoan

Saylou

Panay

I Caburas
Bosrote
I Abuyo
Passge de S. Clara

LAGUS
S. LA

Pulo Camboi
P. de Camboia

P. Catubi

Pulo Citi
Pulo candor
Pulo bube

Tao

Is. dos ladrones
Pulo Fisan
I de S. Maria

Palon
Cavango

ZARI.

Calamianes insula quae te bicta Palon

Trapit Perala

MINDAO
NAO B
G. de Rosarri
cam

Pde Malaqa

I de S. Jonnes
A. de Resurre cam
C. de Bicay
I de Palmeras

Natura

Borneo
Tamnas Iutao
R. de Burule
Malano
Puchavarao
Tamenaeririn
Tamaratos

INSULA

BORNEO

Lave, donde foy Don Manuel de Lima

Arabio

Mon. Praeem

Bacana

S. Michel
Pracel
S. Clara

Candonir
Tagima
Solor

Candinao
Catungo al Sarangan
I de Talaon
Infl de Talay

Mon.
Terrenate

I de Rao

S. Soana
I de Sagiri

Baptuaom

Do. Mou

MOLVCO
Banggica
Manado

GILOLO
INSULAE

I de Dai
Camafo
Maya
Dos G

Succadana ubi adamantes inveniuntur
matchri

Paco

Cabuco
BES

GILOLO
Battachina

Bintan

Bander Lave

Pulo puo Pulo tuio
C. de Mopi
Crimata Surato Pangim
Chinabato

Tisso
Tapoam
Batjos
Ca. pao Asacora
Calamba

Cramata
Suroto
Panangan
Blacana

CE
INSULAE

Saies
Momanias
Curicuri
Mandar
Tobucco
Ciantus
Mahlf
Cam

Supa
Aielato

Pulo al Colla

Sinomao

Burro

I Cenao
Celan

I Cenao Celan
Pulo Gure
Buda

Ceiham

Thomas Cunily

Nisaira
P. Leboe

Agapaos
Tuben

Planet

Burro
Batumbar

Lucapinha

Antonio Pulo

Chyrmaon Java
I Madura

I de S. Mattheo

I de S. Mattheo

Batolaia

Batura

Terra.alta

quae dicitur MAIOR

I Bali

al
Cambab

Cambaba insula nonnullis Iava dicitur

Aram

Partilo insula

Timor

De situ Ia Iaria, est Geographorum sentui ex Marci Pauli Veneti Lib aliqui Sumatram ipsi Paulo Venesse situ, tum ex alijs circumstantijs cu Iavem Minorem dici volunt Nas e

Hic Francisc
Dra. appull.

Foreword

by Sir Malcolm Jack
Royal Asiatic Society, London

❦

Anyone familiar with Kennie Ting's *The Romance of the Grand Tour: 100 Years of Travel in South East Asia* will approach his new book, *The Great Port Cities of Asia: In History*, with a sense of excited anticipation. They will not be disappointed. The unifying thread behind what is an extensive and graphic tour of a large region of the world is Ting's methodology, explained clearly in his introduction. There he tells his reader that he intends to depart from the traditional terrestrial approach of historians, depicting Asian empires as circumscribed cultural entities, and instead to adopt a networked approach, emphasising the interconnectedness of the many civilisations which characterise the vast region. In his own words: 'empires and civilisations in Asia have never existed in isolation. Rather, they have always, by way of trade, conquest and diplomacy, connected, interacted with and mutually enriched each other.'

While in *The Romance of the Grand Tour*, Ting restricted his exploration of his chosen port cities to a hundred years, in this new work the chronological range is much more ambitious. In a series of six, separate but interconnected parts, we are taken as far back as the first millennium CE to the ancient entrepôts of Kedah on the Malay Peninsula and Oc Eo in Funan. Then we follow Tang missions from China to Japan with observations on Tang poetry *en route*. The kingdom of Chola on the Indian south coast; the mysteries of Srivijaya follow. Much later on, we travel East of Suez with European traders to Colombo, Hong Kong and distant Shanghai.

The main impetus for these contacts was trade and commerce. Merchants and mariners linked the peoples of East Africa, the Middle East and India. In the earlier periods, these were primarily Muslim traders but the ports they inhabited were a multicultural mix of peoples of many ethnicities and different religious and language groups. Later, Europeans arrived – at first less intent on imperial acquisition than on setting up useful staging posts for commercial enterprise in India and the Far East, through sea routes via the Cape of Good Hope. The port cities themselves became cosmopolitan centres where people adapted foreign cultures to their own, advancing the progress of their indigenous civilisations. Studying them reveals the constant 'ebb and flow' of practices and ideas across the entire region.

Ting's book is an encyclopaedic history and description of sixty ports in Asia spanning two millennia. Lavishly illustrated with cultural artefacts and architectural gems such as the Nanyang shophouses in Penang, it also tells the story of the individual historical, as well as fictional, characters involved in the development of the port cities. These protagonists add a colourful sub-theme to the description of the locations and the arts and crafts, many imported, to be found in maritime centres across the region. Set in Asia, the book necessarily also goes into detail about food, showing how, for example, Chinese taste infiltrated and influenced Japanese cuisine through trade in Nagasaki.

The Great Port Cities of Asia: In History is more than a richly informed history of Asian port cities. It is an evocative guide, written in a highly readable style, to the kaleidoscope of cultures to be found in this vast region. For this reason, it will appeal as much to the reader with a general interest in Asia and its civilisations, as to the scholar of the last two millennia of its commercial history.

PAGE VI: *Map of the East Indies* (detail). Jodocus Hondius. Amsterdam, 1606.

OPPOSITE PAGE: *Dutchman with a Servant* (detail). Attributed to Kawahara Keiga. Japan, Edo Period, early 19th century. Hanging scroll; ink and colour on silk. 50.2 x 25.1 cm. Gift of Florence and Herbert Irving, 2015. Collection of the Metropolitan Museum of Art.

Introduction

❧

"Go, take ten thousand of our race / Well trained in lore of time and place, / And search the eastern region; through / Groves, woods and hills thy way pursue. / [...] / Go where the silken tissue shines, / Go to the land of silver mines. / Visit each isle and mountain steep / And city circled by the deep, / And distant villages that high / About the peaks of Mandar lie. / Speed over Yavadwipa's land, / And see Mount Sisir proudly stand..."

— Valmiki, 5th to 1st century BCE. *The Ramayana.*[1]

"Tripitaka said, 'Sun Wukong, tell me... when will we reach our destination?' Monkey replied, 'You may walk from when you are young till you grow old, and when you are old till you become young again; and even after repeating this cycle of youth and old age a thousand times, you might still not reach your destination. But if you see the true nature of all things around you, and cultivate stillness in your mind, therein lies the path to the Holy Mountain.'"

— Wu Cheng'en, 16th century CE. *Journey to the West.*[2]

A history of Asia is often told by way of accounts of the rise and fall of its great empires: the Chinese, the Indian, the Persian, the Arab, the Southeast Asian and more; or, more specifically, the Tang, the Mughal, the Safavid, the Abbasid, the Khmer, and many others. The empires highlighted by historians are almost invariably terrestrial. They are held to be the crucibles of culture; the hearts of civilisation. And the progression of time and history on the continent is made out to be the relentless succession of empire after empire, all of them occupying their own proper geographical region, negotiating the boundaries between each other through conflict and diplomacy, but remaining more or less in their specific parts of the continent for millennia.

There is a sense of timelessness and stasis in this method of presenting Asia as a collection of immovable, geographically-circumscribed cultural entities; as though change was anathema to the exotic, oriental mindset, only to be brought to this continent when the Europeans came in the 1500s and disrupted these age-old, unchanging ways with their foreign modernity. But the fact is, empires and civilisations in Asia have never

OPPOSITE PAGE:
Painting of a Street in Bombay. William Simpson. Bombay, 1862. Pencil and watercolour on paper, 50.5 x 35.5 cm. Collection of the Asian Civilisations Museum.

The Monk Xuanzang. Unknown artist. Japan, Kamakura period, 14th century. Colour on silk, 135.1 x 59.9 cm. Collection of the Tokyo National Museum.

existed in isolation. Rather, they have always, by way of trade, conquest and diplomacy, connected, interacted with and mutually enriched each other.

A networked approach to exploring Asian history in the context of world history has only recently gained currency. Academics have begun to re-examine history through the lens of trade, using the phenomenon of the historic Silk Roads as a frame by which to re-interpret global affairs, historical and current. The land-based Silk Roads have been better-researched and used to figure more prominently in popular consciousness. But there were maritime Silk Roads as well – recent archaeological discoveries have since confirmed the existence of oceanic trading routes where goods from China were taken across vast distances, crossing Southeast Asia to the Middle East, even while camels and caravans were plying the deserts and steppes of Central Asia.

Alongside Silk Roads studies is a burgeoning field of Indian Ocean studies, wherein the spotlight is thrown on the vast expanse of water that sits at the heart of the Asian continent. Historically, much more attention has been paid to trade across the Atlantic and even the Pacific Ocean, primarily because the most recent, and thus best-preserved, artefacts and documents pertaining to global trade are in relation to European trade across the world. After all, the Europeans dominated global trade for some 400 years, up until most recently.

Trade across the Indian Ocean, however, is far older, having existed long before our Common Era. For millennia, merchants and mariners have plied the waters here, braving and mastering monsoon winds in their pursuit of glory and opportunity across epic distances. The merchants and the monsoon winds, or *mausam*, in local parlance, linked the peoples and cities along the coasts of East Africa, the Middle East and India in a recognisably Indian Ocean merchant culture, characterised by a distinctly Muslim merchant class co-existing with multicultural, multi-faith local communities. Communities of these Muslim seafaring merchants established themselves as far east as in China, and at every major port city en route.

The maritime Silk Road and Indian Ocean approaches are, in effect, approaches through which history is explored from the perspective of the ocean. From that perspective, history in Asia is recast in a different light: as a timeless ebb and flow of peoples, goods, cultures and ideas across vast expanses. Empires are no longer static, monolithic, monocultural blocs, but are instead fluid and dynamic, changing and shifting as they are shaped through trade and encounter with other cultures, or rather, with a diversity of other cultures. Against this context of trade and the oceans, port cities thus take on a much greater significance than ever before.

Port cities get short shrift in history books, primarily because they often sit at the periphery of terrestrial empires, straddling both land and water while looking like nothing the imperial centre would be familiar or comfortable with. In fact, the imperial centre has frequently viewed port cities as either eccentric or barbaric places, full of strange and undesirable ideas and people, best relegated to the margins, as far away from the capital and from official history as possible.

As the name suggests, port cities are urban agglomerations of people, economy and culture that grow around a port, and which have, as their primary (though by no means only) mode of subsistence, trade. They are critical nodes in the global network of trade and migration, and also feature in histories of conquest and colonisation. A history of maritime trade and commerce in Asia is, essentially, also a history of the many port cities that have played a key role in facilitating and furthering this trade and conquest, and that have grown rich and powerful as a result.

Certainly, the pre-eminent role of the port city in recent historical and contemporary global trade is well-acknowledged. Singapore, Shanghai, Mumbai and Hong Kong are port cities that have remained unchallenged for more than a century, in terms of their dominance of global commerce. But there are far older, pre-colonial equivalents: the likes of Melaka, Aden, Quanzhou, Khambhat (Cambay). And even further back in time: Nagapattinam, Basra, Guangzhou (Canton), Palembang. These ports dominated the global economy of their time. Many have since seen their glory fade away, but some are still powerhouses to be reckoned with today.

Because port cities are open to trade and migration, they are points of contact between the domestic and the foreign. They allow for the inward flow of foreign peoples, cultures and ideas from faraway places, whether peacefully or forcibly; these invariably encounter and irrevocably change local cultures. Port cities also allow for local peoples, cultures and ideas to venture outward in search of new, and often forbidden, vistas.

The result of this to-ing and fro-ing, of encounter and blending, is that more often than not, port cities evolve and boast a unique and colourful appearance. A common defining trait of all Asian port cities is the cosmopolitan, hybrid, multicultural, multi-faith nature of their societies and urban landscapes – in stark contrast to inland empires, which perceive themselves to be culturally "pure". This cosmopolitanism is reflected in the eclectic architecture of port cities, as well as in their material cultures (dress, furniture, decorative arts) and their ways of living (food, faith, languages). It is also reflected in the presence of mixed-race, or creole, communities in these cities, contributing to the diversity of foreign peoples from "barbaric" lands.

Because they are cosmopolitan sites of cultural contact and mixing, port cities are therefore often crucibles of innovation and creativity. The story of Asia's development and progress, whether economic, cultural, social or political, is a story of how new ideas, ideologies, technologies and ways of living were either imported by way of port cities, or invented in them.

Port city societies grow immensely wealthy from trade, and wealth from commerce is invested into an increasingly sophisticated lifestyle. New technologies and consumer products necessarily emerge to cater to constantly-evolving private demand and the ever-shifting needs of the market. Port cities in Asia were showcases for the latest technologies from the European imperium. Singapore, Batavia (Jakarta) and Manila, for example, had electric trams and street lighting very soon after London, Amsterdam and Madrid. Port cities were also showcases for the latest fashions: the modern *kebaya* in the ports of Malaysia and Indonesia, for example, or the *qipao* in 1930s Shanghai and everywhere there are Chinese diaspora communities today. Both the *qipao* and *kebaya* were the products of cultural mixing, blending European tailoring and contemporary silhouettes with Asian styles of dress and textile-making.

Innovation is not necessarily a recent phenomenon, brought on by Europeans establishing themselves in the region. Asian port cities have also been innovating on their own for centuries. Long before Europeans

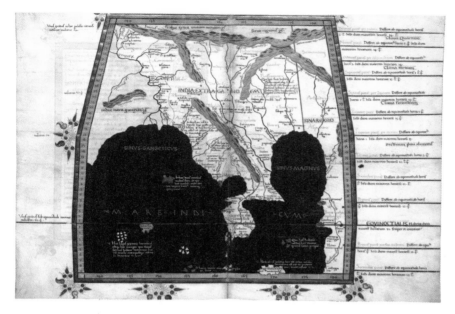

The 11th Asian Map:
The Indian Ocean
(Mare Indicum).
Nicolaus Germanus.
Germany, 1467.
This map is copied
from Ptolemy's
2nd century Greek
work, Cosmographia,
translated into Latin
by Jacobus Angelus.
The Malay Peninsula,
marked Aurea
Chersonesus ("Golden
Chersonese"), is at
centre right. Ink and
colour on parchment,
42 x 57 cm. Collection
of the National Library
of Poland.

mastered the technology, Arab shipbuilders had already developed sturdy ocean-going vessels able to travel immense distances. In China, sophisticated logistics and supply-chain systems had already emerged to manage the transport of Chinese ceramics, themselves a product of innovation and ingenuity, from the interior to far-flung places, in response to global demand.

Newness was, and still is, a defining characteristic of port cities. It can be argued that port cities have played an enormous though under-appreciated role in the development and progress of human civilisation, because it is through them that change has been precipitated and civilisations have embraced novel ways of subsisting and of imagining themselves. Which is why it is time to tell a tale of Asia, from the perspective of its cosmopolitan port cities.

Our journey takes us through 60 port cities across maritime Asia. At the heart of this vast region is the Indian Ocean, the largest water-body in the region and certainly its most important. Abutting this ocean are two smaller water-bodies, the Red Sea and the Persian Gulf, whose trade is inextricable from that of the larger ocean and thus have to be taken as one and the same.

East of the Indian Ocean sits the Southeast Asian mainland and archipelago, with its endless coastline and multiple seas. For millennia, Southeast Asia has been a crossroads of trade between the Indian Ocean world and China. The region has been referred to by various names: Suvarnabhumi ("Land of Gold") in Sanskrit, Nanyang ("Southern Ocean") in Chinese, or the East Indies by the Europeans.

Further east lies the South China Sea, extending to the East China Sea and the Sea of Japan. China's place is unchallenged here. The Middle Kingdom's port cities have traditionally been the termini of trade in Asia, their goods dominating world trade since antiquity. The story of trade has been inexorably one of merchant vessels seeking to establish trading routes across the oceans to China, in order that they may transport silks, porcelains and other luxuries back to their homelands to be sold for immense profits.

Of course, there were other important luxury goods traded across the oceans. Indian textiles were prized for their beauty and the sophistication of weaving techniques used to make them; these textiles lubricated trade and diplomacy, and often stood as a form of currency where there was none. Spices, from India too, but also from Southeast Asia, were another rare and highly sought-after good, shipped in large quantities to China and the Middle East, to be sent onward to Europe. It was spices that lured Europeans eastward, precipitating their violent entry into maritime Asia.

Certain liberties are taken in our journey with regards to geography. A very small number of the port cities we shall visit sits beyond what is geographically part of Asia. For example, we will take a slight detour to the Swahili Coast in East Africa, but only insofar as ports there were intricately enmeshed within networks of trade in the Indian Ocean, and betray significant Asian influence in their cultural make-up. Conversely, the journey does not cover Asian port cities that sit along other water bodies not abutting the Indian Ocean. For example, Middle Eastern ports on the Mediterranean, such as Beirut, Jaffa and Istanbul, do not feature in this narrative as they belong more appropriately to the sphere of Europe-Africa trade in the Mediterranean.

In geographical scope then, our journey is wide-ranging, taking us as far south and west as Cape Town, just north of the Cape of Good Hope in South Africa, which has long held special significance for sailors; to as far north and east as Tokyo. This is the "Asia" circumscribed by our journey, which is by no means *Asia* as we conventionally know it. But then again, *Asia* itself, as a continent and a concept, is a contemporary

invention. Up until very recently, none of
the peoples here saw themselves as *Asian*.
Rather, they were part of fluid, porous,
overlapping spheres of culture in a world of
networks and flows.

The timeframe our journey takes in is
just as sweeping as its geography. We reach
back some 2000 years to great port cities
of late antiquity and forward to those of
the present. This is to illustrate that the

Dhows docked
at Dubai Creek.
Despite the city's
rapid urbanisation,
these trading vessels
continue to ply the
historic waterway, as
they have done for
more than a century.

Asian port city is a timeless phenomenon: the great port cities of today
are not very different, in essence, from their counterparts a thousand
years ago.

As we stop and sojourn at each of the port cities, we will be recounting
the sights and sounds in these climes both foreign and familiar in turn.
In doing so, we would be following in the footsteps of generations of
itinerant explorers and travellers who, since antiquity, have documented
their journeys and experiences in travel journals.

Different words are used to refer to travel accounts in different
traditions. The Greeks referred to these travel journals as *periplus*, or
"wanderings". The Arabs referred to theirs as *rihlah* and the Chinese, as
youji. Today, *rihlahs* belong within the larger literary category of travel
literature; and the writer-wanderers of yore would probably be considered
early manifestations of the contemporary travel writer.

An expansive dramatis personae of travellers and travel writers past
and present makes an appearance in these pages. Likewise, to add colour
to the narrative, I make frequent reference to a full range of *rihlah* from
across the ages. There are early swashbuckling tales, including "The
Story of Sindbad of the Sea", incorporated in *The Arabian Nights*; and
the Chinese novel, *Journey to the West*, based on an actual pilgrimage
to India undertaken by Chinese monk, Xuanzang, in the Tang dynasty.
There are also meticulously-observed eyewitness accounts by famous
explorers like Ibn Battutah and Marco Polo, and many others no less
important, such as Tomé Pires, Isabella Bird and Ma Huan, scribe to the
great Chinese admiral, Zheng He. And finally, there are works by authors
of the 20th century: among them, Somerset Maugham, Graham Greene,
Austin Coates, and Elizabeth Gilbert.

Aside from travel accounts and the occasional work of fiction, this
rihlah also references a very large corpus of research in a wide-ranging

variety of fields: art, archaeology, architecture, anthropology, history, sociology, urban studies, political science, fashion studies, popular culture, and more. It is thus not only a journey through time and space, but also an exploration of ideas, undertaken in the company of the many contemporary thinkers, academics, curators and experts from whom these ideas originate.

I have been deeply inspired by the great minds who have put pen and intellect to the subject of Asian port cities, and I have always dreamt of being able to survey, savour and curate this trove of academic research, as I have done in this book. The intent is to introduce this scholarly wisdom to a mass audience, presenting the great port cities of Asia in a brand new light, refracted through the prism of experience, observation and extensive reading.

The epic trajectory of our wanderings thus plotted on a map both literal and metaphorical, we are now ready to step aboard our vessel: a latter-day, time-travelling Indian Ocean dhow built for comfort and endurance. The southwest monsoon, the *mausam*, is strong, and we must set sail eastward and back in time, to seek trade, glory and adventure.

峡希的折　暹羅國　峡高刺辛

高墨荅城
僉㐀其害官
鳥里舍塔
四指
三角
立歌

骨八丹
佛恩洞
得法難
盆那礁
微迷哈哈
白礁
四指
一角

加密丹
指四
番荅里納
古里國

龍牙葛
利都至俱
電沙八
丹
短㫈蛮
三指角
柯枝國

矣都里潘
加加潘
加平年勝

北辰指

木兒立哈必兒
黑兒
三指角
一角
呵那思刺
哈甫泥
角四指
北辰指
抺兒幹別
木骨都束

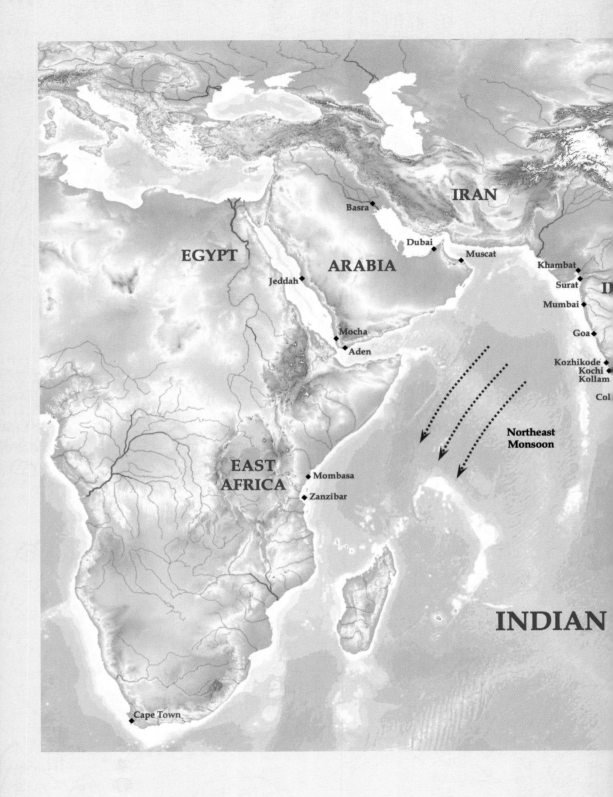

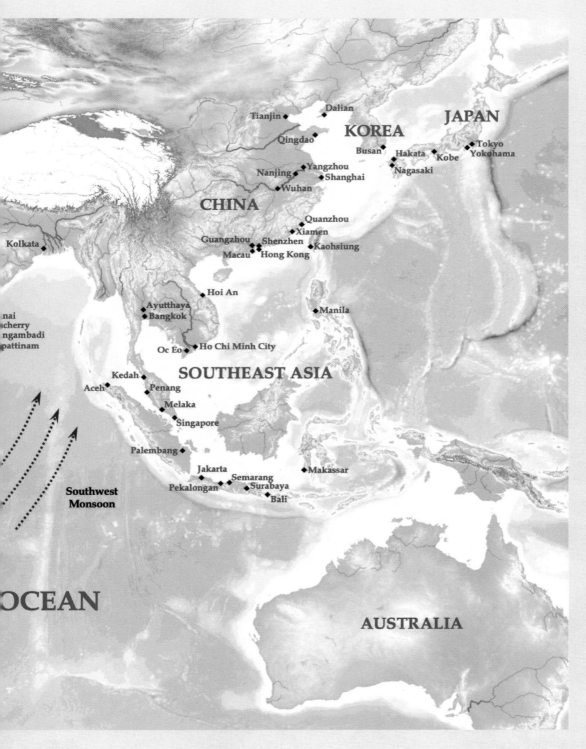

Map of Asia and the Indian Ocean world, with port cities featured on our journey.

PART
I

OF SAILORS
AND
SHIPWRECKS

1st Millennium CE

1. Kedah & Oc Eo
Ancient Entrepôts of Southeast Asia

> "Of Buddhagupta the great sea-captain, resident (?) of Raktamṛttika . . . in every manner, in all cases, absolutely, . . . all . . ., may the voyages be successful!"
>
> — Inscription on the Mahanavika Buddhagupta Stele, 6th century. Collection of the Indian Museum, Kolkata.[1]

In the permanent galleries of Singapore's Asian Civilisations Museum, there is a bronze figurine of the Buddha that hints at ancient maritime links between India and Southeast Asia. The figurine is small but exquisitely cast: the Buddha is depicted with hip gently arched to the right, and right hand lowered to grant a blessing to pilgrims. He is barefoot and smiles serenely; the ends of his robe are draped gently over a raised left arm. His pose is relaxed, languid; his body is sculpted with a nod towards realism.

One's immediate impression is that this is the work of an Indian master craftsman, so closely does the style of this bronze figurine recall that of Buddhist statues during the Gupta Empire, considered a golden age in Indian civilisation. And indeed, the museum's own descriptions of the object note that the figurine most likely dates to sometime between the 5th to the 8th centuries. But they also note that the statue was found in today's Kedah state, to the north of the Malay Peninsula. In fact, scholars believe that the statue was made by a Southeast Asian artisan.

By the early centuries of the Common Era, Southeast Asia was a highly-Indianised region, with civilisations that were Hindu-Buddhist in nature. When and how exactly Buddhism and Hinduism came remains a question. Once, scholars believed in an aggressive Indian colonisation – swords, warships and all – in the pale recesses of antiquity. Now, most believe that the spread of Indian culture was far more complex and gradual, with merchants, Hindu Brahmins and Buddhist monks arriving in the course of centuries, and introducing their ancient faiths to new converts.

In classical Indian texts, Southeast Asia is known by various Sanskrit names, including Suvarnabhumi and Suvarnadwipa. Both names describe the region as a place of great wealth and splendour. The same texts also refer, enigmatically, to a place known as Kataha, which

OVERLEAF: *The Episode of the Whale*, illustration, in *Sinbad the Sailor & Other Stories from the Arabian Nights*. Edmund Dulac. London, 1914.

OPPOSITE PAGE: Bas relief in stone at Borobudur Temple, depicting a Southeast Asian sailing vessel with two tripod masts. Central Java, 9th century.

Buddha. Bujang Valley, Kedah, 5th – 8th century. Bronze, height 20.6 cm. Collection of the Asian Civilisations Museum.

archaeologists today believe is a reference to the ancient kingdom of Kedah.

In the 1830s and '40s, officials of the British East India Company uncovered the existence of a grand and ancient settlement in the Bujang Valley, on the southwestern coast of Kedah. Archaeological excavations of the site would begin in earnest in the 1940s, on the eve of World War II, and led by one Horace G. Quaritch Wales and his wife, Dorothy.

Together, they made extensive discoveries in the region. In fact, it was Dorothy who found the Buddha figurine in an earthenware jar, in a now-ruined Buddhist temple. The many brick structures the Waleses excavated in the Bujang Valley region were determined to be *candi*, or Indian-style Southeast Asian temples – representations, in architecture, of Mount Meru, the sacred mountain in Hindu tradition. The various ages of these structures suggested, to the Waleses, that the region had been continuously inhabited from the 3rd to the 14th centuries.

The *candi* in the Bujang Valley were, in general, modest in size. They were also randomly distributed across the region, rather than scrupulously planned according to a grand cosmic scheme. This randomness implied the lack of an imperial power, and the presence of an entrepôt port, home to communities of merchants dedicating temples to the gods in their good names. A wealth of foreign decorative material like Chinese ceramics, fragments of a Tang dynasty bronze mirror, turquoise-hued Persian earthenware and Arab glass shards, gave weight to the theory that a cosmopolitan port city – one of the earliest of its kind in Southeast Asia – had been located here.

With its strategic location at the northern entry-point to the Straits of Melaka, the Bujang Valley in ancient Kedah would have been the natural stopping point for ships from India. A merchant ship taking a straight-line course between Sri Lanka and Kedah would just miss the northern tip of the island of Sumatra. Arriving on the wings of the southwest monsoon between May and October, it would have sighted Kedah Peak (locally-known as Gunung Jerai) as it approached the coast.

There are few first-hand accounts of Kedah, though one thing is almost certain: it had red earth. Much of the coast of the Malay Peninsula has reddish soil, and there are multiple places in Malaysia named Tanah Merah ("red earth"). In 1834, an ancient stone stele was unearthed in Kedah boasting Buddhist inscriptions that till today remain the oldest such ever found in the region. The stele had been commissioned by a Captain Buddhagupta and dedicated to the Divinity in return for safe passage across the oceans. It referred to the captain's residence as Raktamrittika ("red earth" in Sanskrit).

The Chinese also referred to Kedah as Chitu (赤土 – "red earth").[2] The name was used in the 6th century *Sui Shu* ("History of the Sui dynasty"), and it could perhaps have been a transliteration: the name pronounced in the Hokkien dialect, which sounds closer to the Chinese spoken in the Sui and Tang periods, is *chia'taw*.[3] The relevant chapter in the *Sui Shu* notes that the soil of Chia'taw "was red-hued, hence its name". Situated in the Nanhai (南海 – "Southern Seas") region, 100 days of journeying were required to get there. Chia'taw's main city is described as being a splendid sight to behold, with formidable fortifications, and gates adorned with apsaras, bodhisattvas and mythical creatures from Hindu-Buddhist mythology.

Later in the 7th century (during the Tang dynasty), the Chinese monk, Yijing, sojourns in Kedah while on a journey to the west to study Buddhist scriptures. In his travelogue, he notes that Kedah was the principal stopover in Southeast Asia for travellers bound for India. Yijing refers to the local peoples of Kedah somewhat disparagingly as *kunlun* (昆仑): "dark-skinned barbarians" who were clad in sarongs and had bare feet. They were known for being expert sailors and navigators. In their sturdy sewn-plank vessels, which the Chinese called *kunlun bo* (舶), they dominated trade and travel in the Indian Ocean and South China Sea. These *kunlun* peoples were probably the Malays – the inhabitants of the vast island archipelago making up today's Malaysia, Indonesia and the Philippines. They were, and still are, peoples of the sea: masters of straits and ocean.

From Kedah, *kunlun bo* sailing north to China would have been obliged to stop in the lands of Funan, a far older civilisation located on the mainland, at the point where the Gulf of Thailand meets the South China Sea. Funan is thought to have existed from the 1st to the 7th centuries, and is known only by way of ancient Chinese records.

Map of peninsular Southeast Asia in the 7th century. Merchants travelling east from India would dock at Kedah, cross the isthmus of Kra, and board another *kunlun bo* for Funan. From Oc Eo, *kunlun bo* sailed to and from south China. To the south, Srivijaya held sway.

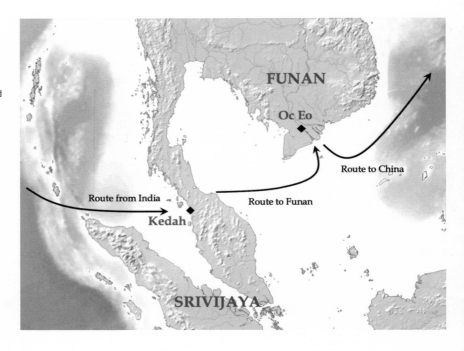

As early as the 3rd century, visiting Chinese merchant, Kang Tai, had been impressed by how sophisticated Funan was, noting in his *Accounts of Foreign States in Wu Times* that people there:

> "...live in walled cities, palaces and houses. They sow one year and harvest for three [...] Taxes are paid in gold, silver, pearls and perfumes [...] There are books and depositories of archives and other things [...]" [4]

The name "Funan" is itself Chinese in origin (扶南 – pronounced *hu-nam* in Hokkien). Some scholars believe it the Chinese transliteration of the Khmer word *phnom*, meaning "sacred mountain". Others believe the name to be a reference to Funan's status as a vassal state in the south, since the characters literally mean "uplifting the South". Certainly, Funan had a distinct privilege and advantage over Kedah: it was allowed to trade directly with China.

Despite its links to the Middle Kingdom, Funan, like Kedah, had a highly-Indianised, Hindu-Buddhist culture. Chinese texts recount that it was originally ruled by a beautiful princess who was the daughter of a *naga*, or magical sea serpent. A Brahmin priest, Kaundinya, travelling across the oceans from India, subjugates her with his magic bow and arrow. He then marries her and sires a line of kings who rule over the kingdom. Interestingly, this origin myth is replicated across many ancient cultures in Southeast Asia, and likely has roots in the actual crossing of Indian Brahmins and merchants and their marrying into local ruling families.

Funan was large and powerful. At its height it probably encompassed most of what is today's Cambodia, southern Vietnam, as well as parts of Thailand and Malaysia.

In 1944, archaeologist Louis Malleret of the École française d'Extrême-Orient began excavations at the fishing village of Oc Eo, situated in the vast plains of the Mekong Delta in southern Vietnam. He would uncover a wealth of artefacts that spoke to the existence of a prosperous and sophisticated civilisation existing here at the turn of the first millennium. His discoveries pointed towards Oc Eo being a major, cosmopolitan port city with trading networks that spanned the known globe at the time. Amongst objects excavated were Han dynasty Chinese bronzes, Buddhist statues from Gandhara and Kushan, Sassanid-Persian artefacts, exquisite, locally-made gold jewellery, and a great number of coins, including Roman ones.

Malleret concluded at the time that this location was likely to be Kattigara, a fabled Far Eastern city described in the early days of the Roman Empire as the port of the "Sinae", or Chinese. Today, Oc Eo is believed to have been the chief port of Funan. Like Kedah, it would have been an entrepôt: a transhipment point for goods bound for China from India, the Middle East and Southeast Asia; and for Chinese goods travelling to India and onward to Rome.

Oc Eo's size and location were extraordinary. Subsequent excavations by French and Vietnamese archaeologists established that it was vast: to this day, the largest ancient port settlement ever excavated in Southeast Asia. The city encompassed some 450 hectares and measured one and a half kilometres by three kilometres. It was surrounded by five rectangular moats and four city walls. More than 30 mounds, some with remains of brick buildings, have been found in its midst; these are likely to be the oldest brick structures built in Southeast Asia.[5]

Located at the foothills of Mount Ba The, Oc Eo sat some 25 kilometres from the coast. It lay at the heart of an ancient and sophisticated network of man-made canals that linked it directly to the sea as well as to the highlands up north. Smaller, specialised vessels would utilise these canals as transport arteries, taking foreign goods up-water from Oc Eo, and highland goods down-water to the sea.

Oc Eo city itself was bisected by the largest and longest of these canals, running some 80 kilometres to the inland city of Angkor Borei. Much larger than Oc Eo, Angkor Borei was distinguished by having a *baray*, or large, man-made reservoir – Chinese records describe communities in Funan being settled around great ponds. Not far from Angkor Borei was Phnom Da, a sacred mountain that was home to an assortment of temples. It was a very important religious site for the worship of Avalokiteshvara, the Bodhisattva of Compassion, believed to offer safe passage across the seas. Both Angkor Borei and Phnom Da also boasted impressive stone statuary, in particular, large and exquisitely-carved Hindu-Buddhist icons.

The Angkor Borei and Phnom Da urban complex was probably, at some point, the capital city of Funan. The earliest examples of Khmer script have been discovered here, suggesting that the people of Funan were Khmers, the ancestors of today's Cambodians. As a matter of fact, the word *angkor* is the Khmer variation of the Sanskrit word, *nagara* (नगर), meaning "city", though the Sanskrit *nagara* differs from the English "city", in that the former implies the presence of a divine and imperial power – a *devaraja*, or God-King – within its demesne.

Funan would decline and fade away into obscurity from the 7th century on, and Oc Eo lose its pre-eminent position as major entrepôt in the trade between China, Southeast Asia and India. The reason it declined is still disputed. One plausible explanation is geopolitics. In the 7th century, Funan lost control of the Indochinese Peninsula as its society split violently into two: the coastal Cham peoples, and the inland Khmers, who chose to turn their backs on the sea and undertake extensive rice-cultivation. Srivijaya would take advantage of the chaos to usurp Funan's position in the region, establishing direct trade with China, absorbing Kedah into its sphere of influence, and introducing new sailing routes along the Straits of Melaka. Funan and Oc Eo would be completely bypassed.

The demise of Oc Eo and Funan was so complete that they would be forgotten entirely, up until French archaeological digs in the 1940s. Archaeology continues to shed light on their sophisticated culture even as the best of their art and heritage is presently displayed in museums in Vietnam, Cambodia and France.

One of the most beautiful works of art from the late Funan period stands presently in the permanent galleries of the Musée national des arts asiatiques-Guimet in Paris. This is a magnificent stone statue of the Bodhisattva Avalokiteshvara, found in My Tho district in the larger Oc Eo region. It is life-sized, standing at more than 170 centimetres in height. The museum has it dated to the late 7th or early 8th century. Like our Bujang Valley Buddha, this statue betrays influence from Gupta India, in the way its hips are just slightly arched, in the flowing, sensual nature of its robes and its voluptuous arms and torso, and also in its serene, languid smile.

It too, was made here in Southeast Asia. Its cross-cultural aesthetic, integrating Indian and local Khmer elements, is known as the Phnom Da style. This style is also referred to as pre-Angkorian, because it would inspire the far more monumental, incredibly stylised, completely Southeast Asian, imperial Angkorian style that would emerge just a century later, as Funan gave way, finally, to the mighty Khmer Empire, ruling over Indochina from its inland capital city of Yasodharapura, better known as Angkor.

2. Basra
Port City of the Abbasid Caliphate

"Having made my resolve, I bought valuable merchandise suited to a sea voyage, packed up my bales and journeyed from Baghdad to Basra. I walked along the shore and saw a large, tall and goodly ship, newly fitted. It pleased me and I bought it. Then I hired a captain and crew, over whom I set some of my slaves and pages as superintendents, and loaded my bales on the ship. Then a group of merchants joined me, loaded their bales on the ship, and paid me the freight. We set out in all joy and cheerfulness, rejoicing in the prospect of a safe and prosperous voyage, and sailed from sea to sea and from island to island, landing to see the sights of the islands and towns and to sell and buy."

— Anonymous, 18th century. "The Story of Sindbad the Sailor." [6]

In the 8th century, two great world powers emerged: the Abbasid Caliphate in the Middle East and the Tang dynasty in China. These two empires would propel global trade by land and sea, in a form of "globalisation" before the term was invented. Baghdad, capital of the Abbasid Empire, was possibly the largest and wealthiest city of its time, equalled only by the magnificent capital of Tang China, Chang'an ("Ever-lasting Peace"). The port city of Basra on the Persian Gulf was the western terminus of an epic trade network reaching across the Indian Ocean to the southern Chinese port city of Guangzhou. The Arabs knew the city as Khanfu, from its full name, Guangzhou-fu, often shortened to just Guang-fu.

Around this time, the Arabs developed the technology and know-how to build and sail ships from the Persian Gulf directly to China, on a continuous journey that was the longest and most epic before the Europeans arrived in the 16th century.[7] This mastery of the oceans may have given Persian and Arab traders an edge over their Malay counterparts, and they settled everywhere there was trade to be found in the larger Indian Ocean region.

In any event, the making of these long-distance ships, or dhows, was only possible through trade, with the technology for building them having been adapted from local, Indian and Malay precedents. The body of the dhow was made either of solid African mahogany, hewn from the African interior and exported from the Swahili Coast, or tropical teak imported by way of India's Malabar Coast. These sturdy planks of wood were sewn tight with coir rope made from coconut fibres; not a single iron nail was used in the vessels' construction. Shipyards specialising in making these vessels were located in port cities along the Gulf: Basra, near the mouth of the Tigris and Euphrates rivers; Siraf, on the Persian coast adjacent to Shiraz; and Sohar, in northern Oman.

Arabs of the Persian Gulf referred to the ships as *marakib al-Sin* (مراكب الصين), or "China ships" (singular *markab al-Sin* مركب الصين) because they returned laden with the treasures of China. Their arrival at port was often cause for celebration, since their journeys would have been long, arduous and very dangerous. In a miraculous twist of fate, one such China ship was found in 1998, having sunk 1200 years ago in the shallow waters off tiny Belitung Island, hugging the coast of Sumatra. The cargo of the Belitung Shipwreck, also known as the Tang Shipwreck, is today exhibited in Singapore's Asian Civilisations Museum, and provides an indication of the kinds of goods carried by the *marakib al-Sin* to the Middle East in the Abbasid period.

And what a cargo! The dhow contained more than 70,000 individual items made in China for export to the Middle East. The bulk of this cargo consisted of Chinese ceramics, featuring elaborate, hand-drawn motifs and patterns echoing those of ceramics produced in Abbasid kilns. Silk would likely have been another commodity on board, though due to its fragile nature, none of it has survived.

The most valuable cargo found on the vessel was a small but stunning assembly of solid gold and silver objects rarely found outside of China. There are wine-bearing vessels, ornamental dishes, cosmetic boxes and a large, solid-gold wine cup decorated with figures of Central Asian musicians at the Tang imperial court. Each and every one of these pieces is a priceless treasure.

These high-quality gold and silver items might have been a form of tribute, offered reciprocally by the imperial court in China to a very

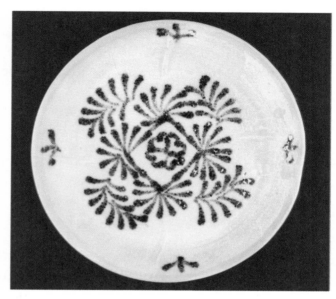

Blue-and-white dish. China, probably Gongxian kilns, c. 830s. Stoneware, diameter 23 cm. Three Tang-era blue-and-white ceramic dishes were discovered on board the Belitung Shipwreck. They had palm frond motifs similar to that of ceramic lusterware made in Basra in the same period. Collection of the Asian Civilisations Museum.

important person – perhaps a merchant-representative of the Abbasid caliph himself. Or they might have been valuable collectors' items, acquired by connoisseurs in Basra or Baghdad: powerful individuals who had the ability to source far and wide, and pay top *dinar*, for rare objects of decorative art.

The great port city of Basra (البصرة - "the all-seeing") has a history as long as that of the *dar al-Islam* (دار الإسلام - "the Islamic World") itself. It was established in the 14th year of the Hijrah, corresponding to the year 636.[8] Its origins were military. It was the headquarters of an important garrison in the early years of the Arab Conquest, and played a pivotal role in the campaign against the Sasanian Persian Empire in the east. It was from here that Arabs would lead their troops to final victory over the Persians, who professed the Zoroastrian faith.[9] Basra would thus be strongly associated with a sense of Arab as well as Muslim identity in the first century of Islam.

When the Abbasids established their new capital, Baghdad, in the 8th century, Basra had already existed for more than a hundred years. It was a hub of trade and manufacturing; and, together with its sister city, Kufa, renowned as a centre of learning, boasting legendary schools of Arabic grammar and Islamic theology.[10] Baghdad would very quickly eclipse Basra in all respects, taking over its privileged position in the *dar al-Islam*, and attracting talent from Basra and beyond. But the latter would retain its position as port of Baghdad and one of the most important ports of the Abbasid Empire – it remains Iraq's chief port today. Its privileged status ensured a thriving economy and cosmopolitan populace that meant, at least for a time, that Basra was the second city of the entire Islamic world, after Baghdad.

With its peerless intellectual pedigree, it also continued to be a major centre of learning, and was regarded by Arab philosophers and commentators to be far more conservative than glitzy and hedonistic Baghdad. It was a place for serious learning and exalted individuals; a place of piety and *adab*, which means courtesy, refinement and a scholarly disposition. The 10th century Arab academic, Abu al-Tayyib al-Lugawi, remarked scathingly (and snobbishly) on the difference between the two cities:

> "The Arabs have no scholarship except in [Kufa and Basra]... Baghdad is a town of rulership, not of scholarship. Whatever scholarship it possesses has been transplanted and imported for the caliphs, their retinue and their

subjects. Apart from that their interest in scholarship is faint, since scholarship is serious and they are people who are predominantly given to jesting."[11]

The Creek at Basra, contained in Nile and Tigris – A Narrative of Journeys in Egypt and Mesopotamia on Behalf of the British Museum Between the Years 1886 and 1913. Budge, E. A. Wallis, Sir. London, 1920. Collection of the Robarts Library, University of Toronto.

Basra sat on the banks of the Shatt al-Arab, the single river formed by the confluence of the Tigris and Euphrates. Located in salt marshes some 100 kilometres from the sea, its viability as a port was only possible by way of a sophisticated system of canals dug and maintained at great effort. This back-breaking work was performed continuously across the centuries by Bantu-speaking African slaves, whom the Arabs referred to disparagingly as the Zanj.

Seen by generations of Arabs as a coastal resort, Basra was known for its immense date palm plantations, producing some of the sweetest dates on earth. Its picturesque, idyllic and inspirational qualities endeared it to poets, artists and intellectuals. It was home, for example, to the legendary al-Hariri, whose magnum opus, *The Maqamat* (variously translated as the *Assemblies* or *Impostures*) was written in the 11th century. *The Maqamat* is considered one of the greatest works of Arabic literature and was hugely popular during al-Hariri's lifetime. It consists of 50 engaging tales written in the *maqama* format – a mix of poetry and stylised prose – and which follow the travels of a roguish wanderer and trickster, Abu Zayd al-Saruji, across the *dar al-Islam*. Indeed, the stories are recounted by Abu Zayd as a means to coax money out of his rapt audiences everywhere he travels, and they reveal much about the everyday lives of Muslims in the great cities of the time. Abu Zayd's tales are wildly entertaining and at times bawdy, but also deeply instructional for the lay reader; they are full of puns, wordplay and twists and turns of language impossible to translate, but which highlight the beauty and flexibility of the Arabic tongue.

Basra was also the homeplace of the revered Sufi poetess, Rabia al-Adawiyya, one of only a few women included in the patriarchal canon of Arab literature. She was born to one of the poorest families in Basra in the early 8th century, and experienced a great famine in her lifetime. She would famously forsake her family to wander the desert as an ascetic, completely devoted to God. Attaining divine enlightenment, she would be moved to write, and be known thereafter for her piety. Most of her work has not survived, and the very little that remains is at best tenuously attributed to her. That said, she commanded great respect from later Sufi poets, most notably Attar, the 12th century Persian poet-author of *The Conference of the Birds*, who also penned a biography of Rabia in his sprawling prose epic, *Memorial of the Sufi Saints*.

Basra's greatest claim to fame would ultimately be its role as the port city from whence Sindbad the Sailor sets sail in *The Arabian Nights*, also known as *Alf layla wa layla* (*The Thousand and One Nights*). *The Nights* are a compilation of folktales with Persian, Indian and Arab origins, set in the Abbasid capital of Baghdad, presented in its full, at turns glittering and sordid, splendour. Most of the stories in *The Nights* take place during the reign of the Abbasid caliph Haroun al-Rashid in the 8th and 9th centuries, widely regarded to be Baghdad's golden age. The caliph himself appears as an occasional lead, frequently disguised and descending into Baghdad's teeming streets for encounters both intellectual as well as erotic. He is accompanied by his sidekick, his long-suffering vizier, Jafar, a cool observer to the caliph's cavalier hedonist.

"The Story of Sindbad of the Sea" ("Al-Sindbad al-Bahri") is one of the most popular tales of *The Nights*, though it was a later addition. Sindbad's story is illuminating because it was likely based on accounts of merchants' and sailors' experiences. The opening paragraph to the Fifth Voyage offers clues about how large ocean-going vessels, such as the wrecked Belitung ship, could have been commissioned and crewed.[12]

The Belitung ship is dated to the second half of the 9th century, more than 50 years after the death of Caliph Haroun al-Rashid and the events of *The Arabian Nights*. It might have been one of the last of its kind. Between 869 to 883, Basra was wracked by a series of uprisings. Legions of Zanj slaves took advantage of civil war within the caliphate to rebel. Coincidentally around the same time (878 – 879), Guangzhou was also struck by a violent massacre of resident Arab and Persian merchants. Both cities would recover in a matter of decades and reclaim their positions in the global maritime trade network. Unfortunately, though, this brief disruption to global trade meant a curtailing of the epic trans-oceanic trading route between the Persian Gulf and China.

By the early 10th century, the *marakib al-Sin* were no more.

3. Yangzhou
The River Capital and the Grand Canal

"An old friend bids farewell at Yellow Crane Pavilion in the west / To head downriver to Yangzhou in the third lunar month, when Spring is in full bloom and willow blossoms fill the air like mist. / His lone vessel steadily disappears into the azure sky / Till one sees only the Yangzi River flowing towards heaven itself."

— Li Bai, 730. "Saying Farewell to Meng Haoran at Yellow Crane Pagoda, As He Travels to Guangling".

One of the most important objects in the Tang Shipwreck Collection is a bronze mirror found alongside some two dozen other mirrors in the wrecked vessel. Corroded and in a poorer condition than the others, it would have been overlooked except for the inscription indicating that it was made in Yangzhou (扬州) on the 3rd of January 759 during the reign of Tang emperor, Suzong. The same inscription also notes that the mirror had been "cast at the heart of the Yangzi River, and by way of being smelted one hundred times".

The mirror's discovery caused a stir in archaeological circles. It was the first and as yet only specimen ever found of an extremely rare type of mirror mentioned in Chinese literary tradition: a River's Heart Mirror. Tang poet Bai Juyi's "Mirror of Perfection: Penned in Tribute to the Emperor" informs us that the casting of such a mirror had to be done "at a time and location imbued with Divine and Imperial Significance". When the mirror was finished, it was offered to the emperor by the mayor of Yangzhou himself. This rare mirror was one of Yangzhou's most prestigious domestic exports. And yet, here it was, stashed on a ship bound for the Middle East.

Aside from the mirror, a trove of exquisite gold and silver objects found on the Belitung wreck was also almost certainly made in Yangzhou. The city had a reputation at the time for gold- and silverware so fine, it was frequently commissioned for the imperial court. Mirror and treasure trove suggest that the Belitung ship could have stopped at Yangzhou, before heading south to Guangzhou, to embark on its journey back west.

In surveys of China's major port cities, Yangzhou is often overlooked in favour of Guangzhou, despite it having enjoyed a glorious heyday during the latter half of the Tang dynasty. Situated at a great distance from Chang'an, Guangzhou had always been regarded as a city of the *fan* (番) – the "foreign barbarians" who came from the south to trade with China by sea. In contrast, Yangzhou was located close enough to China's traditional heartlands along the Yellow River and was thus regarded as a city in China's own image. It also helped that Yangzhou had an ancient pedigree and was a ravishingly beautiful metropolis, set amidst willow-lined canals and picture-perfect pavilions. Thus, Yangzhou figures prominently in China's histories, literature, art, music and popular imagination in the course of centuries.

River's Heart Mirror, with cosmological decoration and inscription. Yangzhou, 759. Bronze, diameter 21 cm. Depicted on the mirror are the eight Taoist trigrams, as well as the cardinal directions in Chinese tradition: the Azure Dragon of the East, the Vermilion Bird of the South, the White Tiger of the West and the Black Turtle of the North. The first part of the Chinese inscription translates to "Made on the 29th day of the 11th month of the 1st year of the Wuxu era of the Qianyuan reign of the Tang dynasty". Collection of the Asian Civilisations Museum.

It appears regularly in the works of Tang dynasty poets, who created a genre of travel-related poetry inspired by the landscapes in and around Yangzhou. The tone of these poems is frequently nostalgic. Yangzhou is often described in pastel shades evoking the halcyon days and too-brief a time spent in the company of one's dearly beloved. It is a place of romance; a lush, verdant, floating dream of a city, in stark contrast to Chang'an's harsh desert environment and its unforgiving political climate. One of the classics of this genre of travel literature is a poem of sweet parting written by that doyen of celebrity Tang poets, Li Bai, who, in the misty, blossomy third lunar month, says goodbye to fellow celebrity poet Meng Haoran as he heads east to Yangzhou.

Yangzhou was also a cosmopolitan city like Guangzhou. Located 250 kilometres from the sea, it was nonetheless open to foreign trade and home to significant communities of *fan* traders. To the Arabs, Yangzhou was known as Qantu, from the Chinese Jiangdu, referring to Yangzhou's alternate name, "River Capital".[13]

The River Capital's rise came due to a combination of politics and geography. In 754, the Tang dynasty was at its zenith. From Chang'an, the great Emperor Xuanzong held sway over a vast dominion that extended south to Annam (today's north Vietnam), and west across

Slender West Lake, with Five-Pavilion Bridge in the distance. This is one of the classic views of Yangzhou today.

much of Central Asia. Tang material culture and lifestyle was the envy of the world. Tang paintings and wall murals that have survived to our day paint a picture of the finer side of life in its cities. Plump, perfumed beauties dress in lavish silks with plunging necklines, sport elaborate make-up, and are coiffed to the nines. They play with pet dogs and goldfish, fan themselves with painted hand-held fans, and sniff at peonies in their gardens. Tang patricians, men and women alike, play rambunctious games of polo in grand playing fields, astride horses imported from Ferghana in Central Asia.

In 755, one of Xuanzong's most loyal generals and advisors rebelled. His name, An Lushan, betrayed his *hu* (胡) origins – the Chinese referred to Central Asians as *hu*, or "foreign barbarians" that came overland (as opposed to the *fan*, who came by sea). The An Lushan Rebellion took close to a decade to be quashed and almost toppled the Tang dynasty. The empire never regained its former splendour and lapsed into a century-long decline.

The aftermath of the An Lushan Rebellion saw major production centres of the north devastated, and economic activity had to shift south. Here, geography was a deciding factor. Yangzhou was a natural choice for relocating merchants, due to its already being a bustling mercantile and manufacturing hub. It also occupied an unparalleled location at the junction of the Yangzi River and China's legendary Grand Canal.

The canal, which the Chinese called the "Great Transport River", was an incredible feat of human engineering, and remains one of China's grandest monuments. Running some 1700 kilometres south to north, it linked China's two great rivers, the Yellow and the Yangzi. First commissioned in the early 7th century by the emperors of China's brief Sui dynasty, the canal's original purpose was to strengthen control of China's vast domains – a perennial concern for China, even today.

By making far-flung provinces accessible, the canal facilitated better governance and administration. Officials – and, on occasion, the emperor himself – could sail the immense distance south from Chang'an to Yangzhou easily, by way of an astonishingly complex system of inland rivers and canals. The canal had a more pragmatic use as well, allowing for grain, rice, salt and other staples from the verdant and fertile Jiangnan and Sichuan regions in the south to be brought to the arid central plains of the north, where China's imperial capitals were traditionally located.

It still serves that function today.

As Chang'an faded, Yangzhou blossomed. China's rich and powerful flocked in droves from the north to take up residence here. The city was home to a large resident population of fabulously wealthy Chinese patricians, merchants and their families, with a sophisticated and unquenchable demand for luxury goods from all over the world. Some of the most wealthy and powerful Yangzhou-ites were salt merchants, who built their fortunes on the backs of the imperial monopoly exerted on salt.

Yangzhou was also a favoured destination for young men of the wealthy literati class who, flirting with a career in the civil service as a matter of familial obligation, found themselves disillusioned with politics at court and desirous of escaping as far away as possible from the oppressive imperial centre. They exiled themselves here to this canal city in the east, to drown themselves in wine, women and poetry, and to lead – in some cases – profligate, decadent, wastrel lives calculated to disgust and disappoint their well-meaning, anxiety-ridden, Confucianist parents.

Fan communities too, began to return; this despite the fact that during the An Lushan Rebellion, Chinese dissident militia had plundered and massacred the modestly-sized local Arab and Persian community. But Tang China was always remarkably tolerant of foreigners. Imperial decrees called for their settlement in specially-designated "foreign quarters", or *fan fang* (番坊), within which they enjoyed freedom of worship and were governed by the laws of their own communities, rather than by Chinese law.

The Persians, many of whom were Zoroastrian scions of former Sasanian nobility, were known as *bosi*. They specialised in jewellery and other foreign luxury items, and were known to peddle their wares in the jewellery quarter of the city. Every year, their trading guild would band together to present a high-profile, luxury trade fair for discerning Chinese customers, who would come from far and wide to partake in the glittering spectacle.

Alongside the *bosi* were the Muslim Arabs, called *dashi*, a term used also to refer to the Abbasid Empire. These *dashi* came in their large ships up the Yangzi River and often stayed for months on end to trade in all manner of exotica: frankincense from Arabia, sandalwood from India, agarwood from Java, ivory and rhinoceros horn from Africa, and blood-red grape wine – a fashionable intoxicant at the time – from Europe.

Yangzhou became China's commercial, financial and cultural centre; its international stock and commodities exchange; its shopping mall of the world; its fashion and lifestyle capital. It was the New York of the Tang with its equivalent of a vibrant socialite scene, trust-fund kids, extravagant parties and fashionable masses.

The Tang poets found themselves captivated by the city's prosperity and decadence post-An Lushan. Poet Wang Jian, in his "Yangzhou Bazaar at Night", vividly captures the spirit of the "floating world" in the city's courtesan quarters; a world that was fleeting, transient and concerned with seizing the moment.

> "The bazaar at night is a sight to see, illumined by a thousand lamps, such that the clouds overhead glow crimson. / In the many-storied pavilions, ladies in red entertain a never-ending stream of pleasure-seeking guests. / Times are not like what they were before; / But here in Yangzhou, the music plays on and revelries continue till dawn."

The Tang dynasty fell in 907, and there was a time of great political upheaval and uncertainty. The River Capital would thrive, however, buoyed along as ever by its strategic location and its inextricable place in China's national consciousness. The pictures of the floating world painted by the Tang poets would endure; even if Yangzhou itself would never again enjoy the pre-eminent status it had during the late Tang, when for a brief moment, it was not only China's most important domestic port, but also China's most cosmopolitan and sophisticated city.

4. Hakata
The Tang Missions and Diplomacy in Japan

"17th Day: In the middle of the night, profiting from a stiff wind,
we hoisted sail and set the ships in motion. At 10 a.m. we reached
the sea east of Shiganoshima [the tip of the peninsula which forms
the landlocked harbor of Hakata Bay on the north coast of Kyushu.]
Because we did not have reliable winds, we stopped for five days."

— Ennin, 838 – 847. *Ennin's Diary: The Record of a
Pilgrimage to China in Search of the Law.*[14]

Any mention of Hakata in today's Japan is bound to evoke cravings
for its world-famous *tonkotsu ramen,* a traditional noodle dish
that is a specialty in Japan's southern Kyushu province and has origins
in China. Lightly-chewy, tensile wheat noodles are steeped in a rich,
white broth that is the end-product of hours of stewing pork-bone, pork
fat and cartilage. The piping-hot bowl of noodles is embellished with a
half-boiled egg and slices of *chashu,* or roast pork cooked in the Chinese
tradition. A sprinkling of sliced Japanese leek and toasted sesame seeds
completes the ensemble. The result is a simple yet hearty meal for a cold
winter's day.

Hakata is today incorporated into the larger city of Fukuoka. The
name Hakata (博多 – meaning "display of abundance") refers to a
specific district that harbours the city's old town and commercial
quarters, as well as its ancient port. This is the best place for visitors
and locals alike to shop for local delicacies like *unagi* (grilled river eel),
mentaiko (spicy cod roe), and *kou-no-mono,* or the variety of seasonal
pickled vegetables that Japanese love taking with their rice. This is,
naturally, also a good place to savour *hakata ramen* – the city's namesake
noodle dish.

Hakata itself is much older than the city that now encompasses it.
In fact, it has the distinction of being one of Japan's oldest cities, having
been functioning as a port since the 7th century. In deference to its age,
the regional dialect spoken in Fukuoka is still referred to today as the
Hakata dialect, and the majestic bay – that sparkling body of water
almost completely enveloped by the city of Fukuoka and its suburbs – is
known as Hakata Bay.

In the 300 years between the 7th and the 9th centuries, Japan would
send 21 formal diplomatic missions to China. Two missions were

dispatched during China's brief Sui dynasty, when the Chinese mainland was first reunified. 19 were sent during the ensuing Tang dynasty, with a planned 20th cancelled in the throes of the Tang itself dissolving into chaos.

The principal port city from which all Tang missions, or *kentoshi* (遣唐使), would depart was Hakata. It was a natural departure point, being the closest port to the Korean Peninsula and thus mainland China. The missions were all dispatched with the blessings of the Japanese emperor, with the intent being for envoys to learn all they could from China and to bring this knowledge back to Japan, so Japan herself might modernise and stand alongside the great power to its west.

The Great Buddha of Nara dates to 752, at the time of the Tang missions. One of the largest bronze statues of the Buddha in the world, it sits in Todai-ji Temple, originally founded in 728.

The glittering Tang dynasty held a particular fascination for the Japanese emperors; and Japan's cultural debt to the Tang is immense. Much of what we recognise as Japanese culture today – its elaborate tea rituals, its dedication to craft and artisanship, its *kimono* and *geisha*, its use of Chinese characters known as *kanji* in its writing, even the practice of eating *sushi* – has roots in the culture of the imperial court and the grand boulevards of Chang'an.

The first Tang missions brought new forms of governance to Japan. Tang law codes, which called for the segregation of religion and state, were adopted. So too, a decentralised bureaucratic form of government, wherein Japan was divided into provinces, each ruled by regional administrations. Tang Chinese forms of architecture and urban planning were also studied closely and adapted. In 710, the capital of Japan was moved to the city of Nara, planned from scratch and modelled after the Tang capital of Chang'an. Tang Chinese art was held up as the epitome of good taste, and returning embassies brought valuable collections of Chinese art back to Japan.

In less than 100 years, the imperial capital moved again, this time to Kyoto, known as Heian-kyo ("Imperial Capital of Peace") at the time. A much larger city was built, again modelled after Chang'an. Kyoto would endure as Japan's capital for 1000 years till the late 19th century, and the Heian period would be regarded as Japan's golden age. Confident in its own identity, Japan began to innovate on and depart from earlier Tang models of governance and culture, introducing its own new alphabetic system, the *kana* – used alongside *kanji*. *The Tale of Genji*, the world's first novel, would be written by a lady of the Heian court, Murasaki Shikibu, using mostly *kana*.

Even though Japan is an island nation, its ability to navigate the oceans beyond its shores was limited at the time of the *kentoshi*. Japanese sailors knew so little about monsoon winds and the Korean Straits that many a Tang mission was actually dispatched when travel was least advisable. Japan also had little mastery of the magnetic compass, used by the Chinese since the Han dynasty. Their one safeguard against inclement weather was prayer and the practice of having communities of Buddhist monks on board ship as a form of divine insurance. It was a miracle any of the *kentoshi* actually made it to China at all.

Of the envoys who did make it, scholar-aristocrat Kibi no Makibi is perhaps the most famous, having made the hazardous journey twice. He first travels as a student on the 717 mission, encountering a China at its zenith during the reign of the Emperor Xuanzong. Makibi remains in Chang'an for 17 years, establishing himself in court and society, before finally sailing home in 735. He returns in 752 to personally escort an old friend back to Japan. This time, his trip is cut short as China lurches into the throes of the An Lushan Rebellion and he becomes an unwitting eyewitness to the end of a golden era.

Makibi's contributions to Japan would include imparting emergent neo-Confucianist thought, imbibed in China, to a generation of young Japanese men in Nara, by way of his treatise, *Shikyo Ruiju*, or *A Private Education*. On "matters in relation to cultivating one's inner and outer states of being", he notes that:

> "Inner cultivation requires five prohibitions – one: no to killing, two: no to stealing, three: no to lechery, four: no to prevarication, five: no to drink. Outer cultivation involves five constants– one: mercy in not killing, two: honour in not thieving, three: propriety rather than iniquity, four: wisdom rather than rashness, five: credence rather than confusion."[15]

These ten commandments meld Buddhist and Confucianist thought. The moralistic tone reflects his own disenchantment with an increasingly decadent Nara society and the growing power and wealth of the Buddhist establishment, exemplified by ever-more opulent and lavishly-endowed temples.

Indeed, two of the most famous travellers on the *kentoshi* were Buddhist monks. Japan looked to its larger neighbour for guidance as to the proper Buddhist rites and rituals, as well as the transmission of Buddhist scriptures and teachings. Aside from the imperial court, only temples could bear the hefty cost of regularly sending envoys across the sea.

The monk, Kukai, departed on his pilgrimage to Tang China in 804, some 50 years after the An Lushan Rebellion. In Chang'an, he would meet with the venerable Yijing, and study Sanskrit with a revered Indian master from Nalanda. Returning to Japan, he would establish the Shingon sect of Buddhism and be given the honorific title *Odaishi-sama*, or "Grand Master". He is said to have founded the Tocho-ji Temple in Hakata in 806.

Another monk, Ennin, travelled on the very last *kentoshi* in 838. He is best known for having written a detailed diary of his travels in China. Unlike official Chinese accounts, which tend towards the opaque and ceremonial, and feature the lives of emperors, noblemen and other important people, Ennin's diary is vernacular and shockingly mundane, featuring everyday people going about their lives in Tang China, particularly in the great metropolis of Yangzhou. We get a hint of how regular folk celebrated local festivals across the Chinese lunar calendar. We sense his awe for the bustling trade on China's Grand Canal and the efficiency of the transport network. And we feel a twinge of sympathy as he attempts, with very little spoken Chinese, to parley and negotiate with the many rude and officious Chinese officials he meets along the way, who mistake him for a Korean.

Ennin's diary, titled *The Record of a Pilgrimage to China in Search of the Law*, would be written in classical Chinese and published in the 850s when he finally returns to Japan and settles down. It remains the only existing foreigner's eyewitness account of everyday life in Tang China.

Hakata Bay provided a natural harbour for ocean-going vessels, and for centuries Hakata harbour was also the principal gateway for any foreign vessel entering Japan. At the time of the *kentoshi*, Kyushu province was administered by a regional government located at the regional capital of Dazaifu ("Official Residence of the Great Governor of the Province"). During this period, the Beihai (北海 – "Northern Seas") trade was dominated by Korean merchants plying Hakata, the Korean port cities of Busan and Gwangju, and the Chinese port cities of

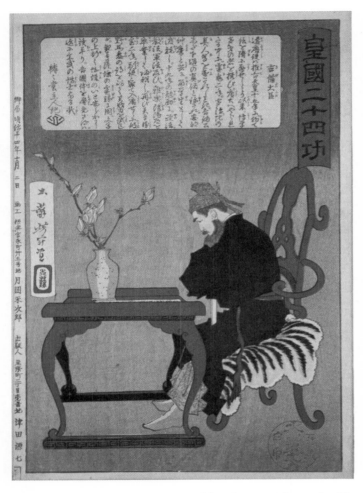

Kibi Daijin (Kibi no Makibi), from the series, *Twenty-four Accomplishments in Imperial Japan (Kokoku nijushi-ko)*. Tsukioka Yoshitoshi. Japan, Meiji Period, 1881. *Ukiyo-e* (Japanese woodblock print). Collection of the National Diet Library, Tokyo.

Mingzhou (today's Ningbo) and Yangzhou. Hakata Bay regularly welcomed Korean ships bearing goods from China and beyond, as well as the latest news from abroad.

At the centre of trade and diplomacy in Hakata was the Tsukushi-no-murotsumi ("Tsukushi Lodge"), the official government guesthouse built by the Dazaifu regional authorities to house visiting foreign guests. It is better known today by an alternate name, Korokan, literally meaning "Great Belly Guesthouse".

For at least 300 years between the 8th and the 11th centuries, the Korokan played a pivotal role in mediating relations between the Japanese and foreigners, mostly Koreans and Chinese. By imperial law, visitors to Japan were obliged to reside at the Korokan, where they were received warmly and entertained lavishly for as long as they stayed. Protocol dictated that government officials resident in Dazaifu would welcome and entertain high-ranking guests from abroad, especially if they were formal diplomatic missions. Occasionally, there would be the opportunity for the highest-ranking guests to travel to Dazaifu itself, to meet with the governor there. But the visitor would never be allowed to step beyond the confines of Hakata and its vicinity. Often, by the end of an extended stay in the Korokan, subject to close surveillance at all times, our intrepid diplomat or trader would be eager to depart Japan, and he would probably reconsider returning to these parts anytime soon.

By the middle of the 9th century, formal diplomacy between China, Korea and Japan ceased. The majority of travellers to Hakata, and those who were the principal guests at the Korokan, became primarily merchants. The fall of the Tang and the rise of the Song dynasty in China saw a shift in Chinese attitudes towards trade. Where the Tang emperors had been trade-averse, the Song emperors encouraged it. Korean merchants in the Northern Seas were eclipsed by Chinese ones, who came in scores to Hakata, setting up shop and residence in what would be Japan's first Chinatown, or *tobo* (唐坊 – "quarters of the Tang people"), located just east of the Korokan. The Great Belly Guesthouse was made obsolete by these developments, and fell into disuse by the middle of the 11th century.

It would be forgotten for almost a millennium, until a dramatic twist of fate in 1987 when, amidst extensive renovations at Fukuoka's baseball stadium, the remains of the Korokan were accidentally unearthed. Subsequent archaeological excavations revealed structural foundations dating back to between the 7th and 9th centuries. Large amounts of imported Chinese porcelain were found, stacked up and remarkably preserved in these foundations. Other foreign trade material discovered included stoneware from Korea and Vietnam, as well as Islamic glassware, suggesting that ancient Hakata's trading networks extended far and wide.

A decision was made by the Japanese national authorities to tear down the baseball stadium entirely. The Korokan site itself was gazetted as a monument and a museum built in situ. Today's Korokan Historical Museum showcases the foundations of the Korokan, alongside artefacts found on site and information related to ongoing archaeological work. Much imagination is required to envision just how forbidding and imposing the Korokan would have looked to travellers to the Land of the Rising Sun. That said, the museum is a welcome spot of ancient calm in a city overtaken by futuristic architecture.

5. Palembang
The Might and Mystery of Srivijaya

"In the fortified city of Fo-che, there are more than one thousand Buddhist monks [who dedicate themselves] to study and good actions. They study all possible subjects [, as one would] in India. [In fact, rules and ceremonial rituals] are identical [in Fo-che and India]. If a Chinese monk wants to travel to India to [study] Buddhist Laws, he must stay in Fo-che [for] one or two years to learn [the proper etiquette and foundations]. [Only then, is he ready to] pursue his travel to India."

— Yijing, 7th century. *Account of Buddhist Law as Practiced in the Southern Seas.*[16]

The tale of the doomed *markab al-Sin* is not yet done. One more mystery remains to be unravelled: that of the puzzling location at which it was wrecked. In the late 9th century, Belitung Island was located near the heart of maritime Southeast Asia's major centre of power: Palembang, capital of Srivijaya. The Belitung ship had probably wended its way south to call there, perhaps to unload and upload some cargo; re-fuel and restock; and undertake repairs and recruit sailors.

Two theories exist for what the ship did next.

It might have been headed towards Java, the rich and fertile playing fields of the Sailendras, a powerful kingdom closely allied to Srivijaya, and best known for having erected Borobudur, the greatest Buddhist monument of all time. The ship, with precious treasures in its hold, was no ordinary trading vessel. It may have also been bound for Java on a tribute mission, unloading more of its cargo once there and offering some of its precious gold and silver trove to the Sailendran kings.

Alternatively, the vessel might have opted to navigate its return to the Indian Ocean via the Sunda Straits (which separate Sumatra from Java). The Sunda and Melaka Straits are the only two entry points by sea from the Indian Ocean into Southeast Asia. They were important "chokepoints" of global maritime trade – anyone who blocked passage through these straits would, in effect, exert a stranglehold on the world economy – and lay firmly within Srivijaya's control. In any event, the Belitung ship's decision to veer east would prove fatal. Shallow waters filled with treacherous reefs would get the better of our captain and his ill-fated passengers and crew.

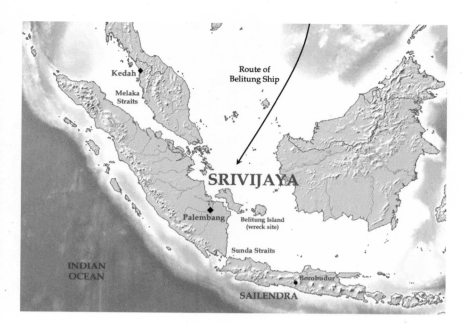

Map of Southeast Asia in the 9th century, showing the route of the doomed *markab al-Sin.*

Srivijaya emerged in the 8th century as the third global power alongside the Abbasid Caliphate and Tang China. It was one of the longest-surviving civilisations in the region, existing in some form for 700 years from the 8th to the 14th centuries. It was large and influential, able to cripple global trade if it wished. It was also an important centre for the study and spread of Buddhism in the region, and had direct links to the holy city of Nalanda. Yet, it remains one of the most elusive civilisations of all time. So little archaeological evidence has been found relating to it that even today, one speaks of Srivijaya in hushed tones of awe, acknowledging its might, as much as the fact that it remains a mystery.

As with Kedah and Funan, we first encounter Srivijaya by way of the Chinese, and from the *Accounts* of one already familiar to us. In 671, Chinese monk, Yijing, stops over for six months at Shi-li-fo-shi (室利佛逝 – *Sia-lai-fut-tsua* in Hokkien) to study the Sanskrit language. He remarks on the presence of a large monastery in the vicinity of the harbour, with innumerable Buddhist monks deeply engaged in the study of Buddhist texts and treatises.

When the monsoon winds turn, Yijing heads north up the Melaka Straits, stopping at the ports of Malayu (Jambi) and Kedah, where he catches his onward vessel to India. 15 years later, on his way back, he notes that both Malayu and Kedah are now part of Srivijaya, suggesting that the latter had significantly expanded its sphere of influence in just over a decade.

At its peak between the 8th and the 10th centuries, Srivijaya held sway over much of western Southeast Asia, including the entire Malay Peninsula, almost all the islands of Sumatra and Java, and possibly also parts of Borneo. Aside from the kingdoms of Kedah and Malayu, the Sailendras of Central Java also paid tribute and fell within Srivijaya's sphere of influence.

Srivijaya was unlikely to be an empire in the traditional sense, wherein an imperial power wields control over a vast territory it has conquered and subjugated. Instead, Srivijaya was probably a complex and close-knit association of city- or region-states willingly submitting to a strong centre-of-power; a circle of kings, rather than a game of thrones.

In fact, Srivijaya referred to itself metaphorically as a *mandala*, in reference to Buddhist conceptions of the cosmos as a geometric configuration of ever larger concentric circles radiating outward from a single point. As one moves away from the centre, its influence begins to weaken. In a nod to the region's Hindu-Buddhist roots, scholars have adopted the term *mandala* as a means to describe this political configuration of strong centre-of-power and subordinate states in the periphery; one that also applies to other empire-like entities like Funan.

Srivijaya's existence was only posited in the 1920s, by French archaeologist George Coedès of the École française d'Extrême-Orient. Coedès argued, persuasively, that the Chinese Shi-li-fo-shi or San-fo-qi (三佛齐 – *Sa-fut-tsuay* in Hokkien) and the enigmatic name, Srivijaya ("glorious victory"), mentioned in passing in ancient inscriptions in Old Malay, referred to one and the same thing: a great Hindu-Buddhist "empire" in Southeast Asia. He also argued that the capital of said "empire" was likely at Palembang, since almost all inscriptions bearing the name had been found in and around the city.

It would take another 70 years for Srivijaya's centre to be more firmly placed at Palembang; this by way of excavations led by another French archaeologist, Pierre Yves Manguin, and which unearthed sufficient material for a stronger case. Aerial photography also uncovered traces of large reservoirs linked by canals to each other and to the Musi River, the city's main waterway. It seemed increasingly clear that a port city had thrived here for at least 1300 years.

Ancient Palembang resembled Oc Eo and the Bujang Valley in that it sat upriver – some 90 kilometres, to be exact. It was also located at the foothills of a majestic peak, Bukit Seguntang, where the greatest concentration of artefacts, including a large and magnificent stone Buddha dating to the 7th and 8th centuries, has been found. The Musi River itself was so deep as to afford Palembang a natural harbour. Even in the 19th century, the largest ocean-going vessels were able to navigate upriver and dock at Palembang with ease. The contemporary Chinese name for the city, in use since the 15th century, is Ju Gang, meaning "immense harbour". Curiously enough, it is not a transliteration of "Palembang", but a description of its once-greatness – a superlative *ju*, rather than *da*, is used. The Chinese appear to have memorialised in the city's name the fact that here, once upon a time, was a large and bustling harbour teeming with ships from all over the world.

Certainly, the question remains: if Palembang was the capital of a great maritime *mandala*, why haven't there been more archaeological traces of its enduring legacy? Perhaps the clues lie in the Malays' mobile, sea-going culture. Visitors to Palembang in the 19th century remarked that much of the population appeared to live in houseboats and houses on stilts lining the banks of the Musi River for miles. In stark contrast to contemporary conceptions of a city as an agglomeration of fixed brick-and-mortar structures, the *nagara* of Palembang had neither brick nor fixed structures, possibly excepting places of worship or the *kedatuan* ("residence of the *datu* / chieftain"). The ephemeral nature of the city meant that it left hardly any permanent trace of itself, since little of it would have been built with stone, brick, or other such long-lasting material.

Stone was used for the making of rather less mundane things. One of the most striking archaeological discoveries related to Srivijaya is a large stone stele found in Sabokingking in Palembang, and housed today in the National Museum of Indonesia in Jakarta. The body of the stele is enveloped by a *nagaraja*, or seven-headed king of the snakes – the *nagaraja* had been adopted by Southeast Asian kings as a symbol of imperial and divine power. The seven heads of this *nagaraja* peek over the top of the stele and cast their steely gaze down at us mere mortals standing before it. Stele and magical serpent are joined at the hip by a trough and spout resembling a tap and sink.

The main body of the stele sports an extensive inscription, possibly dating to 682 – 686, or the early years of Srivijaya. The script used is

Pallava, though the language is Old Malay.[17] Alongside a scattering of Sanskrit terms like *mandala*, Malay words, like *kedatuan*, are also used – this stele is thus one of the earliest to feature the Malay language. The text on the stele is excerpted as follows:

> "All of you, as many as you are – sons of kings, [...] chiefs, army commanders, confidants of the king, judges, foremen, surveyors of low castes, clerks, sculptors, naval captains, merchants and you washermen of the king and slaves of the king. All of you will be killed by the curse of this imprecation; if you are not faithful to me, you will be killed by the curse. [...] However, if you are submissive, faithful and straight to me and do not commit these crimes, an immaculate tantra will be my recompense. You will not be swallowed with your children and wives. Eternal peace will be the fruit produced by this curse which is drunk by you."[18]

Despite the stele being more than 1300 years old, the voice of the king who commissioned it speaks to us loud and clear. So says the Maharaja Jayanaga ("victorious naga"): *Those who have drunk of this sacred water are my allies. If you are loyal to me, you shall be rewarded. If you betray me, you shall be destroyed.* The stele would have been used in an oath-taking ritual, wherein water was ceremonially poured over the heads of the *nagaraja*, and drunk, at the spout, by a faction pledging allegiance to Srivijaya. Facsimiles of this oath stele were found in four other places not far from Palembang and appear to mark out Srivijaya's immediate sphere of influence.

And thus a *sejarah srivijaya*, or annals of the maharajas of Srivijaya, might read as follows...

Sometime during the 7th century, a local Malay chieftain in the Palembang region, consolidating his power over the local peoples and areas of agricultural production, rises to a position of dominance over his peers. Adopting the Buddhist faith and its associated symbols and rituals, by which means he pronounces his own divine legitimacy, he dispatches his vessels to the lands of his fellow *datus*, to request or force their allegiance by oath. His campaign is a resounding success. His fellow chieftains capitulate and acknowledge him as maharaja. His *mandala* thrives for centuries.

Descendants of the maharaja wield consummate diplomatic skill and political acumen, securing and maintaining an intricate network of regional alliances that allows Srivijaya to hold sway for generations. Wealth by way of trade fills Srivijaya's coffers; these riches Srivijaya redistributes to its allied states generously. In the meantime, detractors are dealt with swiftly and viciously – Srivijaya could be war-like when it needed to be. The maharajas, in a stroke of brilliance, co-opt the *orang laut*, or sea nomads, as their navy. The *orang laut* have long had a reputation as fearsome pirates, often striking unsuspecting vessels in the region's many straits and channels; they now strike terror at Srivijaya's behest.

Srivijaya's reach stretches far beyond its immediate *mandala*. The maharajas dispatch formal diplomatic missions to China during the course of the 8th to 11th centuries. Arab and Persian merchants engaged in the China trade know Srivijaya well and write of it in

The Sabokingking stone, or Telaga Batu. Palembang, c. 7th century. 118 x 148 cm. Collection of the National Museum of Indonesia.

their *rihlahs*. Confident in their power and prestige, individual maharajas endow and make gifts to temples in the monastery-city of Nalanda and in Nagapattinam, chief port of a new Asian power: the Cholas.

But then Srivijaya's fortunes change. The Chola king Rajendra I dispatches a vast fleet of warships to Srivijaya, sacking its vassals and forcing it to its knees. In the Far East, the Song dynasty succeeds the Tang. Unlike their predecessors, the Song emperors encourage direct foreign trade with China, and Srivijaya's services as an entrepôt are dispensed with.

By the late 13th century, Srivijaya, a shadow of its former self, is subdued and absorbed into the realms of Majapahit, a Hindu *mandala* centred on the plains of East Java. Majapahit becomes the largest civilisation in island Southeast Asia, encompassing almost all the islands and peninsulas of the Nusantara.[19] Srivijaya is forgotten completely, except in one crucial instance.

The *Sejarah Melayu*, or annals of the Malay kings, tells of a 13th century Srivijayan prince who flees north from Palembang as it is attacked by Majapahit. He lands on an island at the tip of the Malay Peninsula and encounters what he believes is a *singa* ("lion") – a divine symbol of imperial authority in Hindu-Buddhist tradition. He decides to settle there, rallying the *orang laut* and establishing the base of his new domain on the banks of a river, at the foothills of a modest peak.

He calls his new domain Singapura: Lion City.

6. Nagapattinam
The Ainnurruvar and the Chola Kings

> "In the 15th year [of the reign of…] Sri-Rajendracholadeva, who
> […] having dispatched many ships in the midst of the rolling sea and
> having caught Sangama Vijayottungavarman, the King of Kadaram,
> along with [his] rutting elephants, [which were as impetuous as]
> the sea in fighting, – [took] Srivijayam overflown with large heap
> of treasures, which [that king] had rightfully accumulated, and
> possessing the [arch called] Vidhyadhara-torana at the 'war gate' of
> his extensive city, the 'jewel gate', adorned with great splendour, and
> the 'gate of large jewels'"
>
> — *Tirukkadaiyur Inscription* of Rajendra I, c. 1027.
> Amritaghatesvarar Temple, Thanjavur, Tamil Nadu.[20]

Sometime during the 3rd century of our Common Era, the great port city of Kaveripattinam, on the banks of the Kaveri River in Tamil Nadu, was swallowed up by the sea in the aftermath of a massive earthquake. The city had been chief port and capital for the ancient Cholas, Tamil kings of the south. From its vantage point on India's southeastern coast, it welcomed trading vessels from as far afield as the Roman Empire and China. It was known to have been a cosmopolitan entrepôt, with Hindu, Buddhist and Jain communities and their respective places of worship, and all kinds of goods and treasures from all over the world.

Kaveripattinam was a beacon of light and civilisation for the Tamil world during the Sangam Age, a golden age of culture and civilisation, spanning almost a thousand years in antiquity from the 6th century BCE to the 3rd century CE. Long after it was destroyed, the city continued to loom large in an entire corpus of early Tamil literature – legendary lays and epics dating to the Sangam Age and the centuries that immediately follow.

In the aftermath of the great earthquake, trade on the Chola coast shifted south to the city of Nagapattinam (நாகப்பட்டினம்), formerly a small fishing village specialising in conches.[21] It too, sat in the larger delta region of the Kaveri River, a mere 50 kilometres down from its predecessor. And this delta region in turn was the beating heart of the Tamilakam, or ancient Tamil country. Descriptions of the city in the 7th century epic, the *Tevaram*, suggest it had large fortifications, broad streets and opulent buildings. A sizeable merchant community resided there, and in the harbour, ships of all kinds were anchored: monumental ones called *vangam* (வங்கம்) that moved like mountains on the sea, and smaller merchant vessels known as *kalam* (கலம்).

By the mid-7th century, Nagapattinam had also developed into a major transit port for Buddhist pilgrims heading west to the holy city of Nalanda. Xuanzang, the Tang dynasty monk immortalised in *Journey to the West*, passed through the city. As did a disciple of his, our itinerant monk, Yijing, who recounts his arrival at Na-ga-po-tan-na in the latter half of the 7th century, after sailing across the Bay of Bengal in a Srivijayan ship from Kedah.

Buddha Shakyamuni Seated in Meditation (Dhyanamudra). Nagapattinam, Tamil Nadu, c. 12th century. Granite, 160 x 120.2 x 56.3 cm. Collection of the Art Institute of Chicago.

With its strong ties to Buddhist communities in Srivijaya and China, Nagapattinam remained staunchly Buddhist, even as it came under the suzerainty of successive Hindu kings. In the 8th century, one of these kings commissioned and endowed a Chinese-style pagoda, built in honour of the Tang emperor and catering to the religious needs of Chinese pilgrims. The "Chinese Pagoda" would be a fixture in the city over the centuries, figuring largely in visitor's descriptions. Marco Polo saw it in the 13th century; Chinese explorer Wang Dayuan and Arab traveller Ibn Battutah encountered it in the 14th; as did the British in the mid-19th. The pagoda, by then in ruins, was finally demolished by the Jesuits in 1867.

Remarkably, Buddhist statuary dating to as late as the 17th century has been excavated in the larger Nagapattinam region. This suggests that long after Buddhism had ceased to be a major faith in mainland India, pockets of it continued to thrive, by virtue of generous support from pilgrim communities who continued arriving, in significant enough numbers, to seek ancient wisdom.

The city would come into its own during the reign of the mediaeval Cholas, who unlike their ancestors, the Cholas of the Sangam Age, were an imperial power; perhaps the greatest such power in India until the Mughals. At its peak in the 10th and 11th centuries, during the reigns of Rajaraja I and his son, Rajendra Chola I, the Chola Empire's physical territory included almost all of southern India and northern Sri Lanka.

The *Chola-mandala*, or the Chola Empire's larger sphere of influence, extended northeast till the Ganges River delta in Bengal, south to encompass the entire island of Sri Lanka, and east, across the oceans, to Srivijaya. For the first time in the history of the Indian subcontinent, almost its entire coastline, in particular, that of the fertile, verdant, subtropical south, was ruled over by one single empire.

Nagapattinam had been chosen as chief port of the empire due to its location just downriver from the splendid Chola capital, Thanjavur (Tanjore). The Chola kings built magnificent monuments to themselves here, most notably the Brihadishvara Temple, commissioned by Rajaraja Chola I in the early 11th century. This spectacular temple in the Dravidian style, complete with *vimana* tower built out of granite, is one of the largest Hindu temples in South India and regarded as the crowning glory of Chola architecture. This and other spectacular temples dedicated to Shiva stand testament to the prodigious wealth of the Chola kings, accumulated by way of trade at Nagapattinam.

Within these temples stood the other important Chola contribution to mankind's cultural legacy: those sacred and sensuous bronze sculptures of Hindu deities, referred to as Chola bronzes. These served a ritual purpose. Normally ensconced in temple alcoves, they would be swathed in sacred textiles and blossoms during religious festivals, taken out from their temples and paraded down the streets in large processions, to be worshipped by hundreds of devotees.

Of these ritual bronzes, the most startling are depictions of Shiva as *Nataraja*, or Lord of the Dance and of the Cosmos. Here in the south, master artisans, in a departure from traditional practices of representing Shiva as *lingam*, decide instead to depict Shiva in human form.[22] He dances exuberantly, his supple limbs raised in one of the timeless poses of the *Natyashastra*, the ancient Sanskrit treatise on dance, music and performance. His hair is wildly and majestically thrown to the winds, even as the universe itself is simultaneously destroyed and reborn around him.

Of-the-era descriptions of Nagapattinam from the perspective of the Tamils aren't quite so easy to access, at least for the lay English reader. One vivid description of the city appears in the 12th century *Periyapuranam* ("great epic"), recounting the life stories of 63 Nayanars ("saints") in Tamil Saivite tradition. Commissioned by Kulothunga Chola II in the 12th century, and written by the poet Sekkizhar, it features Nagapattinam in the *puranam* ("tale") of the humble fisherman, Athipattha Nayanar.[23]

> "The beauteous city of Naakaippattinam as of right / Belongs to the divine race of hoary and pre-eminent / Cholas who hail from the ever-during solar dynasty. / Verily a blossom of the *karpaka liana*, the realm / Of Ponni [the Kaveri River], abounds in weal and wealth.
>
> Black clouds that have drunk deep the black sea-waters, / Mistaking for hills the gold-bright and beauteous / Mansions, crawl over their sides; many are the raised / Platforms in those mansions where lasses whose / Rows of chains made of pearls dangle low and whose / Locks decked with honey-laden flowers get loosened, / As they play with a ball.
>
> This city is full of glorious sounds; it is / The beloved abode of Lakshmi, the Goddess of Wealth; / It yields all things desired; it looks vaster than / The sea with its waves of elephants, steeds, / Gems and garments and other things thither brought / In barks and barkentines. [...] and as its rich citizens / Are more than a crore, this beauteous and hoary city / Is like unto a mirror mandala which reflects / (Within it) the whole world." [24]

While the city's population did not number a *crore* (ten million), Nagapattinam was undoubtedly a great city with a very large population for its time. With the Chola kings settled in their palaces in Thanjavur, Nagapattinam belonged to merchants and their retinue; and the latter, in upwardly-mobile and nouveau riche fashion, festooned the city with the ostentatious trappings of wealth: palatial mansions, bejewelled wives and daughters, and luxurious textiles and garments.

The most powerful of the merchants were a force to be reckoned with indeed, and were organised in large and influential trading guilds. Two of these guilds are worth noting. The first was the Anjuvannam, representing merchants of Middle Eastern origin: Zoroastrian Persians, Muslim Arabs, Syrian Christians, Jews, Armenians and North Africans who had come to trade in South India. They were active in Kerala as well as in Tamil Nadu, and specialised in precious goods from the Byzantine Empire and the Middle East. The city was a transit point for some of them as they journeyed on to Srivijaya and further east to China.

The second and more powerful merchant guild was the Ainnurruvar, also known as the Five Hundred of Ayyavole.[25] They were a primarily Tamil guild with a network both local and international. In South India, they had a presence in 18 different *pattinam* (பட்டினம் - port cities), 32 *velavula* (villages) and 64 covered bazaars across the country. In inscriptions on copper plates and free-standing steles they had installed across Tamil Nadu, they proclaimed themselves "the Five Hundred of a thousand directions", favoured by Lakshmi (Goddess of Wealth) and other deities.

Their networks would expand greatly during the time of the mediaeval Cholas. From their base in Nagapattinam (and elsewhere), they sailed east and were known to have established fortified settlements wherever they landed. Tamil inscriptions found in Southeast Asia suggest that the Ainnurruvar were active in Sri Lanka, Srivijaya, and even the port city of Quanzhou in China. As a highly-organised guild, they represented their members' interests abroad and likely also employed armed mercenaries to protect them as they travelled east.

Given their power and influence, the Ainnurruvar probably had a direct line of communication to the Chola kings. It's possible that where the guild found its trade compromised or endangered in a foreign land, it would reach out to the highest levels for support or, in extreme scenarios, even military intervention.

In 1025, the 15th year of Rajendra Chola I's reign, the unthinkable happened: the Cholas went to war against Srivijaya. This was extraordinary because it's perhaps the only recorded instance of war between India and Southeast Asia. We know it took place due to a single inscription in the Amritaghatesvarar Temple in the suburb of Tirukaddaiyur in Thanjavur. This inscription provides a blow-by-blow account of Rajendra Chola I's conquest of a dozen cities in Sumatra and the Malay Peninsula, culminating in the sacking and looting of the Srivijayan capital, Palembang, and the installation of a puppet regime in Kadaram (Kedah).

Why exactly the Cholas attacked continues to be debated. One accepted theory is that of competition between the Cholas and Srivijaya for control over the lucrative China trade. The Bay of Bengal was, by the early 11th century, a "Chola

Shiva Nataraja. Tamil Nadu, c. 950 – 1000. Copper alloy, 76.20 x 57.15 x 17.78 cm. Collection of the Los Angeles County Museum of Art.

lake", with Nagapattinam a major stopover for traders en route to Southeast Asia. Once in Southeast Asia, however, these Chola traders had to play by the rules of their counterparts in Srivijaya, who guarded their middleman position fiercely. As the Ainnurruvar's power and influence grew, conflict with Srivijaya probably became inevitable. The historical record suggests relations between the Cholas and Srivijaya deteriorated sharply by this time.

In 1005, Maharaja Chudamarnivarman of Srivajaya would successfully appeal to Rajaraja I for the endowment of a Buddhist *vihara* in Nagapattinam. 10 years later, an offer of precious stones would be made to the same temple and graciously received by Rajendra Chola I. In 1018, yet another gift would be made – of Chinese gold – to another temple in Nagapattinam. These should probably be read as desperate attempts to appease the Cholas and to restore diplomacy, and not as signs of friendly or cordial relations between the two.[26]

Less than a decade later, war would be declared.

Imagine then, the port city of Nagapattinam, bristling with a vast armada of warships.[27] Crimson-hued pennants flap furiously atop the main masts of these fearsome vessels, each large enough to harbour a battalion of soldiers and warrior elephants. These pennants brandish the Chola ensign: a snarling Indian tiger, poised to attack. Purpose-built in an arsenal, the warships have sailed to Nagapattinam harbour, with great fanfare and in full view of resident and visiting merchants. Here they will wait till late December, when the southwest monsoons begin, and they make their timeless way across the Bay of Bengal to Suvarnabhumi, not to trade this time, but to raid and destroy.

麒麟圖

永樂十二年歲次甲午秋九月榜葛剌國進貢臣華亭沈度為

PART
⇸ **II** ⇷

OF MONSOONS
AND
MERCHANTS

11th — 15th Centuries

7. Quanzhou (Zaitun)
Merchant Princes of China's Hokkien Coast

"In deep Spring, with the song of the sea in the background, the entire county is painted a rosy-red / On account of the *tseetung* flowers the Yue People [of South China] plant in abundance here."

— Chen Tao, Tang dynasty (9th century). "An Ode to Quanzhou's Tseetung Flowers, Presented to Envoy Zhao".

Erythrina variegata is a hardy, flowering tree species that originates in the subtropical climes of the larger Indian Ocean region. It grows to just under 30 metres in height and its canopy is sprawling and dense. It is known for its thorns, which grow on the surface of its branches and trunk; and for its flowers, which bloom bright red and occur in dense clusters. The Chinese name for the tree (刺桐) means "thorny *tong* tree" and is pronounced *citong* in Mandarin. The same characters are read *tseetung* in Hokkien.

In the late Tang dynasty, Quanzhou (泉州) was known for its *tseetung* trees, their seasonal efflorescence carpeting the town in crimson. *Tseetung* seeds would have been imported here by hardy, long-distance *marakib al-Sin* from the Middle East. The species proved popular with the city's denizens, perhaps due to the auspicious colour of its blooms, connoting wealth and prosperity in Chinese culture.

The city was home to a large merchant community. This seems particularly apt, given that the southern Chinese province where it's situated is called Fujian (福建), read *hokkien* in the local dialect and meaning "building wealth". The Hokkien people are thus literally "men who build wealth"; and so it seems almost inevitable that many of them would choose trade and commerce as a profession.

Quanzhou's love affair with the *tseetung* tree would endure across the centuries. By the time of the Five Dynasties, the humble but ubiquitous *tseetung* blossom had become the most instantly recognisable aspect of the city. Indeed, Quanzhou had become so associated with the species as to be synonymous with it – "Tseetung City" became a popular, alternative name among the Chinese. Foreigners arriving on its shores would know the city as Zaitun, an arabisation of *tseetung*.[1]

Quanzhou's rise was a product of circumstance. During the Tang dynasty, Guangzhou was the pre-eminent port in China; the official and

OVERLEAF: *Tribute Giraffe with Attendant* (detail). Formerly attributed to Shen Du. China, Ming dynasty, 16th century. Ink and colour on silk. 80 x 40.6 cm. Gift of John T. Dorrance, 1977. Collection of the Philadelphia Museum of Art.

OPPOSITE PAGE: Renshou Pagoda, Kaiyuan Temple, Quanzhou.

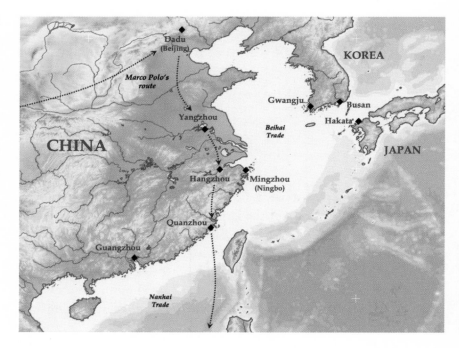

Major port and capital cities in China in the Song and Yuan periods, with Marco Polo's route mapped out. Yangzhou and Mingzhou were ports specialising in the Beihai trade with Korea and Japan, while Guangzhou and Quanzhou saw merchants depart for the Nanhai. Hangzhou was the capital of the Southern Song dynasty while Dadu (today's Beijing) was that of the Yuan.

preferred gateway to the Nanhai. Situated at the furthest possible distance from the imperial court in the north, Guangzhou served as a holding area – keeping the *fan* traders who called at its shores conveniently at bay, segregated from the larger Chinese mainland.

The Tang emperors, inheriting a traditional, Confucian disdain of trade that dated to the earliest days of Chinese civilisation, forbade the Chinese themselves to partake of it.[2] Instead, they instituted an elaborate tributary system that saw "barbarian ships" (*fan bo*) bringing all manner of foreign goods to China's port cities. By imperial decree, a portion of this had to be offered up to the imperial court as tribute; the rest could be sold at the markets in Guangzhou and elsewhere. Quanzhou, situated some distance north from Guangzhou, was a secondary port city. It was deemed distant enough from the imperial courts to be opened up to the *fan*, but it consistently played second fiddle.

The Song dynasty saw a dramatic about-turn in trade and foreign policy. The Song emperors regarded trade as a critical lifeline to empire. Eschewing the aloofness of their predecessors, they sent warm words of welcome to the south, inviting the "barbarians of the world" (诸番 – *zhu fan*) to trade with China. They also encouraged their own subjects to venture forth freely to trade. And so, for the first time in history,

Chinese merchants and Chinese-made vessels would ply the greater Indian Ocean in large numbers, calling at ports in Srivijaya, India, Sri Lanka, and even as far west as the Swahili Coast in Africa. These vessels were called junks, likely from the Chinese word for "boat", *chuan* (船 – read *june* in Hokkien).

Quanzhou's fortunes shifted in the late 11th century. On account of persistent lobbying by resident merchants, the Song emperor appointed a formal Superintendent of Maritime Trade, or *shi bo si* (市舶司), in the city. Prior to this, only Guangzhou, Hangzhou and Mingzhou had maritime trade superintendents. This meant Hokkien merchants needed to make a detour to either of these cities to obtain the necessary permissions to go abroad. The establishment of a superintendency in Quanzhou was a sign that the city's flourishing trade and its mercantile wealth could no longer be ignored. Certainly, this was a huge boon for the Hokkien merchants since there was now a "direct service" from Quanzhou to the Nanhai.

Trade was so important to the Song that members of the royal family themselves partook in it, moving south to take residence in Quanzhou, where they were known as "scions of the Southern branch of the imperial family", or *nanwai zongzi*. These merchant princes engaged avidly in trade, commissioning ships and amassing vast wealth.[3] All manner of goods were traded here, with the most important inward-bound good being *xiang* ("fragrance"). The word referred to a wide variety of plant- and animal-based aromatics originating in the Middle East, India and Southeast Asia, and used as perfumes and incense, spices and flavour enhancers for food, drugs and medicines, and even poisons. At the time of the Song, the Chinese elite were known to import vast quantities of *xiang* to perfume their clothes and residences and to flavour their elaborate cuisine. The rarest and most sought-after *xiang* was ambergris, solidified bile duct secretions from sperm whales. The Chinese believed this to be dried up dragon spittle and called it *Longxian Xiang* ("dragon spittle fragrance"). It was the preserve of royalty.

Quanzhou would surpass Guangzhou as China's pre-eminent port city during the Yuan dynasty. The story of its rise is linked to the remarkable tale of Pu Shougeng, one of its most illustrious citizens, and another of its great merchant princes.

Pu's exact ancestry is hazy. He likely hailed from a community of naturalised Arab-Muslims who had resided in China for generations, adopted Chinese names and spoke Chinese fluently. The surname, "Pu", is likely a transliteration of the Arab "Abu". Pu himself was born and bred in Quanzhou, though his family was said to have emigrated first to Southeast Asia and then Guangzhou, before finally settling down in Quanzhou, where they became prominent and respected representatives of the local Arab-Muslim community.

In 1274, Pu and his brother successfully fended off a pirate attack on Quanzhou harbour with their own private fleets and personal means. In recognition of the Pu family's contributions, Pu Shougeng was bestowed the title of "Superintendent of the Peace in the Coastal Cities of Hokkien Province". This afforded him control over maritime affairs in the province, including naval fleets and military infrastructure. The Song court would further promote him in subsequent years to "Superintendent of the Peace for Hokkien *and* Canton Province", as well as harbourmaster of Quanzhou.

By way of his official appointments, Pu rose very quickly to become one of China's wealthiest and most powerful merchants. He enjoyed strong support from local Han Chinese residents as well as the city's substantial foreign merchant community. During his lifetime, he would own China's largest fleet of private merchant and military vessels, and he built his own watchtowers along Quanzhou harbour to secure safe passage for ships travelling to and from the city. It was widely acknowledged, even at the imperial court, that Pu was de facto Master of Quanzhou.

In 1276, after decades of successful military campaigns in China, Kublai Khan's Golden Horde swept into the Song capital of Lin'an (today's city of Hangzhou), taking the city and forcing the Song emperor south. The emperor and his army came knocking at Quanzhou's city gates, hoping to count on Pu's support. Unfortunately, the ever shrewd and entrepreneurial Pu had already thrown his lot in with the Mongols. He refused the emperor sanctuary, and when Song troops commandeered his ships, retaliated brutally by slaughtering the *nanwai zongzi* and other Song loyalists in the city. Pu would hold firm within the walls of the city for 90 days, until the Mongol army finally arrived to subdue the Song and ride triumphantly through the city gates.

Pu's act of surrender saved Quanzhou. Much of China, including Guangzhou, had been sacked and razed by the Mongols. But in Quanzhou, it was business as usual. Upon attaining the throne, the Mongol emperor, Kublai Khan, made an appeal to the world's merchants, inviting them to trade freely at his imperial port city of Quanzhou. And come they did, en masse. Chinese records remark on the number of countries trading with

Quanzhou's historic Masjid al-Ashab. The structure and floor-plan of the mosque resembles Persian Gulf antecedents, while the generous use of ogee arches and calligraphic inscriptions on the walls echoes contemporary mosque adornment in Sultanate-era India. Constructed in China, the mosque is a cross-cultural product of the Indian Ocean trade.

Quanzhou increasing significantly. Quanzhou, already multicultural in outlook, became even more polyglot and international. Along with cultural diversity came religious diversity. The city counted mosques and churches, Confucian, Buddhist, Taoist, Manichean and even Hindu temples amongst its many places of worship. Much of the city's multi-religious heritage still exists today, and Quanzhou is the first port city on our journey that also happens to be a UNESCO World Heritage Site.

Two sites, in particular, stand out. The first houses the ruins of the Masjid al-Ashab, also known as the Qingjing Temple in Chinese, and the oldest stone mosque still standing in China. Parts of it date back to the Song dynasty, though it had been successively rebuilt during the Yuan and the Ming. The arched gateway and entrance façade to the compound likely dates to the Yuan period, and is distinctively non-Chinese in style. Most notably, the mosque's immediate vicinity contained the *ancien* residential quarters of the local Arab-Muslim community. Pu Shougeng and family would almost certainly have resided near this very spot – perhaps his tomb once stood in the mosque's cemetery.

The second of the city's sites of cross-cultural history is the spectacular Kaiyuan Temple. One of the largest Buddhist temples in China, it has stood in the same spot since the 7th century, though much of it, too, was rebuilt during the Ming dynasty. Its most intriguing feature is a group of stone pillars and fragments that appear completely out of place. Lord Vishnu features in no less than seven of these fragments, which depict scenes from Hindu mythology, in a classic Chola-style.

Scholars now acknowledge that the stone pillars and fragments are likely all that remain of a lost Hindu temple that once stood in the city and was probably destroyed during the Ming. This lost temple would have been endowed by a small but thriving community of resident Tamil merchants: the legendary Ainnurruvar, whose trading networks extended as far east as here.

By the turn of the 14th century, Quanzhou had become one of the largest port cities in the world. Chinese and foreign visitors alike were amazed by its scale and its cosmopolitan nature. The great Chinese explorer, Wang Dayuan, describes the city as the place where the *zhu fan* converged to trade. Quanzhou was the point of departure for his grand tour of the Nanhai. In the course of the 1330s, he would visit the various kingdoms of Southeast Asia and the Indian subcontinent. He is best known for his first-hand accounts of the city of Angkor as well as the Malay island of Temasek (which we know today as Singapore). He would return to Quanzhou to complete his great travelogue, *Daoyi Zhilue*, or *A Brief Description of Islands and Barbarian Peoples*.

A Chinese contemporary of Wang Dayuan, Quanzhou-born Zhuang Mishao, describes his home city as "married to the sea" and part-*fan* in essence: a melting-pot of cultures and the central node in a maritime network of trading vessels from the "ten thousand kingdoms" (meaning "the known world").[4] He notes that in this city (*du*), vessels from all over the world converge and convene with each other (*hui*). The word *duhui* (都会) would later be used to translate the English word, "metropolis", which is precisely what Quanzhou was in its prime.

Into this great metropolis comes another of Wang Dayuan's contemporaries: the great Italian explorer, Marco Polo. Born in 1254 to a family of merchants in Venice, Polo would become one of the greatest explorers of his time. Together with his father, Niccolò and his uncle, Maffeo, he would embark, in the 1270s, on a remarkable journey across the Eurasian continent to Asia, while he was only 17 years of age. The three intrepid explorers managed to reach Khanbaliq, also known as Dadu, the capital city of the Yuan emperors. Marco would remain in China for 17 years, travelling extensively across the country, and purportedly accompanying a Mongol princess across the Indian Ocean to Persia, where she would be wed to the Mongol Ilkhanate rulers of Iran at the time. He would finally make his way home by sea sometime in the 1290s, crossing Southeast Asia and stopping at India, Ceylon and the East African coast, before returning to Venice, by now a very rich man.

Polo's voyages east are recounted in his *Travels*, originally titled *Livre des merveilles du monde* in French, or *Book of the Marvels of the World*. In the *Travels*, Polo arrives at the city of Zaitun after he had taken in the spectacle that was Khanbaliq, as well as the energising dynamism of China's economic capital, Hangzhou (Kinsai in the *Travels*). Nothing prepares him, however, for the immensity of the city on the Hokkien coast.

> "At the end of five days journey, you arrive at the noble and handsome city of Zaitun, which has a port famous for the vast quantity of shipping, loaded with Merchandise that enters it and is afterwards distributed through every part of the province of Manzi [South China]. The quantity of pepper imported here is so great that what is carried to Alexandria to supply the demand of the western parts of the world is trifling in comparison – perhaps no more than a hundredth part. It is indeed impossible to convey any idea of the number of merchants and the accumulation of goods in this place, which is held to be one of the largest ports in the world." [5]

In mediaeval Europe, pepper was the luxury good *du jour,* worth more than its weight in gold. And yet here in this Chinese city was more of the black gold than he had ever seen (and would ever again see) in his lifetime.

Polo is also one of the first Europeans to encounter Chinese porcelain. On a tour of the city's outskirts, he casually notes the production of a strange sort of clay-based material. Then unknown to Europe, Chinese porcelain – particularly the blue-and-white variety – was already one of the Yuan dynasty's most important exports to the Middle East. Enormous volumes of the precious stuff were shipped from Quanzhou to Persia and Anatolia, where they remain today in royal collections in Iran and Turkey. Blue-and-white porcelain would become an important luxury import to Europe only a century later, during the Ming.

Polo concludes, after his brief sojourn here, that all in all, the city of Zaitun was simply delightful, boasting a top-notch quality of life. He remarks with a trace of envy that its inhabitants had all their needs well-met, and that they lived in a general state of ease, prosperity and abundance. And how could they not? This was, after all, China's merchant province, where the business of "building wealth" was not just a profession, but a matter of cultural identity.

8. Khambhat (Cambay)
Indian Trade Cloth and the Gujarati Baniya

> "Cambay is one of the most beautiful cities as regards the artistic architecture of its houses and the construction of its mosques. The reason is that the majority of its inhabitants are foreign merchants, who continually build there beautiful houses and wonderful mosques – an achievement in which they endeavour to surpass each other."
> — Ibn Battutah, c. 14th century. *Rihlah.*[6]

The great Jami Masjid of Khambhat (ખંભાત) stands at the southern edge of the old town, overlooking the port and mouth of the Mahi River. Built in 1325, it is one of the oldest buildings in the city and has been continuously in use for 700 years. The exterior of the mosque is built in sandstone and looks unprepossessing, suggesting a city or fortress wall. But once inside, the mosque's significance is immediately apparent: this is one of the earliest examples of Indo-Islamic architecture in the world, predating the spectacular monuments of the Mughal Empire by some 200 years.

The architecture of the mosque's interior is syncretic, blending elements of Hindu, Jain and Islamic styles and belying Islam's relative novelty in 14th century India. A forest of some 100 pillars - distinctly Hindu or Jain in style - holds up the domes of the mosque. These pillars were culled and re-purposed from former temples that used to stand in the vicinity. The undersides of the mosque's many domes are, likewise, elaborately carved and ornamented, and likely taken from former temples. They make for hours of enjoyable viewing and would be the highlight of any visit here, except for another legendary feature: the mausoleum of Umar bin Ahmad al-Kazeruni, built into the southern side of the mosque complex.

The mausoleum, and its accompanying private mosque and courtyard, is believed to have been commissioned by al-Kazeruni himself. His *nisba* ("patronymic") betrays his Persian origins. Al-Kazeruni means "of Kazerun", with Kazerun being a small town near the city of Shiraz, in the historic Persian heartland of Fars. Once topped with minarets and the largest dome in India in its time, the mausoleum would have dominated the city's skyline. But a series of major earthquakes, the last in 1819, brought down dome and minarets alike.

The tomb of al-Kazeruni still stands at the centre of the mausoleum, though it is now exposed to the elements. It is a beautiful work of art, wrought entirely of white marble and heavily adorned with floral decoration. The tomb is crowned with an exquisite headstone boasting stylised calligraphic script spelling out various *surahs* from the Qur'an. The inscription on the tomb honours al-Kazeruni as "blessed martyr, received in mercy, chief of chiefs, prince of Vazirs, celebrated in Arabia and Persia, pillar of the state and of religion."[7] It suggests that he was a very wealthy and important man indeed.

Al-Kazeruni's white marble headstone, and others of the kind in the city, would have cost a fortune to commission. The marble had to be hewn from mountainous north Gujarat and brought to the city to be painstakingly carved and decorated by local artisans. These headstones are so distinctive to the city as to be known as "Cambay headstones". They stand testament to the wealth and reach of local merchants in their heyday. They were also exported in the 13th to 15th centuries to all around the Indian Ocean rim, where they adorn tombs of nobles from as far afield as Kilwa, on the Swahili Coast, and Gresik, in East Java.

Interior of the Jami Masjid, Khambhat.

Khambhat itself was once better known as the great port city of Cambay, although very little aside from the Jami Masjid and the mausoleum of al-Kazeruni remain in this little town to remind the visitor of its past glory.

Cambay is situated in the northwestern Indian province of Gujarat. First described as a major trading port in the 10th century, it was India's pre-eminent port city till the 16th. Its advantage was proximity to the agricultural and craft heartlands of Gujarat and integration into the maritime trade networks of the Indian Ocean. From Cambay, networks of merchants extended westward to Persia, Arabia, and the Byzantine Empire, southwards to Great Zimbabwe in Africa, and eastwards to Srivijaya and China.

Very little by way of physical architecture or objects remain from this legendary city. We thus have to depend on eyewitness accounts to understand how important it was. Marco Polo arrives in the city in the 1290s, and describes the trade carried on as being very substantial indeed. At the time, Gujarat was still ruled by Hindu kings, the Vaghelas. Polo arrives to witness Cambay's last gasp as a city of "idolaters" (in his words). By 1299, Gujarat, including Cambay, would be brought under the aegis of the Delhi Sultanate.

The city thrived under its new, Muslim sovereigns. Another great world traveller, Ibn Battutah, offers us a telling first-hand account of the city in the mid-14th century. Born to a family of *qadis*, or religious scholars, in the caravan-city of Tangier, Battutah was of North African, Berber origins. Very little else is known about him except for his travels, and he travelled further than any other explorer in the world before the 1500s.

He made three great journeys in his lifetime. The first, he made in the mid-1320s when, en route to Mecca on his first Hajj, he decided to take monumental detours to Baghdad, Muscat and the great port cities of the Swahili Coast. The second took place sometime between the late 1320s to the early 1340s when, suffused with wanderlust, he travelled by land and sea to Yuan China, taking in Zaitun and Dadu, just as Marco Polo did before him. His third journey was made between the 1340s to the 1350s, when he explored Granada in al-Andalus and Timbuktu in present-day Mali. His epic *Rihlah* (رحلة), or "Itinerary", was written after his final journey, and recounts the details of his 29 years of exploring the *dar al-Islam* and beyond. It is considered the definitive example of its genre.

Battutah stopped in Cambay around 1342 while on his second journey across the globe. Cambay was clearly a Muslim city by that time. It probably resembled a *medina* in Abbasid times, furnished with courtyard gardens, fountains and flowing water, elegant arches, *iwans* and minarets, albeit transplanted to the north Indian coast.

Battutah notes that the majority of the city's residents were foreign. And indeed, at this time, the Indian Ocean would more aptly have been described as a "Persian Lake", its trade dominated by Persians (by now Muslim, rather than Zoroastrian) and Arabs of the Persian Gulf. Its lingua franca, or language of trade, would have been Persian or a Persian creole. When Cambay turned to Islam, it became a preferred destination for these merchants, who beautified the city to suit their cosmopolitan taste and culture.

It comes as no surprise that al-Kazeruni appears in Battutah's accounts. Referring to the great man as Malik al-Tujar ("King of the Merchants"), Battutah describes his house as one of the grand buildings of the city, boasting a private mosque built beside it. He recounts al-Kazeruni's murder at the hands of bandits in 1333, and how the city mourned him as a martyr. Battutah's arrival in Cambay comes almost a decade after the merchant-king's death, revealing how the tragic event continued to haunt Cambay society for years.

Sometime between the 14th and the 15th centuries, Gujarati merchants eclipsed their Persian Gulf counterparts in the Indian Ocean. They would not be displaced in turn by Europeans until the early 19th century. In fact, the name, "Indian Ocean", is a nod to their ubiquity, and the overwhelming significance of the Indian trade. Cambay was the principal port city of the Gujaratis. From here, they would fan out across the globe, establishing diasporas in other Asian port cities.

Two groups of Gujarati merchants featured prominently. The first were the *baniya* (વાણિયા): Jain and Hindu merchants. Marco Polo encounters them when he arrives in Cambay, and they continued to thrive under the auspices of the Delhi Sultanate, tolerated by Muslim sultans who reaped the benefits of the immense wealth they brought to the province.

The *baniyas*, as a whole, included closely-knit and very powerful groups of great merchant families. They dominated trade by way of strong networks of kinship, excellent and reliable business practices, expertise in shipbuilding and navigation, ready credit and insurance, and links to artisans and markets. *Baniya* families were known to be prodigiously wealthy, but extremely frugal. They were also fervently religious; strict in their observances of caste and ritual. One of their main pre-occupations, aside from business, was to sponsor the construction and maintenance of Hindu and Jain temples in Gujarat, as well as their adopted hometowns.

A second group of Gujarati merchants emerged later, when the Gujaratis themselves converted to Islam, and as Gujarat was eventually absorbed into the Mughal Empire. They would play an important role not just in trade, but in the spread of Islam across the Indian Ocean. The proliferation of these Muslim Gujarati merchants accounts for the Indian Ocean being referred to as a "Muslim Lake" by the 16th century. Like the *baniyas*, there were different groups of Muslim merchants who operated within their own milieu. Perhaps the most well-known of these are the Dawoodi Bohras, who also established diaspora communities across the Indian Ocean from Mombasa to Singapore.

By far the most valuable commodities traded at Cambay were printed cotton textiles, much in demand for their elaborate designs and exuberant colour, which would not run when the cloth was washed. These light and comfortable Indian fabrics were luxuries compared to the relatively drab and harsh cloth produced in Europe, Africa and Southeast Asia at the time. Large-scale production was possible due to plentiful supplies of cotton from the Gujarati heartland.

The earliest extant examples of Indian trade cloth have been found in the Middle East. 5th century fragments were famously excavated at the Egyptian Red Sea port of Berenike; while thousands of 11th century fragments have been excavated in Cairo. One of the oldest of these Cairo fragments remarkably still retains its sandy-red colour, and features a lotus scroll motif.

In Southeast Asia, high-quality Indian trade cloth was treated as currency and traded for spices. Southeast Asians regarded these textiles as heirlooms, using them as ritual hangings in places of worship, and at important ceremonies and rites of passage. Trade textiles were a mark of status, ancestry and power. Local royalty and nobility draped their bodies with this cloth and tailored fashionable vestments out of it. The textiles themselves were also used as diplomatic gifts or valuable presents bestowed by local royalty upon their subjects.

The process of making printed cottons was elaborate, which explains why they were so valuable. A pattern would first be drawn and painted onto the plain fabric. Sometimes block prints would be used for a repeating motif. A combination of resist and mordant dyeing techniques would then be applied for colour.[8] In the pre-Sultanate period, printed cotton textiles from Gujarat often sported Hindu or Jain motifs: dancing apsaras, warriors fighting mythical beasts, or scenes from *The Ramayana*. By the Sultanate and Mughal eras, motifs would gradually, in the course of time, become geometric and stylised, eschewing human figures (in accordance with Islamic principles), but tending towards highly-elaborate floral compositions.

Of all the trade cloth, fine indigo-hued cloth was likely the rarest and most-prized commodity. Since the 3rd century BCE, Indians had mastered the art of dyeing cloth with organic indigo dye, and these deep blue textiles had been one of the fine products exported to Greece in

ancient times. Marco Polo remarks, wide-eyed, on the great quantity of indigo manufactured in Cambay when he visits, suggesting that the deep-blue dye continued to be a luxury in Europe, more than a thousand years after the Greeks.

The Sanskrit word for indigo is *nila*. As the textile spread across the oceans, the word followed, becoming *al-nila* in Arabic, and *nila* in Malay. The mythical founder of Singapore is referred to as Sang Nila Utama, which possibly translates to "Supreme Lord Indigo" and perhaps refers to this great leader being swathed in indigo cloth, a mark of royalty.

Arriving in the shadow of Marco Polo and Ibn Battutah, the intrepid, world-travelling Portuguese apothecary, Tomé Pires, offers us the best account of this legendary port city of trade cloth and *baniyas*. Immediately after the Portuguese invasion of Melaka in 1511, Pires determines to head east, documenting everything that he sees in his 1515 travelogue, *A Summary of the Orient from the Red Sea to China*, better known as the *Suma Oriental*.

Fragment: female warriors battling mythical beasts. Gujarat, 14th century. Cotton (block printed, drawn and painted, mordant and resist dyed), 156.2 x 102.9 cm. Made for the eastern Indonesian market. From the former Roger Hollander Collection. Collection of the Asian Civilisations Museum.

He stops over at Cambay in 1511, en route to Melaka. He is a keen observer. The *Suma Oriental* serves up one of the most detailed and earnest journalistic accounts of Cambay and its economic potential:

> "It is about three hundred years since the kingdom of Cambay was taken from the heathen; but there are still a great many of them in Cambay, almost the third part of the kingdom [...]. [They] are called Banians. [...] Some of them are men who in their religion lead good lives, they are chaste, true men and very abstemious. [...]

> These [people] are [like] Italians in their knowledge of and dealings in merchandise. All the trade in Cambay is in the hands of the heathen. Their general designation is Gujaratees [...] They are diligent, quick men in trade. They do their accounts with figures like ours and with our very writing. [...] Those of our people who want to be clerks and factors ought to go there and learn.

> ... both the Gujaratees and the merchants who have settled in Cambay [...] sail many ships to all parts [...] where they take quantities of merchandise, bringing other kinds back, thus making Cambay rich and important. [...]

At this point in his reportage, our foreign correspondent makes this legendary remark, quoted down through the ages:

> "Cambay chiefly stretches out two arms, with her right arm she reaches out towards Aden and with the other towards Malacca, as the most important places to sail to, and the other places are held to be of less importance."[9]

From Cambay, all sea roads led either to Aden or Melaka, and the three port cities formed an indomitable axis of global trade up till the 16th century.

9. Aden
Customs-House of the Yemen, Treasury of the West

> "[Aden is] the anteroom of China, [customs-house] of Yemen,
> treasury of the West and mother-lode of commodities."
>
> — Al-Muqaddasi, c. 10th century.
> *The Best Divisions for Knowledge of the Regions.*[10]

Of all the port cities we shall visit on our journey, Aden (عدن) occupies the most dramatic location. It straddles two epic water bodies: the turquoise expanse of the Indian Ocean and the coral-rich sliver that is the Red Sea. The city sits at the southwestern edge of the Yemen, a harsh, arid landscape of mountains and desert to the south of the Arabian Peninsula. This has traditionally been the region of Arabia most associated with seafaring. For centuries, its inhabitants, particularly the Hadhrami Arabs of the Hadhramawt, have departed from here to trade and establish diasporas across India and Southeast Asia.

The city of Aden abuts the Gulf of Aden. Just past it to the west, forming a natural gateway to the Red Sea, lies the infamous Bab al-Mandeb ("Gate of Tears"), so-named because it was a dangerous strait to navigate; many a vessel had been felled by its treacherous reefs and the unpredictable weather in these parts. Local legend has it that once, the Red Sea was no sea at all, and that it was Alexander the Great who created it, by dredging the soil near what is today's Bab al-Mandeb, and allowing the waters of the Indian Ocean to flow in. He did this to create a natural barrier between Abyssinia (today's Ethiopia) and Arabia, whose peoples were constantly at war.[11]

The Bab, and the entrance to the Red Sea, is the narrowest point between Africa and the Arabian Peninsula; only 18 miles across. It is thus a chokepoint for maritime trade, and Aden is its sentinel. The city itself is a sight to behold, nestled impossibly at the foothills of a ring of precipitous peaks. What we know as Aden is actually a minuscule, apostrophe-shaped peninsula that juts out into the water. The peninsula is what remains of a long-extinct volcano, and Aden sits in its crater. Sirah, the city's historic old town, is also known as the Crater district in English.

For more than a thousand years, residents of the city have taken to the top of the crater for exceptional views of sunrise and sunset, and the

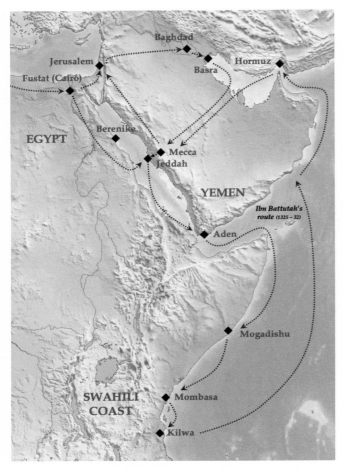

timeless spectacle of vessels at port. These ships used to come and go with the *mawsam* (موسم), the Arabic term for "the seasons" (plural *mawasim* مواسم). The word would be anglicised as "monsoon" and used to describe the coming and going of seasonal winds and rain.

The timing of the monsoons and sailing seasons ran like clockwork. Between August and September, ships bound for India left the city, taking advantage of the last gasps of the southwest monsoon to propel themselves out from the Gulf of Aden to the ocean beyond. Ships from the Mediterranean, wishing to trade in Indian goods, had to arrive in Aden by July. Meanwhile, the return journey from India occurred from late October, with the northeast monsoons propelling ships towards Aden.

Ibn Battutah's travels took him across the *dar al-Islam*, where he stopped at all the major urban settlements of his time. Here, on his first journey east, he travels by way of Mecca to Aden, and southwards to the port cities of the Swahili Coast. His *Rihlah* provides valuable first-person accounts of these places.

From November, the winds stopped and some rains fell to quell the heat. There was no sailing then.

For a city so close to the sea, Aden has always faced a shortage of water. All historical accounts of the city describe it as a barren place, rocky and desolate. Nothing grows here. No crops of any value, nor native shrubs or trees to provide shade and green cover. Water itself has to be captured and stored in cisterns and reservoirs during the rains. And yet despite its obvious disadvantages, Aden has proven so strategic to global trade that it has flourished for most of the second millennium.

Aden's swift rise was built on the slow demise of the Abbasid Caliphate in Mesopotamia. In the early 10th century, a new and powerful Arab caliphate emerged in the fertile Nile River delta in Egypt. Claiming descent from the Prophet Muhammad's daughter, Fatima, they called themselves the Fatimids and established their capital at Fustat (in the suburbs of today's Cairo). In Baghdad, the Abbasids had become but a shadow of their former selves, having been brought to their knees by a regional Iranian power, the Buyids.

Thus, Fustat replaced Baghdad as political and economic centre of the *dar al-Islam*. This westward shift of power meant the nexus of maritime trade in the Middle East also shifted west from the Persian Gulf to the Red Sea. Merchant vessels that formerly brought their wares to Basra and Siraf now took them to Jeddah and Aden. In fact, four major trade routes now converged at Aden: the India route west from Cambay and the Malabar Coast, the Persian route southwest from Khorasan, the African route northeast from Kilwa and Zanzibar, and the Mediterranean route southeast, by way of the Red Sea, from Cairo and Alexandria. Aden became the fulcrum of trade between the Indian Ocean and the Mediterranean Sea.

The 10th to the 16th centuries saw a suite of regional and local sultanates succeed each other in the southern Yemen. Despite prolonged political instability, one thing remained constant: these sultanates allied themselves with Egypt. Aden benefitted commercially from this consistency, and its economic growth was swift. Al-Muqaddasi, in his 10th century encyclopaedia of the known world, *The Best Divisions for Knowledge of the Regions*, refers to Aden as the "*furda* (فرضة) of Yemen", simultaneously describing the city as principal entrepôt of the Yemen, but also, quite literally, its customs-house – port duties collected here made the Yemen rich.

Furda is very likely also a reference to Aden's legendary Customs House building, a major landmark in the city. It stood at a prominent location on Sira Bay, at the city's historic harbour. Arab accounts have the customs-house built into the city's imposing sea walls, which ran all across the shoreline from the hills in the north to craggy Sira Island in the south. The walls sealed the city off from the sea and were an important defence against naval attacks.

The *furda* had two gates: a Sea Gate, through which goods were brought to be assessed for duties by customs officials; and a City Gate, by which goods assessed were allowed to enter the city. It deployed lookouts at watchtowers on the edges of the harbour, built high at the top of the hills. These lookouts were able to spot any vessel approaching the harbour and forewarn customs officials accordingly. Ships arriving would be swiftly and smoothly processed at customs and immigrations.

View of the city of Aden, c. 1572, engraving published in *Civitates Orbis Terrarum*. Georg Braun and Franz Hogenberg. Cologne, 1572 – 1617. The city's legendary Customs House is probably at centre. To the left is Sira Island.

Such unfailing efficiency probably also contributed to Aden's growth. Four centuries after al-Muqaddasi, Ibn Battutah arrives at Aden and describes a port city no less thriving and wealthy, home to Indian and Egyptian merchants. Trade with China had, by this time, given way to trade with India, and "India ships" – *marakib al-Hind* (مراكب الهند) – were now the main vessels of trade.

Battutah remarks on the city's admirable piety, noting that despite great wealth, the merchant community here were humble, dutiful people. They treated their guests hospitably, gave to the poor, and performed their religious duties. The city's religiosity would be corroborated in later accounts. Aden-born historian, Abu Makhrama, in his incomplete *History of the Frontier-Region of Aden*, goes to great lengths to explain how 16th century Aden was a centre of Islamic learning, drawing scholars and pilgrims from across the *dar al-Islam*. Aden's Islamic pedigree – so Abu Makhrama explains – ran deep. One of its earliest mosques had been founded by none other than Uthman, third caliph and son-in-law of the Prophet Muhammad.

Unfortunately, almost nothing of mediaeval Aden remains today. There is no longer any trace of its ancient mosques or madrasas, nor of its customs-house and sea walls. The most enigmatic pre-18th century structure that still stands is the so-called Aden Minaret in downtown Crater. Some say the structure was once part of a large mosque complex. Others believe it an *ancien* watchtower or lighthouse, in operation long before silting and land reclamation moved the waterfront miles out to sea.

The other remaining structure from the mediaeval period is the imposing fortress on Sira Island, believed to have been built in the 12th century. Today, it is still used by the local military, and as such, has eluded archaeological surveys, even as it continues to serve its original purpose.

Aden's central role in bridging the Indian Ocean and Mediterranean trades is vividly illustrated by way of the Cairo Geniza Letters: an astonishing collection of letters written in the 11th and 12th centuries by Jewish merchants resident in Aden and Egypt.[12] Sieved out from amongst hundreds of thousands of religious documents, these letters are written in Judaeo-Arabic script (wherein Hebrew script is used to write the Arabic language). Many are fragmented or physically falling apart due to age. Words are often almost illegible, and the Arabic used is not just antique, but colloquial. Much of the contents of these letters and personal documents come to us today by way of 20th century German-Jewish academic, Shelomo Dov Goitein, who spent his lifetime studying and translating this precious archive.

Some 400 of the letters – a mere fraction of the whole – relate to Indian traders and their *marakib al-Hind*. Most of these are personal letters, many of them written in Aden and sent to various ports in India and the Swahili Coast. They reveal that trade at the time was multi-religious in nature: Jewish merchants operated within a larger trade network that was at once Muslim, Christian and Hindu; and merchants from all faiths regularly transacted with each other.

Amongst the earliest letters to be translated into English was one by Madmun bin Hassan bin Bundar, merchant representative, superintendent of the port of Aden, and head of the Jewish communities of the Yemen. The letter is addressed to Abraham bin Perahya Ben Yiju, a Tunisian Jew who had major business interests on India's Malabar Coast and who appears, like a recurring character, in a few of the *geniza* letters. The postscript of the letter, written in 1149, is its most evocative and illuminating section:

"Please give Sus Siti and Kinbati [and Isha...] and Ishaq the Banyan my best regards, and tell them of my longing for them. Inform them in my name that as for pepper, in this coming year its value, (that is) the price per *bahar* [a unit of weight corresponding to approximately 800 grams], will be thirty dinars, and more, and as for refurbished iron, a *bahar* will be not less than twenty dinars, and that the *raqs* (shining, glittering iron), which was in the city, is completely exhausted. (Tell them also) to dispatch a ship from Mangalore, if they can, and to send in it any available pepper, iron, cubeb and ginger; it should set out at the first opportunity for al-Dyyb [Diu], taking some coir (coconut fibre), fine aloes wood, mango (?), and coconuts, because all these are selling well. If they are equipping a ship in Aden, and they want me to take part, I will share (in it) with them." [13]

Mr Madmun advises on trade in Indian spices and other luxury goods at commodities markets in Aden. He hints at the trade networks between the ports of Arabia (Aden), Gujarat (Diu) and the Malabar Coast (Mangalore). He makes reference to the bustling shipping industry in Aden, and how merchants commissioned ships by way of joint shareholding. He refers to a Banyan (*baniya*), or Gujarati merchant, who would have functioned as his agent or go-between in Diu and Mangalore. The tone of the letter is so personable – it could have been written yesterday.

This warm and reassuring tone belies the geopolitical instability that has plagued the Red Sea region for much of history, even till today. Aden's subsequent history would continue to be marked by conflict and political change. In the 16th century, the Portuguese and Ottomans repeatedly tussle over the city. Then from the 17th century on, Aden declines drastically, losing its predominant position as entrepôt to the Red Sea ports of Mocha and Jeddah. Its fortunes would only recover in the 19th century, by which time it had become a British colony, and first port-of-call for most ships sailing down the Suez Canal.

10. Mombasa
The Dhow, the Island and the Swahili Coast

> "We arrived in Mombasa, a big island, at a distance of two days navigation from the lands of the Sawahil. This island did not depend at all on the mainland; it had plantain trees, lime trees and lemon trees. They don't indulge much in agriculture, and grain is brought here from the Sawahil. They mainly eat fish and plantain. They profess the Shafi'i doctrine, and are a pious, chaste and virtuous people. Their mosques are constructed solidly, of timber. [...] We stayed one night on this island; after which we continued our course by sea to Kilwa, a great city on the coast, whose inhabitants were Zanj for the most part, and had extremely black skin."
>
> — Ibn Batoutah, c. 14th century. *Voyages d'Ibn Batoutah.*[14]

The Swahili Coast is a narrow sliver of land in coastal East Africa, at the western extremities of the Indian Ocean world. It extends from Mogadishu in the north to Sofala in the south, taking in the former and present cities of Mombasa, Malindi, Kilwa and Dar Es Salaam, the archipelagos of Lamu, Zanzibar and the Comoros, and snaking across coastal regions of four nations: Somalia, Kenya, Tanzania and Mozambique.

For over a millennium, the Swahilis of East Africa have been connected by trade to the peoples of the greater Indian Ocean region. Persians, Arabs, Gujaratis and Malays settled here in significant numbers in the course of centuries, precipitating a culture that was heavily cosmopolitan and hybrid. The Swahilis themselves consciously distinguished their culture from that of the African interior. They referred to themselves as having *uungwana*: civilisation, taste, culture, refinement. A *mungwana*, or civilised person, was a townsperson: one who was urbane, immaculately dressed, and had a way with words; one who was also schooled in Islamic tradition, and who contributed to mosque and community. Many of the city-states of the coast were ruled by *waungwana*: great families from noble lineages who preserved Swahili culture, upheld their religious duties and gave back to society.

The opposite of *uungwana* was *ushenzi*. The Swahilis used the word to describe peoples of the interior. *Mshenzi*, they were called: rural, backward peoples with no class or taste. Uncouth and uneducated, they were deemed foreign, even strange, by the genteel, urban folk. The term *ushenzi* likely gave rise to the Arabic *zanj* (زنج), a derogatory term used to describe the dark-skinned peoples of the African coast, exported as slaves for centuries to the Gulf. It must be noted that *uungwana* and *ushenzi* as historically defined are concepts that are deeply passé and politically incorrect today. Both terms are more generally applied in Kenya to distinguish between polite and uncouth behaviour.

Swahili itself is a form of creole. Its roots lie heavily in the Bantu languages of East Africa, but it has borrowed significantly from Arabic and Persian. The term "Swahili" derives from the Arabic word *sahil* (ساحل), meaning "seashore". The plural of the word is *sawahil* (سواحل), from whence "Swahili", meaning "of the coasts". Swahili vocabulary pertaining to the maritime derives from Persian and Arabic antecedents, and betrays Swahili culture's roots in the dhow cultures of the Indian Ocean. The word for "sea" is *bahari*, from the Arabic *al-bahar*. The word for "market" is *soko*, from the Arabic *al-suq* ("souk" in English). *Msimu* is Swahili for *mawsam*, the Arab word for "season".

The Swahili word *nahodha*, meaning "skipper" or "ship-captain", is derived from the Old Persian *nav* ("ship") and *khoda* ("master") – the word recurs as *nakhoda* (ناخدا) in Farsi, Arabic, Gujarati and Malay. Likewise, the Swahili *bandari*, or "port", deriving from the Old Persian *bandar*, occurs as *al-bandar* in the Arabic, *bandara* in Gujarati, and *bandar* in Malay (which also means "city" in that language). By extension, *shahbandar* (شاهبندر), a Persian word also found in all Indian Ocean languages, means "harbour master". The English would encounter the word, *bandar*, in India, spelling it as *bunder*, as in Apollo Bunder in Bombay. The word travels further east, where it becomes *bund*, as in the Shanghai Bund.

A contemporary dhow, seen off the coast at Dar Es Salaam, Tanzania. The triangular sail remains the primary means of propulsion, though many dhows today – like this one – also have engines affixed for extra horsepower.

Swahili contributes one important word to the rest of the Indian Ocean languages: *dau*, from whence the English *dhow*. At once Arab, Persian, Indian and African, the dhow was a fixture in all the ports of Asia, even China. There are many different kinds of dhows, with differing sizes and names in local languages. Traditionally, they would have been constructed without the use of nails. Instead, large wooden planks are painstakingly sewn together with coir rope made from the husks of coconuts. By way of waterproofing, the dhow's outer surface is slathered with fish or animal oil. A lateen sail, traditionally made with palm leaves, completes the ensemble. The sail's triangular shape and angled mounting allow the dhow to catch the winds and sail long distances.

Today, dhows are no longer a ubiquitous sight in the Indian Ocean. Their use is limited to Oman and the Persian Gulf, where they are still made and repaired the traditional way. Up until the turn of the 20th century, however, dhows were plentiful along the East African coast; particularly so in the port city of Mombasa, where the dhow became a symbol of the city itself.

Mombasa is a tiny coralline island situated on the east coast of Kenya and surrounded almost entirely by a vast bay that shelters it from the monsoons. Blessed with a spectacular harbour, it has been a major port city since at least the 14th century. The old Swahili name for the city is Mvita, meaning the "city that was fought over in the course of many wars". And certainly, the history of Mombasa is riddled with war, conflict, and migration.

If asked, the Swahilis of Mombasa would tell you they were once ruled by kings of Shirazi origin, whose names include the *nisba* "al-Shirazi". This suggests that the first traders to the Swahili Coast were most likely Persians or Arabs from the Persian Gulf. They would have taken as their brides young women from the local *waungwana* families, and in the process of intermarrying, anchored Islam to the Swahili Coast. The Shirazi ruling families of Mombasa were most likely already Swahili. They immigrated south from the city of Mogadishu, and north from Kilwa, as each city, in turn, waxed, warred and waned.

New waves of Arabs came in the 13th and 14th centuries, this time from the Yemen and other parts of Arabia. The port city of Aden reigned supreme in the western Indian Ocean during this period, and merchants there monopolised trade with East Africa. Unlike the Shi'a Shirazis from the Gulf, these newcomers were Sunni, professing a strict, Shafi'i doctrine. When our world traveller, Ibn Battutah arrives in 1331, he notes that the dominant faith is Shafi'i Islam, that the Mombasans are pious, chaste and virtuous people, and that Swahili mosques are made solidly of timber.

Battutah's Mombasa is an idyll: a pleasant city of plantain, lime and lemon trees, where fragrant blooms perfume the sea breeze. He doesn't stay long, though he makes a point of remarking that in his next destination, Kilwa, the inhabitants are black-skinned Zanj for the most part. This implies that the Mombasans were lighter-skinned Arabs.

Not having stayed long, Battutah neglects to point out another distinguishing aspect of the city: spectacular, white-washed stone architecture that by the 14th century was already a feature of Swahili port cities. Entire quarters were built of coral hewn from the ground, then plastered and painted over with lime-wash, such that they gleamed under the light. These "stone towns" were often home to wealthy merchant and other elite classes, and typically occupied prime waterfront locations. Part of the experience of arriving by dhow at Mombasa was the sight of gleaming white façades along the city's waterfront as one approached the harbour.

The 15th century was Mombasa's golden age. During this time, the last of its noble Shirazi families ruled the city as an independent state. Kilwa, Mombasa's rival in the south, had begun its slow decline, and buoyed by the influx of wealth and talent, Mombasa began to thrive.

Trade from Mombasa was predominantly of gold, mined from the lands of Great Zimbabwe. Other goods exported include ivory, elephants, large quantities of iron ore and slaves. Inward trade to Mombasa included Indian cloth, Southeast Asian spices, and Chinese porcelain – the usual suspects. The latter was prized by noble Swahili families, and used as expensive tableware, interior decoration, or ritual adornment for tombs of the rich and powerful.

The Mandhry Mosque in Mombasa Old Town is one of the oldest mosques on the Swahili Coast; it dates to the 16th century. It boasts a distinctive, cone-shaped, Swahili-style pillar minaret that is unlike any other form of mosque minaret elsewhere.

Alongside the rise of the Delhi Sultanate, communities of Gujarati merchants established themselves in Mombasa and Aden, playing a critical role in furthering trade between the Swahili Coast and beyond. The first major incursion by a non-Indian Ocean peoples came with the Portuguese in 1498 – they were the first to describe the ocean as Mar Indiano ("Indian Sea"), even as they attempted to supplant the Indians on the high seas. In the course of the 1500s, they attempted to take Mombasa by force, multiple times, succeeding only in the 1590s. Their walled settlement, Fort Jesus, still stands today in

Mombasa Old Town, and was inscribed as a UNESCO World Heritage site in 2011.

"Mvita" would describe Mombasa's subsequent destiny as, in the course of the 18th to 20th centuries, it would be fought over first by the Portuguese and the Omanis, and later by the Omanis and the British. In 1898, the Omani Sultan of Zanzibar surrendered Mombasa to the British, who then made it capital of British East Africa.

A potted history of early-modern Mombasa would end here, if not for another, earth-shaking incursion in the early years of Mombasa's golden age – that of the Chinese in their gigantic junks, questing for tribute and mythical creatures.

In 1414, a strange beast, brought to China upon one of Admiral Zheng He's magnificent treasure ships, was presented to the Ming emperor at court. The event was memorialised by renowned painter Shen Du, in a piece titled *Painting of the Tribute Qilin*. The scroll depicts a foreign man walking the namesake *qilin* by way of a leash tied to its long neck. Shen Du, also a calligrapher, pens an accompanying colophon, "Prelude and Ode to the Tribute Qilin", excerpted below:

> "In the ninth month of the Jia-Wu Year of the reign of the Yongle Emperor, a *qilin* arrived from Bengal, and was presented at court. Court and citizenry alike gathered to admire the beast, and their joy knew no bounds. I have heard that when a Great Sage accumulates wisdom and virtue beyond that of the ordinary, such that his Light shines through the Darkness itself, a *qilin* would appear. The appearance of the *qilin* shows that Your Majesty's virtues are equal to Heaven; your blessings have spread far and wide, such that all life, be it plant, insect, bird, fish or animal, is full of vitality."

In Chinese mythology, the *qilin* was a harbinger of peace and stability. Its appearance at court thus signified divine legitimacy for the Yongle Emperor. The *qilin* was typically described in Chinese tradition as a horned beast with the head of a dragon, the scales of a fish, and the hooves of a deer. It was believed to inhabit barbarian lands far across the Western oceans. Small wonder then, that when they first laid eyes upon the giraffe, Chinese officials on board Zheng He's treasure ships would mistake it for the mythical beast. After all, they had never seen such a bizarre creature in their lives.

The Yongle Emperor was so taken by the giraffe that he would dispatch another fleet of treasure ships out west to the lands of Sengqi (likely a Chinese transliteration of "Zanj"), to trade precious goods for more specimens of the auspicious beast. In 1418, these magnificent ships appeared again on the East African coast, stopping at Malindi and

Mombasa. They brought fabulous things: Chinese porcelain, splendid silks and brocades, and spices from across the oceans. They came twice more in 1421 and 1431, and then stopped coming altogether.

By the time Vasco da Gama arrived with his modestly-sized carracks in 1498, a generation of Swahilis had grown old and despaired of ever encountering the Chinese again. The legacy of the Chinese remained, however, in the Swahilis' penchant for exotic foreign goods. They did not make much of the Portuguese and their gifts, dismissing them as mere trinkets compared to what had been brought half a century ago, by those *other* resplendently-dressed white men, who had arrived in ships as large as mountains, and who had vanished like a dream, never to be seen again.

11. Kollam, Kozhikode & Kochi (Quilon, Calicut & Cochin)
Black Pepper Ports of India's Malabar Coast

> "[Koulam] is the residence of many Christians and Jews, who retain their own language. The king is not tributary to any other. Much good dyewood grows there, and pepper in great abundance, being found both in the wooded and open parts of the country. It is gathered in the months of May, June, and July; and the vines which produce it are cultivated in plantations. […] The heat during some months is so great as to be scarcely endured; yet merchants come here from such various parts of the world as, for instance, the kingdoms of Manzi [South China] and Arabia, attracted by the great profits upon the merchandise they import and upon their returning cargoes."
>
> — Marco Polo, c. 14th century. *Travels*.[15]

Piper nigrum is a tropical vine species native to the Malabar Coast in Kerala. In the wild, it grows profusely at ground level, spreading fast and taking root wherever its stems touch the ground. Where it is cultivated, the vines are held fast by tall trellises, allowing them to grow upwards for up to four metres in height; these vines sprout a profusion of deep-green, heart-shaped leaves.

The fruit of the vine occur as drupes, or small berries. When unripe, the berries are green, but they gradually turn bright red as they ripen. Most of the time, the drupes are harvested while the berries are unripe. They are then blanched in hot water, and laid out in the hot tropical sun, until the skin of each berry dries up, shrivels and blackens. Berry thus becomes black peppercorn.

A trade history of the Malabar Coast is essentially a history of trade in black pepper, once the most traded spice of all. The Romans imported pepper on an immense scale: thousands of tons of it each year. They came, so the ancient Tamil poems recount, in their Yavana (யவனர் - "Western") ships to the legendary port of Muziris, from whence they shipped their "black gold" northwards to Aden and Alexandria, and onwards across the Mediterranean to Italy.

The 1st century Greek *Periplus of the Erythraean Sea* refers to Muziris and its coastal regions as the source of the black pepper trade. Where exactly Muziris lies is a mystery – some think it buried in the vicinity of contemporary Kodungallur and the village of Pattanam. Here stand what are believed to be India's oldest church and mosque – it is said that the former was established in the 1st century and the latter, sometime in the 7th. They attest to ancient Middle Eastern merchant communities resident in these parts.

No one single port has ever held complete sway over the Malabar Coast. Rather, we see port cities succeeding each other in the course of history. Quilon (today's Kollam കൊല്ലം), for example, succeeded Muziris. Existing alongside the latter, it came into its own towards the end of the first millennium. According to local tradition, the port was founded by Saint Thomas Christians (also known as Syrian Christians) in 823.[16] Two itinerant bishops, Mar Sabor and Mar Proth, travelling here from Persia, are credited with seeking and receiving permission from the local Hindu king to establish a trading port.

The ancient Kollam Tarisappali copper plates appear to corroborate this founding story. Inscriptions etched in Old Malayalee date to 849 and lay out a royal charter, issued by the Chera Perumal king to the leader of the Syrian Christian merchant community, granting him land to build a church, and permitting Christians the right to oversee foreign trade. Intriguingly, the copper plates include signatures of witnesses to this charter, variously inscribed in Arabic, Pahlavi (Middle Persian script) and Judaeo-Persian, by gentlemen whose names reveal them to be of Muslim, Zoroastrian and Jewish faith.

825 marks the beginning of the Malayalam Calendar, known as the Kollavarsham ("Kollam Era") in Malayalee. The calendar, purportedly also invented by Mars Sabor and Proth, divides the Kollam Andu ("Malayalee year") into twelve months, with dates for harvest and festivals designated, and names in Malayalee for the seven days of the week. It is still used in Kerala today.

Quilon is situated to the south of Kerala, near the tip of the Subcontinent; and as such it was the nearest port to China. By the 11th century, Song-era junks also started making their way here to trade in black pepper, by then consumed in China on an epic scale. The Chinese called the black pepper *hu jiao*, or "barbarian pepper". The word *hu* suggests that pepper had probably first arrived in China by land, across Central Asia. If it had come by sea, we would know it today as *fan jiao*.

By the 14th century, Calicut (today's Kozhikode കോഴിക്കോട്) had overtaken Quilon. Situated in north Kerala, it would be the greatest port in the region for much of the second millennium. The city was ruled by

Hindu kings known as Zamorins (Samoothiri in Malayalee). Prohibited from seafaring by virtue of their Brahmin caste, they nevertheless grew immensely wealthy from taxing the pepper trade and allying themselves with the merchant community.

The Zamorins suffered foreign trade in the city to be managed by localised Muslim communities known as Mappilas (മാപ്പിള). The Mappilas trace their origins to Arab merchants who arrived in the 7th century from the Yemen; the word, "Mappila", means "son-in-law", and was a reference to how newly-arrived Arab men assimilated by marrying local women.[17]

The Mishkal Mosque in Kozhikode was built in the 14th century by one Nakhoda ("Ship-owner") Mishkal. It is a striking exemplar of Keralan architecture with its tiered and sloping roofs. Note also the open balconies and the slatted sides to allow for air circulation.

Muslim Mappilas played an instrumental role in introducing Islam peacefully to the Malabar Coast. Over the centuries, Islam was gradually assimilated and naturalised as one of many local systems of faith. Malabari mosque architecture is thus syncretic in nature. Traditional Keralan mosques eschew Middle Eastern-style minarets for so-called Kerala roofs suited to the local climate. Local timbers are applied to the creation of two-storey structures with sloping pyramidal roofs and open balconies. Sharply sloping roofs serve to repel heavy rain during the monsoon season and protect the faithful from the searing heat of the sun; while open balconies allow for the circulation of air such that interiors remain cool. A variation of this tropical architectural vernacular can also be found in Southeast Asia, at the eastern edge of the Indian Ocean rim.

Calicut's swift ascent on the Malabar Coast was also due to the ruling Zamorins' respect for private property. Ibn Battutah, sojourning here in the 14th century, observes how, unlike other Malabar ports, Calicut guaranteed ship-owners' rights to ships wrecked along its coast:

> "Then I saw the heathen ruler of Calicut who wore a large piece of white cloth around his middle from the navel to the knees and on his head he wore a small turban. He was barefooted, and a servant held an umbrella over his head. A fire was lit before him on the coast, and his police officers belabored the people so that they should not plunder what the sea has cast up. It is the custom of the country of Malabar that whenever a ship is destroyed whatever is saved goes to the treasury. Such is not the custom in this town alone. Here the lawful proprietors collect whatever is thrown up by the sea and therefore the town is flourishing, and great is the influx of foreigners."[18]

Battutah also remarks on the large numbers of Yuan-era Chinese ships in the harbour; and devotes a long tract to describing the different types and sizes of junks he witnessed. The Chinese presence in Calicut would expand and culminate with Admiral Zheng He's legendary treasure fleets in the Ming dynasty. Calicut's renown as the foremost port of the pepper coast was such that the emperor of China deigned to bestow an imperial mandate upon the Zamorin, affording his kingdom stature as a favoured tribute nation.

After the Chinese, the Portuguese came, lured, like everyone else, by the pepper trade. Unlike everyone else, the Portuguese disregarded a tacit law of free and peaceful trade that governed merchant activity across the Indian Ocean. Instead, they came bearing dangerous arms, intending to wrest control of the spice trade from Muslim merchants. Landing in Calicut in 1498, Vasco da Gama purportedly declared that he had arrived in search of "Christians and spices". His gifts to the Zamorin so failed to impress that da Gama and his retinue were unceremoniously booted out from the city and denied permission to trade. They would eventually establish a toehold further south along the coast.

Silting of the harbour at Kodungallur facilitated the emergence of Cochin (today's Kochi കൊച്ചി) as a major port. For some time, it co-existed with Calicut and Quilon – Zheng He's fleets stopped here too, and the admiral's on-board historian remarked the presence of Chettiars, a Southern Indian merchant caste specialising in jewellery and pearls. The Chinese marvelled at the Chettiars' wealth, noting that they had a fixed and sophisticated system of setting and negotiating prices for their baubles.[19] Bargaining was taken to the level of an artform.

At this time, new waves of Arab and other Middle Eastern merchants had also settled along the Malabar Coast, adding to the diversity of its inhabitants. These Paradesis (പരദേശി - "foreigners") were distinguished from the Mappilas by their lighter skin. Paradesi Muslims, Christians and Jews settled in the multicultural bazaar town of Mattancherry, under the protection of the raja of Cochin. They lived and traded uneasily alongside the Mappila communities, whom they looked down on and regarded as backwards. Being rather more orthodox in their faiths, they frowned on local Mappila religious practices, which were syncretic in nature.

Of the Paradesi communities, the best known are the Jews, settled in Cochin's Jew Town from the early 15th century on. Many of them were Sephardic Jews who had migrated from either Kodungallur, or from Spain in the aftermath of the Spanish Inquisition. Their main synagogue, built in 1568 and known as the Paradesi Synagogue, is one of Cochin's iconic attractions. From the outside, the building looks deceptively unprepossessing, with a whitewashed façade and an 18th century clocktower. Once inside, however, visitors are invariably surprised and delighted by the sumptuous interior. Elaborate glass lamps made in Belgium hang from the ceiling, and every inch of the floor is covered in exquisite, 18th-century blue-and-white porcelain tiles made in Canton.

Among Cochin's iconic attractions are its legendary *cheena vala*, or Chinese fishing nets. These are found north of the city, where the Indian Ocean meets Kerala's backwaters. Fishermen have been operating these gigantic nets for at least 500 years. The nets are manually operated and a sight to behold, particularly in the early mornings

Kochi's historic Paradesi Synagogue sits at the heart of Jew Town in Mattancherry.

when fishing takes place in earnest. Some believe it was Admiral Zheng He's treasure fleets that brought the *cheena vala* here in the early 15th century – they are, after all, called "Chinese" fishing nets, and were once widely used in South China and Vietnam. A more likely scenario is their being a Portuguese import from Macao, particularly since Portuguese names are used for their individual parts.

Cochin's time would come with the Portuguese. Between 1500 and 1503, the Portuguese returned repeatedly to the Malabar Coast in search of a permanent trading settlement. Sensing a strategic opportunity, the raja of Cochin allied himself with the Iberians, granting them land for a trading settlement, in return for protection against rival Calicut.

In 1503, Fort Manuel – the very first permanent European settlement in India – was erected in honour of the Portuguese king, Manuel I. From their base in Fort Manuel (today's Fort Kochi), the Portuguese would wage war against the Zamorins of Calicut for much of the 16th century. The cost of warfare was debilitating for Calicut. By the time the Dutch arrived in the 17th century, Cochin had eclipsed its ancient rival, and it continues to be Kerala's most important port today.

12. Nanjing (Nanking)
Admiral Zheng He and the Treasure Ships of the Ming

"During the sixth Lunar Month of the third year of the Yongle Emperor's Reign [1405], the emperor decreed that Zheng He and the Prince of Qi, Zhu Jinghong – along with many others – set forth as envoys to the Western Ocean. They were accompanied by a 27,800-person retinue, and brought with them a large amount of gold, silver and other treasures. Large ships were built: there were 62 ships measuring 44 *zhang* in length and 18 *zhang* in width. Departing from Liujiahe in Suzhou, they crossed by sea to Fujian province, and then set sail from Wuhumen in Fujian."

— Zhang Tingyu et al, Qing dynasty (17th – 18th century).
Ming Histories – An Account of Zheng He.

In the Zhongbaocun district northwest of Nanjing (南京), there is a popular municipal park situated along the Yangzi River and surrounded by apartment complexes. The park consists of three enormous, rectangular lakes, each more than 400 metres long and some 40 metres wide. There were once thirteen of these lakes, but most of them were filled in sometime in the late 20th century. The three remaining are listed as National-Grade Historical Monuments in China. Right after the park opened to the public in 2005, they were further gazetted as the sixth most important Cultural Heritage Site in the nation.

These lakes are what remain of a huge complex of dry docks that once housed shipyards. The Chinese name for the park, the Longjiang Shipyard, references an ancient shipyard dating from the early Ming dynasty. The English name – Nanjing Treasure Shipyard Relics Park – is far more explicit about the site's heritage.

The Ming treasure ships are the subject of myth. They were reportedly immense. Chinese official records have them sized at some 140 metres in length by 60 metres in width. Boasting nine masts, they were made entirely of wood from China's forested interior. 62 of these ships were built to sail on the admiral's first voyage alone. A good number of them would have been built right here at the Nanjing Treasure Shipyards. Most would likely have been built in Quanzhou, where a longstanding tradition of shipbuilding had existed since the Song dynasty.

His Lord Admiral, the Grand Eunuch Zheng He, was born Ma He. His diminutive name was Sanbao ("three treasures") and he is also

Chinese sea-going junk. Date and original Chinese engraver unknown. Contained in *A propos des voyages aventureux de Fernand Mendez Pinto*. M. A. J. Charignon and M. Médard, 1934.

popularly known today as the Three Treasures Grand Eunuch. His surname "Ma" betrays his Muslim origins – the word is an abbreviation of the Arabic name Mahmud. He was born in China's Yunnan province to a Muslim family of substantial means. Sanbao's grandfather, the Ma family patriarch, had been an official of the Yuan dynasty, and both Sanbao's grandfather and father carried the title "Haji", meaning they had made the pilgrimage to Mecca.

In Ma Sanbao's 10th year, Ming dynasty troops swept into Yunnan. All Yuan dynasty officials and loyalists, including Sanbao's grandfather and father, were deposed and executed. Sanbao, and other young sons of former Yuan gentry, were taken to the imperial court in Nanjing, to be castrated and put to service as imperial eunuchs. In a twist of fate, Sanbao was sent north to serve at the household of Zhu Di, second son of the first Ming emperor, Hongwu. Some 11 years older than Sanbao, the prince and his eunuch would become fast friends.

In 1402, Zhu Di ascended the throne as third emperor of the Ming, after laying siege to the imperial palace at Nanjing, and deposing his nephew, the Jianwen Emperor. He took the reign name Yongle ("Everlasting Joy"); he would later be regarded as the greatest emperor of the Ming. Sanbao was brought to the imperial court, bestowed a new surname, Zheng, and given the title *Tai Jian* ("Grand Director of the Imperial Household"). From thence, he would be known as Zheng He.

He was known for his formidable strength and physical stature. Chinese records suggest that he was seven feet tall, with a waist as thick as a tree trunk, a loud, booming voice, and a searing, ferocious gaze. This was unusual, since, being a eunuch, a lack of testosterone could have limited physical development. It was thus all the more extraordinary that Zheng He was celebrated for his military prowess as much as for his superior intellect.

In 1405, the emperor appointed Zheng He admiral and imperial ambassador on an unprecedented diplomatic and naval expedition to the Xiyang (西洋 - "Western Ocean"). Why exactly he commissioned these epic missions remains a point of debate even today. Some scholars believe the treasure fleets were Yongle's elaborate, roundabout way of searching for his deposed nephew, who had escaped from Nanjing and reportedly lived in exile in the West.

Others argue that the treasure fleets were a means by which Yongle hoped to legitimise his reign – he did usurp the throne, after all. Zheng He's expeditions were calculated to trumpet and reinforce the emperor's pre-eminent position as ruler of *tianxia* (天下 – "all under heaven"). Certainly, by the end of Zheng He's voyages, China's position as Zhongguo, or "Kingdom at the Middle (of *Tianxia*)", would be unchallenged, and knowledge of China's cultural and technological superiority, widespread.

Seven voyages were made in all. The third voyage, made in 1409, was remarkable for Zheng He's erection of a stone tablet at a Buddhist temple in Ceylon, commemorating his journey in three languages: Chinese, Persian and Tamil. On this voyage, Zheng He also violently deposed the reigning king of Ceylon, replacing him with a relative amenable to China.

Ma Huan, a Muslim compatriot of Zheng He's, joined the fleet on its fourth voyage in 1413. Fluent in multiple languages, Ma served as interpreter and scribe for this and subsequent voyages. He later documented his experiences in his travelogue, *Yingya Shenglan*, or *A Triumphant Survey of the Farthest Corners of the Ocean*. On this voyage, too, Zheng He's fleet made it to Arabia, stopping at Hormuz, the Hadhramaut and Aden. He returned with various foreign ambassadors and a giraffe, which he would present to the emperor at Nanjing.

The fifth voyage in 1417 saw the treasure fleets returning ambassadors to their home countries and venturing their furthest, to the Swahili Coast. New ambassadors sailed back with the fleet, together with a full menagerie of animals, including – naturally – more giraffes. The sixth voyage in 1421 whisked these ambassadors home.

Just before the sixth voyage, the Yongle Emperor moved his imperial capital north from Nanjing to Beijing, where it would remain for the next 600 years. By this time, China's global influence was at its peak – trade and soft power had done their job. China had reclaimed its *tianxia*. The traditional system of tributary trade was back on track, except the imperial court itself had a monopoly on trade.

But in 1424, the Yongle Emperor

died even as plans were being made for a seventh voyage. His successor saw little value in continuing his father's vanity projects. The seventh voyage finally took place in 1431, during the reign of Yongle's grandson, the Xuande Emperor. Zheng He, by then 60 years old, made a final voyage, sailing the fleets out to Calicut, where he died in 1433. His body was likely buried there, though an official tomb with his name stands in the outskirts of Nanjing. The Xuande Emperor died soon after, in 1435. With both Zheng He and his patron dead, there was no further impetus to lead these epic voyages to the West, and China turned its back on the world.

Domestically, Zheng He and his legacy were vilified. The Confucian bureaucracy had always regarded these voyages as wasteful and against the natural order of things. They lost no opportunity in banning any further voyages. All related records, including valuable navigational treatises and detailed maps, were burnt. The treasure ships were abandoned and left to rot in the Treasure Shipyard. All other vessels, sailors and ship-hands were redeployed towards naval defence and the transport of grain and other essentials along the Grand Canal.

The last time we hear of the treasure ships is in 1553, more than a hundred years after Zheng He's final voyage. By then, the erstwhile Treasure Shipyards had been successfully redeployed towards the production of ships for domestic use. The new director of the shipyards, Li Zhaoxiang, commendably ensuring due diligence, conducts a full survey of physical assets and human resources. He meticulously records

Historic walls of the Ming imperial palace in Nanjing. The palace, built by the Hongwu Emperor during the second half of the 14th century, stands in ruins today. The Hongwu Emperor's son, the Yongle Emperor, would move the seat of the empire to Beijing in 1420.

his observations in his *Longjiang Shipyards Treatise*. Buried deep within the voluminous tome, in a section pertaining to staff matters, he notes, cursorily, that:

> "There are two shipyard artisans currently deployed to the Treasure Shipyards. In the Hongwu and Yongle periods, ships were built here, to be sailed out across the seas to seek treasure. These shipyards have treasure vaults, and thus these shipyard artisans are deployed there as guards. Today, the shipyards and treasure vaults are overgrown with weeds, and the guards spend their time gambling."[20]

Thus, our tale of Admiral Zheng He and his treasure ships ends, not with a bang but a whimper.

Ironically, by the time Zheng He set sail for the Xiyang, the Ming dynasty had imposed almost fifty years of *haijin* (海禁), or an imperial ban on private maritime mercantile activity. Unlike their Song and Yuan counterparts, the Ming emperors frowned upon trade, espousing a conservative, Confucian suspicion of it and preferring that it be fully controlled by the imperium.

For merchants of the Hokkien coast, this was a tremendous blow to their livelihoods, and millions of them simply left. The Ming dynasty saw the largest outflow of emigrants to the Nanhai and beyond, surpassed only later in the 18th and 19th centuries, during the European colonial period. Most of these emigrants, former merchants and seafarers from Hokkien province, settled in Taiwan, and in the port cities of Japan, Sumatra, Java, Malaya, Vietnam, Siam, Borneo and the Philippines. They were already there when Zheng He arrived with his treasure fleets, and were referred to as the *huaqiao* (华侨), or "Overseas Chinese".

Wherever the Hokkiens went, they brought their culture and their faith with them, most notably the worship of Mazu, goddess of the sea and seafarers. Mazu originated as a minor deity protecting fishermen and sailors in her hometown of Putien in Hokkien province; legend went that she was a powerful female shaman named Lin Moniang. She was first worshipped as a popular folk deity in the Tang dynasty. From the Song dynasty on, the imperial court would co-opt her, promoting official worship of her and canonising her as an important goddess in the state-sanctioned Daoist pantheon. By the Ming dynasty, she had become a much-honoured and very important deity.

Before his first voyage in 1405, Zheng He made quite the to-do about stopping at Quanzhou to pray at a Mazu Temple there. He attributed his safe return from the second voyage to the goddess's divine protection, and appealed to the emperor for the construction of a Mazu Temple in Nanjing. The emperor graciously acquiesced, bestowing upon Mazu the honorific, "Celestial Consort of Sublime Numinosity, Glorious Response, Magnanimous Benevolence, and Universal Salvation, Who Protects the State and Guards the People" – Tian Fei ("Celestial Consort"), in short.[21] She would later be promoted to Tian Hou ("Celestial Empress") by the Qing emperors.

Today, Tianhou, Tianfei or Mazu temples are found in coastal regions across China, East and Southeast Asia and the Pacific, where large communities of Overseas Chinese continue to venerate her. Meanwhile, the Tianfei Temple in Nanjing was progressively destroyed in the course of war and revolution in the 19th and 20th centuries. A massive reconstruction effort was undertaken in the early 2000s, and a brand-new Tianfei Palace inaugurated in 2005, boasting Ming-inspired architecture. Not far from it, within the same temple complex, stands the Jinghai Si ("Temple of the Quiet Seas"), also a contemporary reconstruction, and today a museum dedicated to the history of Zheng He and his voyages to the West.

13. Melaka (Malacca)
The "Muslim Lake" and the Genealogy of Kings

> "Then Sultan Iskandar Shah returned and walked to the beach by a river; Bertam was its name. His Majesty stood under a tree and began to hunt. There under the tree his hunting dog was kicked by a white mousedeer. Said Sultan Iskandar Shah, 'This is a propitious place. Even the mousedeer is daring. Let's build a *negeri* here. [...] What is the name of this tree under which we are standing?' 'Melaka,' replied an officer. Sultan Iskandar Shah decided, 'In that case, *Melaka* shall be the name of this *negeri*.' Thus, the Sultan remained in Melaka, built and extended it. He initiated the ceremonies."
>
> — Tun Seri Lenang, 16th century.
> *Sulalat al-Salatin – The Genealogy of Kings.*[22]

In the beginning, there was a sacred mountain. Seguntang Mahameru was its name, and it was the earthly embodiment of the mythical Mount Meru, the "great mountain" in Hindu-Buddhist tradition. It stood in the ancient city of Palembang, in the country of Andelas, also known as Srivijaya.

One evening, the summit of the mountain turned to gold and gleamed with holy light in the twilight hour. This miraculous event heralded the arrival of three golden princes, descended from the mighty Raja Chulan of the Chola Empire, and from Iskandar Zulkarnain ("Alexander the Great") himself. One of the princes became ruler of Palembang and was bestowed the divine title, Sri Tri Buana ("Lord of the Three Realms"). His other name was Sang Nila Utama, or "Great Leader (swathed) in Indigo".

After some years on the throne, Sri Tri Buana grew restless, seeking to move his court to some other place. Sailing from Palembang, he would chance upon an island, Temasek, at the tip of the Malay Peninsula, not far from the island of Bintan. There, he spied a fantastic creature – a *singa*, or lion – and decided to found his new *negeri*, or capital city, which he called Singa-pura ("Lion City").

Peace prevailed for Sri Tri Buana and his descendants in Singapura for almost a century. But one fateful day, his great-great-great-grandson, the Raja Parameswara, suspecting an imperial concubine of having an affair, decided to execute her in a most humiliating manner. The father of the girl, the *bendahara* ("grand vizier"), called down war upon

Singapura in revenge. A vast naval fleet from Majapahit invaded and sacked the Lion City. Parameswara was forced to flee north where he founded a new *negeri* on the banks of the Bertam River. He named his new *negeri* Melaka.

The *Sulalat al-Salatin*, or *Genealogy of Kings*, is the great epic of the Malays, imbued with the same cultural significance as the *Shahnama* for the Persians. Originally written in Classical Malay, it has often been referred to as the *Sejarah Melayu*, or *Malay Annals*. Certainly, the form of its narrative has the epic sweep and chronological structure of annals. But it is really, at its core, a tale of sacred and royal lineage, and the rise and hubristic fall of sultans.

Any royal genealogy worth its salt blends elements of the historical, the magical and the moral. And thus the *Sulalat* is replete with characters based on fact and fable, even as it follows the illustrious lives and careers of the Melakan kings, and the intricate kinship networks they establish across the Nusantara.

Many of the characters and fables in the *Sulalat* are still well-loved today. Singaporeans would be familiar with the tale of Sri Tri Buana tossing his crown into the sea to calm the waves as he approaches Temasek. Likewise, they would also recall the tale of strongman Badang, who heaves huge rocks into the Singapore harbour; and that of the boy who aids Singapore in fending off a swordfish attack, and whose blood, when he is murdered by the jealous raja, stains the earth red.

Malaysians would know well the legend of Puteri Gunung Ledang, fairy princess of Mount Ophir, who rejects the advances of the great Sultan Mansur Shah by demanding of him seven impossible gifts, including seven trays filled with mosquito hearts and a bowlful of blood from his own son. Malaysians would also recall fondly the heroic figure of Hang Tuah, *laksamana* ("admiral") to the sultan. So dashing and handsome a man was he that married women would slip away from their husbands' arms to ogle at him as he swaggered down the street.

Most academics believe the *Sulalat* to have been commissioned in 1612, during the reign of Sultan Ala'uddin Ri'ayat Shah of Johor, and written by the *bendahara* of Johor, Tun Sri Lanang. The *Sulalat* is thus concerned not only with the genealogy of the Melaka Sultanate, but also that of Johor, successor sultanate to Melaka. This explains why

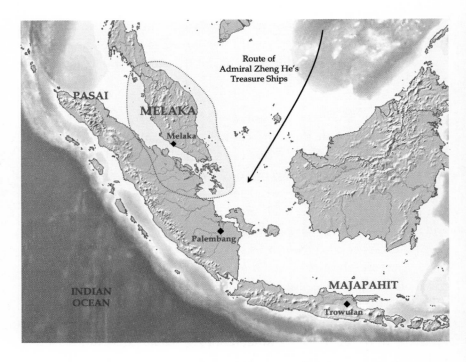

The Melaka Sultanate, at its greatest extent during the reign of Sultan Mansur Shah. To the west is the Sultanate of Pasai – the first Islamic kingdom in the Nusantara. To the southeast is the Hindu-Buddhist maritime *mandala* of Majapahit – successor to Srivijaya – with its capital at Trowulan.

the narrative doesn't end with Melaka's fall to the Portuguese. Instead, it follows the peregrinations of the last sultan, Mahmud Shah, as he flees to Bintan and eventually has his sons establish the Perak and the Johor sultanates.

Indeed, one intriguing characteristic of the Malay kings was their eminent mobility – how they were willing and able to simply drop everything and *move* from island to island in the vast Nusantara. When they did move to establish a new *negeri* elsewhere, court and loyal retinue would follow them – as though court and retinue were appendages to the Royal Person.

We first encounter the ephemeral, impermanent, mobile *negeri* of the Malays at Palembang. The word *negeri* has its roots in the Sanskrit *nagara*, meaning "city", or more accurately, "seat of power". Within the Malay cosmos, heavily influenced by Hindu-Buddhist tradition, power inherent in the *negeri* is invested in the person of the *datu* ("chief"). A *negeri* can thus be seen as the sum total of kinship, fealty and other human relationships that surround the position and the body of the chief. What this means, is that a *negeri* is essentially formless and not anchored at all to the soil. It is instead invested in the person of the king and his subjects. Wherever he goes, there the *negeri* is.

The Sultanate of Melaka was the greatest of all Malay *negeri*, acknowledged as such even today. It wasn't the first Muslim *negeri* in Southeast Asia; that honour falls to the Sultanate of Pasai, in northern Sumatra. But Melaka was important because it was during this time that rituals of Malay kingship were codified, within the religious framework of Islam.

In the early Melakan chapters of the *Sulalat al-Salatin*, courtly protocol is established by Sultan Muhammad Shah soon after his conversion to Islam. He proclaims that only royalty may use the colour yellow and that yellow parasols are to be held aloft only over princes of royal blood. He decrees that only the king may wear golden anklets and that gold itself is forbidden to ordinary subjects, except if it were a gift from the king. And he declares that any man who enters the *istana* ("royal palace") must don a *sarong*, bear a *keris* at his waist, and drape a *sebai* (a shawl-like garment) over himself.

These rituals and protocols were retained and adapted from earlier Hindu-Buddhist tradition. In Palembang, the maharaja had been regarded as a *devaraja* – an earthly avatar of the Boddhisattva Avalokiteshvara. In Melaka, the new faith no longer allowed for king-as-Divinity. As such, the sultan was recast as God's representative on earth, with no less elaborate trappings and symbols of divine authority. From traditions of Islamic world kingship came the principle of *Daulat*, an ineffable and sacred quality of authority that permeates the office and person of the sovereign. *Daulat Tuanku!* was the appropriate address for the sacred person of the sultan. *Hail to the Highest!*

Melaka also defined what it meant to be Malay. Its swift growth into the most successful port city in the region resulted in great wealth that, in turn, precipitated a flowering of culture, literature and the arts. Melaka became a crucible for new ideas, eagerly emulated by other *negeri* in the region. It became the foremost patron of Islam in Southeast Asia, attracting scholars from far and wide. The Malay language was standardised, becoming the lingua franca of maritime trade and diplomacy in the region. Laws were codified, particularly in relation to sumptuary. Regardless, Melaka still became a paragon of style and fashion for men and women alike; a Paris of the Nusantara, setting the standards of dress for the region.

A new Melayu identity emerged. *Orang melayu* was defined by his cosmopolitan, maritime heritage and engagement in international trade; his use of the Malay language and adoption of the symbols and rituals of

Malay culture; his Islamic faith, notwithstanding the syncretic nature of its application and worship; and his loyalty to the Malay king, wherever the *negeri* might move to.

From its inception, Melaka had been founded as an entrepôt, and thus there was never any question of it having a hinterland. It fully depended upon international trade to survive. Its emergence as entrepôt par excellence in 15th century Asia was a product of circumstance and strategy, facilitated by Ming China's reversion to an ancient system of tribute trade abandoned some four centuries ago. Chinese merchants were once again banned from engaging directly in overseas trade. This called for an entrepôt port in Southeast Asia to – once again – supply China with foreign goods. There hadn't been one since Srivijaya declined in the 12th century. Melaka, with genealogical roots in Palembang, deemed itself Srivijaya's natural successor.

But the road to success wasn't quite so straightforward for Melaka's early kings. Ming records indicate that in the early 1400s, a nascent Melaka had been subject to armed raids by Siam. Keenly aware of their precarious position, the first three sultans of Melaka travelled on Chinese ships to pay tribute to the Ming court in Nanjing, hoping to secure China's protection.

These overtures were successful. In 1407, on his second voyage west, Admiral Zheng He stopped in Melaka, and in a great show of pomp and circumstance, bestowed imperial seals and symbols of kingship such as a gold diadem and silk robes upon the sultan. Zheng He also erected a stone tablet proclaiming Melaka a kingdom, in China's eyes. In effect, Ming China had pronounced Melaka "Favoured Trading Nation and Vassal". The Siamese got the hint and Melaka's security was guaranteed, for the moment.

Ming records indicate that Melaka conducted some twenty missions and royal visits in total between 1405 to 1435, including on each of Admiral Zheng He's voyages.[23] Local legend in Melaka has it that on one of the voyages, a princess of royal blood by the name of Hang Li-Po was purportedly brought to Melaka to be married to the sultan. The princess and her entourage settled at the foot of a hill still known as Bukit Cina ("China Hill") today, and which is home to the largest Chinese cemetery in the world outside of China.

But China turned out to be mercurial and unpredictable in its attitudes to trade and foreign policy. Melaka's newfound security would

be short-lived as, in a matter of decades, Ming China would turn its back on the world fully. Foreign tribute trade itself was discouraged and foreigners banned from travelling to the imperial court. Melaka was once again on its own.

Therein came a brilliant stroke of wisdom that would change Melaka's fortunes and secure its success.

By the 15th century, the Indian Ocean had become a veritable "Muslim Lake". For centuries now, Muslims had plied their trade there. Islam itself had been brought to Southeast Asia by way of merchants from the Middle East and India, looking to peaceful trade and commerce with communities here.

Sometime in the mid-1430s, having returned from China where he witnessed, first-hand, an about-turn in Chinese trade policy, the third raja of Melaka decided to convert to Islam. He probably did so for practical reasons, knowing full well the competitive advantages to be gained from the Islamic trade. The deed was done tactically, by his allying himself through marriage to a princess of Pasai, entrepôt of choice at the time for Muslim merchants of the Indian Ocean.

Baju kurung, or long robe, made of *songket* – a hand-woven piece of brocaded or textured fabric with gold or silver threads used in the weave. *Songket* was strictly reserved for Malay aristocracy and royalty. This particular *baju* once belonged to a member of the Johor royal family in Singapore. Behind it hangs a *kain selendang*, or shoulder cloth, which boasts gold *songket* embroidery as well as *limar* – wherein the weft yarns are first tied and dyed before being used in weaving. *Baju kurung* (c. 19th century) and *kain selendang* (early 20th century) were both made in Palembang. Collection of the Asian Civilisations Museum.

Known as Seri Maharaja in Chinese records, he becomes Sultan Muhammad Shah in the *Sulalat al-Salatin*. His conversion is a pivotal scene in the narrative: one night, the Prophet appears to him in a dream to tell him he would be renamed Muhammad. When the sultan awakens, he finds himself miraculously circumcised and able to repeat the articles of Muslim faith. Meanwhile, a vessel from Jeddah arrives conveniently, with wise men on board able to advise and instruct the sultan in Islamic prayer and ritual.

After his conversion, Sultan Muhammad Shah wasted no time in positioning Melaka as the best place along the Straits for business. This came by way of guaranteeing rule of law and private property, and also ensuring efficient harbour management, customs and state administration. As with the maharajas of Srivijaya before, he co-opted the *orang laut* as his navy, thus securing city and harbour.

Islam as state religion allowed Melaka to insert itself into the larger *dar al-Islam*, with its timeless network of monsoons, merchants and merchandise. These merchants came in droves. The *Sulalat* notes that "in time, Melaka expanded, and numbers of traders made it their main port of call. The colonies of Melaka likewise multiplied. [...] It became known in all the countries under the wind that it was a great *negeri*" and "in due time, rajas travelled to Melaka to pay their homage."[24]

Melaka's golden age in the latter half of the 15th century came during the reign of the great Sultan Mansur ("Victorious") Shah. In wealth and power, it surpassed all other Malay port cities before it, becoming one in a triumvirate of powerful entrepôts, including Aden and Cambay, that controlled world trade.

Prosperity made Melaka one of the most cosmopolitan cities in its time. It had not one, but four *shahbandar*, charged with handling foreign maritime affairs at the port. There was one representing the interests of the Gujarati merchants alone – they were the largest community of resident foreign merchants. Another *shahbandar* represented the Chinese, who still came to trade, albeit illegally. Many settled down in Melaka and became the ancestors of the city's Peranakan Chinese, or Baba-Nyonya, community. A third *shahbandar* represented the interests of Burmese and Indians from Bengal, and the Malabar and Coromandel Coasts. Hindu merchants from the Coromandel settled down in Melaka and were the ancestors of today's Peranakan Indian, or Chitty Melaka, community. Finally, the fourth *shahbandar* attended to merchants from elsewhere in the larger Nusantara: Sumatra, Java, Borneo, the Spice Islands, Luzon and Mindanao.

For the most vivid and accurate first-hand account of Melaka in its glory days, we turn again to intrepid world-travelling Portuguese apothecary, Tomé Pires, who arrives here in 1512, soon after the Portuguese occupy the city. On the ground at last, our foreign correspondent remarks, wide-eyed and breathlessly, on the city's cosmopolitanism:

> "…in the port of Malacca very often 84 languages have been found spoken, every one distinct, as the inhabitants of Malacca affirm."

He describes, at length, the detailed vicissitudes of trade in Melaka, including custom duties, exchange rates, and the types of merchandise passing hands in the city. His observations on trade between Gujarat and Melaka suggest just how large in scale and truly global in scope this trade was. Merchandise that changed hands here came from all over the known world. He concludes the *Suma* with these famous last words:

> "Men cannot estimate the worth of Malacca, on account of its greatness and profit. Malacca is a city that was made for merchandise, fitter than any other in the world; the end of monsoons and the beginning of others. Malacca is surrounded and lies in the middle, and the trade and commerce between the different nations for a thousand leagues on every hand must come to Malacca. […] Whoever is lord of Malacca has his hand on the throat of Venice."[25]

His words retrospectively justified Portuguese conquest and occupation of Melaka. Indeed, occupation was necessary, in his view, because Melaka was ruled by Muslims who – so he judged – could not be friends, and thus the only way the Portuguese nation could benefit from the Indian Ocean trade was to take Melaka violently, by any means possible.

Melaka during the Sultanate period is remembered mostly (and nostalgically) by way of text and historical record. Very little in the way of material or archaeological evidence from the period remains. One of these pieces of evidence, a rare artefact from Melaka's golden age, is in the collection of the National Museum of Singapore. Its story is also the story of Melaka's rise and fall.

The artefact in question is the headstone of a tomb, carved in the form of an ogee horseshoe arch. An inscription in elegant Arabic script notes that the "pious deceased" was a certain Nakhoda Haji al-Kambayi bin Jemal-ud-din, and that he had died on the ninth day of the month of Shawal in AH 863 (9th August 1459). The name of our

Headstone of Nakhoda Haji al-Kambayi bin Jemal-ud-din. Melaka, mid-15th century. Stone, 131 x 49 x 9 cm. Collection of the National Museum of Singapore.

pious deceased is a combination of honorific and patronymic. It reveals that he was a ship captain, or more likely a wealthy ship-owner; that he had made the pilgrimage to Mecca; that he was "of Cambay" and thus Gujarati in origin; and that he was the "son of" Jemal-ud-din. This headstone attests to an active and prosperous Gujarati presence in Melaka in the first decades of its becoming a Muslim state. Nakhoda Haji al-Kambayi dies in 1459, the very same year Mansur Shah is crowned sultan.

The story of how the headstone got to Singapore in the first place is intimately related to Melaka's occupation by the Europeans. In the aftermath of the Portuguese conquest of Melaka in 1511, the royal palace and the city's mosques and cemeteries were levelled, and the stones used to build the city's new fortifications. The headstone was among many others embedded in the walls of the Fortaleza de Malaca, which encircled the city for more than 300 years, outlasting the Portuguese (1511 – 1641) and almost outlasting the Dutch (1621 – 1824).

When the British arrived in Melaka in 1807, they blew up most of the walls, leaving only a single gatehouse, the Porta de Santiago, standing. Nakhoda Haji al-Kambayi's headstone, together with a few others, would be moved to Singapore in 1824. They have remained there ever since, and are an eloquent reminder of how Melaka was a turning point in more ways than one.

Not only would it be the greatest Malay-Muslim sultanate, defining Malay identity for centuries to come, it would also, with its demise, mark an earth-shattering shift in the nature and dynamic of the Indian Ocean trade. After Melaka's fall, Europeans would no longer be just an occasional visitor and nuisance in the ports of the Indian Ocean rim. They would swiftly evolve from significant to major presence, and subsequently to violent, oppressive and monopolistic power.

Nakhoda Haji al-Kambayi's headstone doesn't just stand atop the tomb of this pious deceased. It also stands, symbolically, atop the tomb of Melaka itself, and that of the entire Indian Ocean trade as it had been for more than a millennium. After the fall of Melaka come the East India Companies and the inexorable path to colonialism.

OF SPICES
AND
COMPANIES

16th — 17th Centuries

SATIS EST DNE SATIS EST

IHS

INRI

S.P.FRĀCISCUS XAVERIVS SOCIE

14. Goa
The Estado da Índia and the Rome of the East

> "What glorious palms on Goa's isle I see, / Their blossoms spread,
> great Albuquerque, for thee! / Through castled walls the hero breaks
> his way, / And opens with his sword the dread array / Of Moors and
> pagans; through their depth he rides, / Through spears and show'ring
> fire the battle guides. / As bulls enrag'd, or lions smear'd with gore, /
> His bands sweep wide o'er Goa's purpled shore."
>
> — Luís Vaz de Camões, 1572. *The Lusiads*, Book X. [1]

Almost all visitors to Old Goa today arrive overland. It is a pleasant enough ride. Our vehicle trundles along a lovely intercity highway that links the state capital, Panjim, to the old city, and which extends along the waterfront, affording the visitor scenic views of nature and bucolic villages. The most dramatic (and at one time, the *only*) approach to the old city, however, is by water. In the days of the viceroys, the visitor would have arrived at Velha Goa ("Old Goa") by barge, floating up the sluggish Mandovi River, its waters witness to trade and conquest, splendour and decay.

Imagine, if you can, the river cutting a straight path through dense, green jungle. As our barge progresses, we are uncomfortably reminded of Conrad's *Heart of Darkness*. Here and there, a white speck in the canvas of green betrays a church, precariously perched on the edge of the unknown. Suddenly, there is a clearing in the green cover, and one comes face to face with the spectacle of this great city of the Portuguese. The shimmering, multi-hued façade of the Palace of the Viceroys rises impossibly from the waters, its baroque architecture and elaborate adornment designed to strike awe and wonder in all who approach. For almost 300 years, this was the first view of Goa, symbol of its glory, its power and its opulence; and it doesn't disappoint.

Beyond the Viceroy's Palace, the city extends till as far as the eye can see. We gasp in wonder at the panoramic view of gilded domes amidst a sea of reddish-gold, sun-baked roof tiles. We understand, now, why returning travellers always referred to the city as Goa Dourado – "golden Goa". It literally gleams under the light.

For much of the 16th to 20th centuries, Goa was the centre of a vast Portuguese maritime empire known as the Estado da Índia, or the "State

OVERLEAF: *The Castle of Batavia* (detail). Andries Beeckman. Amsterdam, c. 1662. Oil on canvas, 108 x 151.4 cm. Collection of the Rijksmuseum.

OPPOSITE PAGE: *Portrait of St. Francis Xavier.* Unknown Japanese painter. Japan, Edo period, early 17th century. Colour pigments on paper. 61.0 x 48.7 cm. Collection of the Kobe City Museum.

of India". At its greatest extent during the 16th century, the heyday of Portuguese hegemony over global maritime trade, the Estado extended all the way from the Swahili Coast in Africa to southern Japan. It was during this time that Goa, the administrative and commercial centre of the Estado, was at its zenith.

The Estado da Índia wasn't an empire in the normal, terrestrial sense of the term. The Portuguese weren't interested in conquering tracts of land or displacing incumbent sultanates and kingdoms. Instead, they strived to exert control over the high seas and maritime trading networks. As such, the Estado consisted of a string of strategically located port and trading settlements that ringed the greater Indian Ocean world. These ports included Mozambique, Malindi and Mombasa along the Swahili Coast, Hormuz in the Persian Gulf, Diu, Damaõ, Cochin, Calicut, Colombo, Nagapattinam (amongst others) in the Subcontinent, Melaka, Timor and the Moluccas in Southeast Asia, Macau in China and Nagasaki

View of the Market
at Rua Direita, Goa —
engraving published in
Jan van Linschoten's
Itinerario. Joannes van
Doetecum (engraver /
etcher), Cornelis Claesz
(publisher), Pieter
Hoogerbeets (writer).
Amsterdam, c. 1596.

in Japan. At the centre of this vast network of ports and trade was the city of Goa, second only to Lisbon itself.

The Portuguese had been lured into the Indian Ocean world by the spice trade. Spices such as pepper and nutmeg had, by this time, become necessities in Europe, used not just for preserving and thus extending the shelf life of meat and other forms of food for the long winters (as is widely believed), but also for enhancing the flavour of food and drink. The fall of Constantinople to the Ottomans in the mid-15th century resulted in a steep decline in the supply of spices overland from Venice to the European mainland. Trade would resume again very soon between Venice and Constantinople, but with spices sold at exorbitant prices.

The Portuguese hatched a plan to establish an alternative sea-route to India and the great entrepôt of Melaka, which they knew to be the source of spices traded west. They calculated, correctly, that in order to break Venice's monopoly, they needed control over the spice trade at its source.

Up until then, no one had yet successfully sailed around the southern tip of Africa. In 1497, Vasco da Gama made a radical decision to steer his ships west towards Brazil, avoiding unpredictable trade winds near the West African coast, and instead, catching prevailing currents that would swing the ship far enough south and east. Safely and successfully reaching the Cape of Good Hope, he became the first person to sail round the tip of Africa. At Mozambique, da Gama's ships finally encountered the ubiquitous dhows of the Indian Ocean world. They knew, then, that they were on their way.

Goa was taken in 1510, twelve years after Vasco da Gama made landfall in Calicut and seven years after the Portuguese established their first trading settlement at Cochin. At first, the Indians weren't impressed with the Portuguese and saw no benefit in trading with them. But the Iberians persisted, returning repeatedly to India and finally securing their factories by taking advantage of local rivalries and brandishing their advanced firearms technology.

Goa fell to Afonso de Albuquerque, a middle-aged conquistador who had cut his teeth in Morocco and taken Hormuz for the Portuguese just three years earlier. A year after conquering Goa, he would go on to sack and subdue Melaka, thus securing Portuguese control of the spice trade at its source. He would be the first of the viceroys of the Estado da Índia at Goa, holding the title till his death in 1515. His exploits in the East, alongside those of da Gama and other luminaries of the Portuguese Age of Discovery, are immortalised in that most epic work of Portuguese literature, *The Lusiads*, composed by Luís Vaz de Camões in 1572.

In the course of the 17th century, a series of epidemics forced residents of Old Goa to abandon the city and move west to Panjim. The old city was progressively taken apart, stone by stone, and these stones were floated downriver to be used in the construction of the new city. The viceroy himself moved his residence and seat of power to Panjim in the mid-18th century, and the city was finally designated the capital in 1843, and given the name Nova Goa ("New Goa").

What is left of Velha Goa today is a scattered collection of churches and ecclesiastical buildings, spectacularly restored in the 20th century. Though only a handful of structures, they hint at the city's glory in its heyday as the heart of Roman Catholicism and Catholic missionary activity in Asia – a "Rome of the East". The churches and convents of the old city of Goa were collectively designated a UNESCO World Heritage site in 1986.

Three monuments in particular dominate the ensemble. The first is the Church of Saint Francis of Assisi, initially built in 1521 in the Manueline style – the self-consciously opulent architectural style that emerged in Lisbon during the reign of King Manuel I, when Portugal was the undisputed ruler of the high seas, and Lisbon, the marketplace of the world.

Unfortunately, all that remains of the original Manueline church is its exquisitely carved main door, still in use today. The church as it stands was reconstructed in 1661 in a simple, rustic, Tuscan style, its three-tiered façade devoid of ornamentation, and topped with two octagonal towers. Don't be fooled by the simple exterior, however. The Church of Saint Francis of Assisi has the most staggeringly beautiful interiors of all the monuments here. Elaborate floral panels cover the buttresses and pilasters, as well as the rib-vaulted ceiling hanging over the chancel. Large paintings depicting the life of Saint Francis of Assisi hang on both sides of the chancel, flanking the magnificent main altar, gilded in gold in an exuberantly baroque style.

Just beside the Church of Saint Francis of Assisi stands the Sé Cathedral, completed in 1619. Also designed in a rustic Tuscan style, the cathedral would not look out of place in Italy. Its façade has two tiers and is topped by a wide pediment. A single bell tower stands to the south – the north tower collapsed in 1776. Before entering, stand on the threshold of the cathedral and look before you. This was once the main square of the old city. It was here that the city's great processions, including those of the notorious Goa Inquisition, took place.[2] Inside, the church is more simply decorated than its immediate neighbour, though it is considerably bigger – the largest church building in Goa, and one of the largest in all of Asia. The highlight of the interior is the main altar, which is carved and decorated in stucco relief and richly gilded in gold. Dedicated to Saint Catherine of Alexandria, it consists of six panels depicting her martyrdom.

The third of the great churches in Goa is perhaps the most famous of them all: the Basilica de Bom Jesus, the church of the Jesuits. It was completed in 1605 in a baroque style, the dark red laterite of its façade in harmonious contrast with its beige-hued basalt pilasters. It has a three-tiered façade topped by a pediment adorned with the letters, "IHS". The

Basilica de Bom Jesu, Velha Goa. Note the mark of the Jesuits at the top of the basilica's pediment: the initials "IHS" are an abbreviation for the name of Jesus Christ in Greek.

exterior of the church is best admired in the afternoon, when the rays of the sun turn the entire façade a reddish-gold.

The church's main attraction is the preserved body of Saint Francis Xavier, that most legendary of Catholic missionaries in the East. Xavier was a Basque missionary born in the former Kingdom of Navarre, in what is today's Spain. Alongside Ignatius of Loyola, a fellow Basque, he was one of seven founding members of the Society of Jesus (also known as the Jesuits), established in 1540. The Jesuits were a Catholic religious order that placed particular emphasis on the undertaking of missionary activity worldwide, often under extreme duress. Xavier would be best known for having travelled extraordinary distances and gone to extreme lengths in his missionary activities in Asia. Goa was his base out East, and his travels brought him to Melaka and the Spice Islands, to Japan and finally, to China, where he died unexpectedly in 1552. After his death, his body was first brought to Melaka and thereafter to Goa in 1554.

Following Francis Xavier's canonisation in 1622, his remains were transferred to the basilica. And for more than 300 years now, these sacred relics have been venerated here, attracting pilgrims and the faithful from all over the world. The saint's relics are housed and displayed in their own side chapel, to the immediate right of the main altar. The preserved body is encased in an elaborate silver casket made by Goan silversmiths in 1637. The casket in turn is laid atop an elaborate memorial dating to 1698. Made of marble and jasper, and with beautiful bronze plaques depicting the saint's life and death, this memorial had been commissioned by the grand duke of Tuscany, crafted by Italian artisans and imported from Florence.

Visitors often make a beeline to this side chapel and so it can be hard to catch a glimpse of the saint. Every ten years, a formal exposition takes place, wherein the saint's relics are openly displayed to worshippers over a period of 35 days. Once, worshippers were allowed to touch and kiss the remains. But by the mid-20th century, when visitor numbers swelled to the hundreds of thousands, a decision was made to enclose the body in a glass casket and forbid physical contact.

Aside from the Catholic faith, the Portuguese in Goa also introduced Eurasian cultures and communities to the Indian Ocean world. When Goa was taken, the first Portuguese residents of the city, most of them soldiers and sailors, had been encouraged to marry local women converts to Catholicism. This was both a pragmatic and tactical move. Few Portuguese undertook the journey to the East; and so inter-marrying was a necessary step to establishing a permanent presence in India, and to growing local communities of Christians loyal to the Portuguese crown and church.

The result of intermarriage was that by the end of the 16th century, there were significant populations of *mestizo*, or mixed-race, Portuguese in Goa (and elsewhere, like in Melaka and Macau). Their mothers being of local, Indian descent, it was inevitable that the *mestizo* Portuguese would adopt and assimilate local cultural practices alongside Portuguese ones, giving rise to hybrid Goan forms of dress, food and leisure.

Between 1583 and 1588, a young Dutchman, Jan Huyghen van Linschoten, worked as the archbishop's secretary in Goa. He would recount his experiences in his *Itinerario*, published in 1596 in Dutch and subsequently translated into other European languages. The book was valuable for its extensively-detailed navigational routes to the East Indies, as well as its very fine maps of places in the region. It would prove instrumental to the Dutch East India Company's bid to break the Portuguese monopoly on trade in the 17th century, affording them the know-how to sail their own vessels into the Indian Ocean world.

But by far the most enduring aspect of the book is the keenly-observed depiction of life in Old Goa in its heyday. One description of note relates to women's everyday lives:

"[t]he Portingales, Mestiços, and Indian Christian women in India [...] for the most part sit still within the house, and goe but seldome forth [...] When they goe to church, or to visit [any friend], they put on very costly apparrell with bracelets of gold, and rings upon their armes, [all beset with] costly Jewels and pearles, and at their eares hang laces full of Jewels. [Their] clothes [are] of Damaske, Velvet and cloth of gold, for silke is the worst [thing] they doe weare. Within the house they goe bare headed with a wastecoate called Baju (short shirt), that from their shoulders covereth [their] navels, and is so fine that you may see al their body through it, and downewardes they have nothing but a cloth wrapped three or foure times about [their] bodies. These clothes are very faire, some of them being very costly [wrought] with [loome worke, and] divers figures and flowers of all colours, all the rest of the body is naked without any hose, but onely bare footed in [a paire of] moyle (sandles) or pantofles, and the men in like sort." [3]

The Goan woman's revealing, figure-hugging apparel was essentially an early version of *kebaya*, still popularly worn today in Indonesia, Malaysia and Singapore. *Kebaya* was a quintessentially hybrid form of dress that fused elements from cultures around and beyond the Indian Ocean rim. Loose and lightweight, it would have been adopted by women in the port cities of the Portuguese Indian Ocean world as a matter of comfort and practicality in the tropical heat.

In the course of the chapter, van Linschoten highlights other Indianised aspects of Portuguese-Goan culture, for example, the preference for eating rice rather than bread; a love for curry-like potages of fish and meat, accompanied with pickled fruit and vegetables (called *achar* in the local language); and a tendency to eat with one's hands. He also remarks on the chewing of betel as a pastime, amongst ladies and their female slaves alike. Van Linschoten recounts that newcomers from Portugal were often mocked and laughed at until they have "learned the Indian manner, which they quicklie doe". [4] His anecdotes offer early hints as to the array of creole cultures that would emerge as Europeans encroached on the Indian Ocean world.

15. Macau

The Creole Culture of the Macanese

"Thus Macao in the days of its greatness: a city of adventurers enjoying a rich life, confidently aware that at any moment they might have to fight for it. Bold and superstitious, hospitable and remarkably tolerant of outsiders who came in peace, kind to each other, with a strong sense of being one community, they conducted their trade and worshipped in their churches, with their golden-skinned Malacca wives and sun-blackened African slaves, their entire lives the unique, exotic fruit of the grafting of West on East."

— Austin Coates, 1978. *A Macao Narrative.*[5]

Galinha à Africana is one of those classic conundrums of Macanese cuisine. Its name means "African chicken", yet the dish is nowhere to be found in Africa. The origins of the dish are obscure. Some believe it was invented by a local restaurateur in the 1940s; others think it a more recent import from former Portuguese colonies in Africa; yet others say it is a traditional recipe handed down for generations.

There are many variations of *galinha à Africana*, though locals would tell you it generally consists of grilled pieces of chicken, steeped in a fiery marinade preferably made from bird's eye chillies, and slathered with a spicy, curry-like sauce. It is then served either with rice in the Asian fashion, or with potatoes in the European fashion; and accompanied with a glass of Portuguese *vinho verde*. It is a hybrid dish through and through. The form of the dish closely approximates *piri-piri* chicken, a similarly fiery, classic grilled chicken dish from Mozambique; though the liberal use of coconut milk, curry powder and spices betrays Indo-Malay influence from the port cities of Melaka, Goa and the Malabar Coast. Finally, chillies and potatoes are not indigenous to Europe, Asia or Africa at all. They originate in the Americas and travelled from New to Old World by way of the Columbian Exchange.[6]

Thus, while it is most likely a contemporary invention, the *galinha à Africana's* very nature reflects Macau's age-old identity as a cosmopolitan port city with trade and cultural links to former Portuguese-speaking territories in Africa, Asia and the Americas. This identity is also reflected in Macau's Chinese name. *Aomen* (澳門) – read *Ou-Mun* in Cantonese – means "harbour gate"; and indeed, for centuries, Macau has been a gateway between China and the world.

The Praia Grande, Macao, contained in *China, in a Series of Views, Displaying the Scenery, Architecture, and Social Habits, of That Ancient Empire.* Thomas Allom, G. N. Wright. London, 1843.

The Portuguese Age of Discovery involved men, exclusively. Portuguese women were in short supply in all Eastern colonies. In Macau, Portuguese settlers searching for wives initially turned to Goa, Melaka or Nagasaki, where there were already healthy numbers of converted, Asian Catholic women. Filipino wives from Manila were also an option, particularly during the Union of the Portuguese and Spanish crowns from 1580 to 1640. Subsequently, long after the Portuguese had firmly established themselves in Macau, they also began to intermarry with the Chinese.

From this heady mixture of Portuguese, Indian, Malay, Japanese, Filipino and Chinese came the local creole Macanese people – though this is admittedly an over-simplification of centuries of cultural mixing. In Cantonese, the Macanese are referred to as *tou-saang-ian* (土生人), from the Portuguese *filhos da terra* ("sons and daughters of the soil"). They are distinguished from the Cantonese of Macau, known as the *ou-mun-ian*, and the Portuguese, colloquially referred to as *fan-gwai* (番鬼 – "foreign barbarian devil") or *gwai-lo* (鬼佬 – "old devil").

The Macanese are among an array of Portuguese Eurasian communities that emerged around the Indian Ocean rim. There were others; in particular, the Goans in India and the Kristang in the Malay Peninsula. There are also other Eurasian communities which came later: the *mestizo* in the Philippines; the *Indische* in the former Dutch East Indies (today's Indonesia); the Dutch Burghers in Ceylon, *les métis* in former French Indochina, and the Anglo-Indians and Anglo-Burmese in the former British Raj. All these Eurasian communities continue to endure, some just barely, others thriving. Many of them exist as part of a larger diaspora around the world, most notably in Europe, North America and Australasia.

Macanese culture likely draws from that of the Kristang. The Macanese language, Patuá, is a fusion of Portuguese and Indo-Malay grammar and vocabulary. It is a variation on the Kristang language still spoken by Eurasians in Melaka and Singapore today, and was likely imported to Macau when Melaka fell to the Dutch in the 1600s, and a wave of Kristang fled north. Both cultures share and cherish a very similar repertoire of traditional folk songs, such as "Jingkli Nona" ("Fair Maiden") and "Macau sâm assi" ("This is Macau").

Macanese dress also bears a strong resemblance to Malay dress, though with touches of Japanese and Portuguese influence. The Macanese, like the Malays, refer to a "grande dame" as *nhonha* (*nyonya* in Malay) – both terms probably derive from the Portuguese *dona*. The *nhonha*'s traditional dress is the *saraça baju*, consisting of three separate items of clothing: a *baju*, or blouse-top, cut like a kimono from expensive, embroidered fabric; a *saraça* or skirt-cloth wrapped around the waist; and a long veil, or *mantilla*, that is used to cover the head when the lady steps out of the house. *Saraça* is likely derived from the Malay *serasah* and Japanese *sarasa*, both of which refer to printed and brightly-coloured Indian trade cloth.

Needless to say, Macanese cuisine, too, closely resembles that of the Kristang. A case in point is the Macanese *diablo*, cousin to the Kristang *curry debal* – both names mean "devil's curry", and both dishes feature a variety of meats in a rich and spicy stew. A key distinction is that *diablo* uses vinegar liberally and is generally known for being tart; while *curry debal* uses obscene amounts of chilli peppers and is one of the most devilishly fiery dishes in the Eurasian kitchen.

The Portuguese came to China in 1513, settling in the vicinity of the Pearl River Delta. It took some 50 years of diplomacy before Chinese authorities at Guangzhou permitted the establishment of a Portuguese factor at Macau, in return for taxes levied on trade. Unlike in Goa, the establishment of a trading settlement at Macau was a private initiative, undertaken by Portuguese merchants rather than the Portuguese state. Macau was thus neither a colony, per se, nor a leased concession, but Chinese sovereign territory, administered via a semi-tacit agreement, with the Portuguese as managing agent. The Portuguese remained in Macau purely through Chinese sufferance, and they knew it.

Administratively, Macau was unique in being semi-autonomous in relation to the Estado da Índia. Its governor reported to the viceroy at Goa, but was only responsible for defense of the territory. Even then, the defense budget was fully paid for by the private citizens of Macau in the manner of an "outsourced" arrangement. At the same time, Guangzhou authorities refused to recognise or treat with any party other than the city's Câmara ("Municipal Council"), consisting of the most wealthy and powerful Portuguese and Macanese merchant families in the territory. Macau was thus self-governing in most matters other than defense, allying itself more with China – as a pragmatic course of action – than to the distant Portuguese Crown.

Macau experienced its golden age as a trading settlement from 1557 to 1641. Success stemmed from its geographical location, at the confluence of four very lucrative trading routes – the China trade up the Pearl River from Guangzhou; the India trade from Goa by way of Melaka; the Japan trade from Nagasaki, and the Mexico trade by way of Manila. The arrival of a Portuguese *nau*, or carrack, was always a big event in all the ports of the Estado da Índia, for the cornucopia of treasures that the vessel would bring from foreign lands. As go-betweens and intermediaries, the Portuguese in Macau became immensely wealthy.

Portuguese advantage in East Asia faded in the 1600s due to a series of seismic shifts in geopolitics. In 1638, the Tokugawa shogun, irritated by Catholic missionary activity and believing Portuguese Catholics to have played a role in instigating what was then Japan's largest-ever civil uprising, issued an edict banning all Portuguese from his nation.[7] Not long after, the Iberian Union between the crowns of Spain and Portugal dissolved, making Manila and the Mexico trade now out of bounds to the Portuguese. 1641 saw the Estado da Índia lose its major trading settlements of Melaka and Nagasaki to the Dutch VOC. The final blow fell in 1684 when the Chinese emperor, Kangxi, decided to open Guangzhou to foreign trade, thus obliterating Macau's earlier monopolistic position on the Chinese mainland.

For a time, Macau crumbled and decayed, becoming a quaint anachronism: an odd relic from times past, with its beautiful *edifícios* and sprawling villas harking back to lost wealth. The city enjoyed a modest revival in the late 18th century when it became a second home for European and American traders in Guangzhou, forced to leave the city during the winter season. But even this advantage was lost to Hong Kong in 1842, when the island became British territory. After the Portuguese government legalised gambling in Macau in the 1850s, the city became infamous as a gamblers' haven, rife with gangs, opium-smuggling and prostitution.

Macau became a formal Portuguese colony only in 1887, in the aftermath of two opium wars and a European scramble for foreign concessions. One of the earliest European trading settlements in Asia, it was ironically the last relinquished, reverting to China only in 1999 after having been Portuguese for 442 years.

Surprisingly, much of old Macau's architectural heritage remains, and has been preserved and painstakingly restored by the local government. Today, as in the past, the old city resembles mediaeval towns in the Iberian Peninsula, with their winding cobblestoned streets, neoclassical edifices and the many churches that appear, as if out of nowhere, when one turns a street corner.

In 2005, much of the old city was inscribed on UNESCO's World Heritage List as *O Centro Histórico de Macau* ("The Historic Centre of Macau"). The listing consists of two core heritage zones, incorporating some two dozen major monuments and landmarks and many other historic edifices. Only a handful of these monuments date from Macau's 17th century heyday. The most important are the Ruins of Saint Paul's, situated at the heart of the old city, and consisting of the granite façade of the former Church of Mater Dei ("Mother of God"), and the remains of the Colégio de São Paulo (Saint Paul's College). The Ruins stand on a spectacular elevated position right beside the city's Fortaleza de São Paulo do Monte (or Mount Fortress). Church and fortress were built by the Jesuits.

First-hand accounts of the interior of the Church of Mater Dei relate how vast and astonishingly beautiful it was, second only to Saint Paul's Cathedral in the Vatican. It was certainly one-of-its-kind, having been constructed by Christian Japanese artisans fleeing Nagasaki in the wake of the Tokugawa regime's persecution of the faith. Unfortunately, the wooden body of the church was destroyed by fire in 1835, leaving only its granite façade unscathed. But the façade itself is a magnificent work of art, featuring motifs from Western and Eastern tradition – Jesuit saints, Portuguese ships, Chinese lions and Japanese chrysanthemums, to name a few. The first glimpse of this amazing structure, silhouetted against a

View past Portuguese-style edifices to the majestic ruins of Saint Paul's.

clear blue sky, is guaranteed to elicit gasps from the unwary visitor. Small wonder then that the immediate vicinity of Mount Fortress is constantly over-run with visitors.

Another important monument in the city is the A-Ma Temple, just south of the historic centre. This is one of the oldest buildings in Macau. Pre-dating Portuguese arrival, it was probably built in the late 15th century by Hokkien merchants and seafarers trading in these parts. It is dedicated to Mazu, goddess of the sea, known fondly and colloquially here as A-Ma, or "Mother". The temple bustles with activity, particularly on festive occasions when hundreds of the faithful throng its modestly-sized grounds.

Macau gets its name from A-Ma Temple. Legend goes that the Portuguese first dropped anchor right here where the temple stands. Spying local fishermen out and about, they asked: *Tell us, good sirs, what country we've arrived at?* To which the locals replied: *A-Ma Ou* or "Bay of A-Ma". The name "Amacau" stuck, and was shortened to "Macau". Later on, the Portuguese would give the city its formal Christian name: Cidade do Nome de Deus de Macau, Não há outra mais leal ("City of the Name of God of Macau, None is more Loyal"), thus embedding God and Goddess, Father and Mother into a name as creolised as the city itself.

From A-Ma Temple, it is a short walk to what was once the city's most breathtaking landmark: the mile-long, crescent-shaped Praia Grande, or

"Grand Beach". This was formerly the very first view of Macau for any visitor arriving by sea, and it did not disappoint. The Praia Grande was where the territory's most imposing civic and commercial edifices and its most opulent residential villas stood – a sweeping stretch of gleaming, European neoclassical façades fronted by a glistening harbour teeming with sailboats. It was the most iconic view of Macau for much of the 19th and 20th centuries, immortalised by painters and photographers who fell in love with this impossible Mediterranean vista on the South China Sea.

Unfortunately, massive land reclamation in the mid-1900s removed the northern half of the bay and transformed it into a casino precinct; while the southern half has only recently been sealed off from the ocean, creating a lake where a bay once was. Only a few buildings from the past still stand; and thus one must close one's eyes and imagine the view from centuries ago. Floating high above the rafters are the familiar, lilting strains of a classic tune – about sunbaked rooftops, singing girls and freshly baked bread – playing over the radio.

Assi sâm Macau... This is Macau.

16. Manila
Chinese Silk, American Silver and the Manila-Acapulco Galleons

"Raw silk in bundles, of the fineness of two strands, and other silk of coarser quality; fine untwisted silk, white and of all colours, wound in small skeins; quantities of velvets, some plain and some embroidered in all sorts of figures, colours and fashions, others with body of gold and embroidered with gold; woven stuffs and brocades, of gold and silver upon silk of various colours and patterns; quantities of gold and silver thread in skeins; damasks, satins, taffetas and other cloths of all colours..."

— Antonio de Morga, 1609. *Sucesos de las Islas Filipinas.* [8]

The Asian Civilisations Museum has in its collection an exquisite mid-17th century ivory sculpture of the Virgin Mary. She stands upright, gazing up to the heavens in supplication, her palms barely touching in prayer. She is sumptuously dressed in a soft and flowing, presumably silk, gown. Her body is carved from a single ivory tusk – you can see where it curves and how the craftsman (or woman) has expertly teased the form of the Virgin from the curve. The Virgin's flowing robe is tucked in at the back, in a manner known as a *suksok* in the Philippines. Her features are Asian, rather than European, suggesting she would have been made in the port city of Manila, at the height of its glory as an entrepôt port at the time. Her cape and robe are elaborately decorated with gold gilding depicting flowers and foliage – these would have been painted on in faraway Mexico. They resemble similar forms of decoration found in Mexican religious art.

In the mid-17th century, the Philippines and Mexico were linked closely by trade, with enormous Spanish galleons shipping treasures regularly from Asia across the Pacific Ocean to the Americas. This Philippine Virgin Mary was once part of a fabulous cargo, headed east to Mexico, on board one of the legendary Manila-Acapulco Galleons.

The galleons go by a variety of names. In the Philippines and Spain, they are known as the Manila Galleons, or *galeón de Manila*, in acknowledgement of the role Manila played in the trade. In Latin America, however, they are known as *nao de la China*, or "China ships", because these galleons brought the fabled treasures of China – by way of Manila, no doubt – to the Americas. The first galleons to set sail from Manila Bay did so in 1573, only two years after Miguel López de Legazpi took Manila for the Spanish Crown. The last of the galleons sailed in 1815, almost 250 years after. From a contemporary perspective, one may thus regard the Manila–Acapulco Galleons as a shipping line, albeit one with extraordinary longevity.

The galleon route was both epic and exceedingly dangerous. The journey westward from Acapulco, in the Viceroyalty of New Spain (today's Mexico), was the easier leg. A typical galleon would take a straight course across the Pacific until it reached the Philippine Archipelago, arriving after about a hundred days on average. The journey eastward to Acapulco, however, was another story altogether. *El tornaviaje* ("the return journey") was notoriously fraught. It involved the galleon taking a counter-intuitive path, wending

The Virgin Mary. Made in Manila, decorated in Mexico, mid-17th century. Ivory, painted and gilded, height 60 cm. Collection of the Asian Civilisations Museum.

northwest upon leaving the Philippines, rather than sailing straight on, which would have led it right into the infamous whirlwind belt of the Pacific. Hugging the coast of Japan due north, the galleon would finally encounter the North Pacific Current, and be powered across the Pacific to the Californian coast. The return journey took some six to eight months, and even then, the risk of encountering a storm was high.

Manila-to-Acapulco was only one half of a global trade route. Most goods unloaded at Acapulco went on to Mexico City. A good portion, however, were bound for Europe. They were transported overland to the market-town of Puebla and onwards to the port of Veracruz, where they would be packed onto Atlantic galleons and shipped off to Seville in Spain. These Atlantic galleons would return some months later, with European goods bound for New Spain or Asia.

The Manila-Acapulco route expanded networks of Asian trade across the globe. For centuries, trade from China to Europe had flowed westward, via the Middle East. The galleons introduced an unprecedented, eastward flow of goods from the Middle Kingdom to Europe, with a stopover in the Americas. Eastward trade from China across the Pacific, though not quite on the scale as westward trade across the Indian Ocean, was nonetheless regular and voluminous. Hundreds of galleons sailed in the two centuries of the Manila-Acapulco Line's existence. Ships grew in size and tonnage till, at the peak of the run, they were immense – the average galleon weighed some 1000 tonnes, with the largest-ever recorded surpassing 2000.

On the eastward-bound galleon, cargo generally consisted of a wide variety of luxury goods from across Asia, the single most important being silk and other Chinese textiles, highly in demand in the Americas and Spain. Chinese junks from Hokkien port cities or Macau would sail regularly to Manila, bringing their wares. These would be purchased by enterprising local merchants for re-export, with a hefty mark-up in price. In the opening excerpt, Antonio de Morga, a Spanish official in the Philippines in the early 1600s, provides a sense of the dizzying array of Chinese silks traded in Manila.

One of the most famous silk exports was the so-called *manton de manila*, a luxurious, heavily-embroidered silk shawl popular with fashionable women. Draped sensuously around a woman's shoulders and falling down to her knees, it defined the silhouette of Hispanic dress, and remains a classic of Latin American and Spanish fashion today. The name of the shawl makes reference to these textiles being brought to Spain on the *galéon de manila*, though in fact, they were Chinese products originally from Guangzhou.

Aside from silk, porcelain was another important luxury commodity on the galleons. Besides full sets of European-style dinner services commissioned by wealthy merchant or noble families, new and unique porcelain forms were also developed by Chinese potters for the American market. For example, a full range of vessels emerged catering to the consumption of chocolate, including the *chocolatero*, or jars to store chocolate and cacao; and the *mancerina*, distinctive and hybrid cup-plus-saucer vessels used to hold molten chocolate and biscuits for dipping. Blue-and-white porcelain was particularly prized, and attempts to imitate Chinese blue-and-white in the market-town of Puebla led to the creation of a brand-new type of locally-produced, quintessentially-Mexican ceramic, known as *talavera*.

Meanwhile, westward-bound ships carried one singular cargo: American silver in the form of bullion, or later on, minted silver coins known as Spanish silver dollars, or *reales de a ocho* ("pieces of eight"). In his 1699 travelogue, *Voyage Round the World* (*Giro del Mondo*), Italian explorer Giovanni Francesco Gemelli Careri notes, in Volume V on the Philippines, that:

> "…the Emperor of China calls the King of Spain, the King of Silver; because there being no Mine of it in his dominions, all they have there is brought in by the Spaniards in Pieces of Eight."[9]

And indeed, the Chinese were obsessed with the precious metal. China's economy in the late 16th century was on the brink of collapse: wanton printing of paper money had resulted in hyper-inflation and the devaluation of currency. The Ming emperors found it expedient to revert from paper- to coin-based currency pegged to silver. The entire economy was thus overhauled and placed on the silver standard. All transactions, including payment of taxes, had to be conducted in silver. When Europeans first attempted to trade with the Chinese, they found Chinese merchants keen only on silver coinage as payment; no other foreign good was of any interest.

China's limited domestic supply of silver meant large volumes of the metal had to be imported from Japan. As Japanese supplies dried up, American silver filled the gap. Chinese demand for silver was so great that it fueled the flames, night and day, at the great Potosí silver mines in Peru, where almost 60% of the world's silver was mined at the time. With each Manila Galleon able to carry more than two million pesos worth of silver, a staggeringly enormous amount of the coin would be transported from New Spain to China in the course of two centuries. China was referred to as the "graveyard" of silver, a bottomless pit that would empty the New World of its silver deposits.

By the 17th century, the Spanish silver dollar had become the gold standard for not only the Chinese but the world economy. The Spanish dollar was the first international currency: a precursor to the American dollar introduced in the late 18th century. In fact, the American was pegged dollar-to-dollar to the Spanish and minted to the same specifications in terms of weight and quality of silver. So too, the Mexican dollar, introduced in the early 19th century when New Spain became independent Mexico; as well as the Chinese *yuan*, the Japanese *yen*, and the Korean *won* in the late 19th century – the words *yuan*, *yen* and *won* mean "round". In French, the word for "money", *l'argent*, literally means "silver".

So much treasure on the galleons meant that they were fodder for pirates, and inevitably, a small number of these galleons would be commandeered by buccaneers, mercenaries, and the occasional Dutch or English East India Company ship. A larger number would be wrecked somewhere along their epic journey across the Pacific, deep in the ocean or along the shallow coastal waters of the Philippines and eastern Mexico. These wrecked ships and their sunken treasure would attract pirates and treasure hunters across the centuries.

Manila's economy was almost entirely reliant on entrepôt trade. Earlier attempts on the part of Spanish colonials to cultivate spices or mine for precious metals were abandoned when efforts proved futile, and when proceeds from trade outstripped everything else. Manila's wealth depended largely on the galleon trade alone, which, given the high risks involved in each venture, meant that the city's economy was subject to rather dramatic up- and downswings.

The Spanish Crown operated the galleon trade as a monopoly, and permitted an average of only two galleons to sail each year. Sometimes they allowed three; other times, they reduced it to one. All was well if the galleon returned successfully from Acapulco. Silver on board would serve as payment for goods exported and would be used to purchase the next year's shipments. The colony's *situado*, or annual silver subsidy from the Spanish Crown, would be secure, and officials in the government could count on being paid. Should the galleon be wrecked, at least half the year's income and *situado* would be lost, and the city itself could sink into a recession. In the decades where only one galleon was permitted to sail a year, the loss of that galleon could be dire indeed. Entire fortunes would be lost, civil service salaries cut, and the year ahead would see spirits low and festivities muted.

The number of Spanish residents in the city was never very large. They walled themselves off from the rest of the local population in a mediaeval fortress town known today as Intramuros ("inside the walls") and which was the city of Manila proper. Within Intramuros, the Spanish built a thoroughly Hispanic city in the image of those in New Spain. The city was laid out in an orderly fashion along the *cuadricula* ("grid system"), with merchant houses, villas and magnificent baroque cathedrals standing alongside numerous public squares and plazas.

Unfortunately, much of Intramuros was destroyed during the Second World War when Manila was the stage of a decisive battle between the

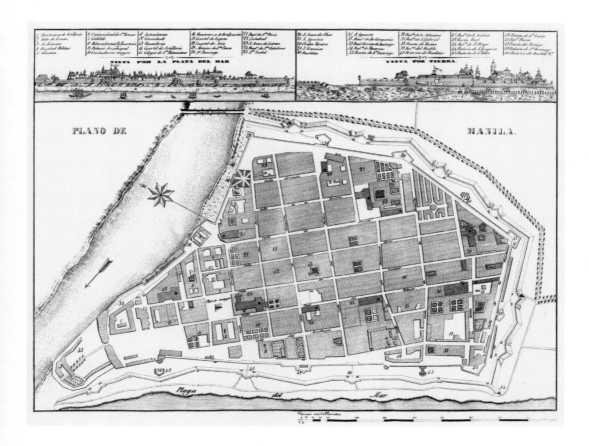

Americans and the Japanese. Of the many churches and cathedrals that used to stand here, only one remains today. This is the San Agustin Church, which, along with a few other baroque-style churches across the Philippines, was designated as part of a collective UNESCO World Heritage site in 1993.

For much of Manila's history, the Chinese had been the largest resident community in the city. Many of them had come here illicitly to trade, given that the Ming emperors maintained a ban on private trade for their subjects. The Spanish called the Chinese *sangley*, a word many believe to derive from the Hokkien word for "doing business" (生理 – *seng li*); though the term could also derive from the words for "arriving frequently" (常来 – *siong lai* in Hokkien).[10] Certainly, from the point of view of the Spaniards and the local Tagalogs, the Chinese were the people who frequently came, with their treasures and their trade.

Much to the consternation of the Spanish, thousands of Chinese chose to settle in the city. They were housed outside and to the west

Map of Old Manila in 1851, contained in the *Diccionario Geografico-Estadistico-Historico De Las Islas Filipinas.* Manuel Buzeta Núñez, Felipe Bravo. Madrid, 1851. The Pasig River is at left. Collection of the University of Texas in Austin Library.

of the walled city, in a foreign merchants' quarter known as the Parían ("market") and which was also the commercial heart of Manila. Later, as numbers continued to swell, the Chinese would move across the Pasig River to the suburb of Binondo, making it the first ever "Chinatown" anywhere in the world.

With resident communities of Spaniards, Chinese, Tagalogs and at various points even Japanese, Africans and Native Americans, Manilan society saw the emergence of a large *mestizo* community. Unlike the Portuguese in Goa, Macau and Melaka, who encouraged intermarrying and considered anyone with Portuguese blood Portuguese, the Spanish frowned upon miscegenation, and were greatly concerned about *limpieza de sangre*, or purity of blood.

A dizzying array of terms was used to describe the full range of pureblood and *mestizo* communities in the city and their respective castes in society. Spaniards from Europe were known as *peninsulares* and stood at the top of the pyramid, followed by *criollos*, or Spaniards born in the colonies. Just below them came many, many different groups of *mestizo*: *mestizo con Española* (native + Spanish blood), *mestizo con China* (native + Chinese blood), *castizos* (Spanish + mestizo), *mulattos* (Spanish + African), *moriscos* (Spanish + Muslim) and so on. The *sangleyes* came after, and almost at the very bottom of the pecking order were the *indios*, the local Filipinos, who ranked only above the *negros*, or African slaves. Except for the *peninsulares*, all of these ethnological terms invariably came coloured by prejudice and racial discrimination.

The most iconic depiction of historic Manila, reproduced in prints, maps and photographs, is the bird's eye view of its eponymous walled city, located at the mouth of the Pasig River, and shaped like an oyster's shell. The earliest known image of this walled city dates to circa 1645, and is a painting in oil by an unknown artisan on the inside of the lid of a wooden travelling trunk. Manila is depicted in its heyday, with its city walls firm and forbidding. Its sea-facing ramparts run straight and strong along the water and are topped by enormous *baluartes* ("bastions"). Within the walls, the city is bustling. Churches, plazas, broad thoroughfares and hundreds of buildings are arranged in an orderly fashion along the *cuadricula*. Spaniards, some of them astride horses, are out and about in the city, dressed to the nines in European-style garments.

Just outside the walled city is the Parían, situated on an artificial island in the Pasig River. Here we spy miniature figures of Spaniards treating with Chinese merchants and their wives, garbed in the latest Ming styles. At the top of the painting, sailing alongside the walls of the city, are Chinese-style junks bringing treasures from the Hokkien coast. Sampans and a European-style sailboat are docked just off the Parían, while at top-right is a large European-style vessel – perhaps the earliest depiction of a Manila Galleon?

The wooden trunk within which this delightful scene is ensconced sits today in the galleries of the Museo José Luis Bello y González in the Mexican city of Puebla. This is one of the most gorgeous decorative art museums in the city, and one with long-standing, historic ties to Asia. The trunk had been made in Manila and dispatched by Christian clerics to Puebla as a gift to the bishop. It is yet another tangible illustration of the far-reaching impact of the Manila-Acapulco Galleons, and the role Manila played in the spread of Asian material culture to the Americas, where it was eagerly consumed and where it precipitated new forms and expressions of Hispanic cultural identity.

17. Jakarta & Cape Town (Batavia & Kaapstad)
Castles, Keramat and the Vereenigde Oost-Indische Compagnie

"In the Name of Allah, Most Compassionate, Most Merciful. This is a statement of Islamic belief [*aqidah*] by the Leader [*Imam*], the Bearer [*hamil*] of the flag of Islam's Divine Law [*Shari'ah*], the ascetic [*zahid*], the worshipper [*abid*], the traveller in the Way [*salik*], the otherworldly [*nasik*], the friend of Allah [*wali*], the pious [*salih*], the Godfearing [*war'*], […], our Master [*Sayyid*], the father of Abdullah, our Patron [*Mawlana*], Muhammad bin Yusuf al-Sanusi al-Hasan, Allah's mercy be upon him and Allah be pleased with him, and may we benefit from his erudition. He is the author of this book whose title is *Umm al-Barahin* [The Demonstrative Proofs]."

— Abdullah ibn Qadi Abd al-Salaam, c. 1781.
The Aqidah of Tuan Guru. Being a transcription, while incarcerated at Robben Island, Cape Town, of the *Umm al-Barahin* of Muhammad bin Yusuf al-Sanusi.[11]

Most visitors to Jakarta today don't come for the history or the architecture. Most visitors don't stop much in Jakarta at all, so notorious is the city for its traffic and its population density, and its immense urban sprawl. This is a pity, for Jakarta still has plenty to offer by way of cultural heritage.

North of Jakarta lies its most historic district. Known as Kota ("City") or sometimes Kota Tua ("Old City"), this district has the largest concentration of historic buildings. Once, it was known as Oud Batavia ("Old Batavia"). And indeed, here, in this northernmost point of the city, closest to the sea and slowly sinking in the mud, stands the oldest – and still reasonably well-preserved – section of the former Dutch East Indies capital.

The visitor would be well-placed to begin his or her tour of Oud Batavia at the former Stadhuisplein, or City Hall Square, renamed Fatahillah Square after a 16th century Javanese general. Here in the middle of the square, facing the stupendous and surreal former Stadhuis ("City Hall"), one is immediately transported to a tropical Amsterdam, notwithstanding the local Jakarta families on brightly-coloured bikes circling the square or picnicking on its grounds. The Stadhuis, built in 1710, is one of the oldest examples of Dutch architecture in Asia. It's completely European in style with its symmetrical form, neoclassical entrance, baroque ornamentation and slender, Dutch dome.

All that remains of Batavia's old city walls is a small section that today flanks Jakarta's Maritime Museum (Museum Bahari). The museum, occupying former VOC warehouses, stands just north of Kota Tua, close to Jakarta's historic Sunda Kelapa port. A fire in 2018 damaged the building but it has since been restored.

North of the Stadhuis is the merchant district, flanked by the former Grootegracht, or Great Canal (today's Kali Besar), which flows north through the old city into the sea. Around the Kali Besar are historic commercial buildings that used to house the offices of merchant establishments here, and which feature a variety of architectural styles from neoclassical, to Indo-European eclectic, to art deco. One of the most important structures still standing is the so-called Toko Merah, or "Red House", a private residence built in the Dutch Patrician style. The building has a severe, blockish structure and is entirely closed in, with small windows that keep out rather than let in the air and the light. This vernacular, imported straight out of the Netherlands, would prove completely inappropriate for the tropical weather.

Perhaps the most storied historical edifice in Old Batavia was the former Kasteel Batavia. A mediaeval European-style fortress, Batavia Castle had been completed by the Dutch United East India Companies in 1627, less than a decade after their ships first dropped anchor here. The castle sat right on the waterfront, facing the sea to the north, and flanking the entrance to the Grootegracht to its west. It was shaped like a four-pointed star, with each point being a formidable bastion. These were named after precious stones: *Parel, Saffier, Robijn, Diamant…* Pearl, Sapphire, Ruby, Diamond.

One of the most iconic and fascinating early views of Batavia is Dutch painter Andries Beeckman's *Het Kasteel van Batavia* ("The Castle in Batavia"), completed in 1662 and presently in the collection of the Rijksmuseum in Amsterdam. In this painting, the castle is situated in the distance, illuminated by sunlight. The Grootegracht runs diagonally across the canvas, dividing it into foreground and background. In the foreground is the famed former Chicken Market, or Hoenderpasar, bustling with all sorts of people. Locals from Java can be seen playing a traditional ball game. Two moustached Chinese gentlemen reach out to greet each other. A Japanese gentleman in a blue kimono and black top hat strolls by, his right hand wielding a sword. Not far from him stands a Mardijker man in his eye-catching striped shirt and trousers.[12] Finally, taking pride of place in the scene is a Dutch gentleman in European clothing, promenading with his Eurasian or Asian wife, dressed in *baju* and *sarong*. A slave trails behind them, shielding them from the sun with a parasol, a symbol of authority in Malay cultures.

From this heady mix of cultures came the local Orang Betawi, or Betawi people. These were the "indigenous" peoples of Batavia, "sons and daughters of the soil" here. A Muslim community distinct from the Javanese, their ancestors were slaves brought from all across the Indonesian Archipelago and Indian Ocean to this imperial city. Their language, Betawi, is a creole form of Malay; and their food and material culture, celebrated today as an essential part of Jakarta's identity, are hybrid in nature, incorporating Dutch, Portuguese, Sundanese, Balinese, Ambonese, Bandanese, Arabic, Chinese, Japanese, Indian and other influences.

Most of Batavia Castle was demolished in the early 1800s, when the colonial government moved the centre of administration south to the district of Weltevreden. By that time, Oud Batavia, with its canals and putrid, stagnant water, had become a death-trap of malaria and dysentery. There being a shortage of building material, the castle and its walls were taken apart and the stones used to build new civic and administrative buildings down south. For much of the 19th and early 20th centuries, all that remained of the castle was the ornate, neoclassical Amsterdamse Poort, the castle's former front gate, built in 1744. Sporting statues of Mars and Minerva, it used to stand just north of the Stadhuis, but had to make way for a vehicular road expansion in the 1950s.

The Vereenigde Oost-Indische Compagnie, or the United Dutch East India Companies, thrust itself onto the global stage in the 17th century, intent on supplanting the Portuguese Estado da Índia. The company was formed in 1602 by way of a directive from the Dutch government, forcibly merging competing merchant houses into one single trading company.

The VOC, as it is more commonly known, was given a charter to trade exclusively, on behalf of the Republic of the Netherlands, in the oceans between the Cape of Good Hope and the Straits of Magellan. It was one of the first great European East India Companies, unprecedented in organisational structure. As a joint stock company, it had permanent share capital owned by multiple investors, and shares traded at the Amsterdam Stock Exchange. At its peak, the VOC was the largest trading company in the world, owning hundreds of ships, employing thousands of people, and ruling over trading settlements and maritime networks that stretched halfway across the earth. It more than fulfilled its initial intent of ousting the Portuguese, and would only be eclipsed by its closest competitor, the Honourable (English) East India Company, in the 19th century.

The company was governed by an elite, rotating group of merchants, known as the Heeren XVII, or the Gentlemen Seventeen. These gentlemen merchants functioned as the company's board of directors, and were exceptionally powerful. They set policies and prices; they decided on the nature and volume of goods to be traded, the number of vessels in each fleet, the routes that must be taken to Asia. They were more like kings than merchants. The decisions they made had an impact on tens of thousands of people in the VOC's territories worldwide.

What first drew the VOC to Asia was a trio of spices: nutmeg, mace and cloves. All three were used to preserve meats or spice wine and other victuals for the winter, and they had become absolute necessities in Europe. Unfortunately, these rare plants were only to be found in the Spice Islands, a remote archipelago known as the Moluccas (Maluku in contemporary Bahasa Indonesia), situated in the eastern part of today's Indonesia. Cloves were cultivated in Tidore, Ternate and other neighbouring islands; but nutmeg would only grow in the Banda Islands, the most remote and isolated island group in the larger Moluccas chain.

Up till the late 16th century, the Portuguese, operating from their regional trading settlements in Ambon and Ternate, and from their entrepôt port of Melaka, had enjoyed a monopoly on the export of these precious spices. The Dutch would supplant them in all these ports, and go one step further in controlling the supply chain.

In 1617, the VOC named as fourth Governor-General of the East Indies one Jan Pieterszoon Coen, a ruthless and ambitious man who, by any measure today, would be regarded as a genocidal maniac. Coen had earlier secured trading privileges for the Dutch in the Spice Islands, but it had proven impossible to police these privileges without a more permanent settlement in the region, and in the face of the rival Portuguese and English. Already in a statement to the Heeren XVII in 1614, Coen had argued for the use of violence in achieving the VOC's interests, stating that:

> "Your Honours should know by experience, that trade in Asia must be driven and maintained under the protection and favour of Your Honours' own weapons, and that the weapons must be paid for by the profits from the trade; so that we cannot carry out trade without war, nor war without trade." [13]

In 1619, Coen set sail for the city of Jayakarta on the north Javanese coast, then a vassal state to the adjacent Sultanate of Banten. Razing the city to the ground, he erected in its place a Dutch factory and fortress named Batavia, supposedly after a legendary Dutch-Germanic tribe that existed during the Roman period. From Batavia, Coen captained a fleet of East Indiamen to the Banda islands in 1621, where he ruthlessly tortured and massacred local Bandanese – men, women and children alike. After exiling whoever else resisted, he turned over the cultivation of nutmeg to Dutch settlers exclusively, in effect transforming the islands into a vast Dutch-owned plantation and making the Bandanese slaves in their own land. He would do the same in Ambon and Ternate for the purpose of cultivating cloves. This ruthless, war-like approach meant the Dutch had full control of the production of spices at its very source. The VOC was therefore able to exert its monopoly effectively, setting prices in a manner that would make it immensely profitable, and its shareholders prodigiously wealthy.

Batavia would be designated the Asian headquarters of the VOC trade. From this base, the VOC would expand their networks in the region, taking Melaka, the Moluccas and Ceylon from the Portuguese, establishing footholds at Surat, Bengal, Cochin and Pulicat in India, setting up shop in Guangzhou and Nagasaki, and establishing a supply station at the Cape of Good Hope. From Batavia also, the Dutch would eventually colonise all of what would become the Dutch East Indies – today's Indonesia – by the early 20th century. Coen would be remembered as the founder of Batavia, though his legacy today has been cast in a far more critical light.

Batavia was ostensibly second only to Amsterdam; though, in reality, in matters pertaining to the VOC's Asian trade, it was second to none. For starters, Batavia was the central transhipment point and entrepôt for all of the VOC's Asian trade. Everything traded out of the VOC's settlements in the East had to be brought to Batavia to be transhipped onwards to Amsterdam. This ruling applied even to VOC settlements in India and Ceylon, which were much closer to Europe.

All the Company's officials in the East reported to Batavia as their headquarters – appointments, transfers and promotions were decided here. The Raad van Indië, or Council of the Indies – the highest governing body in Dutch Asia – counted amongst them representatives from all the secondary settlements, including Ceylon, Melaka, and even Cape Town. The governor-general and his Raad van Indië ruled de facto over all the VOC's Asian territories. After Coen's death, the post of governor-general would be selected by local council representatives in Batavia and submitted to Amsterdam merely for confirmation.

During its heyday in the 17th century, Batavia was the most important entrepôt port in the entire Indian Ocean world, eclipsing Goa and Melaka before her, and rivalling Manila and its Pacific trade. The centre of all this power, the place where governor-general and Raad van Indië held court, was the Kasteel Batavia. Unfortunately, all that remains of this concentration of power is a grand meeting table and accompanying set of armchairs once used by the governor-general and his council. These were relocated from Kasteel to Stadhuis when the former was demolished, and have been preserved there to this very day.

Amsterdam and Batavia being of great distance from each other, there was a need for a half-way house: a supply and refreshment station for East Indiamen to stock up on manpower and supplies, and for crew to rest and recuperate, before continuing their arduous journey. The Cape of Good Hope, at the southern tip of Africa between the Atlantic and Indian Oceans, was seen as the perfect stopover. The Cape had been the gateway to the Indian Ocean trade ever since the Portuguese first made their way there in the late 15th century.

In 1652, the VOC established a permanent settlement in Table Bay, at the foothills of the spectacular Table Mountains. They called it Kaapstad ("Cape Town"), and it would be a stopover on the Amsterdam-Batavia route until the opening of the Suez Canal in 1869 rendered the Cape route obsolete. All ships travelling to the East necessarily stopped here.

The city was thus at the crossroads of East and West, its architecture and material culture blending elements from Europe, Africa and Asia.

The material culture of Cape Town's elite society had similarities with those of Batavia and other VOC settlements in Asia. The big patricians' houses boasted luxury goods from all over the East, brought here by the VOC. There were full dinner services made of expensive china, exquisite Japanese lacquer furnishings, brightly-coloured printed cotton textiles from India; elaborate tables and chairs, chests and cabinets made from ebony and other hardwoods and carved in Ceylon, Batavia or the Coromandel Coast; and of course, an abundance of spices from Southeast Asia to enhance the flavour of food and wine.

People too, were imported to the Cape. Aside from officials of the VOC, thousands of slaves from across the Indonesian Archipelago and the Indian Ocean were also shipped here. Many of these enslaved Asians were either Muslims, or converted to Islam when they arrived. Malay was then the lingua franca of trade in the Indian Ocean world, and as such, wherever these Asians may have hailed from, they all spoke a version of the language.

The Cape was also a penal colony. Many political prisoners – those who dared oppose VOC rule in their native lands – were exiled here. Amongst these were members of East Indies royalty, scions of the kings of Macassar, Tidore and more, who fervently resisted Dutch rule. They would become influential and revered *imams*, or spiritual leaders, for the burgeoning Muslim communities of the Cape, their tombs in the city becoming *keramat*, or sacred places for the faithful. Today, some twenty of these sacred places form a "circle of *keramat*" that surrounds the city and – so locals believe – protects it from harm.

These exiled, enslaved, but later, emancipated, Asians would form the seed of the Cape Malay community. Resembling their distant cousins, the Orang Betawi, the Cape Malays too have a hybrid culture blending elements of Dutch, Portuguese, Indian, Arab, African, Bugis, Bandanese, Ambonese, Sundanese and other Indian Ocean cultures. They are best known for their heady cuisine, which has strong Indian Ocean flavours, and features *roti, biryani*, spicy curries, *sambal* and *achar*. A highlight of the cuisine is the *bobotie*, a sort of shepherd's pie equivalent made with minced meat, fruit, chutney and curry, and finished with a thin layer of egg custard on top.

Cape Malay culture is centred on the Bo-Kaap district in Cape Town – once a racially segregated district for "coloured" peoples, today one of the most vibrant, historic and distinctive attractions in the city. The Bo-

Kaap is known for its pastel-coloured facades and its cobblestoned streets, and of course, for the preponderance of Cape Malay food to be found here. At the heart of the Bo-Kaap, not far from each other, stand the Auwal Masjid and the *keramat* of revered imam, Tuan Guru. These two historic sites serve as spiritual and religious centres for the community, and feature strongly in Cape Malay history. Abdullah ibn Qadi Abd al-Salaam, better known as Tuan Guru ("Esteemed Master"), was a member of the royal family of Tidore, in the Moluccas. Exiled to the Cape in 1780, he established the Auwal Masjid, Cape Town's first mosque, in 1794.

Like Batavia, Cape Town also housed a VOC castle-fortress, completed in 1679. Unlike Kasteel Batavia, the Kasteel de Goede Hoop ("Castle of Good Hope"), shaped as a five-pointed star, still stands today and is the best-preserved example of its kind anywhere in the world. Once, like Kasteel Batavia, it stood at the edge of the water, poised to welcome or repel vessels approaching Table Bay. Today, due to extensive land reclamation, it stands just over a kilometre from the seashore.

Entrance gateway to the Castle of Good Hope, Cape Town. Note the VOC monogram emblazoned on either side of the entrance, just below the pediment.

The Castle of Good Hope was the seat of power in VOC-era Cape Town. The governors of the Cape Colony resided here, as did the local courts and other arms of government. Throughout the settlement's history, the castle also served as a prison for political dissidents and prisoners of war. Up until 1993, non-whites were forbidden from entering the castle, on account of apartheid policies put in place by the South African government.

Today, the visitor approaches the castle by land, crossing a moat and entering by an imposing gate and bell tower, erected in 1684. We catch our very first glimpse of the VOC monogram on this gateway. The simple but distinctive corporate logo, featuring the letters "V", "O" and "C" intertwined, was ubiquitous in Dutch Asia, stamped on flags and documents, gateways and buildings everywhere the VOC established their trading settlements. It signified that the Dutch were here to stay, and they would do anything in their power, even resort to war and genocide, in order to secure a permanent place in the Indian Ocean world.

18. Ayutthaya & Hoi An
Canal Cities and Grand Emporiums of the Southeast

"The king has his court in the city of Odia which is girded with a brick wall and located inside two deep canals. This city is located some forty leagues from the sea on the bank of a tributary of the Ganges [sic]. The biggest ships come close to the outworks. Medium-sized vessels can enter the city which is traversed by canals in which swim innumerable and sometimes enormous crocodiles."

— Jacques de Coutre, 1640.
Memoirs of Jacques de Coutre.[14]

In 1431, the city of Angkor fell to Ayutthaya after a seven-month siege. With that, the great Khmer Empire came to an end, after over six centuries of hegemony. Ayutthaya stepped in to fill its shoes, though it would be a very different sort of empire from the Khmers, oriented seaward rather than landward, and dependent on trade rather than agriculture.

The Ayutthaya kingdom was named after its capital city, Ayutthaya (พระนครศรีอยุธยา). The name itself is a Thai variation on "Ayodhya", a sacred city in India, and fabled birthplace of Prince Rama in the great Hindu epic, *The Ramayana*. The city was dream-like: a floating realm of golden *wats* and bejewelled palaces on a large island in the middle of the Maenam ("River") Chao Phraya. Europeans referred to it as the "Venice of the East" because it was a canal city, criss-crossed by *klongs*. Many of these *klongs* were thronged with people, living and making a living. Ayutthaya was famed for its floating markets where everything on earth could be bought, sold and bargained for. One needed to navigate the *klongs* with care though. These waterways were famously teeming with enormous crocodiles, basking in the tropical sun, and grown fat on the wealth of the city's denizens.

Like Oc Eo, Ayutthaya was a riverine port city, located some 100 kilometres upriver, north of Bangkok. Its inland location ensured it had access to goods from the Thai and Cambodian interior, and that it was secure from invasion via the sea. The route to Ayutthaya was fiendishly fraught and difficult. The river itself was meandering and shallow, and filled with countless shoals, rapids and a notoriously dangerous sandbar guaranteed to deter the most intrepid adventurer.

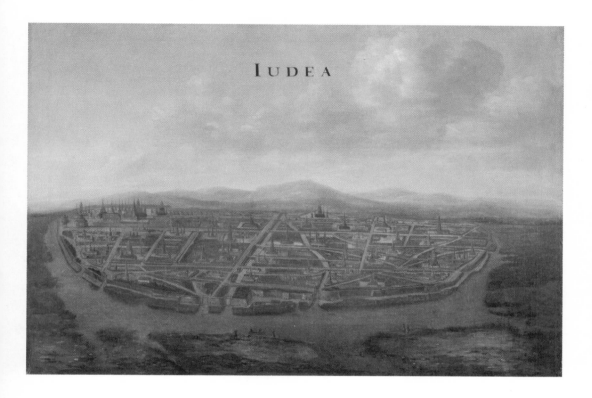

IUDEA

But the destination was well worth the danger. Visitors reported being awestruck when, at a bend in the river, the city appeared like a mirage, gleaming in the distance, as though conjured up by magic.

When Melaka fell to the Portuguese in 1511, Ayutthaya filled in the vacuum, emerging as *the* major Southeast Asian entrepôt for the China trade in the 16th and 17th centuries. Located far inland, it is often seen as a terrestrial rather than a maritime power. In fact, it played an important role in facilitating trade and free movement for Asian merchants, long after Europeans had muscled their way into the arena, attempting to cut these Asian merchants off. It also successfully managed to evade European conquest where other regional Southeast Asian kingdoms succumbed.

Three main groups of Asian traders resided in the city. The Chinese were the most important and numerous. Many were Hokkien merchants from Quanzhou, Xiamen (Amoy), and other port cities of South China's merchant coast; they'd been trading here since the late 14th century. The Ming dynasty's *haijin* had less of an impact in the Hokkien province, separated from the Chinese mainland by precipitous mountain ranges.

View of Judea [Ayutthaya], the Capital of Siam. Attributed to Johannes Vinckboons, c. 1662 – 1663. Oil on canvas, 97 x 140 cm. Collection of the Rijksmuseum.

Scores of these merchants traded with and settled down across Southeast Asia, including in Ayutthaya, where they had their own special Chinese quarter *inside* the walls of the city. When the Ming *haijin* was repealed in 1567, they breathed a sigh of relief.

The Japanese were the second most important group of merchants here. The lifting of the Ming *haijin* did not apply to trade between China and Japan, and Ayutthaya became one of the few places in the world in which Chinese and Japanese merchants could meet and trade freely. Despite an icy diplomatic relationship between the two Eastern powers, there was strong mutual demand for each other's goods: the Japanese desired raw Chinese silk, and the Chinese desired Japanese silver. Around the turn of the 17th century, the Tokugawa Shogunate started issuing red-sealed letters to Japanese merchants, permitting them to trade with Southeast Asia. So-called *shuinsen* (朱印船), or "red-seal ships", were commissioned by merchant families or private individuals in Japan. A community of Japanese merchants settled down in Ayutthaya in their own special quarters just outside the city walls.

They came alongside Persians from Safavid Iran, and Indo-Persians from the Deccan in India. Ayutthaya's name in Persian was Shahr-e-nav, or "City of Boats". In the late 17th century, during the reign of King Narai the Great, the shah in Iran famously dispatched an embassy to the floating city. The journey is recounted in the *Safineh-e-Solaymani* ("*The Ships of Suleiman*"), which provides a unique, Middle Eastern, eyewitness account of the city, including its floating markets and water-bound way of life.

The Persian community in Ayutthaya, though small, wielded significant political influence. Some of them became the closest advisors to the kings themselves, particularly in matters of trade and commerce, in which Persians were regarded as neutral parties to East Asian and European interests. Persian taste and aesthetics also influenced the city's architecture and courtly style.

The kings of Ayutthaya themselves partook openly and avidly in trade, commissioning and sailing ships from local docks to China, Southeast Asia and Japan. Trade was managed as a royal monopoly, and trading privileges dispensed to local – often Chinese – merchant families in return for a substantial portion of the proceeds. The kings profited immensely from this carefully dispensed privilege.

Ayutthayan kings were also known for being shrewd diplomats. Bloody courtly intrigues meant they couldn't trust their own kinsmen, least of all their royal siblings. They were forced to look outwards in their court administrations, employing foreigners on home ground: Persian or Chinese trade advisors, Japanese guards, Portuguese armies deployed to defend the border, French architects, even a Greek chief minister, famously in the employ of the charismatic King Narai. They sent tribute missions not only to China (repeatedly and more than anybody else at the time), but also westwards. The first Thai Embassy to Europe stopped at Holland in 1609, the intent being to offer Ayutthaya's services in facilitating VOC entry into the China market. In King Narai's time, embassies left for Iran, India, Rome, England and, most notably, France. There, in the endless salons of the palace of the Sun King in Versailles, the Thais, with their elaborate courtly dress and mannerisms, caused a *grand frisson* in fashionable royal circles.

Time and again, the European powers – especially France – would scheme to bring Ayutthaya squarely under their control. But the Ayutthayan kings never failed to outwit the Europeans by playing one European power against the other while absorbing and assimilating the best that each nation had to offer. This deftness and willingness to adapt and modernise would also characterise the foreign and domestic policies of the Chakri kings later on in Bangkok.

Ayutthaya would eventually be sacked and overcome by the Burmese in 1767, who attacked the city from the mainland rather than from the sea. The city's ruins still stand today as a park and UNESCO World Heritage site (inscribed in 1991). They can be taken in as a daytrip from Bangkok and are well worth the journey, if only to gaze in a mixture of awe and melancholy at the ruins of *wat* and *prang* (reliquary stupas), monastery and palace, once gilded with gold and now crumbling in their majesty.

East of Ayutthaya, the Vietnamese port city of Hoi An held court as another Southeast Asian entrepôt. Like its Thai counterpart, it was also a canal city, bisected by a man-made waterway that allowed vessels to sail right into the city's heart. It was as important as Ayutthaya for the same set of reasons: facilitating continued intra-Asian trade and evading European conquest, at least till the 19th century.

Hoi An is located on fertile alluvial plains near the mouth of the Thu Bon River in today's central Vietnam. The entire city was designated a UNESCO World Heritage site in 1999, for being one of the best-preserved examples of a Southeast Asian trading port from the 15th to the 19th centuries. The city is best taken in at sunset, on a boat floating gently down the river and main canal. On either side of the water stand dozens of old shophouses, functioning simultaneously as warehouses, residences and shopfronts; these elegant buildings turn a burnished gold in the light of the setting sun and contribute greatly to the city's historic charm.

Hoi An's links to China run deep. For almost a thousand years from the Han dynasty to the end of the Tang, north Vietnam had been governed as the southernmost province of China – known as An-nan, which means "peace in the south", but also implies "the south has been suppressed". Vietnamese culture thus draws significantly from the Confucian traditions of its northern neighbour, with the Vietnamese language written in a localised variation on Chinese script known as Chu Nom, and employing sounds and tones reminiscent of those in southern Chinese dialects like Hokkien and Cantonese.

Hoi An's full name is Hoi An Pho (会安府), often shortened to just Hoi Pho: this the Europeans, when they arrived later on, latinised as Faifo. A brief occupation of northern Vietnam by the Ming dynasty between 1407 and 1427 was followed by the Later Le dynasty, which nominally ruled a kingdom that was, in effect, split into two powerful regional factions. The Nguyen lords, situated in the Quang Nam province, grew strong, expanding their territory by seizing Hoi An and its environs from the Chams further south, and declaring their own breakaway state in Central Vietnam. Shrewdly recognising trade and commerce as a means of guaranteeing their survival, the Nguyen lords wrote letters to China and Japan in the late 16th century, inviting merchants to trade at Hoi An.

These overtures were successful. Like in Ayutthaya, scores of Chinese merchants settled in the city. In particular, when the Ming dynasty fell to the Manchus in 1644, thousands of Ming loyalists – generals, soldiers, and mandarins at court, mostly men – would flee south. Many took refuge with existing merchant communities here in Hoi An, intermarrying with local Vietnamese women, and maintaining Ming forms of dress as an assertion of their loyalties. Some of these Ming loyalists rose to take on important positions as ministers and advisors to the Nguyen lords, who shrewdly welcomed them with open arms.

Today, descendants of these ancient Chinese communities are referred to as the Minh Huong (明乡), meaning "those of Ming descent". They are distinguished from later communities of southern Chinese that arrived here from the 18th and 19th centuries on. Those are referred to, in the Hokkien dialect, as *sinkheh* (新客 – "new guests") in Chinese communities across Southeast Asia. The Minh Huong are "old guests" – a mixed-race, Chinese-Vietnamese community who have long since lost the ability to read and write Chinese or speak any of the southern Chinese dialects.

Hoi An is known today for its many *huiguan*, or Chinese clan associations, equivalent to clubs and chambers of commerce for the Chinese. Organised along linguistic lines, they started out as safe spaces for resident communities to gather, to do business and to practice their rituals and traditions. Clan associations were typically situated in communal halls and hosted temples dedicated to ancestral worship and the veneration of Daoist deities such as Mazu or Guangong, the god of war.

Located on the east side of the city's main canal, the clan associations' communal halls and temples are excellent examples of vernacular Chinese architecture. Colourful, exuberant and full of life, they are a highlight of any visit to the city. The usual suspects are here: the Cantonese, the Teochew, the Hainanese – the great southern Chinese diasporas that established themselves in Southeast Asia from the 19th century on. The oldest, largest and grandest of these halls and temples is that of the Hokkiens, and rightly so, since they were, and continue to be, the largest Chinese diaspora in Southeast Asia.

It is here, too, that the Minh Huong have their ancestral hall and temple where, amongst the statues and icons of major Taoist deities, one finds ancestral tablets dedicated to the "ten elders, six clans and three great families" – *ancien* Ming mandarins, loyalists and refugees who were the pioneers and first families of the local community. Unfortunately, many of the Minh Huong left the country in the aftermath of the Vietnam War; and the Minh Huong being officially categorised as "Vietnamese" rather than "Chinese" in the national census, many of the remaining community have lost touch with their roots. As such, the present Tuy Tien Duong Minh Huong serves perhaps only a hundred or so individuals who still identify themselves as "old guests", and who come in on the rare occasion of a festival celebrating the community's ancestors and patron deities.

Visitors to Hoi An in the 17th century remarked on it being a divided city, with merchant settlements on either side of the city's main canal. Italian Jesuit missionary, Christoforo Borri, in his 1631 *Report of the new mission of the P.P. of the Society of Jesus to the Kingdom of Cochinchina,* notes that:

> "[Faifo] is a pretty large [city] as one part belongs to the Chinese, another to the Japanese; they live separately, each having their own governor. The Chinese living according to the laws of China, the Japanese to those of Japan. This seems to be two different cities."[15]

Aside from the Chinese, the other important resident community was that of the Japanese. They had originally settled on the east bank of the canal, today's Tran Phu Street. This side of the canal is where the Chinese clan associations are located today. The first Chinese settlement had actually been to the *west* of the canal, along today's Nguyen Thi Minh Khai Street. When most of the Japanese community left in the 17th century, the Chinese moved in to fill the void.

For a time, Hoi An was the most important port in Asia for the China-Japan trade. Japanese records indicate that the majority of red-seal ships stopped in the Jiaozhi, or central Vietnamese region, which included the port of Hoi An. Trade between Hoi An and Japan continued post-*sakoku*, by way of Chinese-operated merchant junks from the city plying the route to Nagasaki. After the Portuguese, Spanish and Dutch arrived to trade, these Chinese-operated junks continued to ply the lucrative Japanese route, well into the 18th century; and, like their Thai counterparts, the Nguyen lords would manage to shrewdly guard their sovereignty in the face of foreign influence.

Hoi An's Japanese heritage remains by way of the city's most iconic landmark. Perched across the main canal, joining the city's erstwhile Nihon-machi ("Japan Street") to its Chinatown, is an ancient pedestrian-footbridge-with-integrated-temple known as either Chua Cau ("Temple Bridge") or Cau Nhat Ban ("Japanese Bridge"). The temple-bridge is believed to have been commissioned by the resident Japanese merchant community in the late 16th century and the entire structure completed in the mid-17th century, soon after Japan slipped into *sakoku*. It could thus be read as a symbol of hope for the local Japanese community, cast adrift and forced to abandon their old home for a new one.

Certainly, the bridge is luminous in its beauty. It stands at the entrance to the canal, where the latter joins the Thu Bon River, and cannot be missed by any visitor taking to the water. Stylistically, it blends Chinese, Japanese and Vietnamese elements in terms of motifs used, as well as in the adaptation and localisation of traditional bridge and

The Japanese Bridge in Hoi An stands, evocatively, over a canal that runs through the city. It is one of the rare historic sites in Southeast Asia built by an overseas Japanese community.

roof architecture. The roof structure of the entire bridge, for example, is adorned with a row of blue-and-white porcelain plates that allude to the city's trade with China and Japan.

The temple is dedicated to the deity Xuanwu ("Dark Warrior"), also known as Zhenwu ("True Warrior"), from whence its Vietnamese name, Tran Vu. He is one of the great celestial emperors of the Chinese Daoist pantheon, and a most powerful deity. Xuanwu is venerated across China, Japan, Korea, Vietnam and where there are significant East Asian diaspora communities in Southeast Asia – in Japan, he is known as Genbu. Being associated with the compass and the weather, he is venerated in relation to the sea and to travel.

In traditional East Asian fashion, the doorway to Xuanwu's shrine is flanked on both sides by a poetic couplet that serves as an invocation or blessing. In this case, it calls for smooth and successful passage across ten thousand *li* of sea and sky. Above the doorway is a plaque with three Chinese characters in elegant calligraphic script. This was a gift from Lord Nguyen Phuc Chu at the turn of the 18th century. The plaque spells out the temple-bridge's official name, Lai Vien Kieu – a poetic and evocative name, tinged with melancholy, and meaning "bridge of those who have come here from afar."

19. Nagasaki
Sakoku, Dejima and the Tokugawa Shogunate

"a spring breeze / to and fro they bustle / the sailboats"
— Hendrik Doeff, c. 1800s. *Haiku.* [16]

I n the galleries of the Kobe City Museum, there is a spectacular and arresting pair of six-fold *byobu* depicting an unusual scene: the arrival of the Portuguese in Japan. [17] The *byobu* is a masterpiece, and was evidently made for a great and wealthy patron. Its surface is meticulously gilded in gold leaf and shimmers under the light. The pomp and circumstance of the Portuguese arriving at port is vividly captured in painting, with the artist, Kano Naizen – a master of the genre – depicting the Portuguese as curious and exotic strangers. They are seen disembarking from their legendary black ships, dressed in outlandishly-comical costumes that would have put a smile upon the face of the *byobu*'s beholder. Accompanying the Portuguese are slaves from Africa and the larger Indian Ocean world; deckhands unload all sorts of precious cargo from the south – bales of cloth, spices from Southeast Asia, horses and other exotic animals from India and the Middle East.

The Japanese referred to the Portuguese as *namban* (南蛮), or "southern barbarians". These specific types of *byobu* are referred to as *namban byobu* and belong to a larger cross-cultural tradition of *namban* works of decorative art, wherein Japanese traditional craft and artistic techniques were used to depict Portuguese and other Western subjects. *Namban* was thus a kind of *reverse-Japonisme*, for lack of a better term: the opposite of the West's later obsession with Japan in the 19th century. First came Japan's own fascination with and objectification of the West.

To understand how Japan first came to encounter the West, one needs to tread the boards of the grand *kabuki* theatre that was trade and geopolitics in East Asia, to explore Japan's vicissitudes of fortune upon that gilded but uneven stage.

Maritime trade in East Asia was governed by very different principles from those in the Indian Ocean world. In the latter, trade was a laissez-faire, equal opportunity, free and easy affair. Merchants were civilians and free agents. They were welcome to stop and trade at any port around the ocean rim – no one port or kingdom was seen as ranking higher in a hierarchy than another. At least, this was the case before the Europeans arrived.

In East Asia, however, maritime trade was circumscribed by a formal, hierarchical, almost feudal structure heavily influenced by Confucianist thought. The Chinese conceived of this structure as a proverbial *tianxia*, or "all under heaven", believing that the entire known world fell within China's sphere of influence as the Middle Kingdom. Let's refer to this structure in more mundane terms, as the East Asian Order of Things.

At the very top of the order was China, in the role of the August and Benevolent Ruler (*jun*). One rung down were Korea and Japan, while a further rung down were Ryukyu and Vietnam. These were the sinicised kingdoms traditionally in China's cultural sphere of influence. They took on the roles of Most Loyal Officials (*chen*). Others outside of this sphere were *fan*, or barbarians, but also had their own rung on the pecking order, depending on how "favoured" they were as a nation.

In this unequal system, trade thus couldn't simply be trade but had to be dressed up as *chao gong*, or "imperial tribute". All foreign nations (天下诸番国 - *tianxia zhu fanguo*, or "all barbarian nations under heaven") needed permission from the emperor to trade in China. This was achieved by way of diplomatic tribute missions paid regularly to the imperial court. The most precious goods were offered to the emperor, and in return were bestowed far more precious and valuable treasures from the imperial vaults, as well as official recognition (or renewal of recognition) of the nation's rights to trade with China. In other words, the tributary nation was bestowed a rightful place in the Order of Things, but at a rung below that of the *chen*, naturally.

In 1591, after decades of civil war and disunity, Japan was united by the powerful *daimyo* ("feudal lord"), Toyotomi Hideyoshi. Emboldened by his success, Hideyoshi would directly challenge Ming China's position as *jun* in the East Asian Order by waging a campaign to conquer Korea. What ensued was only to be expected – the Ming Empire sent its far larger and more technologically-advanced armies in defence of Korea, subduing and vanquishing Hideyoshi's troops. As punishment for its brazenness, Japan was expelled from the East Asian Order of Things, summarily kicked off its pre-eminent first rung. For some 300 years, there would be no more direct trade between China and Japan.

Hideyoshi was succeeded by the charismatic Tokugawa Ieyasu, who established the powerful Tokugawa Bakufu ("Shogunate") in 1603. The

new shogun ("Generalissimo") wasted no time in attempting to mend ties with Korea and China, but to little avail. Despite contrite letters and diplomatic embassies to China in a desperate bid to pacify the emperor, the Son of Heaven stood firm: Japan was out.

Tokugawa and his scions thus had no choice but to establish their own, parallel, Japanese Order of Things, operating smoothly alongside that of the Chinese and without intervention from them. The Japanese *tianxia* (天下— read *tenka* in Japanese) had Japan at its apex; but the operating principle was modelled after that of the Ming. Trade was initially sanctioned as a royal privilege. The Tokugawa shogun issued red-seals to private merchants wishing to trade down south (China was off-limits). Their *shuinsen* would be fixtures in East and Southeast Asia, some 350 of them stopping off at port cities across the region within a 30-year period. They were only permitted to sail from a single port in Japan: Nagasaki (長崎), on the west of Kyushu Island. Nagasaki was also the port designated to receive trade missions from foreigners.

Arrival of the Southern Barbarians. Kano Naizen. Japan, Momoyama period, c. 1600s. Six-fold *namban byobu* (lacquer and gilded screen), 154.5 x 363.2 cm. Collection of the Kobe City Museum.

Unfortunately, by this time, the Portuguese had long made their grand entrance on stage, establishing a foothold first in Hirado in 1550 and subsequently, in Nagasaki in 1571. They would come to Japan by way of their legendary black ships – hence the popular depiction of Portuguese arrival at port. Much later when the *shuinsen* system came to be, they would arrive also, and frequently, by way of returning red-seal ships. Initially welcomed as one of many foreign nations wishing to trade with Japan, they would prove a threat to the shogun with their active attempts to convert the locals to Catholicism (called *Kirishitan* in Japanese). Having gotten wind of Portuguese conquests in Goa and Melaka, the Japanese were eager to avoid a similar fate. They knew that the only means of eradicating the Portuguese and Catholic threat once and for all was to shut down trade.

In 1635, the national system of red-seal ships was abolished by the third Tokugawa shogun – Ieyasu's grandson – only 30 years after it had been introduced. A *kaikin* (海禁 – after the Ming *haijin*) was put in place. All Japanese were forbidden, on pain of death, to leave the country. All Japanese living abroad were forbidden, on pain of death, to return. The practice and promulgation of *Kirishitan* was banned, on pain of death. Four years later, in 1639, a subsequent edict was issued for the expulsion of the Portuguese and the ban on any Portuguese ships coming to Japan, on pain of death. "Hereafter", so the edict for the *Expulsion of the Portuguese* went:

> "entry by the Portuguese *galeota* is forbidden. If they insist on coming [to Japan], the ships must be destroyed and anyone aboard those ships must be beheaded. [...] With regard to those who believe in Christianity, you are aware that there is a proscription, and thus knowing, you are not permitted to let padres and those who believe in their preaching come aboard your ship. If there is any violation, all of you who are aboard will be considered culpable. [...] This memorandum is to be given to those who come on Chinese ships. (A similar note to the Dutch ships.)" [18]

An embassy was hurriedly dispatched from Macau to Nagasaki to plead the Portuguese case — everyone on board was put to death when they arrived. Japan had entered the era of *sakoku*, or seclusion (鎖国 – literally "locked nation"), and it was dead serious about it.

Sakoku would last for more than 200 years from 1635 to 1853. The term itself was a latter-day invention used to describe this long period of Japan's seclusion. Japan wasn't entirely "locked up", by any means. Trade still flowed, albeit tightly controlled by the central government, and limited to four Japanese ports: Tsushima for trade with Korea, Satsuma for trade with Ryukyu, Matsumae for trade with the Ainu peoples in Hokkaido, and Nagasaki for trade with *karafune* and with the Dutch.

The term *karafune* (唐船 – "ships of the Tang") referred not only to Chinese junks from the mainland, which in the last, waning years of the Ming were few and far between due to the trade ban; but also to junks sailed by Overseas Chinese merchants. Thus, the ships that sailed here came too from Ayutthaya, Hoi An, Luzon and everywhere else the Chinese had a foothold.

Initially allowed to trade freely in Nagasaki, large numbers of *karafune* flocked to the city, and many Chinese chose to reside here. The fall of the Ming dynasty also precipitated an influx of Ming loyalists and refugees, particularly from the Hokkien province. Alarmed at this influx, the Nagasaki government decided to severely limit Chinese junks permitted to anchor, and to compel the resident Chinese to move to an artificial island reclaimed from Nagasaki Bay and completely segregated from the mainland. Called the Tojin Yashiki, or Chinese Settlement, the island was adjacent to what is today's bustling Shinchi, the oldest Chinatown in Japan.

Traces of Nagasaki's Chinese legacy continue to exist today in the vicinity of Shinchi, in the form of temples dedicated to Mazu, Confucius and the Deity of the Earth, as well as the presence of a historic Hokkien Clan Association. Nagasaki is also credited for the invention of a classic Sino-Japanese dish known as *chanpon*, which is a kind of pork and seafood noodle. The name of the dish likely comes from the Hokkien word *jiak peng*, literally meaning "to eat rice", but generally referring to "having one's meal". The most famous of these *chanpon* restaurants, Shikairo, which created the dish, still stands in its original location just off the Nagasaki waterfront, and continues to run a brisk business today.

In the early 17th century, the Dutch VOC made their way to Japan. When the edict came to expel all Portuguese, they managed to convince the shogun that they were not at all like the Portuguese. For starters, these Dutch Calvinist-Christians did not proselytise as zealously, if at all. And they demonstrated that they would be ever pliable and amenable subjects of the shogun. When they were told they could not ever, on pain of death, preach their faith, they complied. When they were told they had to move, almost overnight, from their initial settlement in Hirado to Nagasaki, they simply nodded and got a move on. It helped that they looked so different from the Portuguese. The Japanese were intrigued by their pale faces and flaming-red hair, and called them *komo-jin* (紅毛人 - "red-haired people") rather than *namban*.

In 1641, the Dutch VOC settlement relocated to an artificial, fan-shaped island just off the coast of Nagasaki. The Japanese had finished reclaiming the island from the sea only a few years before, and they had penned up all the remaining Portuguese in these tiny confines only to expel them a few years later. The island was known as Dejima, or "Exit Island", and for the next 200 years that Japan remained in *sakoku*, all VOC trade, warehouses and merchant residences were limited to this tiny island, the sole point of contact between Japan and the West.

From Dejima, Japanese luxury goods would be exported first to Batavia, and then onwards to Amsterdam to be delivered to eager European buyers. Through Dejima and the Dutch, Western technology, books, medicine, ways of thinking and modes of leisure were imported gradually across the decades to Japan. The Japanese referred to all Western learning as *rangaku*, or "Dutch learning" – an indication of just how significant a role the Dutch had played in the early modernisation of the island kingdom. Indeed, much later, when other foreigners came to Nagasaki, the lingua franca for trade and negotiations with the Japanese, the only European language the Japanese could speak, was Dutch.

Free movement in Dejima was heavily proscribed, with the Dutch, who were all men, forbidden to leave the island, and the Japanese, except for cooks, servants, interpreters and women of pleasure, banned from entering. Within the enclave, however, everyday life was materially rich, if a little monotonous. The ship from Batavia would arrive a few times each year with its new stock of wine and victuals. In the meantime, officials of the VOC would revel and wait, served by their Malay servants and slaves.

One of the best accounts of life in the island enclave was written by Hendrik Doeff, the *opperhoofd*, or "settlement chief" of Dejima from 1803 to 1817, who published his *Recollections of Japan* in 1833. A miniature portrait of him by the celebrated painter Kawahara Keiga portrays him as a stern and intense young man, bent on defending this distant outpost of the Dutch Empire. Doeff was also a poet, and amongst dozens of lines of poetry written in Dutch, he wrote two haikus in Japanese, one of which is quoted at the beginning of this chapter.

The VOC trading post on Dejima was abolished in 1858 when the Americans forced Japan out of *sakoku* and Nagasaki was thrown open to all foreign merchants as a treaty port. As trading activities shifted onshore, Dejima became obsolete; it was abandoned and subsequent land reclamations resulted in the island eventually being absorbed into the Nagasaki mainland. In recent years, however, interest has revived, and the Nagasaki authorities have reconstructed Dejima as it would originally have looked in the early 1800s. While rebuilt based on maps of the former settlement and historical records related to everyday life in the enclave, the new Dejima feels somewhat less than authentic and has the air of a theme park.

The most tangible legacy of the VOC period in Nagasaki comprises the thousands of luxury objects shipped out of Dejima, and that still remain today, in private and museum collections around the world. The most voluminous type of trade was in Japanese porcelain, in particular, *kraakporselein*, or simply *kraak*. This was a form of blue-on-white porcelain first commissioned by the Portuguese in Ming China.

When the Ming dynasty fell, the supply of *kraak* porcelain from China plummeted, and the VOC turned to Japanese potters to fill the gap. Initially churning out only excellent copies of Ming-era *kraak*, the Japanese potters eventually evolved their own exquisite and distinctive style.

The distinguishing characteristic of a *kraak* plate is a border of foliated, radial decorative panels that surround a central motif. This central motif could be an animal, a landscape, a figure from Chinese literary tradition, or a European-style coat of arms. Each of the radial decorative panels is also decorated, with varying motifs such as flowers and fruit, Buddhist symbols, or human figures. *Kraak* was a florid and exuberant style highly in vogue in Europe and the Middle East, but not at all in China or Japan, where domestic taste tended towards the austere. It would go on to inspire local imitations in Europe and the Middle East that eventually became ceramic traditions in their own right.

One of the most intriguing examples of *kraakporselein* can be found in the collection of the Asian Civilisations Museum. It is of a type that was frequently commissioned by *opperhoofds* and high-ranking officials of the VOC for their own personal use. The typical attributes of *kraak* are all there: radial decorative florets surrounding the border of the dish. But instead of a figurative element or landscape at the centre of the plate, one spies the monogram of the Vereenigde Oost-Indische Compagnie – the letters, "V", "O" and "C" intertwined and emblazoned in cobalt blue on the pure white surface of the porcelain, which upon closer examination, reveals underlying texture and shades of grey.

VOC Kraakware Dish. Arita, Japan, late 17th century. Porcelain with overglaze, 3.5 x 22 x 22 cm. The name "kraak" is believed to be an approximation of the Portuguese word (*carraca*) for the trading vessels these porcelain objects would have been shipped in. Collection of the Asian Civilisations Museum.

20. Mocha & Surat
The Coffee Capital and the Auspicious Port

"Be aware that of the coffee of Yemen, in summary, is among that which is legally permissible, and that its drinking is absolutely allowed. Whosoever makes the legally permissible thing legally prohibited deserves ignominy and exemplary punishment, and the claim of making something legally prohibited results from mere stubbornness and error which is caused by the illusion of the mind. This is particularly true since the Islamic community is unanimous on the legality of drinking it, as the hadith says: "Clearly my community does not agree on an error."

— Murtaḍa Al-Zabidi, 1758. *A masterpiece for the fellows of the age in explaining the legality of the coffee of Yemen.*[19]

Caffe mocha, or mocha, for short, is a *caffe latte* with chocolate in it. It is easy to make: a combination of *caffe espresso*, full cream churned till frothy, chocolate syrup, and generous sprinklings of cacao or chocolate powder. Even as they partake of the heady brew, most contemporary coffee aficionados don't realise that the word "mocha" is derived from an actual place: the Yemeni port city of Mocha (المخا – al-Mukha) which, for some 200 years from the late 16th to the late 18th centuries, was the coffee trading capital of the world.

Coffea arabica is believed to have first been cultivated in Ethiopia, before spreading across the Red Sea to the Yemen. It is a low-growing, flowering tree. The fruit of the coffee tree turn deep red when they are ripe, and are thus known as cherries. When the cherries ripen, they are harvested for their seeds, which are dried and roasted such that they become the dark-brown coffee beans we are familiar with. By the early 15th century, Sufis in the Yemen had discovered the stimulating effects of coffee, particularly when the bean is boiled in water. Drinking the resulting brew had the effect of transporting the drinker to another plane of consciousness, elevating the senses and banishing sleep, allowing the Sufis to practice their ritual devotions well into the night. Coffee was an intoxicant; consuming it was seen as little different from consuming wine.

By the early 16th century, coffee had spread very quickly across the Islamic world, and become a staple of social life in its cities. Coffee-houses, or *qahwa-khanah* (*kahvehaneler* in Turkish), popped up across the fashionable metropolises of the time: Cairo, Damascus, Istanbul,

Baghdad, Isfahan and Delhi. The spread of coffee as a beverage was greatly aided by the growth of the Ottoman Empire, which encompassed a vast area bordering the Mediterranean Sea, the Black Sea, the Red Sea and the Persian Gulf. Intermittent *fatwas* on drinking coffee, on the part of concerned orthodox Muslims in the course of the 16th century, did little to stop its spread.[20] The cultivation of coffee as a crop proved to be so profitable that the bean was imported from Ethiopia and cultivated on a grand scale in the highlands of the Yemen, which would become the world's leading cultivator and exporter of coffee beans.

Middle Eastern methods of drinking coffee differ significantly from that in the West. In the Arab world, coffee beans are generally roasted before being ground and boiled, and the ensuing brew is spiced with cardamom to enhance the flavour. There is a dizzying number of regional variations, such that the coffee one gets occurs in a range of shades from golden-brown to almost jet-black. Coffee is often served without sugar and so the bitterness of the beverage is balanced by it almost always being accompanied by dates and other kinds of dried fruit and nuts. Turkish coffee, or *kahve*, is prepared very finely ground and boiled with water in a pot made specially for that purpose. Sugar is added to varying degrees and the coffee is drunk as a thick shot, akin to an espresso. Both Arabic and Turkish coffee are unfiltered: the grains remain as residue in the drinking cup.

For more than a thousand years, Indian and Southeast Asian spices and aromatics had been brought westwards to Europe by way of a laborious though predictable route. Ships would first take the valuable cargo up the Red Sea or the Persian Gulf to Egypt or Iraq respectively. This cargo would then be transferred to caravans and taken overland to Constantinople in the Byzantine Empire. From there, more ships would take the cargo onwards across the Mediterranean to Venice, where it was sold to European traders.

The early decades of the Ottoman Empire in Constantinople saw the sultans and their sophisticated, cosmopolitan subjects facing a shortage of spices and other Asian luxury goods as the Portuguese directed these away from Islamic lands to the faraway Cape of Good Hope. It was difficult for the Sublime Porte to re-establish the older Red Sea routes from its Mediterranean location. Diplomatic ententes with the Portuguese were always rejected, and forays into the Indian Ocean met with aggressive, armed Portuguese resistance. The only way for the sultans to regain access to this trade was to control the Red Sea and strengthen the empire's maritime and military presence in the Indian Ocean rim.

By the mid-16th century, the Ottomans – under the reigns of Selim I and the great Suleiman the Magnificent – had defeated the Mamluks in Egypt, taken Baghdad and Basra from the Safavids, and occupied almost all of coastal Arabia, including the holy city of Mecca and much of lowland Yemen. The Red Sea was now, finally, an "Ottoman Lake". When the Ottomans took the Yemen in 1538, they chose to establish their regional trade centre and naval headquarters, not at Aden, but at an unremarkable fishing village located further north, well past the notorious Bab El-Mandeb. This was Mocha.

Trade through the Red Sea once again opened up, and even though private merchant ships were heavily taxed, Muslim traders from across the region and from India returned. The Ottomans themselves got actively involved in trade, establishing a fleet of state galleys that sailed regularly between Suez and Mocha – these were the only ships in the Red Sea exempt from taxes and duties.

Mocha rose swiftly to become the main entrepôt of the western Indian Ocean. Alongside spices, Yemeni coffee became one of the most important goods traded, with Mocha being the sole source of coffee beans for the international market. The actual trade in coffee beans took place at Beit al-Faqih, a caravan town to the north of Mocha, at the foothills of the Yemeni Highlands. Coffee growers would bring their produce here from the highlands, in great sacks and on camel caravans. Here too, would come Arab and Turkish merchants from the Hejaz, Egypt, Syria, the Maghreb and Anatolia; Persian merchants from Iran; Gujarati *baniyas* and *bohras* from Surat in India, and by the early 17th century, Dutch, English and other European traders, newly addicted to the bean.

In 1635, not long after the VOC and its contemporary, the English East India Company (EIC), established their respective factories in Mocha, the Ottomans lost the Yemen to the local Qasimi Imams. Northbound trade in coffee to the Mediterranean was diverted to the northern Yemeni ports of al-Hudaydah and al-Luhayyah, while trade at Mocha became increasingly dominated by Indian and European merchants active in the Indian Ocean. By association, Yemeni coffee thus came to be known by European traders as "coffee mocha", in reference to the port from which it was traded rather than to its source. (This was probably just as well, since the Europeans, unable to pronounce Beit al-Faqih, referred to it as "Beetlefuckee".) Yemeni coffee was known for its distinctive chocolatey

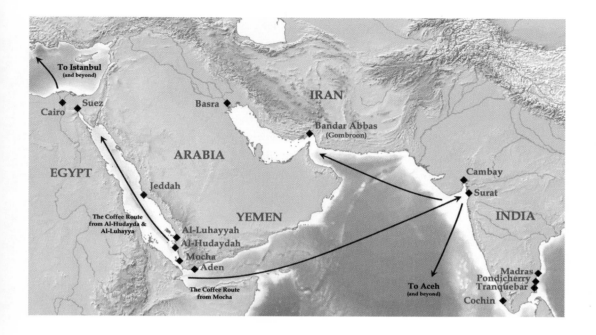

flavour; and so, much later on, the name "mocha" would be applied to a specific type of *caffe latte* with chocolate added.

Mocha and the Yemen enjoyed a monopoly on the coffee trade well into the late 18th century, when the Europeans succeeded in cultivating coffee as a cash crop in their tropical colonies. In the face of stiff competition from these other new and cheaper varietals, the Yemen lost its pre-eminent position in the international market. As swiftly as it rose, Mocha declined. By the early 1800s, visitors to the city remarked on how its lovely skyline of minarets and merchant houses had become just a façade, and how the city itself had fallen into filth and poverty. Much of Mocha's built heritage – its mosques, its merchant houses – was destroyed by war in the 20th century, and almost nothing remains. Today, city is once again village, forgotten by all even as its namesake beverage, the *caffe mocha*, has become one of the most ubiquitous drinks in the world.

At the turn of the 16th century, the Western Indian Ocean region was ruled by three major Muslim empires: the Ottomans in Arabia, the Safavids in Iran and the Mughals in India. To the East, in Southeast Asia, was Muslim Aceh. All four were also trading nations. Even as these empires contended with the Portuguese Estado da Índia, maritime trade between them remained strong, with the Gujarat province in India

Trade routes across the Red Sea, Persian Gulf and Indian Ocean, 16th century.

retaining its position as a major entrepôt for spices and textiles bound for the Middle East. The Portuguese never managed to achieve the monopoly they wanted on the spice trade. The Ottomans, Mughals and Acehnese guarded their routes fervently and ensured that Asian trade continued to thrive, mostly unharried.

Surat (સુરત), on the banks of the Tapi River, rose in importance in the early decades of the 16th century, when it was ruled by the Sultanate of Gujarat. A pivotal turning point for the city was the decision made around 1539 by Sultan Mahmud Shah III to build an extensive and imposing fortress along the coast of the city, in order to defend Asian merchant ships arriving in the city against Portuguese attack. A 16th century, of-the-era account by the Mulla Abdul Badayuni recounts the conditions surrounding the building of the castle, which still stands today. His account demonstrates that the Gujaratis were no pushovers, but like the Ottomans, resisted the Portuguese incursion with military innovations borrowed from the Portuguese themselves.

> "They say the reason for Khudawand Khan's building this fort was, that the Portuguese used to exercise all kinds of animosity and hostility against the people of Islam, and used to occupy themselves in devastating the country, and tormenting the pious. [...] On the bastions which overlooked the sea they made a gallery, which in the opinion of the Europeans is a specialty of Portugal and an invention of their own. The Europeans were very much opposed to the building of that Chaukandi, and endeavoured to prevent it by force of arms. But at last they resorted to peaceful measures, and agreed to pay a round sum of money, if they would leave off building that Chaukandi. But Khudawand Khan, through his love and zeal for Islam gave the reins to his high spirit, and would not consent, and in spite of the Christians soon carried out his purpose of completing that building."[21]

At the time of the Mughal emperor Akbar's triumphant entry into Surat in 1573, Surat was already a port to be reckoned with. Recognising its significance, the Mughal court itself appointed the city's *quilledar* ("commander of the fort"), who functioned as the city's military governor; and its *mutasaddi* ("revenues collector"), who functioned as the city's civic governor and had charge of customs revenues. With its special administrative status, military protection from the Mughal state, and access to craftsmen and raw materials across the entire Hindustani hinterland, Surat rose to become not only the Mughal Empire's most important port, but also one of the most important port cities in the world. It helped that Surat was also the preferred port of departure for millions of Muslim Indians departing on the Hajj. In honour of

The Castle, Surat. Unknown photographer, 1886 – 1889. Albumen silver print, 19 × 24.4 cm. Collection of the J. Paul Getty Museum, Los Angeles.

its achievements, the Mughals bestowed upon it the name, Bandar-e-Mubarak, or "Auspicious Port" in Persian.

Certainly, the city, like all other port cities, was home to a vibrant and multicultural community of merchants. Hindu and Jain *baniyas* were the most numerous, followed by Muslim Gujarati traders like the *bohras* earlier encountered in Cambay. There were quarters for Turks, Persians, Egyptians, Jews, Armenians and Parsis, and at any point in time, there were also resident merchants from the Nusantara, Madagascar, the Swahili Coast and China.

Aside from merchants, a large segment of society consisted of craftsmen and artisans of all kinds, supporting local and foreign taste and demand. There were also skilled and experienced *nakhodas*, or ship captains, able to pilot the many ships that sailed from the docks. And finally, there were the Mughal nobles, who reaped the profits of trade and tax revenues in the city, and led opulent and indolent lives.

Interestingly, it was the Mughal emperors themselves who first invited the *firangis* (فرنگی), or Europeans, to trade, by way of trade concessions and relief from duties levied. The Europeans in turn saw Surat as a neutral place – setting up shop here became a means of giving the Portuguese a run for their money. In 1608, the EIC arrived in Surat, establishing its first Indian factory here soon after. Before long came the Dutch and the

French, and much later in the 18th century, the Danes, the Swedes and the Prussians. Surat would become a "United Nations" of sorts, at least until the EIC seized full control of the city in 1759.

All kinds of goods were exported and re-exported through Surat. There were Southeast Asian spices, naturally, and the legendary printed cotton textiles from Gujarat. There was also ivory: vast amounts of elephant ivory from Africa and Southeast Asia, re-exported to Europe and the Middle East, but also consumed domestically as a luxury item. There was gold and silver bullion imported from the Red Sea, the Persian Gulf, and from as far away as New Spain in the Americas – some of this was used to mint coins for the Mughal Empire. And of course, there were enormous quantities of coffee – Surat controlled its re-export to elsewhere in the world.

The city itself became phenomenally wealthy and was known for its many beautiful merchants' houses with splendid gardens, as well as for its civic buildings and monuments. Many of these mansions and gardens have long since been lost, but much of the city's vernacular trade and residential architecture, including its erstwhile European factories, continues to stand today, in the shadow of its impressive castle. The city's historic district of Nanavat is well worth a wander, particularly as so many of its historical buildings still stand, and since Surat itself is far off the mainstream tourist's beaten path.

Surat would inevitably decline by the middle of the 18th century, along with the decline of the Mughal Empire. It would be eclipsed by yet another rival entrepôt further south on India's Malabar Coast: the English-controlled port city of Bombay.

21. Chennai, Puducherry & Tharangambadi (Madras, Pondicherry & Tranquebar)
The English and Other East India Companies on the Coromandel Coast

> "Dupleix Square retains traces of a garden in the French style, though a dust-strewn thicket of coarse weeds has effaced the noble parterres of yesteryear; the statue of the Conqueror of India stands over nothing more than a vast, sun-scorched esplanade. White Town extends parallel to the sea, with its elegant residences boasting roofs constructed at equal height, with its lovely [grid- and sight-] lines of a grandiose regularity; a city built in the drunken throes of Victory, in honour of Louis [XV,] the Well-Beloved, but whose splendour is now no more than a ghost [of itself]."
>
> — Georges Delamare, 1938. *Trouble in Pondicherry.*[22]

Some 30 kilometres north of Nagapattinam, perched on the edge of a rocky beach and looming portentously over turbulent waters, stands a mediaeval Danish fortress, right out of the pages of *Hamlet*. Channelling Elsinore at Coromandel, Fort Dansborg was indeed built by the Danes and ranks as the second largest Danish fort in the world, after Kronborg Castle in Helsingør. Built some half a century after its European cousin, the similarities between the two are apparent. Dansborg was built in the Renaissance style quite in fashion in the 17th century, hence its pronounced castle-like air, inspired by French *chateaux* in the Loire valley. The grounds of the fort are square-ish in shape and enveloped by thick, enormous walls calculated to repel attack from the sea.

Like the Batavia and Cape Town castles, Fort Dansborg formerly held the offices of the governor and administrative arms of the local Danish government. Today the structure houses the Tranquebar Maritime Museum. Once, the castle would have been surrounded by an entire city bustling with mercantile activity. It now stands alone and incongruous in a large empty field, hosting the occasional group of tourists and young boys playing a makeshift game of soccer. The little hamlet in which Dansborg stands is known as Tharangambadi (தரங்கம்பாடி), its lilting Tamil name meaning "the place where the waves sing". But this sleepy little place has another name: Tranquebar, capital of Danish India for over 200 years between 1620 and 1845.

Fort Dansborg, Tranquebar. Made of sand-hued stone, its forbidding watchtower looks out to sea like an eternal sentinel.

At the turn of the 17th century, the great European East India Companies competed for dominion over this expanse of tropical Indian coastline that once, long ago, formed part of the *Chola-mandala*, or sphere of influence of the Chola kings. The Europeans mispronounced this as "Coromandel" and the name stuck. Since ancient times, the Coromandel had been distinguished by its many glittering port cities, serving great Indian empires and doing a brisk business as entrepôts between east and west. The Europeans would systematically take these cities out with a toxic cocktail of conquest and competition, such that the old Indian ports were invariably replaced by new European ones, and *Chola-mandala* would eventually cease to exist.

The Portuguese were the first to arrive. By the 1530s, the Estado da Índia had successfully established a handful of factories here. The most important was at Nagapattinam, taken in the 1550s. Another was at São Tomé de Meliapore (Mylapore), better known today as the suburb of Santhome in the city of Chennai. Here, Portuguese missionaries had come in search of the sacred remains of Saint Thomas the Apostle. Notwithstanding the local community of Saint Thomas Christians, the Portuguese would erect a church over the saint's tomb, claiming it for Roman Catholicism. The church would be accompanied by a Portuguese settlement, which they named after the saint.

The Dutch VOC arrived in the early 1600s. First settling in Pulicat (today's Pazhaverkadu), they shifted their principal factory and administrative capital south to Nagapattinam, after successfully wresting it from the Portuguese in 1690. The VOC's single-most important trade from their Coromandel outposts was in chintz, or Indian printed cottons. By the 16th century, Mughal influence had precipitated new, exuberant styles of cotton textile produced here in the Coromandel Coast. These were highly floral in nature, embellished with all manner of blooms real and imaginary. Some of the most sought-after of these textiles sported elaborate, flowering "trees of life", and were referred to as *palampores* and used as decorative hangings in Europe and Southeast Asia.

Initially, the VOC exported these textiles solely to Southeast Asia, trading them in Sumatra, Sulawesi and the Moluccas in return for spices. European taste for chintz would catch up in the late 17th century, when the Dutch (and English) began shipping these textiles regularly to Europe. These would greatly influence European style in domestic interiors, with Indian chintz being imitated by European textile manufacturers, and the floral, chintz style being popular even today.

The Danes arrived soon after the Dutch, in 1619. The Danish East India Company, or Ostindisk Kompagni was formed by Royal Charter and operated as a monopoly akin to that of the Estado da Índia. For as long as the Danes were here, the success of their trade depended on war in Europe. Twice in its 200-year history, Tranquebar would experience a "golden age", first during the 17th century Nine Years' War between England, Spain, France and the Netherlands, amongst others; and once again in the late 18th century. Both times, Denmark took advantage of its neutrality to run a brisk and almost virtual monopoly on the Indian Ocean trade, fulfilling European demand on behalf of the maritime powers, whose resources were diverted or drawn down by war.

In the course of its second golden age, Tranquebar grew to be a formidable port indeed, and the Danes expanded their presence on the Subcontinent, annexing the Nicobar Islands and establishing a factory at Serampore in Bengal. This period of a veritable Danish India lasted more than a hundred years till 1845, when the Danish king sold Tranquebar and all remaining Danish possessions to the English Crown. The Dutch had already done as much two decades earlier. The Danes and the Dutch would vanish altogether from the Indian subcontinent, their ghostly legacy remaining in the form of forts, churches and cemeteries that continue to stand today, in various states of preservation or decay.

The Chepauk Palace was designed and built by British engineers around 1768. In 1855, the last Nawab died without an heir and the British promptly absorbed the Carnatic into the Raj. The Nawab's palace was then repurposed for civic, educational and government use.

The English East India Company bursts onto the scene in 1601. Also called the Honourable East India Company, and known colloquially as "John Company", the EIC was established by way of a royal charter granted by Queen Elizabeth I. It had been the culmination of sustained petitioning by a small group of private merchants, alarmed at the inroads both the Spanish and the Portuguese had made into Asia. Initially structured as a small-scale enterprise, limited to a tiny group of private merchants with the backing of the English Crown, the EIC would be restructured as a joint stock company in 1657, like the VOC; though it continued to enjoy a significant investment from the State.

The EIC's first factory on the Coromandel Coast was at Madraspattinam (i.e. "port of Madras"). The location of this settlement, near the mouth of the Cooum River, some 45 kilometres south of Dutch-controlled Pulicat, was not an obvious one since there was no deep harbour suitable for a port, merely a sandy expanse of beach. The area at the time fell within the larger *mandala* of the Vijayanagar Empire, then in its twilight years. In 1639, the EIC received permission from the emperor and the local ruling Nayak to build a fort here. 50 years after, they exacted a Royal Charter from the English king to establish a town corporation:

> "We, The said Governor and Company, having found by Experience and the Practice of other European Nations in India that the making and establishing of Corporations in Cities and Towns that are grown exceeding populous tends more to the well-governing of such populous places and to the Increase of Trade, than the constant Use of the Law Martial in trivial concerns, We have therefore for the speedier Determination of small contraversies of Little Moment, frequently happening among unarmed Inhabitants, thought it convenient to make, ordain, and constitute Our Town of Fort St George commonly called the Christian Town and City of Madrassapatam upon the coast of Coromandel in East Indies, and all the territorys thereto belonging, not exceeding the Distance of Ten Miles from Fort St George to be a corporation under Us by the Name and Title of the Mayor, Aldermen, and Burgesses of the town of Fort St George and citty of Madrassapatam... [30 December 1687]"[23]

Madras would morph and grow into the most important port on the Coromandel Coast, and one of the three biggest presidencies in British India, together with Calcutta and Bombay. Renamed Chennai

(சென்னை) in 1992, it remains one of the largest and most important cities in India and is the capital of Tamil Nadu state.

Madras' urban form would provide the template for other cities in Company-ruled India. At the heart of the city stood its fort, the oldest part of the city and the centre of government. In the fort's immediate vicinity would be its "White Town": the English and European quarters of the city. Adjacent to it, typically occupying land of less favourable topography, ventilation and value, would be so-called "Black Town": the residential, religious and commercial centre of the local Indian community. Within or on the periphery of Black Town would subsist "grey areas" where other alien trading communities resided – Arabs, Chinese, Parsis, Armenians, and Portuguese Eurasians. This segregated urban plan had roots in Portuguese and Dutch Indian antecedents, but the British, obsessed by class and difference, frowned deeply on miscegenation, and went further in the way of segregation along racial and religious lines.

Madras is also where one finds the earliest examples of the Indo-Saracenic style, a distinctive, syncretic style of architecture that emerged in the late 19th century. Flush with the trappings of empire, architects of the British Raj took elements of Mughal, Gujarati, Byzantine and neoclassical styles and combined them to form an entirely new, absolutely imperial vernacular utilised to grand effect in its colonial metropolises.

In fact, the Indo-Saracenic style actually originates here, along the city's seafront thoroughfare, South Beach Road. Here stands the Chepauk Palace complex, once the residence of the Nawabs of the Carnatic. In the late 18th century, these local kings were forced by the British to move from their ancestral seat of Arcot to Madras, where the reigning Nawab commissioned a British architect to construct a brand new palace. The palace, with its fusing of Deccani and neoclassical elements, would serve as a prototype for the Indo-Saracenic style, setting a trend that would accelerate in later years.

Not far from the Chepauk Palace is the Senate House building, one of the finest examples of the Indo-Saracenic style anywhere in the city. Constructed in reddish-orange brick, with four minaret-like towers blending Byzantine and Mughal elements, the Senate House channels a latter-day Mughal Red Fort in Delhi. This resemblance was no coincidence, but deeply calculated: a case of architecture as propaganda. The monumentality of the Indo-Saracenic style symbolically trumpeted the arrival of a grand and nouveau regime: the British were the legitimate successors to the Mughals; they had the mandate and the power to rule all of Hindustan.

And rule it they did. From Madras, the British would expand their empire in the course of the 17th to 19th centuries, displacing all other Europeans, save the Portuguese and the French in their tiny enclaves, and extending the shadow of imperialism over the entire Subcontinent. India became synonymous with the British Raj, also known as the British Indian Empire.

France arrived late to the Company game. The Compagnie française des Indes orientales was formed in 1664 by way of a royal charter granted by Louis XIV, the Sun King. After multiple attempts to secure a foothold in India, and in the face of stiff competition from Portuguese, Dutch and English incumbents, the Compagnie secured rights to establish a factory at Pondicherry in 1674. Located almost halfway between British Madras and Danish Tranquebar, Pondicherry's existence was precarious from the very beginning, and the French had to fend off attacks by the Dutch and the English for much of the 17th and 18th centuries.

The result of frequent wars between the British and the French was that by the late 19th century, the settlement of Pondicherry would consist of a cluster of some dozen enclaves entirely surrounded by British Madras; a messy hodgepodge of small villages and towns totally disconnected from each other. Today, the heart of Pondicherry is the old town that sits on the waterfront. A walled settlement used to stand here; but now only a tiny fragment of the wall continues to exist.

Pondicherry is laid out on a strict, cartesian grid system, the application of which betrayed the grandiose, self-congratulating, civilising mission (*mission civilisatrice*) of the French. Like Madras, the city was divided into "White Town" and "Black Town", or *Ville blanche et Ville noire*, in French. The latter was separated from the former by a grand canal that still runs through the city today. In size, it dwarfs the former, being a good three to four times larger; and in typical colonial fashion, it is further segregated into Hindu, Christian and Muslim Quarters, all of which have their own unique architecture and spectacularly beautiful places of worship.

Ville Blanche itself is small, extending only four blocks deep from the waterfront. Most of the buildings here date from the mid-1800s, after the British razed the city in one of many tit-for-tat skirmishes for domination. The heart of Ville Blanche is Avenue Goubert, the city's lovely though sleepy waterfront. The statue of the man most associated with the city, the Marquis Joseph Dupleix, governor-general of French India from 1742 to 1754, still stands in its own *petit jardin* on the sun-scorched esplanade. He is dressed fashionably in the style of his time, with long wig and tailcoat. Installed in 1870, he watches vigilantly over his

The Hôtel Lagrenée de Mézières in Pondicherry, with its neoclassical columns supporting a large balcony, and high doors and ceilings for better ventilation in the tropical heat.

erstwhile dominion, much of it diminished and crumbling by the early 20th century, a ghost of its former self. Thanks to the combined efforts of local authorities as well as the French government, much of the city has now been extensively restored. Behind the Marquis is a rocky waterfront. In the evenings, the locals emerge to take in the sunset and the sea breeze, and to bathe in the tepid seawater.

On the whole, the city lacks the kind of monumental imperial architecture that Madras boasts. Instead, it has a quiet, provincial feel which is not unpleasant for the visitor. The streets here maintain their French names, spelt out on blue and white signs of the sort also found in Paris. They are lined with verdant trees, low-rise colonial edifices and dozens of old French-style villas that are a delight to explore. There are the typical trappings of a French colony: a metropolitan cathedral; civic, commercial and cultural institutions like a French-style public park, a local branch of the Banque de l'Indochine, a *bibliothèque publique*, a *lycée français*; and a *cercle sportif* – the equivalent of the gentleman's club in the Francophone world.

Perhaps the most intriguing of the city's landmarks is the Hôtel Lagrenée de Mézières: built in 1774, its swashbuckling name sounds like something from the pages of an Alexandre Dumas novel. The former residence of a French East India Company official, this building is one of the earliest that features *créole* architecture, blending neoclassical and Tamil elements, and designed with large balconies and other features that accommodate the humid, tropical weather. Today it houses the Cluny Embroidery Centre run by the Sisters of Saint Joseph, a local convent and charitable organisation that offers shelter and rehabilitation for orphaned girls, and impoverished and vulnerable women. Remarkably, the centre has been in operation for almost 200 years, since it was first founded in 1829. Stepping into the compound is thus like stepping back in time, and affords much-welcome respite from the heat.

After India gained its independence from the British in 1947, Pondicherry and other territories of French India – the coastal enclaves of Karaikal and Yanam on the Coromandel Coast and Mahé on the Malabar Coast – remained French till 1962, when the French Parliament agreed to cede these territories to India to form the Union Territory of Puducherry (புதுச்சேரி).[24] The transition was peaceful; unlike the British and the Portuguese, the French had been more than willing to repatriate its territories. As a reward, they were allowed to stay; and even today, one sees a strong presence of French schools and non-government organisations, such as the École française d'Extrême-Orient and the Institut français. Meanwhile, the city still oozes a Gallic atmosphere, and the food here is perhaps the best one can get along the Coast, a heady mix of classic French and *créole* Tamil cuisine. Certainly, this is the only place in India where a hearty *steak-frites* in the French style can be found everywhere you look.

There is a short but all-important coda to this tale of forts and factories. From these colonial port cities of the Coromandel Coast and nearby Ceylon, millions of ordinary Tamils from all walks of life – merchants, moneylenders, administrators, bookkeepers, teachers, labourers and prisoners – would travel to Southeast Asia from the 19th century onwards, in yet another major wave of migration from the Subcontinent.

The Tamils constitute a major diaspora community in Malaysia and Singapore, where Tamil is recognised as a national language, and to a lesser extent in the port cities of Thailand, Myanmar, Vietnam and Indonesia. Their presence is particularly strong in major cities in Peninsular Malaysia such as Penang, Melaka, Kuala Lumpur and Ipoh, and also in Singapore, where one finds many beautiful Hindu temples with Dravidian-style architectural elements; in particular, elaborate *gopurams*, or tower-gateways festooned with sculptures of deities and sacred animals. Perhaps the most spectacular temple of all is the Batu Caves complex on the outskirts of Kuala Lumpur, where the temple proper, built around the late 19th century, sits within a limestone cave and requires a steep climb of some 270 steps to get to.

Wherever they went, the Tamils also brought with them their distinctive material culture, food and festivals. *Saris* and *dhotis* are commonplace in Malaysia and Singapore – they are everyday and formal wear for many Tamil Malaysians and Singaporeans. One can find some of the most exquisite Indian textiles in the shops here, particularly in "Little India", or the ethnically Indian commercial quarters that exist in all the big cities. Malaysia and Singapore are also home to some of the most delectable South Indian food outside of India, with localised classics, such as *roti prata* (or *roti canai* in Malaysia), that are quite different from their Indian equivalents.

The same major festivals in India also make an appearance, though with some differences in how they are observed. For example, the festival of Thaipusam is one that is particularly important for the Tamil diaspora, though it is also observed and celebrated in southern India. The festival is held annually in *Thai*, the tenth month of the Tamil year (corresponding to January or February), and during the full moon. It is a festival honouring the deity Murugan, son of Lord Shiva, and the god of power, discipline and victory. Murugan holds a special place in Tamil Hindu worship and religious culture.

Mylapore – today a suburb of Chennai – has existed for millennia along the Coromandel Coast, and it was likely a major port city from which Tamil merchants took their culture and language across the Indian Ocean to Southeast Asia. Mylapore is home to the spectacular Kapaleeshwarar Temple, which has existed on the site from at least the 7th century, though its present form dates to much later.

Thaipusam involves a spectacular devotional procession, wherein the faithful carry *kavadi* ("burden"), large and dramatically-decorated canopies that are attached to the body by way of dozens of sharp spikes and hooks, pierced directly into the skin. Sometimes, spikes are even pierced through the tongue and cheeks. Bearing their painful and heavy ritual burden on their backs, they march for long distances and for hours on end, to and from the temple, their endurance a testament of their faith, and a means of fulfilling their sacred vows to the deity. To ease the ritual, music is played constantly, joyously and riotously around them by itinerant drummers and musicians. The festival is a burst of colour and a sight to behold for anyone who has the opportunity to witness it.

OF TREATIES AND EMPIRE

18th — 19th Centuries

22. Aceh & Makassar
Acehnese Queens and Bugis Seafarers in the Lands Below the Winds

> "The port of Aceh was never quiet, being very busy where ships, junks and boats from many other lands came to trade throughout the year. Bandar Darus Salam was very prosperous and food was very cheap and every person lived in peace and obeyed all [Sultanah Tajul Alam Safiatuddin Syah's] instructions. She was fair in all matters of the law and had firm conviction (*tawakal*) in everything she did…"
>
> — Nuruddin al-Raniri, c. 17th century. *Garden of Sultans.*[1]

After Melaka was taken by the Portuguese in 1511, the Melakan Sultan Mahmud Shah fled south to Johor, where he established a new but fragile *negeri*. He would have no rest: defending his new demesne against Portuguese assault would occupy the remainder of his reign. Meanwhile, to the northwest, a new power rose to take advantage of the vacuum left behind in the lands *di bawah angin*, or "below the winds". This new power was Aceh, at the northern tip of Sumatra, standing vigil over the entrance to the Straits of Melaka, to which came trade from the *negeri atas angin*, or countries that lay "above the winds".

The concepts of *di bawah angin* and *ke atas angin* relate to the traditional Malay view of the world. The term "lands below the winds" refers to the heartlands of the *orang melayu*, or Malay peoples, and roughly corresponds to the geographical reach of Srivijaya. The countries "above the winds" include all other foreign places north, northwest, northeast and east of the lands of the Malay peoples. These lie "above the winds" since their merchant ships were brought down here by the monsoons.

Swiftly conquering the ports of Pasai and Pidie in the early 1500s, Aceh rose to become the de facto entrepôt in the Straits of Melaka, inheriting the role from Melaka and Palembang. By absorbing Pasai, Aceh became a major exporter of pepper as well as the region's custodian of Islam.[2] It was known as the *serambi Makkah* ("verandah of Mecca"), given that it was the port of departure for Malay Muslims making the Hajj, and also a centre for Islamic learning. It became home to religious scholars fleeing Portuguese Melaka or settling here from India and the Middle East. Its fame spread far and wide *dari atas angin hingga ke bawah angin*, or "from above the winds to below the winds".

OVERLEAF: *Hookah.* Marked by Hamilton & Company, Calcutta. Calcutta, c. 1900. Silver, nautilus shells, 46.5 x 17 x 14 cm. Collection of the Asian Civilisations Museum.

OPPOSITE PAGE: *Mesh bracelet.* Aceh, Sumatra, 19th century. Gold, enamel, diamonds. Gift of Mr Edmond Chin. Collection of the Asian Civilisations Museum.

Aceh, at its greatest
territorial extent in
the early 17th century,
flanked by Malay
sultanates which
were part of its larger
sphere of influence.
Portuguese Melaka
eked out a precarious
existence, surrounded
by Aceh and its allies.

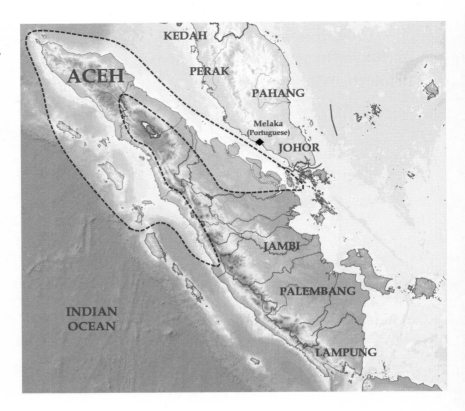

Aceh, at its greatest territorial extent in the early 17th century, flanked by Malay sultanates which were part of its larger sphere of influence. Portuguese Melaka eked out a precarious existence, surrounded by Aceh and its allies.

In their attempts to monopolise the spice trade at Melaka, the Portuguese ironically undermined the city's pre-eminence as a port for Asian trade. Gujarati, Turk, Persian, Arab and Chinese traders shifted their business elsewhere, to Aceh, such that a new triumvirate of entrepôt ports – Aceh, Surat and Mocha – emerged, replacing Melaka, Cambay and Aden before them.

Aceh would prove a shrewd and powerful adversary to the Portuguese. Not only did it successfully resist Portuguese attack, it would also dare to attack Melaka in the initial years of its occupation. Much of its derring-do stemmed from its being part of a larger, global Islamic *umma*, or community, that took in the greatest empires of the time: the Ottomans, Mughals and Safavids. Aceh saw itself as subject to the Ottoman Sultan, referred to in Malay as the *Raja Rum*, or the Emperor of Rome – a nod to the Ottomans being legitimate successors to the Byzantine, or Eastern Roman, Empire.

Early sultans of Aceh actively sought Ottoman protection through diplomatic missions to Istanbul. Turkish and European records of the time indicate the presence of Acehnese envoys on board pepper ships plying the Red Sea. In the meantime, Portuguese disruption of the pepper trade from India meant Muslim traders had to turn to Aceh. Interest in securing lucrative pepper routes encouraged the Ottomans to respond positively to Aceh's entreaties, dispatching much-needed military assistance to the region on more than one occasion.

The 17th century saw Aceh's star rise, particularly during the reign of Iskandar Muda, whose name meant "Alexander the Younger" and was a reference to Alexander the Great. Sultan Iskandar's reign ushered in a golden age for Aceh, when the sultanate was at its greatest geographical extent, taking in most of the lands below the winds. The turn of the 17th century also saw the Dutch and British East India Companies arriving in Southeast Asia with their appeals to establish regional factories. Sultan Iskandar's approach to treating with them was to decline in the first instance. This would greatly aid Aceh's resistance to European encroachment, enabling it to maintain its independence, for a time.

In 1636, Iskandar Muda died without a male heir. He'd had his only son, the crown prince, killed for having dared to plot a coup against him. His son-in-law, whom he designated king, proved deeply unpopular, and died in a matter of years, suddenly. The throne passed instead to his eldest daughter, paving the way for an astonishing period of Acehnese history, wherein queens, or sultanahs, ruled the kingdom in their own right, and with the broad support not just of the local aristocrats or *orang kaya*, but also of the *ulama*, or Islamic religious leaders.

For a good half a century between 1641 and 1699, four queens ruled over Aceh, carefully stewarding the legacy of their illustrious ancestor. Sultanah Tajul Alam Safiatuddin Syah, Iskandar Muda's daughter, enjoyed the longest reign: some thirty years between 1641 and 1675. During her time, the VOC and the EIC could no longer be ignored; their armed presence and influence in the region had become a threat. Reversing an earlier decision her father had made, she would permit the East India Companies to establish a trading settlement in the port and capital city of Bandar Aceh Darus Salaam ("Port of Aceh, Abode of Peace" – today's Banda Aceh). She stood firm, however, on forbidding permanent, stone fortifications being built. She had witnessed how, elsewhere in the lands below the winds, wherever Europeans had been allowed to build permanent fortifications, the local *negeri* would eventually succumb to European control.

Sultanah Tajul Alam's reign was marked by significant territorial concessions to the Dutch, British and other regional powers. She has thus been regarded historically as weak and ineffectual, especially coming after her aggressively expansionist father. Recent scholarship has somewhat reassessed these opinions, positioning her as a mistress of realpolitik, one who understood that diplomacy was not a zero-sum-game but a strategic give-and-take. The Europeans were allowed in, but on Aceh's terms.[3]

Certainly, Aceh during her time grew in wealth and prosperity, if not in geographical extent. European visitors to her court were bedazzled by just how opulent it was. They remarked on how the sultanah had the full respect of her court, and that she was charming, curious, intelligent and elegant. In fact, so many Europeans came during her time and that of her successors that for a while, Europeans were under the impression that Aceh had always been ruled by a queen! Most importantly, it was due to her foresight and adroit diplomacy that Aceh would resist European domination for another 200 years.

In the aftermath of Melaka's fall, Malay merchants and traders also fled eastward, in search of a new base from which to pursue their trade. They found this at the port city of Makassar, some 3000 kilometres east of Aceh, on the island of Sulawesi. There on the southernmost peninsula of the island, the sultan of Gowa welcomed these expatriate Malay traders with wide-open arms, knowing full well that riches brought from trade would make his sultanate wealthy and powerful.

For some 50 years at the turn of the 17th century, Makassar dazzled as a cosmopolitan entrepôt to the east of the lands below the winds, standing alongside Banda Aceh as successor to Melaka. The Sultanate of Gowa, by way of its influence over international trade, came to dominate South Sulawesi, managing to subdue its greatest competitor, the powerful Bugis kingdom of Bone, just to its north. As in Aceh, the East India Companies came a-knocking to seek permission to establish factories. Unlike the Acehnese, the sultans of Gowa afforded the Companies permission to establish trading settlements and permanent stone fortifications in Makassar, unwittingly heralding their own downfall.

In 1669, the Dutch VOC, allied with factions from the Bugis kingdom of Bone, vanquished the Sultanate of Gowa, sacking the royal castle-cum-fortress at Somba Opu and occupying the capital city of Makassar. The taking of Makassar, and thus the end of Gowa's golden age, is recorded in the annals of the Gowan court by way of a simple, throwaway remark: "people agreed by the new river."[4] This was a reference to the sultan's surrender by the side of a man-made canal dug by Bugis labourers forcefully conscripted from Bone. The Gowan royal scribes were probably unable, for shame and sorrow, to say more.

The end to the Makassar War saw widespread devastation and the loss of thousands of lives and livelihoods. The Dutch and the Bugis kingdom of Bone, victors of the war, consolidated power over South Sulawesi as joint rulers: the Dutch had jurisdiction over external affairs and international trade, while the Bugis, led by Arung Palakka, a charismatic and authoritarian prince of Bone, had authority over internal matters. Over the next 30 years, Arung Palakka would rule South Sulawesi with an iron fist, ousting hordes of opposing Makassarese and Bugis aristocratic families along with their retinue, even as he linked all the royal courts of South Sulawesi to his bloodline by way of strategic marriage alliances. In the meantime, the Dutch, in a bid to tighten monopolistic control over the spice trade, would forbid South Sulawesian ships from sailing eastwards to the Moluccas or even to elsewhere in the island of Sulawesi.

Thousands of Bugis and Makassarese were forced to flee their homelands and seek refuge from the late 17th century onwards. They set sail en masse from Makassar to seek honour and opportunity out west in the traditional heartlands of the *orang melayu*. Many of the Makassarese refugees were high-ranking nobles who refused to adapt to their new and reduced circumstances elsewhere. Unable to fit in or get along, Makassarese émigré communities across the Nusantara were driven out by local chieftains and repatriated to their homeland not long after their flight.

The Bugis, though of noble blood themselves, proved far more adaptable and amenable to changed economic circumstance, establishing themselves as a formidable diasporic presence across the archipelago. In the course of the 18th century, Bugis culture and civilisation underwent a spectacular metamorphosis, shifting from being largely agrarian, coastal and rooted, to being immensely maritime and mobile. From farmers and fishermen, the Bugis transformed themselves into the greatest long-distance seafarers and the greatest seafaring nation the Nusantara had ever seen.

Such is the deep association between the Bugis peoples and the sea that it is hard to imagine that up until some 300 years ago, very few Bugis would have been willing to settle permanently far away from their ancestral lands. Anchored in rich, rice-growing lowlands north of the south Sulawesi peninsula, the Bugis were unique in having an ancient culture that was little-touched by the Hindu-Buddhist faith imported to Southeast Asia by the first millennium. Instead, there emerged an indigenous and entirely unique faith and belief system, startling in its scope and complexity, and captured in the oral and written traditions of the great Bugis epic and creation myth, the *La Galigo*.

No one quite knows exactly how long the *La Galigo* is. No copy of it exists in its entirety. Instead, there are some 6000 pages of extant text – about 300,000 known lines – written in the Bugis language, making the *La Galigo* longer than its great Hindu equivalent, *The Mahabharata*. An excerpt from the text reads thus:

> "There is no one / to call the gods Lord, / or to offer praise to the Underworld. / Why, Lord, don't you have one of your children descend / and incarnate him on the earth, / do not leave the world empty, / the earth uninhabited. / You are not a god, Lord, / if there are no humans / under the heavens, above the Underworld, / to call the gods Lord."[5]

In gist, the *La Galigo* tells the tale of a race of god-like beings who live in the divine realms of the Upperworld and the Underworld. Casually observing the state of the Earth one day, the Datu (or Lord) of the Upperworld remarks on it being recently populated with lesser beings: these *humans* who, the gods felt, needed some-One to rule over them. Convening a council, the gods decide to send two of their kind to Earth as its first rulers: the Upperworld god, Batara Guru, and the Underworld goddess, We Nyiliq Timoq. The narrative thus follows some five generations of semi-divine rule by the offspring of the divine couple. It climaxes with a sort of *Götterdämmerung*, when the gods decide to quit Earth in grandiose fashion, only to change their minds and send another generation of gods back to rule. When these latter-day god-kings too decide to abandon the Earth, the narrative comes to an abrupt end.

Of the many divine characters featured in the epic, La Galigo, from whence the title, is one of its most important protagonists. The great-grandson of the original god-king and god-queen, La Galigo is the archetypal Bugis hero: a skilled warrior and intrepid wanderer, but also a trickster and rebel, temperamental and unpredictable; and above all, an expert seafarer, like his father before him. In the world of the epic, the Bugis nation has not yet extended its influence into the Sulawesi heartlands, but like other ancient Southeast Asian port polities, is centred around the mouth of a large river, where boats from across the Nusantara come to trade.

Perhaps the seed of the remarkable latter-day maritime culture and heritage of the Bugis peoples lies, after all, in this ancient epic with its seafaring protagonists. Certainly, the Bugis would be known, for much of the 18th and 19th centuries, as much for their navigational expertise and wisdom as for being fearsome warriors of the sea – both dreaded and respected by Nusantarans and Europeans alike, and often referred to, somewhat unfairly, as pirates. Their strong cultural ethos, encapsulated by the mantra, *siri na pacce*, wherein *siri* means individual as well as community honour, and *pacce* means a deep feeling of pain or empathy for a member who has been shamed or who is suffering, meant that they were often driven to act with impunity and sometimes with violence. It also meant that they were fiercely protective of their own, and constantly striving to ensure that they not only survived, but thrived economically.

A fuller exploration of Bugis seafaring and navigational wisdom, which was finessed and attained its apogee in the 18th century, would require an entire book of its own. Suffice to say that for the Bugis, navigating the seas was a science as well as an art. Bugis *nakhodas* had to have *ilmu*: an accumulation of knowledge that came from apprenticeship and experience. This involved technical expertise such as how to steer a ship, how to navigate by the stars, and knowledge of the monsoons, the winds and the tides. It also included wisdom of a more spiritual and esoteric nature, such as knowing when to sail, reading signs and omens, offering prayers for safe passage, and understanding that to sail successfully, a sailor needed to be at one with God and the environment.

Majestic *pinisi* schooners, docked at the Paotere port in Makassar, South Sulawesi. *Pinisi* schooners continue to trade goods across the Indonesian archipelago, docking at specialised harbours in almost all of Indonesia's major port cities.

The Bugis were also expert shipbuilders, with the most well-known of Bugis vessels being the legendary *pinisi* that still plies the waters between islands in Indonesia today. Though often believed to have an ancient pedigree, *pinisi* boats were actually invented sometime at the turn of the 20th century and perfected in the 1920s and '30s. They are large

trading ships made entirely of wood, with planked decks, sturdy masts and large sails. Originally made to sail by wind, today they are also fixed with engines to boost speed and efficiency. They are primarily constructed in South Sulawesi today, with the art of building *pinisi* inscribed in 2017 on UNESCO's Representative List of the Intangible Cultural Heritage of Humanity. For much of the 18th and 19th centuries, however, Bugis ships – precursors to the *pinisi* – were also built everywhere across the Nusantara where there were sizeable Bugis diaspora communities. Most notably, many were made in southeast Borneo, from whence they sailed to all the glittering port cities of the Nusantara. All kinds of Bugis ships were a visible presence in Jakarta, Surabaya, Palembang, Johor, Singapore and elsewhere, up until the 1960s.

Wherever the Bugis went in their ships, they managed, by way of their fierce commitment to community advancement, to insert themselves into local power structures at an astonishing speed, often by way of exploiting crises of succession. In Aceh, the last sultanah's abdication in 1699 was followed by an interregnum wherein a dynasty of Arab *sayyids* took the throne. In 1727, the leader of the émigré Bugis faction overthrew this dynasty and placed himself on the throne. His descendants would rule Aceh until the sultanate's demise in 1903.

Elsewhere in the Nusantara, Sultan Mahmud Shah II, the last of the Melaka line, named after his illustrious ancestor who had fled Melaka in 1511 for Johor, died without issue. Powerful Bugis factions in Johor supported the ascension of the *bendahara*, or "grand vizier". The position is a hereditary one, but in this case the *bendahara* was also the sultan's cousin and arguably a legitimate heir. In return for support, the new sultan (of the *bendahara* line) bestowed the title, Raja Muda, or "Junior King", upon the *capitan* of the Bugis, and offered him the Riau islands, just south of Johor and Singapore, as his noble seat. In Riau, the Raja Muda and his descendants would establish a brand-new, Bugis-controlled port, that together with Johor, would succeed Banda Aceh and Makassar in the 18th century as the dominant entrepôt in the lands below the winds.

The Bugis would settle easily into their new role as custodians of Malay culture and heritage in the Johor-Riau Sultanate, moulding and shaping a distinctive court and material culture that was as much *melayu* as *bugis*; and intermarrying into the Johorean royal family such that it became difficult to distinguish *melayu* from *bugis* in the royal bloodline. Descendants of the Bugis still rule Johor today.

23. Guangzhou (Canton)
Chinese Tea, the Thirteen Hong and the Canton System

> "…[A]s for the Western countries who come from across the seas, mark my words well. We may not see it now, but I have a premonition that sometime in the distant future, the Middle Kingdom will succumb to their aggression."
>
> — Emperor Kangxi, 1716. *Annals of the Qing Imperial Grand Master*, Folio 270.[6]

In the Trade galleries of the Asian Civilisations Museum, one particular object takes pride of place. This is a Canton *hong* bowl, a classic type of export porcelain traded from the port city of Canton (广州 – Guangzhou). In essence a European-style punch bowl made of high-quality Chinese porcelain, the *hong* bowl is so-called because of the exceptional view of the Canton waterfront with its thirteen *hong* (行), or European factories, painted in brightly-hued enamels around its exterior.[7] It would have been a high-end souvenir, most likely commissioned by a European buyer from afar.

The scene painted on the bowl is full of life. Dozens of Chinese houseboats throng the river alongside Chinese junks and European-style East Indiamen. Along the shore, Chinese coolies huff and puff as they offload cargo from the vessels. European merchants in breeches and wigs stand about supervising the workers, negotiating business with each other, or promenading with their canes.

The thirteen factories are the highlight of the scene. These were the Chinese headquarters of various European East India Companies, physically housing offices, warehouses and residences for officials of the companies. The factories are invariably built in a European architectural style, complete with neoclassical columns and pediments. Colonnaded verandahs on the ground and upper floors of most of the factories betray Anglo-Indian influence. If it weren't for the Chinese-style sampans on the river, one would have thought this a view of Calcutta. This fusion of European neoclassical, Anglo-Indian and local Chinese elements in architecture became known as the China Coast, or Compradoric, style. Originating in Macau, this was the style popularly found in all East Asian treaty ports in the late 19th century.

Hong bowl. China, c. 1785. Porcelain; height 15.5 cm, diameter 36 cm. Collection of the Asian Civilisations Museum.

Above the thirteen *hong*, the flags of the Western nations fly at full mast. We spy the British Union Jack, as well as the Dutch, Danish and Swedish flags. The Austrian double-headed black eagle makes an appearance, as does the white pennant of Bourbon France. Two important flags are missing, however – that of the Spanish Empire and the United States of America. This suggests that our *hong* bowl was possibly made in the 1780s, before the Americans and the Spanish arrived.

Of all the port cities in East Asia, Canton, situated at a strategic location on the Zhu Jiang, or "Pearl River", is by far the greatest and most ancient, and has been known as a major port since the 1st century (during the Han dynasty). It was a true global city; a cosmopolitan, multicultural, polyglot melting pot of a metropolis with traders from all over the Indian Ocean world.

For a good eight centuries before the advent of the Europeans, Canton and its sister city Quanzhou, in Fujian province, would reign supreme as the foremost trading capitals in China. In Chinese accounts, Canton is the city of the *fan* par excellence, with sizeable resident communities of Arab, Persian and other non-Chinese merchants domiciled in ethnic quarters in the city. The city was, in turn, a window to the world for the Chinese themselves, the main maritime gateway by which foreign goods, peoples, cultures and ideas had flowed into the empire for centuries.

Canton's history as a major port of European trade began in 1684 when, overturning the *haijin* ("trade ban") in place since the Ming dynasty, the Emperor Kangxi of the succeeding Qing dynasty opened the seas to foreign trade once more. Canton became one of a few ports of call for European ships, alongside Amoy (Xiamen), Foochow (Fuzhou) and others to the north. Emperor Kangxi remained ever ambivalent about foreign trade, however. Some three decades after throwing the Middle Kingdom's bejewelled gates open, he would predict China's downfall at the hands of the Western barbarians that were now thronging in unprecedented numbers at its eastern port cities.

In 1757, threatened by a wave of missionary activity in China, the Qianlong Emperor – Kangxi's grandson – decreed that henceforth, all Western trade with China would be limited to Canton only. Between 1757 and 1842, China traded with the European powers based on a "one port principle" (*yi kou tong shang* in Chinese), known as the "Canton System" in English. All trading activities and foreigners were relocated to a tiny waterfront location, no longer than 1000 feet across, and situated to the west of the walled city of Guangzhou-fu. Here in this tiny foreign settlement, thirteen factories were established, representing the commercial interests of the various European trading companies in the city, with Parsi, Armenian and Indian Muslim traders also having a significant presence.

Trade in Canton was highly regulated by the Qing government and thus very complicated and restrictive for would-be European traders in the city. By law, Europeans were forbidden to trade directly with the Chinese, but had to conduct their business through a government-appointed intermediary, also known as a *hong*. The same Chinese word referred simultaneously to the foreign trading company (洋行– *yeung-hong*, or "foreign *hong*") as well as to the Chinese intermediaries. The latter were appointed by the imperial court as informal overseers or "chaperones", ensuring that the Foreign Barbarians didn't get up to no good.

Each trading company was assigned to one *hong*, with all the *hongs* forming a guild-cum-cartel known as the Co-hong, answerable to the customs supervisor of Guangdong Province – *Yuet Hoi Kwan Bou Kin Dou* in Cantonese, often also referred to as the *Wubou* (户部 – "revenues department"), from whence the anglicised "Hoppo". The Hoppo and Co-hong established what was in effect a monopoly on all foreign trade in the city. All business transactions had to be made through the Co-hong, at prices negotiated by the Co-hong with Chinese buyers in the interior. The land on which the factories were built and situated was rented from the Co-hong merchants. In the meantime, all foreign vessels entering and leaving the Canton area had to pay steep customs duties to the Hoppo. To make it even more complicated, foreign ships themselves were not allowed to enter Canton. They had to dock at the island of Whampoa, in the outskirts of the city, while their goods (and accompanying traders) were painstakingly ferried upriver in sampans. Foreigners also couldn't remain in Canton all year, but had to repair to Macau after the trading season, which lasted six months when the winds were favourable.

Without exception, the monopoly the Chinese *hong* merchants had on foreign trade made them rich and powerful. European accounts of the city frequently make mention of a few of these extremely important merchants. Four of the most powerful and famous of them were Howqua, Mouqua, Ponkequa and Yanqua, known collectively as the "Wealthy Magnates of Eastern Guangdong". Note that the *hong* merchants were often referred to by their family name, as well as the honorific title *guan*, meaning "Sir" or "Official", mispronounced as *qua* by the Europeans.

By the turn of the 19th century, the factories on the Guangzhou waterfront numbered more or less around thirteen, with each of the factories retaining an official English as well as Chinese name. The most well-known of the thirteen factories included the Dutch Factory (Jaap-Yit Hong), seat of the Dutch VOC in China; and the New English Factory (Bo-wo Hong), seat of the English EIC. Chow-Chow Hong, also known as Fung-tai Hong, was another important factory, being the preferred operating headquarters of the Parsee and other Indian merchant communities. Finally, the Creek Factory (E-wo Hong), would eventually become the local headquarters of Jardine, Matheson & Co., one of the largest and most important British merchant houses in the world, dominating the China trade after the EIC's monopoly was abolished in 1833.

Everyday life in the factories was made possible only through the support of hundreds of Chinese porters and compradors, or middlemen, who supplied the foreigners with everything from food and provisions, to ship supplies, to "chops" (or visas) for their travel documents, to furniture and art. The Chinese who earned a living supplying essentials to foreigners lived in the hundreds of houseboats moored permanently by the banks of the Pearl River. Whole families would live entire lives on these boats, which, in turn, constituted a floating suburb of the city.

As trade grew and thrived in Canton, a new lingua franca emerged, reflecting English dominance, as well as Canton's pre-eminent position, in global trade. By the 1730s, this new tongue, known as Pidgin English, had all but replaced Portuguese and Malay as the language spoken by traders. Having first emerged in Macau, it became popularly used in Canton as well, and would later spread to Shanghai, Hong Kong and other treaty ports on the China coast. It was, in essence, a hybrid form of English that took in Cantonese mispronunciations as well as vocabulary – the word, "pidgin", itself was believed to be the Cantonese mispronunciation of the word, "business". Throw in relevant expressions from Portuguese, Malay, Hindi and Hokkien, and one gets a sense of just how riotously rich and complex the language was.

Unfortunately, use of this language died out in the late 19th century, when proper English instruction began to be offered in China. For a taste of Pidgin English, a good place to turn to is an of-the-era *Pidgin-English Sing-Song*, published in 1876. One of the jaunty – and perhaps more than a little politically incorrect – pieces contained therein goes as follows:

> "Ping-Wing he pie man son, / He ve*lly* worst chilo állo Can-tòn, / He steal he mother picklum mice, / And th*lo*wee cat in bilin' rice. / Hab chow-chow up, an' 'Now,' talk he, / 'My wonda' where he meow cat be?'

> Ping-Wing he look-see, tinkey fun / Two piecee man who shleep in sun, / Shleepee sound he yeung-ki, fáta, / Ping tie 'um pigtail allo togata, / T'hen fi*lee* c*l*acker an' offy *l*un, / T'hat piece ve*lly* bad pie-man son.

> Ping-Wing see gentleum wailo - go / He sc*l*eamee, '*Hai yah --- fan-kwei lo!*' All-same you savvy in Chinee, / 'One fo*l*eign devil lookee see!' / But gentleum t'hat pidgin know, / He catchee Ping and floggum so / T'hat állo-way f*l*om that day, maskee / He ve*lly* good littee Chinee."[8]

At first glance, all this might appear completely inscrutable. But when one attempts to read the excerpt out loud, one more or less gets the gist of the narrative, which is one of local resistance to imperial oppression. Our humble everyman, Ping-Wing, portrayed as a mischievous troublemaker, screams something to the effect of *Look at that foreign devil!* to a passing European gentleman, and is flogged and chastised for his audacity.

Despite the complex, bureaucratic restrictions, trade in Canton was still extremely profitable. The single most important product traded from the city, and one of the most important Chinese products of all for much of the 18th and 19th centuries, was Chinese tea.

An evergreen shrub that occurs in a dizzying array of subspecies, *Camellia sinensis* is native to subtropical China and Southeast Asia, and has been drunk there for at least a millennium. The prevalent means of preparing it today is to steep the dried and roasted young leaves of the plant in hot water. Another, older preparation method – one that dates to the Tang dynasty – involves grinding the dried tea leaves to a powder and dissolving this powder in water. This is how *matcha* is drunk in Japan.

Europeans first encountered tea in the 16th century, when the Portuguese arrived in Macau and had their first taste of the heady brew. It began to be commercially exported in a big way to Europe in the 17th century, via the Dutch VOC and the English EIC, trading at Amoy. The Chinese word for tea is pronounced *cha* (茶) in Mandarin and Cantonese. In Amoy, however, the Hokkien merchants called it *teh* in their local dialect – hence the word *tea* in English, rather than *cha*.

One of the earliest records of anyone drinking tea in England occurs in the pages of the *Diary* of Samuel Pepys in 1660. On Tuesday 25 September, Pepys, having been engaged in conversation with some acquaintances in their offices, "did send for a cup of tee (a China drink) of which [he] never had drank before."[9] By the middle of the 18th century, tea, introduced by way of coffeehouses in London, had overtaken coffee and infused itself firmly into British taste and consciousness. Up until then, tea had been the preserve of the wealthy classes. But a relaxation of taxes in the 1780s made tea accessible to the masses, such that it became Britain's national drink, and British demand for it, completely insatiable.

All that volume of tea exported from Canton made for a massive trade imbalance between Britain and China. The silver mines in America had, by this time, been exhausted; and with China accepting not much else by way of payment, Britain urgently needed solutions to its growing trade deficit. One solution was to cultivate tea elsewhere, as a means to reduce dependency on China. In the 1840s, seeds of the tea plant were smuggled to India where they would be cultivated on a large scale in the highlands of Darjeeling and Assam. Indian varietals of tea, given thoroughly English names such as "English Breakfast" and "Earl Grey", became a staple of English and Indian culture – they still are today.

In the meantime, another solution was found in opium, cultivated in India and exported in increasingly large quantities to China, where an eager Chinese public became hooked on the drug. Silver bullion, used by the British to pay for Chinese goods, was in turn used by the Chinese to pay the British for opium. The scale of opium addiction in China meant it wasn't long before Britain's trade deficit became a resounding surplus. But the drug brought with it a host of challenges that would lead inevitably to crisis and war.

24. Jeddah
Port of Mecca, Bride of the Red Sea

> "Djidda is well built; indeed, better than any Turkish town of equal size that I had hitherto seen. The streets are unpaved, but spacious and airy; the houses high, constructed wholly of stone, brought for the greater part from the sea-shore, and consisting of madrepores and other marine fossils. Almost every house has two stories, with many small windows and wooden shutters. Some have bow-windows, which exhibit a great display of joiners' or carpenters' work. [...] In general, it may be said that Djidda is a modern town; for its importance as a market of Indian goods can only be traced to the beginning of the fifteenth century, although it had been known in the most ancient times of Arabian history as the harbour of Mekka."
>
> — John Lewis Burckhardt, 1829. *Travels in Arabia: Comprehending an Account of those Territories in Hedjaz which the Mohammedans Regard as Sacred.*[10]

For millions of Muslims worldwide, the Hajj (الحج), or pilgrimage to Mecca, is the most profoundly spiritual experience one can ever have in one's lifetime. It is the fifth of the Five Pillars of Islam, the core tenets of the faith to which all the faithful must adhere. All able-bodied and financially-able men and women are obliged to undertake the Hajj once in their lifetimes, and it is so important that those who have completed it are afforded the right to affix the honorific, Haji (for men) or Hajjah (for women) to their names. In olden days, and especially for Muslim communities far from the Arab world, only the aged were able to accumulate enough wealth to make the pilgrimage; and so those who returned were often revered highly in their home communities.

Mecca, the object of the Hajj, is the first city of Islam, its most sacred city, the centre and origin of the faith. In the Qur'an, the city is referred to reverentially as Umm al-Qura, or "Mother of all Settlements". Certainly, for a month each year, Mecca is at the very heart of one of the greatest spectacles of faith in the world: that of millions of Muslim pilgrims circling the Kaaba in the city's Grand Mosque, in an extraordinary expression of their devotion to God.[11]

For centuries, one arrived in Mecca either by land or by sea. Those who took the land route would journey by camel over ancient caravan trails across the deserts of Arabia, stopping off at oases and caravanserais for rest and water. Those who took the sea route would journey by ship across the Indian Ocean and up the narrow expanse of the Red Sea, where they would necessarily stop at the port of Jeddah (جدة).

Jeddah itself has an ancient pedigree, having been designated the port of Mecca since 647, and by none other than Uthman ibn Affan, third caliph of the *dar al-Islam* and son-in-law to the Prophet Muhammad. Like many ancient cities of the Middle East, its fortunes have risen and fallen. In the 11th century, the Persian traveller Nasir Khusraw described Jeddah as a wealthy and bustling coastal town and trading port, surrounded by formidable walls. By the 12th century, Arab traveller Ibn Jubayr's accounts describe it as having declined considerably, with the remnants of its past glory strewn around the city, and nary a trace of its encircling walls. Jeddah's fortunes would rise again from the 16th century on, when, in the wake of Ottoman conquest of Arabia, it became not only a major port of pilgrimage, but also of trade.

Jeddah lies in the Hejaz, a hot and arid coastal region situated to the west of the Arabian Peninsula, and flanking the Red Sea. Since the 10th century, the Hejaz had been ruled by local *sharifs* ("nobles") of Mecca; stewards charged with safeguarding the Holy Cities as well as ensuring safe passage to generations of pilgrims on the Hajj. The *sharifs* traditionally allied themselves to the prevailing Islamic caliphate of the day, who in turn, guaranteed them their autonomy. On the part of the caliph, recognition by the *sharifs* of Mecca meant political and spiritual legitimacy in the eyes of the global *umma*. The caliph's name would be mentioned in the *khutbah*, or the religious sermon that precedes the Friday prayer in Mecca. He would be styled *Khadim al-Haramayn al-Sharifayn*, or Custodian of the Two Holy Cities, charged with protecting the faithful and the faith itself.

In 1517, the *sharifs* of Mecca accepted the suzerainty of the Ottomans, and the latter thus claimed caliphal authority, with Sultan Selim I becoming the first Ottoman caliph. Almost immediately after, he

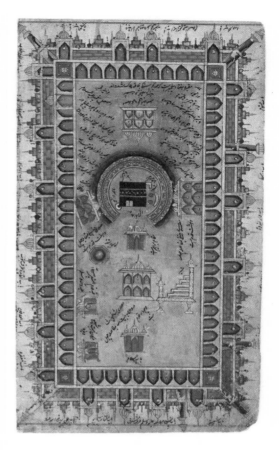

Illustration of Mecca, from the pages of an illuminated manuscript. India, 17th century. Ink, colours and gold on paper. 20 x 11.5 cm. The Kaaba is depicted at centre. Collection of the Asian Civilisations Museum.

found himself having to live up to his obligations. Since the turn of the century, the Portuguese, in a bid to exert a stranglehold on Muslim trade in the Red Sea, had made repeated attempts to blockade the entrance to the sea and cut off Muslim traders. Such a blockade would have seriously impacted the Hajj; and as such, the sultan was obliged to keep the sea routes free, by any means possible.

That same year, Ottoman and Portuguese naval forces clashed at Jeddah. Succeeding in repelling the Portuguese, the Ottomans took the city, fortifying it and stationing a military garrison there. Knowing full well that the Portuguese would strike again, the Ottomans, in the course of the early 16th century, would consolidate their power in the Red Sea region, advancing significantly in terms of naval and navigational prowess, and securing diplomatic ties with Islamic kingdoms in the East. They expanded their presence in coastal Arabia, taking Aden and the Yemen, establishing their regional maritime headquarters at Mocha, and capturing the ports of Suakin and Massawa on the Sudanese and Abyssinian coasts. By the 1550s, the Portuguese had all but given up and the Red Sea was well and truly an Ottoman Lake.

For much of the 17th and 18th centuries, peace and stability brought wealth and prosperity to Jeddah. The Hejaz being an arid region, Jeddah (and the Holy Cities) had long depended on Egypt for grain and other essential supplies. Under the Ottomans, it became an entrepôt port between Egypt and India, functioning as a sort of dividing line between the northern and southern parts of the Red Sea. Danish traveller Carsten Niebuhr, in his 1792 *Travels through Arabia, and Other Countries in the East*, observes this unique state of affairs:

> "Although the trade of Jidda is so considerable, yet this city is no more than a mart between Egypt and India. The ships from Suez seldom proceed farther than this port; and those from India are not suffered to advance to Suez. The matter of a vessel from Surat, being driven one year too far north to enter the harbour of Jidda, proceeded to Suez, and there discharged his cargo. But he was put into prison, next year, at Jidda, and obliged to pay the full dues that would have been charged at Jidda, upon the goods which he had disposed of at Suez." [12]

A prodigious amount of trade was thus artificially concentrated in Jeddah, and the city collected enormous amounts of customs revenues. First-hand accounts remarked on Jeddawi merchants being extremely wealthy, and the city itself being better-built than any other Turkish city of the same size in the Ottoman Empire.

In the meantime, advancements in maritime shipping technology meant more pilgrims would choose to make the Hajj by sea. Jeddah benefited from waves of Muslim pilgrims from all over the world stopping at its harbour and sojourning at the city before making their way on foot to Mecca. Pilgrims often stayed for months at a time, awaiting favourable monsoon winds before departing for their home countries. Many stayed on as permanent residents, serving the needs of their own ethnic communities, who arrived en masse during the Hajj season, and required the impeccable hospitality so well-engrained in the culture of the Islamic world.

Jeddah was thus an extremely cosmopolitan city, with a Muslim slant to this multiculturalism. At any time of the year, there were resident Muslim communities here from all over the Ottoman Empire: Turks, Egyptians, Syrians, Arabs, Yemenis. There were also Muslims from elsewhere in the world: Persians, Indians, Central Asians, Africans, Malays and Chinese Muslims. Jeddah being open to merchants of all faiths, there were even small resident communities of Greeks, Jews, Armenians, Dutch, English and other Europeans. The city's population swelled enormously, particularly during the Hajj, when all the world would descend upon its streets and pass through the ancient Bab Makkah ("Gates of Mecca") to the House of God.

Jeddah ghayr, so an old saying goes in Jeddah, one that is readily repeated by Jeddawis today: "Jeddah is different."[13] Certainly, Jeddah's maritime character and multiculturalism, even as it remained staunchly Muslim, resulted in a unique cityscape and way of living.

Jeddah's cosmopolitanism is vividly expressed in its Old Town, simply known as al-Balad, or "the City". Miraculously, al-Balad clings on today in contemporary Jeddah, where oil revenues and economic development have fuelled decades of modernisation and skyscraper building.

Al-Balad is age-old. On its outskirts stands a historic site that is supposedly the tomb of Hawwa, or Eve, in the Biblical tradition. The old town may likely have stood here since Jeddah's initial years as a port city in the 7th century; though the oldest buildings still remaining were probably erected in the 16th century, during the time of the Ottomans. The town was once surrounded by city walls, built by the Mamluks and reinforced by the Ottomans to defend against the Portuguese. These walls were demolished in the 1940s to much local chagrin; only a few sections remain. At the heart of the old town is the *souq*, or bazaar, with three residential quarters surrounding it: al-Mazlum, or "quarter of the oppressed", al-Sham, the "Levantine quarter", and al-Yaman, the "Yemeni quarter". Incidentally, the largest immigrant community in the city, even today, is that of the Hadhrami Arabs from the Yemen.

Jeddah is quite different from other major Islamic cities, in that up until recently, it lacked a grand mosque or other form of monumental civic architecture in its city centre. This might have been due to its being the port for Mecca, the heart of the faith and of administration, where all things monumental were to be found. In contrast, Jeddah was oriented towards the harbour, and its activities closely tied to the comings and goings of goods and diverse peoples at port. This resulted in it being more like an agglomeration of many small hamlets, served by modestly-sized mosques in quaint little public squares.[14]

The most distinctive and celebrated architectural elements of al-Balad are its tower houses, traditional five to six-storey private residential houses constructed by the city's elite – its wealthy, often expatriate, mercantile families. Though largely erected in the late 19th century after the opening of the Suez Canal, Jeddah's tower houses are based on earlier two-or-three storey antecedents found widely in the ports of the Red Sea. Many examples of these older forms still stand in Jeddah and are almost all that remains of a "Red Sea style" once prevalent in other regional ports such as Suakin, Massawa and Mocha, and which was an amalgamation of Egyptian, Ottoman, Indian and local architectural elements.

Echoing the white stone houses earlier encountered in Mombasa, these Red Sea-style houses are also fine examples of coralline architecture. The main building material is white coral stone, referred to as *hajar manqaby* locally, on account of its being quarried from the al-Manqabah lagoon located northwest of Jeddah. The white coral would be cut into cube-shaped bricks of some 25 to 30 centimetres in length. Dark brown clay dredged from the lagoon would have been used, like cement, to lay these bricks together. The exterior façades of the coral houses would then be painted in white, reflective lime plaster. The plaster protects the façade from salt and humidity, while also serving to reflect sunlight during the day, thus reducing heat transmission through the walls and keeping the interiors of the house cool.

These Red Sea coral houses would be indistinguishable from their Swahili Coast cousins, if not for their spectacular and much celebrated *mashrabiyya*, or bay windows – known locally as *rawshan*, plural *rawashin*. A *mashrabiyya* is a classic architectural element in Islamic architecture:

a boxy projection jutting out of the front or side of a residential building, and often located in its upper floors. Highly ornamented and featuring louvred, slatted or latticed wooden panels, it allows for ventilation and enough light to enter the house, while ensuring that its interior remains cool. On the inside of the house, it functions essentially as an alcove, allowing family members in the house to peer outside onto the street without being seen.

The *rawshan* in Jeddah is typically made of teak, or other tropical hardwoods imported from India and Southeast Asia. The name *rawshan* itself probably originates from Persian, the ancient lingua franca of the Indian Ocean trade. *Rawashin* are also often exuberantly and gaudily painted, boasting ornamental woodwork of an exceptional quality. They were used self-consciously by residents of the coral houses to show off the family's wealth and taste. In other words, they were a form of architectural "bling": everyone who was anyone in town had to have them. Rich, local merchant families competed to tack on as many exceptionally-ornamented *rawashin* as they could possibly afford on a single building façade. Some of the tower houses in Jeddah today have frontages that are so exaggeratedly covered in *rawashin* that the white coral façades have become mere frames for the heavily ornamented bay windows.

Beyt Nassif, al-Balad, Jeddah. Note the mahogany-hued *rawshan* on its second floor, obscured by the towering *neem* tree that stands before it.

Al-Balad in its entirety was designated a UNESCO World Heritage site in 2014. Since then, a massive restoration project has breathed new life into its once majestically-crumbling tower houses and *rawashin*. A walk through the streets of Old Jeddah today is a delight for the senses. The city is alive with the bustle of visitors and Jeddawis alike. There is a dizzying array of wares both quotidian (pots, pans and kitchen equipment) and touristy, and the delicious scent of local food, spices and perfumes. Naturally, a highlight of any tour is the overwhelming array of immaculately-restored *rawashin* painted in their traditional shades of green, blue-green and brown.

Taking pride of place in the restored old town is the Beyt Nassif ("Nasseef House"), built in 1881 as a residence for Omar Nasseef Efendi, Ottoman Governor of Jeddah and patriarch of one of the city's wealthiest merchant families. It stands on Jeddah's main street, Suq al-Alawi, overlooking a public square, and houses a museum and cultural centre today. Unlike other more exuberant tower houses, Nasseef House has an understated quality to it, having only two elegant, mahogany-hued *rawashin* on its façade. Uniquely for Jeddah, it also hosts a large, towering tree in its front yard. Once, this was the only tree in the city. Jeddah's arid climate and the scarcity of water meant that only the wealthiest of the city's denizens could afford to upkeep a tree; particularly as this is a *neem* tree, a thirsty, subtropical species native to coastal Africa and India. Its presence here is yet another nod to the trade and mercantile networks that linked Jeddah and Jeddawis indelibly to the Indian Ocean world.

By the latter half of the 18th century, the Ottoman Empire would face a new adversary from within Arabia itself. Deep in the Bedouin heartlands of Najd, a radical young scholar and cleric by name of Muhammad ibn Abd al-Wahhab began preaching a fundamentalist form of Islam in its oasis towns. The young cleric decried Sufism and any form of religious practice that smacked of polytheism, for instance, the veneration of saints. He called for a return to the strict monotheism of the early decades of Islam, more than a thousand years ago; any form of modernisation was frowned upon. All who did not adhere to this austerity were branded as infidels. The cleric and his followers called themselves Muwahhidun, or Unitarians; others would refer to them as Wahhabis.

In 1744/45, ibn Abd al-Wahhab allied himself with Muhammad ibn Saud, a young tribal leader in the oasis settlements at Diriya. The alliance was strategic: the Wahhabis provided the young ibn Saud with religious legitimacy, while he in turn offered them military assistance for their *jihad*, or Holy War. This alliance gave rise to the first Saudi state, which expanded its domains swiftly but violently across the Najd heartlands and Mesopotamia.

The Saudis took the Hejaz in 1805. They imposed deeply unpopular rules and restrictions upon pilgrims, including banning music and visits to saints' tombs. They also raised fees on pilgrims' caravans, and blocked access to Mecca and Medina for Ottoman pilgrims. In Jeddah, trade declined as foreigners avoided the port. The city's denizens took flight and the city began to fall into disrepair.

The Ottomans responded swiftly to this challenge to their sovereignty. Ultimately, the Saudi hold on the Hejaz proved weak and difficult to secure. On 11 September 1818, the Saudis surrendered to the Ottomans, and the Saudi stronghold of Diriya was destroyed. Seeds would be sown for a much stronger and more formidable Saudi-Wahhabi alliance. This second Saudi state rose in 1824 upon the ashes of the first. It would sweep into Jeddah and the Hejaz just over a hundred years later, in the aftermath of World War I and the dissolution of the Ottoman Empire. Conquering most of the Arabian Peninsula, it would declare its independence in 1932 as the Kingdom of Saudi Arabia.

25. Kolkata (Calcutta)
Nawabs, Sahibs and Babus in the City of Palaces

"Where the sober-coloured cultivator smiles / On his byles; / Where the cholera, the cyclone, and the crow / Come and go; / Where the merchant deals in indigo and tea / Hides and ghi; / Where the Babu drops inflammatory hints / In his prints; / Stands a City – Charnock chose it – packed away / Near a Bay – / By the Sewage rendered fetid, by the sewer / Made impure, / By the Sunderbunds unwholesome, by the swamp / Moist and damp; / And the City and the Viceroy, as we see, / Don't agree."

— Rudyard Kipling, 1887. "A Tale of Two Cities".

For the first-time visitor, Calcutta (কলকাতা) is patently old-world, oozing imperial splendour and decadence with its majestic, monumental, though sadly crumbling buildings everywhere you look. At the same time, it is also a city of extremes, with abject poverty existing side by side with fabulous wealth. It provides a quintessential though stereotypical picture of India: its streets bursting with life and colour, its air perfumed with fragrance and odour; locals playing cricket on the Maidan at midday despite the sweltering heat, and beggars (many of them children) and ramshackle roadside stalls everywhere you turn, selling everything you can possibly imagine.

The city was established in 1690, when the merchants of the Honourable East India Company, led by one Job Charnock, sailed up the Hooghly River and dropped anchor at a small town on its banks. By 1706, the EIC had finished building Fort William, which still stands at the heart of the city today. Around the fort, they would steadily build Calcutta up, brick by brick, in the course of a century. They would also occupy most of the province of Bengal in 1757, in the aftermath of the Battle of Plassey (Palashi in Bengali), when the Nawab of Bengal was forced to relinquish his sovereignty. Company rule proper began in 1773, when the EIC assumed the role of a colonial power and began to govern its Indian dominions directly. In 1772, Calcutta became the capital of British India, and it held on to that title till 1911, when the capital was moved to New Delhi. All this time, Calcutta grew swiftly, becoming the second city of the British Empire by the turn of the 19th century, after London itself.

Like other British Indian cities, Calcutta was divided into two quarters: White Town to the south, where the British and other Europeans lived;

and Black Town to the north, where Bengalis, rich or poor, resided. Both were segregated and self-contained settlements, in that they held residences, places of worship and commercial establishments serving their respective ethnic communities' needs.

The heart of White Town is at former Dalhousie Square, renamed Benoy-Badal-Dinesh Bagh post-Independence, after three early 20th-century Bengali independence fighters: Benoy Krishna Basu, Badal Gupta and Dinesh Chandra Gupta. Right here at BBD Bagh in Central Kolkata stand the most imposing colonial-era buildings anywhere in the city. A case in point: the innocuously-named Writers' Building, erected in 1777 in a neoclassical style. Its exposed red brick façade extends for 150 metres in length, dominating the entire northern side of the BBD Bagh. Topping the structure are classical statues of the Roman goddess of wisdom, Minerva, as well as the personifications of Agriculture, Commerce, Justice and Science. Originally built by the EIC as barracks and accommodations for its employees, it was eventually converted in the 19th century into the Colonial Government Secretariat. It is a sight to behold indeed.

Around the Writers' Building are other civic institutions such as the General Post Office, the High Court building, the Calcutta Collectorate building and the headquarters of the Eastern Railway – built much later, in the second half of the 19th century, they collectively represented the engines of empire. Around the BBD Bagh, White Town sprawls generously. To the southwest lies the vast expanse of the Maidan, the city's parade ground and green lung. Flanking the Maidan is glamorous Chowringhee Road, the centre of the city's leisure and entertainment scene, with its art deco cinemas, high-end residential apartments and the gleaming white neoclassical pile that is the Indian Museum, sister to the British Museum in London.

Midway down Chowringhee is fashionable Park Street, residential quarters to the city's elite, with its (once-)glitzy apartment buildings and fancy cafes channelling New York on the Hooghly. Finally, at the southern end of Chowringhee stands that most ostentatious and obsequious of monuments to the British Raj: the Victoria Memorial, commissioned in 1901 by Lord Curzon, Viceroy of India, in honour of the late Victoria, Empress of India. Resembling the Taj Mahal in Agra, it was only completed in 1921, long after the seat of imperial power had been moved to Delhi.

This misplaced island of European gentility in India was the domain of that species of colonial known as the *sahib*, and his female counterpart,

Victoria Memorial, Calcutta, resembling a cross between the Taj Mahal and a neoclassical Italian palace. The building is constructed of white marble hewn from Rajasthan, and is designed in the Indo-Saracenic style. Its architect was Briton William Emerson. Standing atop the dome is the Angel of Victory.

the *memsahib*. The word *sahib* has origins in Arabic, where it refers to a "companion" to the Prophet. From thence, it travelled by way of Persia to Mughal India, where a form of it was used as an honorific for elegant and sophisticated princes of royal blood. It eventually became a polite form of address, translating to "master" and used by ordinary Indians for those above their status, Indian or otherwise. During Company Rule and the British Raj, the term was appropriated and used exclusively for white European gentlemen, and especially officers of the military, with *memsahib* being a conjoining of "Ma'am" and *sahib*.

One of the most celebrated *sahibs* of all time was the author, Rudyard Kipling, who was born in Bombay in 1865, and made his name by lovingly preserving and perpetuating a classic image of British India. The mainstream popularity of *The Jungle Book* notwithstanding, Kipling's India was one where *sahibs* and *memsahibs* ruled supreme and where Indians, even the highly-educated ones, were incapable of taking care of their own nation's affairs. "Take up the White Man's burden", so said he in the spirit of benign imperialistic paternalism. "Send forth the best ye breed" to "serve your captives' need".[15] He would loathe Calcutta for its seething Bengali resentment against European rule, and for the appalling filth and poverty everywhere he looked. He thought it a black hole, in more ways than one.[16]

For those given to spotting resident Europeans, *sahibs* and *memsahibs* were known to make an appearance in their neoclassical enclosure primarily in the evenings, when the heat and light were rather less harsh on the eye and fair skin. They would emerge in their horse carriages or promenade in their splendid white suits and their voluminous frocks that were spectacularly ill-suited to the climate, in a scene straight out of an Austenian novel, except that this was sweltering Bengal. *Never mind the climate*, they seemed to be saying, stiff upper lip and all. *This is India – English territory to be re-made in England's image.*

For they were princes of this land, after all, these *sahibs*. They had made sure of that, wresting control from the local Nawabs, the Bengali princes who were the rightful rulers of the land. The latter were unceremoniously unseated, bankrupted, forced to pay the Company for damages due to wars fought in a bid to relieve them of their burdensome lands and sovereignty. The Company replaced the Nawabs in the age-old feudal structure that saw the Mughal emperors above, and *zamindars*, or landed gentry, below. Taxes once collected by *zamindars* and paid to the Nawab were thus paid unto the Company, which saw it fit to tax unrelentingly.

In the early 1770s, Bengal was in the throes of a great famine. In response to losses of income, the Company raised land taxes, and used the takings to adorn their brand-new capital city. Millions of Bengalis died even as Calcutta rose from the muddy banks of the Hooghly. Thousands of the rural poor – men, women and children alike – thronged the city in search of opportunity, and, in scenes straight out of a Dickensian novel, ended up as beggars and other denizens of the city's seething underbelly, eking out a meagre living in the shadow of its increasingly magnificent monuments and mansions.

Indeed, by the early 19th century, Calcutta was at its zenith and was known by all and sundry as the City of Palaces, a reference to the fabulous wealth of its residents, and to the general elegance and opulence of the city – seething underbelly notwithstanding. All around White Town were the sumptuous, palatial residences of the *sahibs*, administrators and merchants alike.

The most palatial of these city palaces was Government House (today's Raj Bhavan), located just south of BBD Bagh, and as massive and awe-inspiring an edifice as the Writers' Building to its north. It was built in 1803 as the residence for then Governor-General of India, Lord Wellesley. Modelled after Kedleston Hall, an 18th-century country manor in Derbyshire and the ancestral seat of the Lords Curzon, it would coincidentally be official residence to one of the Lords Curzon when *he* became viceroy in 1899. Upon its completion, it caused a scandal in political and high-society circles because of how much it had cost to build it, and how luxurious it was despite it being ostensibly the residence of a civil servant.

Men came to make names and fortunes in Calcutta. Many a *sahib*, upon returning to the home countries, found himself fabulously wealthy and in possession of newfound titles and country estates. They styled themselves nobles. Others called them *nabobs*. Once a term used by the English to refer disparagingly to the local Bengali Nawabs, the word eventually took on new meaning, referring equally disparagingly to an Englishman who had made his wealth in India, and who flaunted this wealth and newfound status flagrantly. "New money", as it were, attempting to emulate the gentried upper classes.

Obscene wealth wasn't just the preserve of Europeans. Bengali *zamindars*, merchants and other entrepreneurs who threw in their lot with the British found themselves profiting to a significant degree. A new breed of local aristocratic families emerged in the city, becoming extremely prominent and influential. The history of these great families was intertwined with that of their city, and they continue to wield great influence even today in Bengali political, cultural and social life. Some of these great families were actual nobility: old, gentried families who shrewdly and calculatedly found ways to work with the British. Others had no such distinction, having built their wealth through commerce, and having had titles bestowed upon them by the British.

The traditional relationship between *zamindar* and peasantry had been one of mutual interdependence. *Zamindars* kept one foot planted firmly on their rural estates, while the peasantry paid their taxes to the *zamindars*. In years when the harvest was poor, the peasants could count on their *zamindars'* generosity, and expect them to waive taxes and provide food for their struggling families. Under Company Rule, a new Permanent Settlement Bill was introduced in 1793 that made it compulsory for taxes to be paid, regardless of circumstance. Scores of peasants and their *zamindars* were ruined in bad years, and rural estates had to be sold to new owners. Many buyers were newly-rich *babus* in Calcutta, who were absentee landlords and didn't care a toss about these estates, except insofar as they continued paying dividends. The result was a countryside that was increasingly impoverished even as Calcutta itself grew fat.

The term "babu" had Persian origins, and, like *sahib*, was used as a polite and respectful term of address for men with high social-standing, or who were highly-educated and sophisticated. The quintessential *babu* for much of the 16th to 18th centuries was the resident Nawab or the benign and highly-respected *zamindar*. By the late 19th century, the term "babu" had taken on a negative and disparaging tone, referring to a gentleman Bengali (read: an affected, local Bengali dandy) who took on British ways indiscriminately. The great Calcutta families, ever eager to please and emulate the British (from whom they derived their wealth), took to adopting aspects of European culture with gusto. They wore European clothes, incorporated European-style architecture in their family homes, and even celebrated European festivals like Christmas (though they were Hindus). They were British through and through in their behaviour and mannerisms, but Bengali in terms of faith and adherence to traditional family values.

"Babu culture" referred to the hedonism and excess that characterised the lives of many of these urban rajas and their scions, who squandered their wealth on expensive clothes and furnishings (exquisitely-tailored suits, chandeliers from Venice), elaborate parties, and extravagant antics like perfuming their villas with rose water and procuring zebra-drawn carriages.

The *babu's* domain was North Kolkata, formerly Black Town. Today, as in the past, its main thoroughfare, Chitpur Road, presents an everyday Calcuttan scene of poverty and bustle. But look past the immediate dereliction and you will find secreted behind the main street, on either side, the city's most awe-inspiring urban palaces, erected by its great families. Right here, off Chitpur Road, was Calcutta's City of Palaces proper, what people *really* referred to when they used this moniker.

These palatial residences are unique for their hybrid style of architecture, which some refer to as Bengal baroque. European neoclassical, Mughal Indian as well as Hindu elements are melded together in an exhilarating and extravagant style. The façades of these palaces are typically British, featuring neoclassical elements such as Corinthian columns, and Palladian pediments recalling Government House. But woven into the architectural vernacular are local decorative elements: a sitar, for instance, or floral details drawn from Mughal architecture. Inside these great houses were features adapted for local culture and climate. There would be a private Hindu shrine for worship, and multiple courtyards that allowed for ventilation. Some of these great houses had latticed windows concealing *zenanas*, or womens' quarters – elements borrowed from Mughal palaces.

The magnificent Marble Palace, boasting eclectic architecture that blends neoclassical elements with traditional Bengali courtyards and adornment. The house is full of Victorian-era antiques and artworks collected by the family. Members of the family still live in the palace today.

Built some two or three centuries ago, almost all of these erstwhile palaces have been unoccupied for decades and have sadly become decaying skeletons of their former selves. But in those that still stand, one gets a sense of the fairy-tale lives once led behind their walls.

The most spectacular of the palaces still standing is the Marble Palace, built in 1835 by Bengali merchant Raja Rajendra Mullick, and so-called on account of its floors and walls being made almost entirely of imported marble. The house is located at the end of a small but busy street. It is impossible to miss given how it suddenly appears, abracadabra: a Roman or Tuscan villa seemingly transported thousands of miles away from where it ought to be. A massive porte-cochère fronts the entire complex, channelling the Pantheon in Rome. Just beside it is another monumental structure, with two floors of fourteen Corinthian columns each, topped by an elaborately-stuccoed pediment – this is Bengal baroque at its most theatrical.

The sumptuousness continues inside where walls and floors are indeed paved with all sorts of imported marble, and where there are glittering mirrors, chandeliers of Venetian glass, and furnishings from Europe every which way one looks. There is also an impressive collection of European oil paintings, including a rare Rubens. The house stands today much like it was when its patriarch died. Shrewdly, he had included a clause in his trust preventing any changes or additions to the original building. This ensured that the building and its contents have remained intact through the years. Though still owned by the family, part of the Marble Palace is open to the public as a museum.

Not far from it stands another great house, better known for its former owners rather than its architecture. This is Jorasanko Thakur Bari, the 18th century family home of the legendary Tagores, and birthplace of the great Indian poet and Nobel Prize winner, Rabindranath Tagore.

The Tagores were a Brahmin *zamindari* family whose family wealth had been consolidated and expanded by Rabindranath's grandfather, Dwarkanath, an extraordinary entrepreneur and perhaps the greatest Bengali industrialist – a Rockefeller of his time. At his peak, he was director of the highly-profitable Calcutta Steam Tug Association, responsible for the tugboats that sailed goods up the unruly Hooghly River. He also had his own fleet of clippers sailing in international waters and trading at Canton and London. He had a monopoly on coal mining, introduced tea cultivation to Assam, was director of banking and insurance corporations, and also owned local English-language newspapers. He was, furthermore, a patron of culture and the arts, having been one of the first Bengalis to be admitted to the Asiatic Society, a staunchly European establishment.

While *babus* were indeed excessive in their show of wealth, it wasn't all just fêtes and frivolity. Dwarkanath and his peers also contributed significantly to education, laying the foundation for English-style schooling in Calcutta. This precipitated the emergence of a generation of young Bengali men educated in Enlightenment philosophy and Western political thought, and who agitated for reform and modernisation of traditional Bengali culture.

Reform invariably led to nationalism, though rumblings of Bengali nationalism were initially (and paternalistically) held up by the British as a mark of success in "civilising" India. There was an about-turn in this attitude in the aftermath of the 1857 Indian Rebellion, when Company Rule was replaced by British Raj, and any form of nationalistic zeal was no longer tolerated. The great families and their scions thus turned to literature and the arts as a means of expressing their national pride.

Already flowering by the turn of the 19th century, the great Bengal Renaissance thrived in earnest towards the end of the same century, with Bengali poets, novelists, musicians and choreographers experimenting with traditional forms and creating new modes of expression. This efflorescence culminated in the poetry and cosmopolitanism of Rabindranath Tagore; in particular, his 1910 magnum opus, *Gitanjali*.

In this collection of poems, Tagore articulates his radical vision of an India without shackles, and human beings free to love and dream:

"Where the mind is without fear and the head is held high; / Where knowledge is free; / Where the world has not been broken up into fragments by narrow domestic walls; / Where words come out from the depth of truth; / Where tireless striving stretches its arms towards perfection; / Where the clear stream of reason has not lost its way into the dreary desert sand of dead habit; / Where the mind is led forward by thee into ever-widening thought and action— / Into that heaven of freedom, my Father, let my country awake." [17]

In acknowledgement of Rabindranath's contributions to mankind, Jorasanko Thakur Bari has today been transformed into a university for the arts and humanities. It also houses a museum dedicated to the life and times of this most celebrated of Bengalis.

26. Hong Kong
Opium, Treaties and Taipans at the Fragrant Harbour

> "Harbour of many ships, haven of people from China, squatter's colony, fun fair, bazaar and boom town. Hong Kong, where people come and go and know themselves more impermanent than anywhere else on earth. Beautiful island of many worlds in the arms of the sea. Hong Kong. And China just beyond the hills."
>
> — Han Suyin, 1952. *A Many-Splendoured Thing.*[18]

Our account begins, *in medias res*, with the destruction of a large cargo of opium on the banks of the Bocca Tigris (Humen in Chinese), not far from the port city of Canton. Our main protagonist is Imperial Commissioner Lin Zexu, a stern and principled man in his 50s. He stands frowning and gesticulating before the fuming pyre as his associates, carrying chests of the drug, toss the contents upon the fumes. The air is pungent with a sickly-sweet odour that goes straight to the head, muddling the senses. Commissioner Lin inadvertently raises his mandarin's sleeve to his nose, keeping out the noxious smell. Around the pier, held some distance back by guards, are hundreds of onlookers: fishermen and farmers from the village. Some are wailing, ruing the loss of the much-coveted substance.

It is 1839. Around China, millions of Chinese are now addicted to opium. The addiction afflicts all levels of society, from the humble peasant to the emperor himself, so it is said. In opium dens around the Middle Kingdom, men and women lie sprawled sideways on daybeds, puffing at opium pipes. Their eyes are glazed over; they look lost to the world. Though opium had been consumed in China for well over a millennium, it was the importation of tobacco from the West that galvanised its mass consumption. A small pellet of the black substance is mixed with tobacco, before being burnt and smoked. The result is bliss: the drug affords euphoria and relaxation. But there is a sinister side effect: an intense and insistent withdrawal, causing one to consume more and more of it.

The drug is derived from the seed pods of *Papaver somniferum*, also known as the opium poppy. A flowering shrub, the poppy has very attractive, medium-sized blooms in a variety of colours, the most well-known being bright red. It is widely grown and cultivated across parts of Europe, India, the Middle East and Southeast Asia. When cut, the seed pods of the poppy ooze a white sap; and it is this sap that, when processed and dried, becomes opium itself.

As demand for opium grew in the Middle Kingdom, the British began to cultivate it on a massive scale in Bengal and Bihar. The opium was processed and made into balls in massive opium factories, before being shipped downriver to the port city of Calcutta. From thence, opium clippers – swift-sailing, long-distance vessels specialised for this purpose – would ship the opium direct to Canton. These clippers were so small and nimble, they were able to smuggle the drug up the Pearl River to one of its many islands, where they would be met by local Chinese "fast craft" able to transport the drug inland by way of China's extensive riverine networks.

The opium trade was illegal in China. But insatiable demand meant large profits; and so British and foreign merchants got in on the trade, as did the Chinese merchants of the Co-hong in Canton. At one point, most of the *hong* merchants in Canton, foreign or Chinese, were probably, in some way or another, smuggling the drug into China. By the late 1830s, some 40,000 chests (or 2800 tons) of opium were being shipped a year between Calcutta and Canton.

In 1839, the Daoguang Emperor, bowing to internal pressure to ban opium consumption and trade, appointed Lin Zexu imperial commissioner to Canton and charged him to eradicate the drug from China. Lin was a highly respected official of Hokkien descent, known in imperial circles for his incorruptibility and doggedness. As governor-general of Hunan and Hubei provinces in 1837, he had already commenced a successful campaign against the trade and use of the drug. Upon his arrival in Canton, Lin wasted no time in expelling errant British merchants from the city, but not before demanding they surrender all their opium holdings to him. More than 20,000 chests, or some 1400 tons, of the drug were duly surrendered, and very publicly destroyed. This represented a loss of some three million pounds sterling, an enormous amount of money.

Victory was thus short-lived for Imperial Commissioner Lin. Diplomatic ties between China and Britain deteriorated sharply in a matter of two years, leading to all-out war. Just before war was declared, Lin would write a letter to Queen Victoria, decrying British hypocrisy in banning the cultivation and use of the drug domestically, while

Painting of Hong Kong Island from the Harbour. Chinese artist, late 1850s. Oil on canvas, 67.2 x 112.3 cm. Collection of the Asian Civilisations Museum.

encouraging its sale in the "Inner Lands" of China. In the letter, he also gave fair warning that trade in opium would be banned, and all smugglers of the drug executed. Not surprisingly, the letter never reached the queen – the British Foreign Office refused to accept it.

The Anglo-Chinese War, also known as the First Opium War, lasted three years from 1839 to 1842, and ended with China's defeat and surrender. On 29 August 1842, the Qing government signed the Treaty of Nanking, the first in a series of so-called "unequal treaties", wherein China would be forced to accede to trading privileges and other demands made on its sovereignty. Under the terms of the Treaty of Nanking, China was made to pay 21 million silver dollars in reparations to Britain, and to abolish the Canton System altogether. Instead of a single port of call, China would be obliged to open up four additional coastal ports to foreign trade: Amoy, Foochow, Shanghai and Ningpo. It would also be made to cede Hong Kong Island in perpetuity to Britain. An important component of the treaty was the principle of extraterritoriality, wherein Britons residing in China's "treaty ports", as they became known, would be subject to British rather than Chinese law.[19]

The Opium War and the Treaty of Nanking introduced gunboat diplomacy to Asia. Following the British example, the Americans and the French also negotiated unequal treaties of their own in China in 1844, allowing for trading privileges and extraterritoriality for American and French merchants. Nor was the First Opium War the final one. Between 1856 and 1860, Britain and France would wage a Second

Opium War against China, notorious for the Anglo-French sacking and looting of the Summer Palace in Beijing. The war was concluded by way of China ratifying yet another set of unequal treaties at the 1860 Convention of Peking, conceding several more treaty ports (including Tientsin, Nanking, Swatow and Hankow), and allowing for foreign legations (or embassies) to be established in Beijing, just outside the walls of the Forbidden City.[20] The Kowloon Peninsula was, at this time, ceded in perpetuity to the British at Hong Kong; and the opium trade was also, finally, legalised.

The Chinese would look back on the 100-year period from the First Opium War and the Treaty of Nanking as a "century of humiliation". In fact, textbook histories of modern China often commence with War and Treaty, and frequently play out as narratives of heroic struggle against an untrustworthy and belligerent West. Indeed, for much of the 19th century post-1842, China would see itself encroached upon on all fronts by hostile Western powers and an imperialistic Japan. In 1898, following China's defeat in the First Sino-Japanese War, France, Germany and Russia secured large and important territorial concessions at Kwang-chou-wan, Kiautschou Bay and the Liaotung Peninsula respectively. Meanwhile, under the terms of a Second Convention of Peking, the New Territories were leased to Britain for 99 years and annexed to the colony of Hong Kong.

One of the earliest views of Hong Kong harbour may be seen in the Trade galleries of the Asian Civilisations Museum. This is a reasonably large China trade painting of Hong Kong Island that dates to the late 1850s, some two decades after the territory was ceded to the British. As with other paintings of this genre, the landscape is executed by way of Western oil painting techniques imported into Canton in the 19th century. The painting would likely have been commissioned by a foreign merchant, and painted by a Cantonese artisan in one of the many local workshops specialising in paintings of this nature. It is, in essence, a "postcard" of the city, albeit of a high-end, luxury variety.

In this view of Hong Kong, the main island rises stalwartly in the distance, its many ridges silhouetted against a cloudy sky. In the foreground are all manner of ships, including Chinese junks of various sizes, three-masted, European-style sailing ships flying the flags of Britain, France and the United States, an American-style paddle steamer, as well as smaller vessels owned by the city's boat people, known as the Tanka.

The message is clear: though less than twenty years a British territory, Hong Kong was already bustling.

This dramatic and awe-inspiring view of Hong Kong Island would have greeted any visitor arriving into the narrow straits that separated the island from the Kowloon Peninsula. In 1878, intrepid English lady explorer, Isabella Bird, stopped over at Hong Kong en route to Southeast Asia. In her famous travelogue, *The Golden Chersonese and the Way Thither* (published 1883), she had this to say about the epic vista, revealing, as she does, how quickly Hong Kong had established itself as a convenient stopover for Western tourists headed East.

> "Victoria, which is the capital of the British colony of the island of Hong Kong, and which colloquially is called Hong Kong, looked magnificent, suggesting Gibraltar, but far, far finer, its Peak eighteen hundred feet in height – a giant among lesser peaks, rising abruptly from the sea above the great granite city which clusters upon its lower declivities [...] A forest of masts above the town betoken its commercial importance, and "P. and O." and Messageries Maritimes steamers, ships of war of all nations, low-hulled, big-masted clippers, store and hospital ships [...] great high blocks of commercial buildings, huge sugar factories, great barracks in terraces, battery above battery, Government House, and massive stone wharves, came rapidly into view, and over all, its rich folds spreading out fully on the breeze, floated the English flag."[21]

The island didn't always move its English visitors to waxing proud and lyrical. The EIC had originally intended to establish its permanent Far Eastern base at Chusan, which had a much superior location and geography. But instead, British naval forces had found themselves occupying Hong Kong in 1841, in the midst of war. Initial British responses to Hong Kong's acquisition were icy. Hong Kong was seen as a fatal and costly mistake, a wretched and pestilential island compared to the beautiful and salubrious place that was Chusan – this despite the name "Hong Kong" in Chinese (香港) meaning "Fragrant Harbour". Lord Palmerston, the British foreign secretary presiding over the Opium War, described Hong Kong famously and scathingly as a "barren island with barely a house upon it", adding that it seemed "obvious that Hong Kong will not be a Mart of Trade, any more than Macao is so."[22]

The popular conception of Hong Kong as a godforsaken place swiftly gave way to a measure of imperialistic pride as, against all odds, a thriving port and city was built up on the foothills of the island's precipitous peaks. There was nary any flat ground on the island capable of being used for agriculture; but the natural deep-water harbour was one of the best in the Far East, allowing for ocean-going ships to dock right in the heart of the city. A policy of free trade, first introduced in Singapore, meant that all the world's ships and merchants called here, and Hong Kong became regarded as a city of opportunity, a "boom town" where one came to seek wealth and opportunity, and a place where trade and commerce were paramount.

At the heart of Hong Kong's economic success were the great British *hongs*, or merchant houses earlier established in Canton, and which also set up shop here at the earliest opportunity. In Hong Kong, they would come into their own, becoming truly vast corporations that spanned the globe. At the helm of the great Hong Kong *hongs* were tycoons and business magnates known, in Cantonese, as *taipan* (大班), meaning "big shot" or "top management". They were mostly British of Anglo-Saxon descent, though there were also *taipans* who were of Armenian, Jewish, Parsi, Eurasian and much later on, Chinese descent.

Taipans were the historical equivalents of today's CEOs of multi-national corporations, except that in a city like Hong Kong, where commerce was king and money moved mountains, they were veritable emperors, prodigiously wealthy and extremely powerful. It is no exaggeration to say that Hong Kong was literally built by its legendary *taipans*, whose names – Keswick, Swire, Kadoorie, Sassoon, Mody, Ho Tung and more – continue to reverberate in the city today, etched upon its streets and many of its buildings.

The most important of Hong Kong's *taipans* was Scotsman William Jardine, founder of the city's greatest *hong*, Jardine, Matheson & Co. Originally trained as a ship surgeon, Jardine would found his namesake corporation in 1832 with business partner and fellow Scotsman, James Matheson. Initially registered at Canton, it was the first British firm to establish a presence in Hong Kong. It went by the Chinese name, E-Wo, meaning "Pleasant Harmony" Trading Company.

Jardine, Matheson & Co. would build its empire on the back of the opium trade, becoming the largest importer of opium, as well as the largest British *hong* by far, by the 1840s. William Jardine was a shrewd, powerful and ruthless man; one of the most notorious and determined smugglers of opium. He played an instrumental role in lobbying for the use of war against China, in order to protect and expand his trading interests. He went so far as to advise Lord Palmerston on military strategy, and even suggested some of the terms eventually incorporated into the Treaty of Nanking.

In the course of the 19th and 20th centuries, Jardine, Matheson & Co. would hold true to its core business of trade while also functioning as a one-stop service provider for all related ancillary services such as shipping and freight, banking and insurance. An ever-shifting global economic landscape would see it diversify its holdings, expanding into real estate, food and beverage, textiles, railways and hospitality; and eventually growing into a massive global conglomerate. The company still exists today as Jardine Matheson, headquartered in Hong Kong and run by a fifth-generation *taipan* of the Keswick family, related to William Jardine (who died a bachelor) by way of his older sister.

Early 20th century postcard of a junk in Hong Kong harbour.

Besides merchant houses, Hong Kong also became headquarters to a number of major Asian banking corporations, the most notable of which was the Hongkong and Shanghai Bank. The bank began operations simultaneously in Hong Kong and Shanghai in 1865 to provide credit and financing for trade and commerce between China and the rest of the world. Not long after it was incorporated, it opened in major cities across the globe where there were significant Chinese trading interests, including London, Yokohama, San Francisco and New York. It went by the Chinese name, Wayfoong, meaning "Abundant Exchange" Banking Corporation.

Perhaps the most influential *taipan* of the bank's history was Sir Thomas Jackson, chief manager between 1876 and 1902. Under his charge, the bank grew to become the most important in Asia in its time; and it also became de facto central bank to the Hong Kong government, issuing banknotes for the colony – a role it continues to play in today's Hong Kong Special Administrative Region. In 1989, the bank was renamed the Hongkong and Shanghai Banking Corporation, or HSBC.

Of all the *hongs* in Hong Kong, HSBC has had the most enduring impact on the city's urban landscape. Excepting a brief London phase in the 1990s, it has remained staunchly headquartered in the city; and since its earliest days, the bank's headquarters has itself been an architectural icon of the city.

The HSBC Main Building has stood at the same address, 1 Queen's Road Central, since 1864. It has been demolished and rebuilt three times in its history. Today's Main Building is a 47-storey skyscraper designed and executed in 1985 by British architect, Norman Foster, in a breathtakingly contemporary style. The chief conceit of the building's design consists in the displacement of its core to its edges and exterior; and the laying bare of elements of the building's internal structure and machinery – its weight-bearing trusses, building services and elevator shafts – for all to see. Glass-clad façades and lightweight materials afford the skyscraper a sense of lightness and transparency, not to mention spectacular views of harbour and city for anyone inside it. In a masterful stroke, the entire structure is lifted entirely off the ground, such that the "ground floor" of the building presents itself as a public plaza, integrated with pedestrian and circulation networks in Central.

The implicit message conveyed by this daring and revolutionary architecture is that HSBC remains inextricably entwined with Hong Kong's past, present and future. Towering over city and harbour, and visible for miles to any ship sailing into Hong Kong waters, the HSBC Main Building is an ode to Hong Kong's status as East Asia's global financial hub, and HSBC's pre-eminence as architect of its success.

27. Xiamen (Amoy)
Coolies, Towkays and the Overseas Chinese in Nanyang

"There are, probably, three hundred junks of all sizes trading at this port – many of them are the property of Amoy merchants. They trade with the northern and southern ports of China, with the island of Formosa, in the Straits of Singapore and ports in that region. A daily communication by means of small vessels is kept up with the principal cities which can be reached from Amoy by water, and boats go and come laden with passengers and merchandise."

— Nicholas Belfield Dennys, ed., 1867. *The Treaty Ports of China and Japan: A Complete Guide to the Open Ports of those Countries, together with Peking, Yedo, Hongkong and Macao.*[23]

In the aftermath of the Treaty of Nanking in 1842, five treaty ports were forced open to foreign trade: Canton (Guangzhou, already open), Amoy (Xiamen), Foochow (Fuzhou), Shanghai and Ningpo. From the first three port cities, millions of Chinese would emigrate to the Nanyang (南洋 – "Southern Ocean") to seek wealth, opportunity and a better life.[24] They would form a second great wave of Chinese immigration to the south, after an earlier one in the Ming dynasty. Even today, a majority of Overseas Chinese (*huaqiao*) in the Nanyang are southern Chinese of Hokkien, Cantonese and Teochew descent primarily, but also, to a lesser degree, of Foochow and Hakka descent.

The development of these five first treaty ports was uneven. Shanghai, initially deemed to have the least economic potential, would go on to become a financial and economic powerhouse, surpassing even Hong Kong in due course. Canton would be avoided in the initial years after the First Opium War on account of the seething resentment against the British. Foochow and Ningpo never really developed into major port cities – the former filled a niche as a "boutique" inland port for the tea trade, while the latter became the focus of European missionary activity. And then there was Hong Kong, which the British possessed outright, and where most of the *hong* merchants would focus their capital and attention.

Aside from Canton, Amoy had the strongest trading pedigree of the ports. Since at least the 16th century, first the Portuguese, and then the Dutch and the English, had sailed their ships to the city to trade in tea.

Panoramic view of Gulangyu Island and mainland Xiamen from the top of Sunlight Rock. In the near distance is the Bagua Building, with its distinctive neoclassical dome.

Amoy also had the distinction of being erstwhile capital of Ming loyalists in the early years of the Qing dynasty. The formidable general Zheng Chenggong, also known as Koxinga, made Amoy his capital; and from there he wreaked havoc along the southern Chinese coast in a bid to destabilise the fledgling Manchu state. From Amoy, Zheng would also wage battle against the Dutch VOC in Taiwan (then known as Formosa), defeating the latter in 1662 and claiming Taiwan for his breakaway Kingdom of Tungning. Unfortunately, he would die of malaria soon after, and his short-lived kingdom was subdued by the Qing in 1683. He is remembered in today's Xiamen by way of an immense granite statue looking out to sea (and Taiwan), greeting any ships entering the harbour.

Like Hong Kong, Amoy is an island city. It is located in China's Hokkien province, just south of the ancient port of Quanzhou. The word "Amoy" is actually an anglicisation of "Ay-mng", which is how "Xiamen" is pronounced in the Amoy variation of the Hokkien dialect spoken in these parts. The name, Xiamen (厦门), means "gateway to the mansion", which seems an apt moniker since the city would be home to many a palatial mansion in the course of its history.

Amoy Island is modest in size, some 150 square kilometres. Recalling Mombasa on the Swahili Coast, it sits in a crystalline bay and is almost entirely sheltered on three sides by the mainland. To the east of it is its sister island of Quemoy, or Jinmen in Mandarin, which though belonging to the same cultural sphere as its sibling, today forms part of Taiwan rather than Mainland China. Old Amoy, including the former foreign concession area as well as the historic Chinese commercial quarter, sits to the southwest of the island. Just off the old city is an islet known as Gulangyu, or Kulangsu in the Amoy dialect; its evocative name means something to the effect of "drum wave islet", referring to the drum-like timbre of the sound of waves when they hit the reefs.

Post-1842, trade in Chinese tea returned to Amoy, given the city's much closer proximity to the traditional tea-growing heartlands of the Hokkien province. Ever wary of depending too heavily on China for its tea, the British had already experimented with cultivating it in the highlands of India and Ceylon. Success meant that by the mid-1870s, Indian and Ceylonese tea began to be exported on a large-scale, resulting in a steep decline in the Amoy tea trade.

In the meantime, Amoy became the main port in China for the trade in "coolies": low-skilled, very poor Hokkien labourers shipped by agents to European colonies worldwide.[25] The abolition of slavery meant the need for cheap manpower, particularly in the Americas, and this new form of indentured hard labour emerged to fill the gap. Millions of coolies were transported to the Straits Settlement ports of Penang, Melaka and Singapore, to Batavia, Semarang and Surabaya, to San Francisco and Honolulu and even to far-flung Lima and Havana, where they were put to back-breaking work in silver and gold mines, and in the construction of roads, railways and buildings. It is no exaggeration to say that these cities were literally built on the backs of these nameless young men, many of whom laboured under excruciating and grim conditions.

The history of Amoy as a foreign settlement took off in 1903 when Kulangsu Islet was established as an International Settlement, the only other one aside from that in Shanghai. Kulangsu's status as a foreign concession was thus formalised, and it was run by a 13-country municipal council that oversaw infrastructural development on the islet, as well as security, cleanliness and hygiene. Less than two square kilometres in size, the islet housed consulates representing these 13 countries. Britain was naturally here first in 1843, and it was gradually joined by the Netherlands, France, Spain, Germany, Italy, Denmark, the United States of America, and Japan. As a matter of interest, the move to establish an International Settlement had been motivated by intimations of the Japanese wishing to take over the settlement entirely.

The high concentration of European cultures on this Chinese islet resulted in a singular cultural fusion, best reflected in the variety of architectural styles present on the island. Today's Gulangyu Islet is an outdoor museum of sorts, entirely pedestrianised and accessible from the main city of Xiamen by a very short ferry ride. It was designated a UNESCO World Heritage Site in 2017 and is one of the most popular tourist destinations for domestic tourists.

The island contains almost all of the city's Western-style architecture, in particular, the so-called Compradoric, or China Coast, style involving neoclassical adornment, colonial-style verandahs with high ceilings and long balustrades, and local red-brick architecture. The best examples of the style are the many former consulate buildings that still stand on the island and have been immaculately restored and repurposed as boutiques, cafes, restaurants and the like.

Other architectural styles are also present, in particular, Amoy deco, a fusion of art deco, China Coast and the traditional Minnan-style featuring curving roofs, stone and wood carvings, and Chinese decorative motifs. This style is exuberantly seen in the dozens of erstwhile residential mansions built here in the early 1900s by returning Overseas Chinese tycoons from the Nanyang. These mansions, too, have almost all been completely restored, with ample information available at most of these premises about the luminaries who once lived in them.

The Qing court's reversal, in 1893, of long-standing edicts banning emigration and forbidding Chinese immigrants from returning to China, encouraged a good number of wealthy *huaqiao*, particularly from Southeast Asia, to return to China and invest in the development of their homeland, albeit by way of the treaty ports they settled in. Many of these wealthy tycoons, referred to in the Straits Settlements port cities as *towkays* (头家) – meaning "big bosses", or literally "head of the family" – returned to settle, or at least, establish a second home in Amoy.

Having either grown up or been born in colonial Southeast Asia, they were hybrid and cosmopolitan in their cultural identity, absorbing the best of Chinese culture – such as a love for Chinese arts and deep respect for Confucian traditions – as well as European (or American) culture. Many were, in effect, British (or European or American) citizens, by virtue of their being born or resident in the colonies. They thus preferred to live with the foreigners on Kulangsu in part because they felt comfortable within this cosmopolitan milieu, but most importantly because the International Settlement guaranteed protection of their personal wealth and private property, while the Mainland Chinese regime did not.

With all these returning émigré millionaires building mansions so close to each other on the islet, Kulangsu was at one point in the 1920s literally the wealthiest place on earth, per square foot. It was also once referred to as Piano Island, because of an inordinate number of pianos on the islet, belonging to its many *towkays*, and speaking to a certain degree of gentility in this microcosm of a society. Former residents recall many an evening of being serenaded by the sound of pianos being played across the island, under the moonlight.

A few of these millionaire mansions are worth a special visit for their extraordinary architecture. The first of these is the magnificent Huang Rongyuan Villa on Fujian Road, built in 1920 as the private residence of a Filipino *towkay*, Shi Guangming, but later transferred to a returning Vietnamese *towkay*, Huang Zhongxun, who named the villa after his company. With its expansive front porch and its forest of classical columns, it resembles a Roman villa, except it is placed in the midst of a traditional Chinese-style landscaped garden with delightful ponds and ornamental rock formations. It is the Chinese equivalent of the Marble Palace in Calcutta.

On the very same road is the Sea and Heaven Villa, likewise built for a returning Filipino *towkay*, Huang Xiu Liang, in 1921. It is a classic example of the Amoy deco style, with its dramatically upward-curving Minnan-style Chinese roof, neoclassical façade adornments, large and airy China Coast-style verandahs framing the front and sides of the building, and a mix of red-brick and granite used in its core structure. Echoes of this form of architecture would travel to Singapore, Penang and Melaka, though nothing quite as striking and elaborate as this.

The single most important Overseas Chinese *towkay*, whose name is indelibly etched upon Xiamen, is Tan Kah Kee. Once regarded as the "Henry Ford of Malaya", no other Asian tycoon has made such a huge impact on contemporary East and Southeast Asian history. His legacy was truly global, as evidenced by the many places and buildings named after him in Singapore, China and even in California.[26]

Born in the village of Jimei in Greater Amoy in 1874, he moved to Singapore at the age of 16 to support his father's rice trading business. From thence, he built his own trading and business empire, dabbling in shipping, rice trading, canning (of food products), manufacturing, real estate, and in particular, rubber and rubber products. He became one of the wealthiest and most influential merchants and industrialists in British Malaya in the 1910s, and a respected figure in Singapore's business and social scene.

Tan's rise and success spoke of the tremendous opportunities available in colonial Southeast Asia at the time, and also a sea-change in Asian society: the emergence of a wealthy Chinese merchant class able to hold their own alongside the Europeans. Tan was the quintessential Nanyang Chinese *towkay*, existing in a fluid and dynamic space 'twixt East and West. A 1936 account by a British observer provides the most vivid description of this curious, culturally-hybrid figure, rendered all the more realistic by its being purportedly inspired by Tan Kah Kee:

> "...the towkay of today is a very different being from the courteous pig-tailed gentleman of two generations back. Externally, at least, he is Westernised from the soles of his brown shoes to his tie and collar, and in the evening he can wear his boiled shirt and dress-coat with the best European. More often than not he wears horn-rimmed glasses.
>
> [...] He runs banks and newspapers. He has the stock exchange quotations of the world's bourses at his fingertips. He is an authority of commodity prices. He owns rubber estates and tin mines. His factories turn out [all manner of products], and by the latest methods of modern salesmanship he contrives to export his goods to nearly every country in the world.
>
> Outside of business hours, he plays a considerable part in the social life of Singapore, owns houses, takes his wife to the races, and plays golf. [...] He is, too, a patriotic citizen and keen Rotarian, is grateful to the British raj which protects him, and gives valuable service both to the Government Legislative Council and to the various municipal boards to which he may be a member.
>
> Above all, he is a generous giver to local institutions, and like American millionaires, is fond of endowing hospitals, colleges and other educational institutions.
>
> He is expatriated, [...] But [...] it would be a mistake to imagine that he has forgotten his homeland. [...] Already some of his profits go to help his struggling country, and there is more than one university, including Amoy, in China that has been founded with Chinese money from Singapore."[27]

Motivated by staunch Confucian values stressing the importance of doing good in society, Tan began to give generously to various causes from the early 1900s. Though supportive of anti-imperialist and revolutionary movements in China throughout the early 20th century, he would focus his philanthropic efforts significantly on education, believing in education as the best avenue for uplifting society, as well as modernising China.

In Singapore, he was one of the founders of many Chinese-language schools, including the Tao Nan School, the first Chinese-language school

Statue of Tan Kah Kee, standing before Xiamen University's main administration block.

in Singapore, and the Nanyang Girls' School. He is best remembered, however, for being the main patron and founder of The Chinese High School, a Chinese-language secondary school for boys. Established in 1919, the school today occupies one of the largest campuses for any secondary school in Singapore, and is also highly regarded as one of the nation-state's foremost educational institutions.

Tan would travel regularly between Xiamen and Singapore in the 1910s for business and charitable work. In his hometown of Jimei in Greater Xiamen, he would fund kindergartens, elementary and secondary schools, and vocational institutes catering to all ages and a wide variety of subject areas. The crowning glory of his career as a philanthropist was his establishment of Xiamen University (formerly Amoy University) in 1921 – two years after The Chinese High School was established in Singapore. The university was the first modern tertiary institution in China, grounded in academic inquiry and research. Largely funded out of his own pocket, and also by way of funds raised from Nanyang Chinese philanthropists, the university would be nationalised and taken over by the Republican government in 1937.

Today, Xiamen University remains one of the foremost academic institutions in China, and also a major landmark in Xiamen. Located southeast of the former Xiamen foreign concession area, it is a must-visit for any tourist. A highlight of the visit is the architecture, which, alongside Amoy deco, emerged in the 1920s and '30s, and belongs to a larger domain of nationalist styles of architecture marrying Chinese traditional elements with a Western structural form. It is variously known as the Chinese Renaissance style, or the Kah Kee style, honouring the fact that many of the buildings Tan Kah Kee erected are classic examples of this vernacular.

A good place for a pause and ponder is right in front of the main administration block, a great example of the Kah Kee style. Here, in front of the structure, is a bronze statue of the great man himself, impeccably dressed in a western-style three-piece suit, holding a hat in one hand and a walking cane in another. A companion to this statue stands, thousands of miles away, in front of The Chinese High School's Clocktower Building in Singapore. There, Tan is depicted looking visibly older and without a hat, but holding his walking cane and sporting a pair of horn-rimmed glasses. His left foot is placed just slightly forward and he looks resolutely ahead, in the spirit of his oft-repeated mantras on the importance of progress through education.

28. Yokohama & Kobe
Black Ships, Boom Towns and the End of Japan's Seclusion

"The scenery visible from [the Bluff] is as follows: one looks down on all the foreign residences; from there, the Customs House and officials' residences, then to Hon-cho, Benten dori, Ota-cho, all as though they could fit in the palm of one's hand. Ahead, one can see everything from the residences of the officials in Tobe, and the rooms of the inns at the Kanagawa post station, to the girls in the rooms of the Daimachi tea house. [...] At sea, ships of the five nations enter [the harbour]. As everything within two *ri* in all directions is in one's purview, this is surely the number one scenic spot in the area."

— Nansoan Shohaku, 1862.
Curiosities of the Five Nations: Yokohama Tales.[28]

Yokohama-e, or "Yokohama pictures", refer to Japanese-style woodblock prints in the late Edo period, depicting the fledgling treaty port and its denizens in their full and foreign glory. This sub-genre of the more general *ukiyo-e* only existed for a brief period of time, between 1859 to the early 1870s. It was an expression of Japanese curiosity and fascination with the West. After the Meiji Emperor's restoration in 1868 and Japan's headlong dive into industrialisation and Westernisation, Yokohama pictures, with their depictions of foreigners in strange dress, were no longer quite so exotic since the Japanese themselves began to dress in a similar fashion.

Yokohama prints themselves were extremely popular, with more than 500 different designs created, and some 250,000 prints produced over a short period of time. Their subjects were wide-ranging, from bird's-eye-view panoramas of port and foreign concession, to portraits of foreign residents from China and the Five Nations (the United States, Britain, France, the Netherlands and Russia), to general views of the city's various bustling streets and esplanades.[29]

A great master of this genre was Utagawa Sadahide, who produced some of the most complex and compelling pictures of the city of Yokohama; these provide a window into life in treaty-port Japan in its initial decade. One of his masterpieces is the *Picture of Western Traders at Yokohama Transporting Merchandise*, produced in 1861 as a panorama requiring five sheets of paper to capture in full. The harbour is a burst of activity – great black ships of all kinds can be seen. The flags of the

Five Nations flap above their respective vessels. In the foreground, to the left, an American ship looms. Its multi-ethnic crew busily loads chests of valuable cargo, brought to the ship on smaller boats. In the foreground, to the right, is a Russian ship, its port windows providing a glimpse into the luxuriously-appointed interiors. In the background are an English ship and a Dutch ship, one a traditional East Indiaman, the other a more recent invention: a steamship. The port of Yokohama had only been open two years; but already it was a picture of growth and great possibility.

On 8 July 1853, Commodore Matthew Perry sailed four black ships into Edo Bay, dropping anchor just off the village of Uraga, not far from the city of Edo itself. The Americans, in the wake of Britain's success at forcing China open to trade, decided they had to take on Japan, the final frontier. Just five years ago, Mexico had ceded California to the United States of America in the aftermath of the Mexican-American War. San Francisco was thrown open to trade not long after and became America's most important port city on the Pacific Coast. With San Francisco open, East Asia was now immensely closer, and Japan beckoned.

Commodore Perry's *kurofune* (黒船 – "black ships") had not come as a surprise to the Japanese. The Dutch at Nagasaki had alerted the *bakufu* of these foreign warships' incursion into Japanese waters. The Japanese, however, looked on in helplessness and shock, unprepared for what was to come.

Perry and his crew came ashore at the fishing village of Yokohama to deliver a letter to the *bakufu*, demanding that Japan open up to trade with America. In a classic case of gunboat diplomacy, he threatened to return later for his positive answer – with more warships and guns. Return he did in March 1854, with a much larger crew and fleet of ships, bristling with cannons. Some of these ships were steamships, the most advanced type of vessel the Japanese had seen. The *bakufu* was forced to relent and on March 31, they signed the Treaty of Kanagawa, in the shadow of an ancient Japanese bay tree (*tabunoki*) in the modest fishing village of Yokohama. The treaty called for two ports – Shimoda and Hakodate – to be opened to trade, and for a resident American consul in Japan.

After 200 years of self-enforced seclusion, this was earth-shattering for the Japanese, though not quite enough for the Americans. Four years later, the first US consul, Townsend Harris, wrangled another treaty, called the Treaty of Amity and Commerce, which forced four more ports open to foreign trade: Nagasaki, Kanagawa, Hyogo and Niigata. The treaty also provided for extra-territoriality and freedom of religion for foreign residents. As in China, the American treaty was swiftly followed by other unequal treaties with the Western powers, chiefly Britain, France, Russia, and the Netherlands (who were loath to give up their advantage at Dejima). The Gokakoku ("Five Nations") would have a major presence in Japanese treaty ports.

Yokohama wasn't initially one of the ports opened for trade. The *bakufu* unilaterally substituted it in place of Kanagawa, given that the latter was a post town situated directly on the Tokaido, or eastern highway that connected Edo to the imperial capital of Kyoto. The Tokaido was frequently used by local *daimyo* and samurai, and the *bakufu* feared that situating the foreigners so close to local warlords would result in violent clashes of culture and arms.

A brand new planned city, with an orderly grid, granite piers and solid houses, was swiftly built in a few months on reclaimed swampland at the village of Yokohama in 1859. The foreign consuls objected to this deviation from treaty terms, but the merchant community accepted these new accommodations readily, pointing out that Yokohama's deep, natural harbour was far better than Kanagawa's. And so the treaty port of Yokohama (横浜) – meaning "broad beach" – came to be.

By 1864, the foreign population had outgrown the original town of Yokohama, and so the *bakufu* gave permission for Europeans and Americans to build their residences on the nearby hills. This premier location became known as the Bluff, and was the equivalent to Hong Kong's Peak, being a much cooler and more salubrious location than the waterfront. As with treaty ports in China, the waterfront of Yokohama was developed as a bund, with the offices of merchant houses, banking corporations and other commercial establishments occupying prominent locations on the esplanade. Chief of all were the premises of Jardine, Matheson & Co.

Meanwhile, with trade came a huge influx of Chinese compradors from the Chinese treaty ports; these middlemen who had played a critical role in facilitating commerce and contact between Chinese and

The Former British Consulate (1931 – 1972), Yokohama, was built on the site where the Treaty of Kanagawa between Japan and the USA was signed.

Westerners. Japanese being, in large part, still written in Chinese characters (or *kanji*), these enterprising gentlemen found themselves at an advantage and of use to the Westerners here, who could neither read nor write the language. Yokohama's Chinese population thus swelled, and the city also became home to a large Chinatown, only the second Chinatown in Japan after that in Nagasaki.

The Great Kanto Earthquake of 1923 destroyed almost everything that stood from Yokohama's treaty port era. All the historic architecture in its old downtown and erstwhile foreign settlement was flattened. Everything that remains today dates from the late 1920s. That notwithstanding, the spirit of the foreign settlement still remains in the city, evident in the numerous examples of historic Western-style architecture.

A walking tour of historic Yokohama today needs to begin at the Yokohama Archives of History, the former British Consulate built in the 1930s. The building would be just another neoclassical European-style building in Japan, if not for the fact that the towering *tabunoki* that stands in its courtyard marks the spot where the Treaty of Kanagawa was signed between Commodore Perry and officials of the *bakufu* in 1854. In fact, this tree is a direct descendent of the very tree under which the treaty was signed. The original burnt down in the Great Kanto earthquake, but a sapling survived and was replanted at the same spot.

Ten-minutes on foot from the Archives lies Yokohama's Chinatown, the largest Chinatown in Japan today. Stop here for a visit to the city's Kanteibyo, or Temple to Guandi, the ruddy-faced god of war and wealth. A temple to the deity is said to have stood here since 1862, though the present temple is its fourth incarnation. The crowds in the temple attest to it being the spiritual heart of the local Chinese community; these days, it is thronged by more Chinese tourists than locals.

Another ten-minute walk from the temple takes us to Yamate, formerly known as the Bluff. Historical first-hand accounts of this precinct note how it resembled an American town, with low-rise, wooden homesteads channelling the New England coast. Unfortunately, no buildings from the treaty port era still stand. The remaining *yokan* ("Western residences") either date from the mid-1920s or were transplanted here from elsewhere. Those that do belong here, such as the Ehrismann Residence (1926) or Berrick Hall (1930) were designed in a consciously American rather than British style. The former was the work of an assistant to American designer, Frank Lloyd Wright, who travelled to Japan frequently in the early 1900s; the latter boasts a Spanish Colonial Revival-style architecture popular in California in the 1910s and '20s.

The Yokohama General Foreign Cemetery is the only part of the Bluff that survived the earthquake. It is a good place for a wander, since many of its permanent residents played prominent roles in the city's history. A case in point is Briton, Charles Lenox Richardson, slain on 14 September 1862 by a *daimyo* of the Satsuma clan, with whom Richardson had the misfortune to cross paths on the Tokaido. One thing led to another, and British forces eventually retaliated by levelling Kagoshima city, the ancestral seat of the Satsumas. Ironically, the Satsumas, impressed by Western arms technology, would later ally themselves with the British and turn against the Tokugawa Shogun, whom they blamed for haplessly allowing foreigners into Japan in the first place. The Satsumas would play a pivotal role in toppling the Tokugawa Shogunate in 1867 and calling for the restoration of the Meiji Emperor at Kyoto.

Yokohama's opening was followed nine years later by that of Kobe, in 1868. Like Yokohama, Kobe was a new build entirely. Hyogo, the original port stipulated in the treaty, had been a much older, highly-established Japanese port, close to Kyoto and Osaka, the commercial capital of Tokugawa Japan. Again wishing to avoid contact and conflict between local and foreign, the *bakufu* called for the construction of a new port and settlement immediately east of Hyogo, calling it Kobe (神戸), or "Gate of the Gods".

The city was planned and built in Yokohama's image, with many of the same trappings. Along the waterfront was a Kobe Bund; foreigners were allowed to reside in the nearby Kitano hills; and the Chinese too came in droves to the city, such that Kobe soon also became home to a significant Chinatown and resident Chinese population. Kobe's growth was swift, and it would be a serious rival to Yokohama throughout the two cities' history.

First-hand accounts of Old Kobe include that of intrepid English lady wanderer, Isabella Bird, who visited here in 1878, ten years after the treaty port was open. In her travelogue, *Unbeaten Tracks in Japan*, she notes how the city also appeared to be modelled after those on the English and New England coasts:

> "The Foreign Concession, beautifully and regularly laid out on a grand scale
> for the population which [it] has never attracted, is at the east end. It is a
> "model settlement," well lighted with gas, and supplied with water, kept

methodically clean, and efficiently cared for by the police. The Bund has a stone embankment, a grass parade, and a magnificent carriage-road, with the British, American and German Consulates, and some 'imposing' foreign residences on the other side. [...] The foreign houses are spacious and solid, and the railroad, and the station and its environments, are of the most approved English construction. [...]

A number of foreign wooden houses straggle up the foot-hills at the back, some of them unmistakeable English bungalows, while those which look like Massachusetts homesteads are occupied by American missionaries. In spite of the solitude and stagnation of the streets of the settlement, Kobe is a pertinaciously cheerful-looking place." [30]

A far cry from the exotic Japan she was expecting to encounter, the transplanted landscapes in Yokohama and Kobe struck Bird as tedious and not worth her attention; merely pale copies of the real thing in far-off Europe and America.

It is thus surprising to find so much of this historic architecture lovingly preserved in the city today. The Great Kanto Earthquake did not impact Kobe like it did Yokohama, and so many of the city's historic buildings still stand. Unlike Yamate with its dozen or so Western residences, Kobe's Kitano-cho still boasts some thirty-odd *ijinkan* ("foreigners' residences"), all of which were built in situ, and many of which have startlingly original architecture that dates to the first decade of the 1900s, just after treaty ports were abolished (though the foreigners were permitted to stay on).

The most famous of these *ijinkan* is the Weathercock House, built for a German merchant, and perched on a prominent spot in the hills with an outstanding view of Kobe city. Its Saxon-style architecture, complete with turret and weathervane, adds a generous dose of Alpine charm to Kitano-cho. Not far from here is the Uroko House, or House of Scales, unique for its twin turrets and for being covered in a proliferation of slate tiles that resemble fish scales. It was built for yet another German resident of the city, and also houses a lovely museum today.

Elsewhere on the hills, there are at least a dozen other residences open to the public, though many have been turned over to cafés, boutiques and (oftentimes kitsch) museums, resulting in an atmosphere that is more Disneyland than dutifully authentic; but this appears to appeal to local tourists, who come in droves to take photos of themselves against the exotic backdrops.

The only actual merchant house dating to the treaty port period and still standing in the city is the matter-of-factly named Kobe Foreign

Settlement Building No. 15. Built in 1880, and once housing the US Consulate, it stands near Kaigan-dori ("Beach Road"), which was and still is the main thoroughfare in downtown Kobe. The two-storeyed building, with neoclassical elements such as pediments and columns, and large verandahs on both floors, is a classic example of the Compradoric-style structures seen earlier in Amoy, and imported to Japan's treaty ports.

The building houses a fine-dining restaurant today and is well worth a visit for a taste, however fleeting, of life in a time of treaties and empire. The fact that the oldest remaining Western-style building in the city once housed the US Consulate speaks to the long legacy of American intervention in Japan in the course of the 19th and 20th centuries.

PART

V

OF STEAMSHIPS
AND
MODERNITY

Late 19th — Mid-20th Centuries

29. Colombo
East of Suez to Galle Face Green

"At the extreme southern end of the Galle Face Esplanade and in close proximity to the sea stands the luxurious Galle Face Hotel. In many respects this fine hostelry is unequalled in the East. It enjoys the advantage of a site as perfect as could be found, bearing in mind the great desideratum of sea breeze. Its hall, verandahs, dining-room, ballroom, drawing-room, billiard-rooms and reading-rooms are palatial, while the supreme attraction to many is an excellent and spacious sea-water swimming-bath. Whether we are staying at this hotel or not we ought at least to explore it and make our way by means of the electric lift to the top floor in order to enjoy the fine panoramic view from the front windows."

— Henry W. Cave, 1908. *The Book of Ceylon: Being a Guide to its Railway System and an Account of its Varied Attractions for the Visitor and Tourist.*[1]

The Suez Canal Company, or Compagnie universelle du canal maritime de Suez, was originally a Franco-Egyptian corporation. The idea to build the canal had come from French diplomat, Ferdinand de Lesseps, who secured a concession to undertake the project from Sa'id Pasha, the Ottoman viceroy of Egypt. Lesseps also persuaded the latter to take on the herculean task of securing funding for the project, a task met largely by way of appealing to French and other European creditors.

Construction began in 1859 and took ten years, the canal opening to great fanfare in November 1869. The *pasha* hosted an extravagant international soirée graced by French Empress Eugénie, alongside other members of European and Middle Eastern royalty. Unfortunately, not long after the opening, Sa'id's successor, Ismail Pasha, found himself saddled with crippling debt on account of his uncle's massive borrowing towards the canal project. He was forced to sell Egypt's substantial shares to Great Britain, such that the canal became an Anglo-French company. Egypt would thus, in a tragic stroke of irony, find itself cut off completely from this canal that sliced through its sovereign territory, deriving no financial benefit from its phenomenal commercial success.

The opening of the Suez Canal changed the face of maritime trade and travel. For starters, there was now a shortcut between Europe and India. Where once a traveller had to round the Cape of Good Hope and circumnavigate all of Africa to reach the Indian Ocean, the new

OVERLEAF: Historic postcard depicting *P. & O.S.S. "Syria"* at *Port Said*, by W. L. Willie, probably 1870s.

OPPOSITE PAGE: Covered walkway at the entrance to the Galle Face Hotel.

canal cut a path from the Mediterranean right through to the Red Sea. A 20,000-kilometre journey between London and Bombay was now reduced to some 11,000 kilometres. A journey by ship from London to Colombo could be undertaken in just twenty-one days; faster, if one travelled by train to Marseille and boarded a ship from thence. Suddenly, long-distance travel was no longer quite such a huge undertaking.[2]

At the same time, the advent of steam engine technology meant the emergence of passenger steamliners that were so large and well-equipped that sailing itself became a predictable and comfortable affair. Where sailing vessels once depended on monsoon winds and fair weather to travel, these steam-powered behemoths could travel in any season; their steel hulls were built to withstand rough weather. They were particularly good for sailing up and down the rough waters of the Red Sea, any time of the year.

These advances in long-distance travel technology gave European powers superiority over the East and facilitated the expansion and consolidation of colonial empires. In the aftermath of the Suez Canal and the steamship, the furthermost reaches of Africa and East Asia were no longer out of reach for Europeans and Americans. Africa was swiftly swallowed up and parcelled out between the European powers. Japan was forced open to foreign trade by the United States. China was brought to its knees by a humiliating scramble, at gunpoint, for foreign concessions.

Alongside the spread of imperialism came mass long-distance leisure travel. Commerce and colonialism bred a new generation of affluent middle-classes in the West, who took keen advantage of the advances in long-distance travel, their new-found wealth, and their access to previously-foreign-but-now-colonial territory to take to the high seas with abandon. In the course of the late 19th century, shipping companies such as the British Peninsular & Oriental Steam Navigation Company (better known as P & O), the French Méssageries Maritimes, and the Dutch Koninklijke Paketvaart-Maatschappij (or KPM) competed with each other to offer the best service, experience and value-for-money on board their cruise liners, which became extremely luxurious indeed, akin to five-star hotels on the water. Round-the-world tours offered by tour agencies, most notably the legendary Thomas Cook & Sons, appeared as early as the 1910s, seducing would-be tourists with exotic, orientalist descriptions of a "mysterious East".

A brand-new term – "east of Suez" – was coined to refer to these exotic lands east of the Suez Canal, which had opened up to Western tourism (and colonisation). The phrase itself had first been used by Rudyard Kipling – that doyen of all things Indian and imperialistic – in his poem, "Mandalay".

Wherever east of Suez steamships and cruise-liners docked, tourists would disembark to be accommodated at legendary grand hotels. These were European-style luxury hotels offering the most modern amenities to the discerning tourist, and reproducing the glamorous, cosmopolitan lifestyles to be had in the imperial metropolitan centres of London, Paris and New York. Within these grand hotels, European and American tourists could enjoy familiar experiences like afternoon tea and French cuisine, smoking rooms and high society balls, and impeccable Swiss or German-style hospitality. The hotels were a high-end home away from home, affording tourists the fantasy of being able to live like kings and queens, for a time and for a fee.

The most famous of these hotels were very famous indeed in their time and continue to be household names today: the Raffles Hotel in Singapore, the Oriental Hotel (today's Mandarin Oriental) in Bangkok, the Manila Hotel in Manila, the Hotel Continental in Saigon, the Hotel Des Indes in Batavia, the Peninsula in Hong Kong, the Cathay Hotel (now the Fairmont Peace Hotel) in Shanghai, the Imperial Hotel in Tokyo, the Taj Mahal Palace in Bombay, the Great Eastern Hotel in Calcutta... The list goes on. These hotels were the centre of glamorous, albeit colonial, society. They were also often crucibles for new and innovative technologies. For example, many of them were often the first establishments in their home city to boast electric lighting and Otis elevators.

Galle Face Hotel, Colombo.

Early 20th century postcard of the Galle Face Hotel.

One of the most illustrious and possibly the oldest of these grand hotels was the Galle Face Hotel in the port city of Colombo (කොළඹ), on the island of Ceylon. The hotel is situated at an epic waterfront location on the southernmost edge of Galle Face Green, a vast, 12-acre green expanse that serves as public park and esplanade. It is widely regarded as one of the most ravishing and evocative grand hotels anywhere east of Suez. And it is still in operation today.

Galle Face Hotel was established in 1864, five years before the opening of the Suez Canal. Initially, it occupied Galle Face House, a colonial bungalow belonging to a former Dutch resident of Colombo. Major competition in the city and the boom in tourism post-Suez saw the hotel undergoing a massive reconstruction and expansion exercise in 1894. Subsequent additional renovations in the course of the 20th century transformed it into the sprawling, four-storey, neoclassical palace it is today. Designed by Englishman Edward Skinner, the hotel adhered to the Anglo-Indian colonial idiom, with a large *porte cochère* at its entrance, colonnaded verandahs and walkways, and high-pitched roofs adapted to the tropical monsoons. Boasting 180 rooms, the hotel was enormous for its time; and even then, like the other hotels in the city, it was so fully subscribed that the corridors could sometimes be seen dotted with hastily put-up beds.

In the post-Suez world of steamships and modernity, Colombo thrived as a major port of call. It was a critical coaling station for steamships traversing the Indian Ocean, and with its scenic vistas and beautiful cityscape, it was also a convenient and popular stopover for tourists. American diplomat Frederic Courtland Penfield's 1907 travelogue, *East of Suez: Ceylon, India, China and Japan*, notes, albeit with colonial overtones, that:

> "No part of England's great realm [...] is more beautiful than the crown colony of Ceylon in the Indian Ocean. An Eastbound traveller during the long run from Aden hears much of the incomparable island of palms, pearls, and elephants; and every waggish shipmate haunts smoke room and ladies' saloon waiting for the opportunity to point out the lighthouse on Minecoy Island in the Maldives as "the Light of Asia." Four hundred miles further and your good ship approaches Colombo. The great breakwater [...] is penetrated at last, and the polyglot and universal harbour of call unfolds like a fan." [3]

Sri Lanka had long been known by sailors and seafarers. The ancient Greeks called the island Taprobane, the Arabs and Persians, Sarandib, purportedly derived from its Sanskrit name, Simhaladvipa, or "Island where the Lions Dwell". In the colonial period, the island was referred to as Ceylon, from the Portuguese Ceilão. Since the earliest days, Sri Lanka had been fought over by a succession of kingdoms and empires both local and foreign. In the course of the first millennium, the island would be ruled mainly by Buddhist kingdoms, culminating in just under a century of occupation by the mighty Chola Empire in the 11th century. Various polities held sway between the 12th to the 18th centuries, with the Kotte and Kandy kingdoms being perhaps the most significant.

The Portuguese would arrive in the 16th century, requesting to trade in cinnamon (*Cinnamomum verum* - once Sri Lanka's most important export), and establishing a fortified settlement in Colombo, where there was already a resident community of Arab merchants. They were supplanted by the Dutch VOC in the 17th century and the English EIC in turn in the 18th century, with Ceylon gaining independence in 1948 and changing its name officially to Sri Lanka in 1972.

All this history means Colombo, the island's capital city and main port, is a literal palimpsest; it resembles an ancient manuscript, on which successive authors have etched their own writing in a different script and language, without fully erasing any of the text earlier inscribed. All of Colombo's layers of history are still present in the city itself, making for a rich and surprising journey of discovery for any heritage buff.

A grand heritage tour of the city best begins in the downtown districts of Pettah and Fort, where the Dutch and British legacies remain palpably etched into the urban landscape. "Pettah" is derived from the Sinhalese *pita-kotuwa*, which means "outside the fort". This exactly describes what Pettah was and still is today. In the Dutch era, this area was known as the *oude stad* ("Old Town"), and was a residential suburb where Dutch colonials had their villas and residences, erected along a tidy grid of verdant, tree-lined streets. When the British took over, much of the "Dutch-ness" of Pettah was gradually lost, and the district became a multicultural melting pot of communities and religions; as well as the location of the city's main bazaar.

All that remains of the Dutch in Pettah are two important buildings. The first is the former residence of Dutch governor, Thomas van Rhee, on Prince Street (formerly Prinsestraat). It was built in the late 17th century and features Dutch East Indies-style architecture with an internal courtyard, high ceilings and colonnaded verandahs. Formerly used as a post office, it was the first building in Colombo to be

Wolvendaal Church, Pettah, with its distinctive cruciform plan and bright red roofs.

officially conserved and restored; and it houses a museum today. The other important Dutch-period building in Pettah is the Wolvendaal Church, also known as the Dutch Reformed Church. It was built in 1757 and was the primary place of worship for the Protestant Dutch. On its grounds and inside the church building lie the graves of many erstwhile Dutch residents of Colombo.

Fort, as the name suggests, was where the Portuguese first established their fortified settlement. It has been the centre of government administration since the Portuguese occupation of the city in the 16th century and is one of the oldest built-up areas in downtown Colombo. Once, there were actually walls that surrounded the district. Parts of these walls were destroyed and others reinforced by the Dutch; most of them were demolished by the British in the late 19th century, in order for the city to expand.

Today, much of Fort consists of monumental civic and commercial buildings erected in the late 19th and early 20th centuries during the British period, with some of the most spectacular landmarks found along and not far from York Street. Here we find the Grand Oriental Hotel, erstwhile competitor to the Galle Face Hotel, and still doing a brisk business today. Afternoon tea on its terrace is absolutely recommended for the spectacular view of the Colombo Port. Not far from the GOH (as it is colloquially referred to) is the iconic, Edwardian, red-brick confection that is Cargill's, a departmental store built in 1906 by Walker, Sons & Co and still a household name for Sri Lankans today. Elsewhere, one major exception to the British heritage is the Old Dutch Hospital, built in the 17th century. It has been lovingly restored into a posh lifestyle precinct.

British Colombo extends into Cinnamon Gardens, a pleasantly laid-back and walkable district built on land that belonged to VOC-era cinnamon plantations. The venerable Colombo National Museum stands here, at the edge of the former Victoria Park, known today as Viharamahadevi Park.

The museum is an excellent place to contemplate Colombo's precolonial history, with three objects in particular warranting attention. The first is a splendid Chola-period Shiva Nataraja, or Shiva as Lord of the Dance. We last encountered him in the ancient temple city of Thanjavur; and here he is, in his untrammelled splendour, the entire cosmos framing his wildly-flailing hair, his feet trampling the dwarf Apasmara, representing ignorance.

Elsewhere in the museum stands a Chinese-style stone tablet with an inscription in Chinese, Tamil and Persian, and dated to 15 February 1409. This was the very tablet commissioned by the eunuch-admiral Zheng He and dedicated to a Buddhist temple in Galle. The tablet attests to the presence of Chinese, Middle Eastern and South Indian traders and resident communities in Sri Lanka long before Europeans came. Rediscovered in Galle in 1911, it was brought to the museum, where it continues to be displayed.

A further stroll through the museum brings us to the magnificent royal throne of the kings of Kandy, the last of Sri Lanka's local Sinhalese kingdoms. The throne is elaborately carved and dripping with gold. It was actually a gift from the Dutch governor to the king in the late 17th century. As such, its style is eclectic, marrying Sri Lankan as well as European elements. The back of the chair depicts the sun, radiant, resplendent and flanked by two divine beings in Buddhist tradition seated in *padmasana,* or the lotus position. The arms of the chair are carved in the form of roaring lions, a symbol of royalty as well as a reference to Sri Lanka's ancient Sanskrit name.

Emerging from the museum after a full day of time-travel, the history buff would be well-placed to stop in at one of Colombo's most under-visited yet most intriguing historic sites: the tiny Dutch Burgher Union building, dating to 1913 and located at the southwestern edge of Cinnamon Gardens. Here, one may learn more about the history of the Dutch Burghers, or Dutch Eurasians – one in a rich diversity of creole cultures in Asia; cousins to the Macanese, the Goans and the Kristang. The Burghers have been here for a long time, at least since the 17th century; and they have retained a surprisingly strong sense of identity, particularly in relation to their unique material culture and cuisine.

The highlight of a visit to the DBU (as it's affectionately called) is a meal of authentic *lamprais* at its modest little café. *Lamprais* is a quintessentially Sri Lankan dish with Dutch, Malay and Ceylonese influences. The name is the English approximation of the Dutch *lomprijst*, which literally means "a lump of rice". Don't be fooled by the ·humble appearance of this most complex dish: comprising rice accompanied by side dishes including a meat curry, an eggplant *moju* (spicy and tart pickle), *frikkadels* (deep-fried Dutch-style minced-beef meatballs), *pol sambola* (spicy grated coconut) and more, all wrapped up and baked in a banana leaf. Every morsel of it is steeped in the history of the Indian Ocean, and Colombo's central role as a crossroads of cultures and civilisations.

30. Muscat & Zanzibar
Stone Town, Slavery and the Sultans of Oman

"Bet il Mtoni, distant about five miles from the city of Zanzibar, lies on the sea coast, surrounded by most beautiful scenery, and quite hidden in a grove of palm and mango trees, and other gigantic specimens of tropical vegetation. The house of my birth is called "Mtoni house" after the little river Mtoni, which rises only a few miles inland, runs through the whole palace into numerous fountains, and flows directly behind the palace into the splendid and animated inlet which severs the island from the African continent."

— Emily Ruete, *née* Sayyida Salama bint Said,
Princess of Oman and Zanzibar, 1886.
Memoirs of an Arabian Princess: An Autobiography.[4]

In 1650, the Omanis wrested control of Muscat (مسقط) from the Portuguese, in an extraordinary case of an Asian naval power triumphing over a European one. This defeat marked the beginning of the end for the Estado da Índia in the Western Indian Ocean.[5] By the turn of the 18th century, the Omanis would succeed in ousting the Portuguese from Mombasa and imposing colonial rule over much of the Swahili Coast north to Somalia, south to Mozambique, and including the great port cities of Kilwa and Malindi.

At its height, the Omani Empire was vast, including continuous swathes of territory around the Persian Gulf, the entire Swahili Coast, and the waters in between. The political capital of the empire was at Muscat, strategically located at the southeastern tip of the Arabian Peninsula and standing sentinel over the entrance to the Gulf. During this time, the legendary Omani dhows – warships and trading vessels alike, built in all shapes and sizes – plied the ancient routes joining the Indian Ocean, the Red Sea and the Gulf. They brought their goods, peoples and cultures from across the world to Muscat and also increasingly to Zanzibar (زنجبار), which grew to become the empire's economic capital.

Geographically, Zanzibar is an archipelago situated off the coast of today's Tanzania. It consists of two main islands, Pemba to the north and Unguja (commonly known as Zanzibar) to the south. The capital of the archipelago is at Zanzibar City; and historic Stone Town is its oldest and most evocative district. Stone Town is situated on a triangular peninsula to the west of Unguja Island, just 40 kilometres off the African mainland, and it enjoys a sheltered, natural harbour perfect for anchoring vessels.

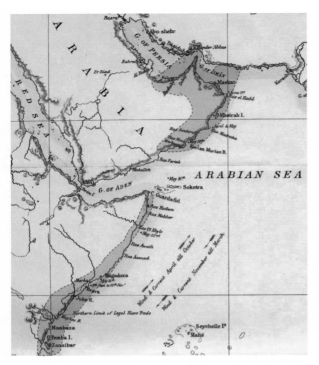

ARABIA

G. OF PERSIA

Abu-shehr

Bander Abbas

Bahrein

Er-Riad

Al Bidia

G. OF OMAN

Maskat

Karachi

G. o

Sur

June I⁴

Ras el Hadd

Masirah I.

Ras Sankira

Jird & Maj

Ras Moraba

RED SEA

Ras Nous

Maj 15th Nov⁴

Kurian Murian B.

Ras Fartak

Mukalleh

ARABIAN SEA

Maj 15th

Sokotra

Aden

G. OF ADEN

C. Guardafui

Ras Hadoon

Ras Mabber

Ras Ul Khyle

Maj 22nd

Ras Awath

Ras Asunad

Wind & Current April till Octobr

Wind & Current November till March

Magdoxa

Maj 15th

Nov⁴

Marka

Ava

Juba R.

Northern Limit of Legal Slave Trade

Seychelle Iˢ

Mahé

Mombaza

Pemba I.

Zanzibar

The Omani Empire at its peak, in the mid 19th century.

For at least a millennium, Zanzibar had played the part of an entrepôt, where treasures from across the Indian Ocean, and from as far away as China, had been brought to be traded for gold, ivory, animal skins, slaves and other goods from the African interior. Here too, the ancient cultures of the Indian Ocean and the African heartland collided and melded with each other, giving rise to the Swahili peoples.

By the turn of the 19th century, Zanzibar had eclipsed Muscat to become the largest and most bustling city in the empire, a great emporium and cosmopolitan gateway to the African continent. In a dramatic turn of events, Seyyid Said bin Sultan of the ruling al-Busaid (or Busaidi) clan moved the empire's political capital from Muscat to Stone Town in 1840.[6] The intent was to allow for better administration of his East African holdings, and to afford greater proximity to the true centre of trade. This convergence of the political and economic at Zanzibar would prove instrumental to the city's growth and prominence.

Seyyid Said wasted no time in inviting *baniyas* and other merchants to settle in the city, to supply much-needed credit and insurance services, and to secure trade networks with Bombay and other port cities of the Malabar Coast. He offered European merchant houses concessions to establish factories on the main island, and signed a series of treaties with the West by the 1830s. The sultan himself engaged in trade and diplomacy, investing in trading ships and dispatching embassies to far-flung London, Marseille and New York. Remarkably, his 1840 embassy to the United States of America was the first-ever from an Arab nation.

It was during Seyyid Said's time that Zanzibar secured its spot in the European popular imagination as an exotic and prodigiously wealthy port settlement in the East, a jewel of a city ruled by a powerful and enigmatic Oriental potentate, the sparkling, balmy waves of the Indian Ocean lapping on its pristine white beaches – in other words, an island paradise.

Zanzibar's wealth in the 19th century was built upon cloves and slaves.[7] Earlier in the 17th century, the Dutch had succeeded in transplanting cloves from elsewhere in the Moluccas to Ambon, refashioning the latter into a vast plantation island. The late 18th century saw French colonists smuggling clove seedlings to the islands of Mauritius and Réunion in the Indian Ocean, and introducing similar plantation economies there. It wasn't long before clove cultivation also spread to Zanzibar.

The climate in Zanzibar proved remarkably suitable for cloves. Ever the shrewd entrepreneur, Seyyid Said promoted cultivation of the spice on a grand scale, enticing new colonists from Oman with offers of land for cultivation. In the course of the early 19th century, large tracts of land were acquired from local Shirazi families, sometimes by force, and cleared for cultivation.[8] Zanzibar was transformed into a vast plantation island like Ambon, with the sultan and his associates as its largest landholders. By the mid-19th century, Zanzibar had become the world's leading exporter of the spice.

Clove cultivation was highly labour-intensive and depended heavily on African slave labour; the locals would not be persuaded to undertake the backbreaking work. Enormous numbers of African slaves were imported from the mainland, and employed in the harvesting and care of the precious crop. While the average plantation employed a few dozen slaves at most, some of the larger ones were known to harbour thousands of slaves.

The resounding success of the clove-based plantation economy precipitated a boom in the local slave trade. Swashbuckling English explorer, Sir Richard Francis Burton, in his 1872 travelogue, *Zanzibar: City, Island and Coast*, remarked on how extensive and horrifying this trade was.

> "The slaves on Zanzibar Island are roundly estimated at two-thirds of the population; some travellers increase the number to three-fourths. The annual loss of males by death, export, and desertion, amounted, I was told, to 30 per cent, thus within every fourth year the whole gang upon a plantation required to be renewed. The actual supply necessary for the Island is now estimated at a total varying from 1700 to 6000, and leaving 12,000 to 16,000 for the export slave market. As usual in Moslem lands, they may be divided into two distinct classes: first, the Muwallid or Mutawallid, the Mazaliya of the Waswahili, the famulus or slave born in the family, or rather on the Island; secondly, the captive or imported chattel."[9]

For the record, the slave population on the island was estimated at 200,000 to a total island population of 300,000 by the end of the 1850s, making for an island society that was overwhelmingly and appallingly constituted of indentured labour.[10] For some, Zanzibar was an island paradise; for most of its residents, it certainly wasn't.

Slavery in the *dar al-Islam* had deep roots. For centuries, African slaves had been traded along caravan routes, or shipped by Arab and Persian dhows to the various empires of the Middle East – we have already encountered them in the port city of Basra. The Arabs referred to these slaves as *Zanj*, and thus the Swahili Coast came to be known to the Arabs as *Zanj-Bar* (meaning "lands of the black peoples"), from whence the name, Zanzibar.

The Indian Ocean slave trade reached its peak in the mid-19th century, with Zanzibar as its largest and most notorious slave market. The demand for slaves was such that Arab and Zanzibari slaver settlements were established not only along the Swahili Coast, but also deep in the African heartlands. Colonies of these slave traders sprung up around Lake Tanganyika, Lake Malawi and Lake Victoria, and even along the Congo River. Unsuspecting young men and women would be kidnapped, shackled and transported by caravan across the harsh African terrain to Zanzibar, where they would be corralled into underground pens, whipped, starved and tortured, and sold like chattel at the city's great slave markets.

A good proportion of male slaves brought to Zanzibar were either deployed domestically in its vast clove plantations or shipped south to French Mauritius and Réunion; others were sent to Oman to toil in date palm plantations there. Yet others were transported in dhows to Egypt and the lands of the Ottoman, Safavid and Mughal Empires, where they were employed as servants, gardeners, guards, soldiers and other forms of domestic and military help. Female slaves would be shipped off to the palaces and mansions of the wealthy ruling classes in the region, where they would spend their days in the harems as ladies-in-waiting or concubines. They would be closely watched over by generations of eunuchs, castrated male slaves put to work as chaperones and guardians of the harems.

Britain's interventions in Oman and Zanzibar were ostensibly motivated by its interest in curtailing the slave trade. In 1856, Seyyid Said's sudden death sparked a crisis of succession, and his empire was contested heatedly between two of his sons. The British were brought in as intermediaries and after intense politicking, they finally ruled in 1861 to partition the empire into two halves. Thuwaini bin Said succeeded his father as sultan of Muscat and Oman, while his younger brother, Majid bin Said, became the first sultan of Zanzibar. The split barely impacted Zanzibar at all – not long after, the opening of the Suez Canal would herald Zanzibar's golden age. Muscat, on the other hand, declined and greatly lost its significance in international trade.

Zanzibar's fortunes are etched indelibly upon historic Stone Town, designated a UNESCO World Heritage Site in 2000. Echoing al-Balad in Jeddah, a majority of the low-rise structures here are constructed of coral rag and lime mortar. Their façades are plastered with limewash and painted white, such that they gleam under the sun and present a coherent, beautiful vista of white for any visitor arriving by dhow. Stone Town was the abode of the wealthy and powerful in the city: the Arab and Shirazi landowners, Indian *baniyas* and merchants, and later, British colonials. Africans and the non-Shirazi Swahili lived in Ng'ambo, meaning "the other side" – a district that lay just beyond Stone Town.

A large majority of the buildings here are Omani-style houses: low-rise, multi-storeyed, residential mansions, often distinguished by decorative crenellations along the roof. The houses are introverted, with central courtyards enclosed on all sides by rooms, balconies and walls, ensuring the family's privacy. They are also known for their Zanzibari doorways – large, elaborately-carved wooden double doors and door frames, adorned with traditional motifs harbouring symbolic meaning, and with beautiful Arabic calligraphy spelling out quotes from the Qur'an. In a nod to local Swahili architecture, the houses also sport *baraza*, or stone benches, just outside their front doors. These facilitate the exchange of conversation and gossip between members of the community.

Indian architecture too, informs the vernacular here. Indian merchants brought Anglo-Indian-style verandahs to these parts, as well as so-called Gujarati doors, distinguished from the Zanzibari ones in their being much less ornate, and structured rather more like four-panelled, shuttered French doors. Later on, British architects would import the Indo-Saracenic style popular in British India and use it in the design of major civic monuments such as the local Supreme Court and General Post Office.

Two structures are worth a mention for their historic significance. The first, and by far the most impressive, is the Beit al-Ajaib, or House of Wonders, which occupies a prominent spot on the Stone Town waterfront. It had been commissioned by Seyyid Barghash bin Said, who succeeded his half-brother as second sultan of Zanzibar when the latter died suddenly at the age of 35. Barghash's reign from 1870 to 1888 was a time of great prosperity in Zanzibar, coinciding with the opening of the Suez Canal, and marked by the young sultan's own energetic efforts to modernise his kingdom.

Barghash initiated, in Zanzibar, a form of the rapid and far-reaching societal and cultural transformation experienced in the imperial metropoles of London, Paris and New York. The island would be linked by telegraph to the rest of the world – the first place in East Africa to have such connectivity. Stone Town would have paved roads and tramways, streets illuminated by public lighting, and railway tracks that linked it to the interior. Barghash ignited a literary renaissance, setting up Zanzibar's first printing press and encouraging new forms of religious and political thought. A nascent class of Zanzibari elite gained access to luxury goods enjoyed in the West: fashionable dress, exported textiles, lavish furnishings for domestic interiors and the like. They would cultivate a taste for promenading in public and enjoying public forms of entertainment.

The crowning glory of Barghash's modernisation juggernaut was the construction in 1883 of the Beit al-Ajaib, conceived originally as a ceremonial palace, but repositioned later on as an exhibition space in which new technologies and products from all over the world were displayed; a sort of "Crystal Palace on the Swahili Coast". The ground plans for the palace were informed by traditional Omani palace architecture, with two major distinctions. The first was the sheer scale of it all – the Beit al-Ajaib was, and still is, the largest structure in Zanzibar. Another was the Beit's outward-orientation – the three-storey building had extra-high ceilings on each floor, and large, deep Anglo-Indian-style verandahs that ran around the entire building. These functioned as viewing galleries, allowing the sultan to ostentatiously preside over elaborate street parades and festivals, even as his subjects down below were suffered to remark and stand awed by the royal personage. In a further nod to architectural eclecticism, the verandahs were held up by prefabricated Greek-Revival-style cast-iron columns imported from the United Kingdom.

Today, the Beit al-Ajaib is seen by scholars as an exemplar of early African modernism, demonstrating how local African elites were willing and able to incorporate foreign ideas into a thoroughly new African architectural style. The European powers would hijack this natural trajectory of progress as they scrambled to colonise Africa and to impose their own frames of modernity onto the continent. In 1890, not long after Barghash's death, Zanzibar became a British protectorate. The British would append a Victorian-style clocktower to the Beit al-Ajaib, thoroughly ruining the aesthetic, and in so doing, undermining the progress Barghash had wrought. They would appropriate the Beit for their own use as the headquarters of colonial administration.[11]

A short walk away from the Beit al-Ajaib stands Christ Church, the city's historic Anglican church, and the second most significant

Beit Al-Ajaib (House of Wonders), Stone Town. Unfortunately, part of the building collapsed in 2020, though the entire structure is presently being restored.

site in Stone Town. Built in 1879, the church also features an eclectic design, fusing Victorian-style elements with Omani-style crenellated roof decorations, and built with a mixture of Zanzibari coral rag, Portland cement, and lime plaster. Its significance, however, lies in it standing atop what had been Stone Town's last operating slave market, notorious for being the cruellest of all Zanzibar's slave markets. When the British shut the market down for good in 1873, the local parish decided to purchase the site and erect a cathedral here.

The church's altar was built right over the market's infamous whipping post, where male and female slaves alike were tied up to be whipped in a test of endurance – those who bore the searing pain in silence fetched a higher price. A white marble circle marks the spot where the whipping post had been; it is surrounded by red tiles symbolising the blood of the hundreds of slaves who died here. At a historic mansion just next door, fifteen underground cellars remain which bear witness to a cruel practice, wherein slaves newly imported to the island would be imprisoned for days with little food and no air circulation. Those who survived the ordeal would be judged sturdy enough for sale.

Between church and mansion lies Zanzibar's Slave Market Memorial. Created by Swedish artist Clara Sörnäs and completed in 1998, the memorial consists of a pit in which statues of five enslaved persons – men, women and a child – stand shoulder-deep. They are chained at the neck, by actual neck collars and chains once used on slaves. The expressions on their faces are chillingly bleak: they look completely worn out, beaten down and devoid of all hope. The memorial is a stark reminder that there was a dark and brutal side to trade and commerce in Asia's cosmopolitan port cities.

31. Tianjin, Qingdao & Dalian (Tientsin, Tsingtao & Dalniy / Dairen)
Northeast China and the Scramble for Foreign Concessions

"You, dear city on the yellow sea, / Ringed all around by hills, / How ancient you are, and yet how young! / Some fifteen years have passed, / Since Diedrichs' ship pulled into the bay, / And our Prince's flag flew in the East. / Let us all remember that happy day / And lift our mugs up with a cheer!"

— "Tsingtao Then and Now". Sung to the tune of "O Alte Burschenherrlichkeit". Performed in honour of Prince Heinrich of Prussia on 16 October 1912. [12]

On the banks of the Hai He ("Sea River") in the northern Chinese city of Tianjin lies a quaint Italian town resembling a suburb of Rome or Florence. Piazza Elena Regina, a delightful little town square, sits at its heart (it is now named Marco Polo Square). Named after Elena of Montenegro, wife to King Victor Emmanuel III of Italy, it is graced by a monumental fountain topped with a neoclassical marble column and a statue of Vittoria, or Winged Victory. Just off the piazza is the former Sacred Heart Church, built in 1922 in a neo-Renaissance style, with its striking clock tower extending high into the sky and visible from across the river. From the circular piazza, the town radiates outwards, resolving itself into a strict and rational grid plan. Here stands a profusion of elegant villas variously adorned with elaborate loggias and civic towers, and recalling 15th-century mansions in northern Italy.

Initially built to further colonial business interests in China, the Italian Concession in Tianjin later became primarily residential. Italian residents in the concession never numbered more than a few hundred, while some six thousand Chinese residents moved in and made it their home. In a twist of circumstance, the concession thus became a gated community – an exclusive, high-end residential enclave for former Chinese aristocrats fleeing in the aftermath of the fall of the Qing dynasty, as well as wealthy Chinese business magnates, warlords, political activists and members of the literati. European accounts of Tianjin relate how the Italian Concession had an "aristocratic" air. It was certainly the most elegant and well-planned of the concessions in the city. [13]

Tianjin occupies a strategic location at the northern terminus of the Grand Canal, where it meets the Hai He. Its location has thus afforded it the distinction, since at least the 15th century, of being the port of the imperial capital of Beijing. The name "Tianjin" (天津) itself means "heavenly ford" and is believed to have been bestowed upon the city during the Ming dynasty, when the Yongle Emperor succeeded in fording the river at this very location. The old city of Tianjin was a walled city, or *cheng*, built on a rectangular grid plan on a strict north-south axis; it still stood when the Western powers arrived.

In the aftermath of the Second Opium War, Tianjin was forced open to foreign trade by the Treaty of Tientsin (1858). This was later ratified by the Qing government during the Convention of Peking in 1860. The city formed part of a second wave of treaty ports established on the Chinese coast. The word for treaty port in Chinese was *shang-bu* (商埠), which means "port of commerce" (*bu* literally means "jetty"). It makes no reference to the fact that these ports were administered by foreigners or that they were forcibly opened.

Like Shanghai – to which it would forever play second fiddle – Tianjin originally consisted of just three foreign concessions, British, French and American. A concession, as the term suggests, was a sizeable area of land *conceded* by China in perpetuity to the Western powers (and later on, Japan) for the purposes of trade, and in return for an annual lease payment. The Chinese name for "concession" was *zujie* (租界), which literally meant "leased territory".

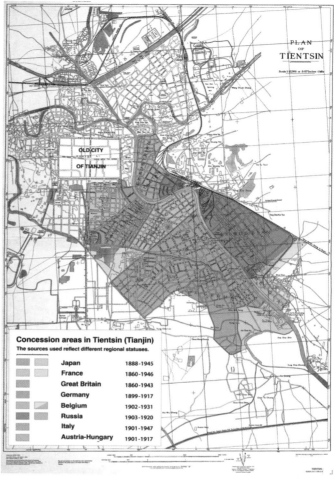

Tientsin Foreign Concessions, with the Walled City at left. Based on a 1945 map of Tianjin, printed by the US Army Map Service.

Concession areas in Tientsin (Tianjin)
The sources used reflect different regional statuses.

Japan	1888-1945
France	1860-1946
Great Britain	1860-1943
Germany	1899-1917
Belgium	1902-1931
Russia	1903-1920
Italy	1901-1947
Austria-Hungary	1901-1917

Though leased, a concession was sovereign territory of the occupying power, in principle if not in name. Extraterritoriality applied, in that within these concessions, foreign jurisdictions held sway and all residents, foreign or Chinese, were protected by foreign laws. Many Chinese fleeing conflict and dynastic change at the turn of the 20th century took up residence in foreign concessions, on account of laws that granted them immunity and protected private wealth and property.

Tianjin grew substantially in size between 1895 and 1901, when China was wracked by war and civil unrest, and fell prey to a scramble for concessions by the great powers. Germany and Japan secured concessions here in 1895 and 1898 respectively. In the course of the Eight-Nation Alliance occupation of Tianjin and its subsequent suppression of the Boxer Insurrection from 1900 to 1901, Russia, Italy, Austria-Hungary and Belgium too secured their concessions, while the existing powers – Britain, France, Germany and Japan – expanded theirs.[14] The result was a patchwork-like urban landscape, with nine sovereign territories occupying a continuous swathe of land along the Hai He, and existing alongside the traditional walled Chinese city. A turn-of-the century visitor wishing to take in the entire city would thus be technically crossing ten different sovereign territories on a single tour. American journalist, John Hersey, recounts in his 10 May 1982 article in *The New Yorker*:

> "What a weird city I grew up in. For three or four Chinese coppers, I could ride in a rickshaw from my home, in England, to Italy, Germany, Japan, or Belgium. I walked to France for violin lessons; I had to cross the river to get to Russia, and often did, because the Russians had a beautiful wooded park with a lake in it."[15]

The concessions became showpieces for the colonial powers. They were *tabula rasa*, or blank slates, on which the powers would impose Western frames of urban development. It was by way of the concessions in Tianjin that new and modern forms of housing, sanitation, banking, transport, communications, legal, educational, military and government administrative systems, know-how and technology were imported into China. From Tianjin, railway lines were built to connect Beijing to the rest of China, greatly reducing the time taken to travel vast distances. Steamships began to ply not only the China coast but also its major riverine networks, particularly the Yangzi River. Electric street lighting gradually spread from Tianjin and other treaty ports to cities in the interior.

Architecturally, the Western powers and Japan imported their own distinctive, nationalistic vernaculars into their respective concessions, experimenting with eclectic styles that drew on elements from the European past as a way to articulate contemporary imperial identities. Thus, the British Concession boasted monumental neoclassical edifices and Anglo-Indian verandahs like those found elsewhere in Shanghai, Bombay and Singapore; the French Concession channelled Paris on the Hai He, with its Beaux-Arts *hôtels* and bourgeois *bâtiments*; the German Concession resembled a Bavarian town at the foot of the Alps; the Austro-Hungarian Concession replicated imperial Vienna as stupendous waterfront vista; and the Japanese Concession saw the wholesale borrowing and blending of European-style neoclassical architecture into a brand-new expression of Meiji-era imperial might.

Though legally and architecturally distinct, the concessions were nonetheless united in their being bases for the exploitation of China's vast market and resources. As a symbol of this common thread, a single commercial high street could cut through each of the concessions but change in name and flavour as it passed through each sovereign territory. Thus Wilhelmstrasse became Victoria Road became Rue de France. Tianjin was a sort of permanent World Fair, at a time when the Universal Exposition first emerged as a means by which the great powers trumpeted their colonial territories and imperial might to the world.

At the turn of the 20th century, the great powers referred to China condescendingly as "the sick man of the East". The reality was that it was a very large nation and society in the throes of great change; and the waves of war and conflict were symptomatic of a great civilisation struggling, like the metaphorical butterfly, to emerge from its cocoon. The fact was also that China was swiftly modernising, adapting and developing local versions of new technologies earlier imported from the West.

The late 19th century saw China introduce its own banks and telegraph companies, its own steamships and railroads, its own universities and armed forces, its own new forms of art, literature and leisure. In promulgating the idea that China was a moribund kingdom, the great powers were ironically betraying their own insecurities: their fear that China would leapfrog them developmentally, and no longer need their business. The Middle Kingdom thus had to be stopped in its tracks, before it got too technologically advanced.

China's defeat in the 1895 First Sino-Japanese War emboldened the colonial powers. In 1898, Germany summarily invaded and occupied Jiaozhou Bay, a natural harbour located on the southern side of the Shandong Peninsula. The excuse was the killing of two German missionaries by local Chinese. The Qing government was forced to pay an indemnity and to concede Kiautschou Bay (as the Germans transliterated it) and its main port city of Qingdao (青岛 – Tsingtao in German, meaning "green island") on a 99-year lease. Unlike Tianjin, Qingdao was thus not a treaty port but a colony proper, the German equivalent of Hong Kong; and the Germans were determined that the city give Hong Kong a run for its money.

In Qingdao, with its dramatic landscape of forest, mountain and seashore, the Germans found a place that reminded them of home; the perfect location for the model colony. The forest – *der Wald* – spoke to a primal part of German identity. The figure of the lone wanderer or innocent child rambling through a dark and primeval forest recurs in Teutonic literature and popular imagination; one need look no further than the fairy tales of the Brothers Grimm to find this recurring image.

Qingdao's location right on the sea also allowed the Germans to indulge in another trope from their cultural imagination: that of the seaside resort or sanatorium – *das Seebad*, closely related to *das Bad* ("Bath"), which refers to a kind of rehabilitative facility where one bathes in restorative or medicinal waters as a form of therapy.

Mining deeply into their cultural roots, and sparing no cost nor effort, the German Empire created the city of Tsingtao both in the image of a familiar mediaeval fairy-tale town, as well as that of a popular seaside sanatorium. Mostly inhabited by military and naval personnel, the city birthed a new genre of popular songs, the *Tsingtao-lied* – *lied* from the German *lieder*, or traditional song. Akin to pub ditties, these invariably waxed lyrical about the fair region of Kiautschou that was *die deutsche Heimat im Osten* ("the German Homeland in the East").[16] They would undoubtedly have been popular during Oktoberfest, when they would have been accompanied by mugs of rich German lager and a healthy dose of Bavarian good cheer.

The entire old town of Qingdao has been lovingly preserved, researched, documented and restored by the municipal authorities. The visitor today would still be charmed by the quaint and surreal landscape of mediaeval-ish castles, replete with turrets and Anglo-Indian verandahs, on every street corner. These housed civic and commercial institutions like the Post Office, or the Seamen's Guesthouse (*Seemanshaus*), or the headquarters of the Hamburg-America Line. The sense of the magical is heightened when the mists roll in from the sea, blanketing the entire city

The Governor's Mansion in Qingdao continues to channel a Bavarian castle today.

in white, and one has the impression of stumbling upon a fairy city in the middle of an ancient wood.

One of the most impressive monuments in the city is the former Governor's Residence, perched high up on a hill, and looking like a mix between hunting lodge and modest version of Neuschwanstein Castle. Built for an astronomical sum in 1903, it is an exemplar of *Jugendstil*, the German version of art nouveau, which originated in the Bavarian city of Munich and was prevalent in the late 19th and early 20th centuries. Its distinctive look is achieved through the generous use of large and imposing grey blocks of Qingdao granite in its façade, resulting in an overall aesthetic that is neo-Teutonic, for lack of a better term. One almost expects a group of blonde young men to come huffing and puffing up the slope in their shorts and *lederhosen*. That said, the building also contains hybrid elements such as a pagoda-like roof sporting Chinese ceramic tiles and the heads of stylised dragons – a nod to the significance of dragons both in mediaeval European as well as traditional Chinese culture.

The Germans held onto Qingdao and the Jiaozhou Bay Concession for only 16 years. In 1914, in the midst of World War I, the Japanese overran the colony and held it till 1945 (with a brief interregnum between 1922 and 1938). They would keep much of the German architecture in the Old Town, adapting many of the buildings for their own use. In the meantime, they built their own new city adjacent to the German Old Town, adopting the mixed Japanese-European style that characterised Meiji, Taisho and Showa Japan and many of Japan's other colonies.

Not to be outdone by Germany or any of the great powers, Russia had already, in 1860, secured what was possibly the largest concession of all. By the terms of the Treaty of Aigun, also ratified at the Convention of Peking, China had been forced to cede a vast tract of Outer Manchuria to Russia. This territory was bordered by the Amur River in the south and the Stanovoy Mountain Range in the north, and extended Russia's Far Eastern coast all the way south to the border with Korea. That very same year, Vladivostok was founded as the major Russian port on the Pacific coast and it remains Russia's largest and most important eastern port city today.

Unfortunately, for four months of the year, Vladivostok's harbour would freeze over, rendering shipping and trade impossible. Thus would the Russian Empire hanker for that elusive ice-free port in the Far East – one which would finally set the course for their imperial ambitions straight. Their opportunity came in 1898 when, following the German lead, they occupied the southernmost tip of the Liaodong Peninsula, on the Bohai Sea. The Chinese were persuaded to cede the Kwantung Leased Territory to the Russians on a 25-year lease. Here, the Russians would found the port of Dalniy (Дальний), meaning "remote", alongside pre-existing Port Arthur, which they designated a naval base.

Determined that Dalniy should be a showpiece of Russian Imperialism, the empire invested huge sums in its development. An urban plan inspired by St Petersburg and informed by "Garden City" principles was conceived, and the Russians set about clearing the land and laying out the basic grid plan for the city.[17] The centrepiece of their city plan was a grand, circular city square, which they called Nicholas Square (after the Tsar Nicholas II). In the vicinity of the city square, they erected residential mansions and a handful of monuments. Of these, only two still stand today, including the former Dalniy City Hall and a former shipping company headquarters that houses today's Dalian Art Gallery.

Then, just seven years after 1898, it was all over for the Russians as, in the aftermath of the Russo-Japanese War, the triumphant Japanese occupied Dalniy. In 1905, China handed Dalniy and (what came to be called) the Kwantung Leased Territory to Japan, and they would hold it till the end of World War II in 1945.[18] The Japanese kept the name Dalniy but transliterated it to Dairen, meaning "Great Connection". This is the name that continues to be used today – the Chinese pronounce it "Da-Lian" (大连).

Over the next forty years, the Japanese would transform the city, against all odds, into a cosmopolitan metropolis in the north, retaining and building on the Russian urban plan. The city became known for its wide boulevards and its stately European-style buildings that featured Japanese decorative elements. These eclectic forms of architecture had become a hallmark of Japanese imperialism and were to be found in other colonial cities such as Keijo (today's Seoul) in Korea as well as in the Japanese metropole, Tokyo.

The city's heart remained at Nicholas Square, which the Japanese renamed Ohiroba, meaning "Grand Plaza". Around the square, they would build ten of the most imposing pieces of Japanese imperial architecture west of Tokyo. These housed the headquarters of Japanese banks and merchant houses, as well as the British and other European consulates.

Amongst these buildings, perhaps the most iconic was the Yamato Hotel, depicted in countless picture postcards of the city, and built in 1914 in a grandiose imperial style characteristic of the Taisho era. It was the equivalent of the Cathay Hotel in Shanghai and the Raffles Hotel in Singapore, a high-end luxury hotel hosting celebrities and members of royalty who passed through Dairen en route to Japan on their round-the-world tours. The Yamato Hotel chain was owned by the Mantetsu, or Southern Manchuria Railway (SMR) Company, which had a mandate from the Japanese imperial government to develop the entire city. The SMR played a pivotal role in expanding Japanese imperialism on the Chinese mainland. Later in the 1930s, it would build other Yamato Hotels in the Japanese colony of Manchukuo (Manchuria, today's Northeast China), though its Dairen branch remained the flagship.

The other iconic building on the Ohiroba stood directly opposite the Yamato Hotel – this was the headquarters of the Yokohama Specie Bank, built in 1909 as a late exemplar of exuberant Meiji-style architecture. Crowned by three imposing green domes that channel an Orthodox church, it inadvertently also evokes the city's earlier Russian past. Like the Yamato Hotels, branches of the Yokohama Specie Bank around the world were also a symbol of Japanese imperialism. Founded in Yokohama in 1880, the bank financed Japanese overseas trade, and played a pivotal role in lubricating Japanese expansion into China and subsequently, the rest of Asia.

Driven by a deep veneration for nature, the Japanese created a garden city that was startling in its modernity, while fully integrated

Former Yokohama Specie Bank Building, Zhongshan Square (former Nicholas Square and Ohiroba). The square was renamed Zhongshan Square in honour of Dr Sun Yat Sen (who was also known as Sun Zhongshan).

with its natural landscape of mountain, forest and sea. Of-the-era postcards depict Dairen as a verdant and thoroughly modern metropolis, with impeccable sanitation, paved and tree-lined streets, wide boulevards, and monumental Western-style buildings. Electric tramways were introduced here in the 1900s and were an iconic attraction in the city – they continue to run today.

Dairen was particularly known for its acacia trees, which the Japanese imported and planted en masse in the city centre. Called *akashiya* in Japanese, their white blooms carpeted the city and made it a pretty sight indeed; they were the equivalent of *sakura*, or cherry blossoms in Tokyo and Kyoto. Long after the Japanese had been expelled from their ex-colony, a generation of authors, filmmakers and songwriters would reminisce fondly about the city's ubiquitous acacias, immortalising them in a genre of nostalgic works celebrating *akashiya no dairen* ("Dairen of acacia flowers").

Dairen's gentle beauty, however, belied steely determination on the part of imperial Japan to trumpet the city as a showpiece of its advanced technology, and its right and readiness to take its place amongst the great nations of the world. From the 1930s on, Japan would accept nothing less than full subjugation of China, from which it had been estranged since Tokugawa times, and towards which it harboured mixed feelings of respect and animosity. This unquenchable need to bring China to its knees would pave the way towards World War II.

32. Bangkok & Ho Chi Minh City (Saigon)
From Charoen Krung Road to Rue Catinat

"But the most important event that influenced Siamese thought about Western Culture was the first Chinese war with England, which occurred in 1842. Most Siamese at that time believed the Chinese propaganda that the Chinese Government only granted the treaty to England as a compromise in order to avoid annoyance. But there were three men who not only believed that the Chinese had been defeated in the war but were convinced that Western power and influence were to increase in the future in this part of the world. The three men were King Mongkut, […] his young full brother Phra Pin Klao, […], and also [a young nobleman called Luang Sidhi, who became Regent at the beginning of the reign of King Chulalongkorn]. These three men considered that the Siamese should begin to try and acquire knowledge about the Western peoples so as to be prepared for future eventualities."

— "The Introduction of Western Culture in Siam".
A paper read by H. R. H. Prince Damrong Rajanubhab at the
Rotarian dinner of the United Club, on August 7th, 1925.[19]

The Asian Civilisations Museum has in its collection a golden, embroidered *sua khrui*, or Thai official robe, typically bestowed upon officials of high rank and illustrious service. This particular robe was given, in 1901, by King Rama V of Siam (better known as King Chulalongkorn), to the admiral of the Royal Siamese Navy, a Danish gentleman by the name of Andreas du Plessis de Richelieu. De Richelieu had arrived in Siam in 1875 to offer his services to King Rama V. He would become the king's adviser on matters of trade and maritime affairs, playing an instrumental role in modernising the Royal Siamese Navy. In the Paknam Incident of 1893, he led Siamese naval forces against the French, who had sailed up the Chao Phraya River within firing range of Bangkok's Grand Palace, in an attempt to force Siam to relinquish territory to French Indochina.

The *sua khrui* itself is an astonishing work of Thai craftsmanship. Only worn at court, and for ceremonial occasions such as coronations and investitures, its form probably has Indo-Persian roots and harks back to the days of Ayutthaya, when expatriate Persian and Indian merchants introduced fashionable styles of dress and architecture to Siam. The robe is made of cotton tulle and adorned with elaborate gold thread embroidery depicting maritime motifs such as whales, ships' wheels and anchors, secreted amidst a glorious proliferation of twirling vines and flowers. Echoing European-style military uniforms, the *sua khrui* is also decorated with a large, blue-and-silver royal insignia in the form of an eight-pointed star.

An of-the-era photograph of the Admiral du Plessis de Richelieu in ceremonial garb has him draping the golden *sua khrui* like a cape over his European-style naval admiral's uniform – the very picture of poise and power. De Richelieu would retain his position as admiral for only a year from January 1900 to 1901. Stricken with malaria, he would retire and return to Denmark in 1902, though he would remain ever loyal to the Siamese king.

King Chulalongkorn's appointment of a Danish admiral was in keeping with a tradition, since the days of Ayutthaya, of Thai kings employing foreigners at court, particularly to advise in matters of trade, defence, diplomacy, science and architecture. The Chakri kings continued the practice of learning from the West in order to consolidate their own positions of power. King Rama IV, better known as King Mongkut, would initiate a process of Westernisation from within, on Siam's own terms, in an effort to stave off colonisation by the Western powers. By way of setting an example, he was the first Thai king to speak and write English – amongst other languages; and he took to acquiring knowledge in a range of modern subjects such as geography, science and astrology. Most famously, he would engage an English governess, Anna Leonowens, to teach his children English.

Official robe (sua khrui). Thailand, 1902. Cotton tulle, gold netting, gold bullion threads, sequins and soutache, 104 x 58 cm. Collection of the Asian Civilisations Museum.

Mongkut's reign in the mid-19th century marked the beginnings of Bangkok's stark transition from a city of canals and waterways like Ayutthaya before it, to a largely terrestrial city in the image of imperial metropolises in the West. The Chakri kings strived to evoke the glory of Ayutthaya in their new capital city on the Chao Phraya River. In fact, the very foundations of their Grand Palace in present-day Bangkok had been built with rubble taken from the ruins of Ayutthaya and floated downriver. 18th century accounts of Bangkok resembled 16th century accounts of

Ayutthaya, in that both described the city as a "Venice of the East", and both told of how, rounding a bend in the river, travellers would see a glorious city of golden temples and gleaming palaces suddenly appearing upon the horizon. Incidentally, Bangkok goes by multiple names. The Chakri kings called their city Rattanakosin, which means "receptacle of the precious gems". The Thais themselves call their capital city Krung Thep Maha Nakhon (กรุงเทพมหานคร): "City of Angels".[20]

The new Bangkok would be a city of roads and boulevards. By the mid-1850s, under the terms of various treaties signed between Siam and the Western powers, Bangkok had accumulated a sizeable community of foreigners settled at a riverfront location to the south of Rattanakosin. The various foreign consuls in the city banded together to sign a petition to King Mongkut, arguing that Europeans were unaccustomed to traversing the city in boats; they had to have proper roads on which they could ride out in carriages and horses. The king graciously acquiesced.

The first major thoroughfare in the city, and still its most important, was Charoen Krung ("Prosperous City") Road, built in 1864 and running more than eight kilometres parallel to the Chao Phraya. New Road (as it was called in English) linked all the major districts in the city: the European district at Bang Rak, Chinatown at Yaowarat and the Royal Precinct at Rattanakosin. Very quickly after its inauguration, it became the city's main artery of commerce and trade, displacing the river itself. European trading houses established their neoclassical edifices along New Road; while the local Chinese erected their Nanyang-style shophouses.

King Chulalongkorn built on the foundations set by his father. His long and illustrious reign saw massive reforms in all aspects of governance and society, be it in courtly protocol, education, transport and communications, or law and city planning. Soon after he was crowned in 1873, the young king issued a decree that henceforth, no subject need ever prostrate him or herself before the person of the king. Like his father, he travelled widely across the globe, eager to imbibe new ideas for application back home, while presenting himself as a thoroughly civilised monarch in the European fashion, able to hold his own amongst his peers.

Like his father, he too understood the power of architecture as a symbol of progress and modernity. Returning from a grand tour of Europe in 1897, during which he had been hosted at many a royal palace in grand style, he set about commissioning his own European-style palace complex to the north of the city, hiring Italian and German engineers to undertake the task. His brand new palace complex, named Wang Suan Dusit, or "Celestial Garden", sported a mix of European styles such as neoclassical and Italianate, fused with traditional Thai elements in a hybrid imperial scheme that refashioned the Thai monarchy as one that was future-oriented and unafraid of change.

During Chulalongkorn's reign, European encroachment upon Siamese territory intensified. For a moment in the 1890s, it seemed Siam might end up as a French or a British protectorate, or worse yet, be carved up in two to appease the two great powers. The Paknam Incident would prove a turning point. The years leading up to it had seen French and Siamese forces clash violently over lands to the left of the Mekong River, constituting what is today's Laos. These lands had traditionally fallen within Siam's *mandala*, or sphere of influence. Unfortunately, they were coveted by an expansionist *la France impériale*.

The Paknam Incident was defused by way of Siam capitulating to French demands. The left bank of the Mekong was conceded, much to Chulalongkorn's chagrin. Over the next two decades, Siam would be forced to concede more territory to France and Britain. In 1907, Siam ceded the Cambodian provinces of Battambang and Siem Reap, including the temples of Angkor, to French Indochina. The southernmost Muslim provinces of Kedah, Kelantan, Perlis and Trengganu were relinquished to British Malaya in 1909. This loss of territory and nationalistic pride hit Chulalongkorn hard, though he continued to observe his duties tirelessly. Unfortunately, he passed away from a long illness in 1910, at only 57 years of age and after having ruled Siam for 42 years.

Chulalongkorn had believed these concessions painful but necessary ones in order that Siam's sovereignty be preserved. He would ultimately be proven right. Their territorial acquisitions secured, Britain and France turned their attentions elsewhere, content to have Siam remain a buffer state between their spheres of influence. Today's Thailand remains the only nation in Southeast Asia never to be colonised by a western power. The Chakri kings' far-sightedness and efforts paid off.

Things would be starkly different in Vietnam, Siam's chief rival on the Southeast Asian mainland at the turn of the 19th century. Not long after the Chakri dynasty consolidated their rule over Siam, the erstwhile Nguyen lords of Hoi An successfully conquered all of Vietnam, becoming the Nguyen emperors. They would be the last ruling Vietnamese dynasty.

Nguyen Phuc Anh, scion of the Nguyen clan, unified the kingdom against great odds and became the first of its emperors in 1802, adopting the reign name, Gia Long ("Great Prosperity"). Observing the age-old East Asian Order of Things, the new emperor sought imperial China's blessing for his new dynasty. The Qing emperor bestowed a gold imperial seal upon him, signalling China's acknowledgement of the Nguyens as loyal vassals. The emperor suffered Gia Long to call his new domain Viet Nam, meaning "the lands of the Yue (pronounced *Viet* in Vietnamese) peoples to the south".

Emperor Gia Long had counted on French military aid in his quest to subdue his opponents and conquer all Vietnam. Throughout his reign in the early 19th century, he would honour this debt to the French, affording them a place at court, and allowing their missionaries to build churches and proselytise freely in his kingdom. His successors reversed this position, expelling the French, and eventually banning Catholicism. Vietnam would instead be moulded into an already-outdated form of centralised state modelled after China's, and governed by a traditional, Confucianist bureaucracy with the emperor affixed at the centre of "all under heaven" (*tianxia – thien ha* in Vietnamese), surrounded by his most loyal officials and courtiers.

The Second Opium War coincided with the reign of the fourth Nguyen emperor, Tu Duc ("Heir to Virtue"). Where his predecessors had made some effort to understand and learn from the West as a means of self-defence, Vietnam under Tu Duc turned its back on the world. Fearful of Western powers securing concessions as they had done in China and Japan, Tu Duc, ill-advised by his traditionalist court, closed Vietnam entirely to foreign trade, attempting a latter-day version of Japan's *sakoku*. Tu Duc was a contemporary of Chulalongkorn, and the difference between the two couldn't be more striking. While the latter was actively travelling the world, absorbing new knowledge and transforming his kingdom, the former remained ensconced and isolated in his Chinese-style imperial palace, the Purple Forbidden City, at his royal capital of Hue.

In 1858, using the execution of two Spanish Catholics as an excuse, French troops occupied Da Nang, at the Vietnamese coast, before moving south to capture the port city of Saigon. Tu Duc would be forced to cede Saigon and three of Vietnam's provinces in the aftermath of this skirmish in 1862. It was a downhill slide thereafter, as the French gradually forced the emperor to cede all of Vietnam to France by 1884. In their ultimatum, the French left no doubt as to the consequences should the emperor not concede:

> "Now here is a fact which is quite certain; you are at our mercy. We have the power to seize and destroy your capital and to cause you all to die of starvation. You have to choose between war and peace. We do not wish to conquer you, but you must accept our protectorate. For your people it is a guarantee of peace and prosperity; it is also the only chance of survival for your government and your Court. We give you forty-eight hours to accept or reject, in their entirety and without discussion, the terms which in our magnanimity we offer you. [...] If you reject them, [... the] Dynasty, its Princes and its Court will have pronounced sentence on themselves. The name of Vietnam will no longer exist in history."[21]

Tu Duc would be forced to melt down the gold seal bestowed upon the Nguyens by the Qing emperor, symbolically ending Vietnam's centuries-old relationship with China as a tribute nation in the East Asian Order of Things.[22] The Nguyen emperors themselves were henceforth propped up as puppet monarchs subservient to France.

Vietnam was split into three territories, Tonkin (to the north, centred at Hanoi), Annam in the centre (with imperial Hue at its heart), and Cochinchina to the south (with Saigon as its capital). In 1887, the Indochinese Union, better known as l'Indochine française, or French Indochina, was formed as a merger between Tonkin, Annam, Cochinchina and Cambodia. Laos joined in 1893, and the tiny Chinese Concession territory of Kouang-Tchéou-wan in 1898. Hanoi was anointed political and administrative capital of the Union in 1902, though Saigon remained its economic capital. In fact, where Tonkin and Annam were administered as French protectorates, Cochinchina was an outright colony of France. Thus, Saigon became the centre of French commerce and culture in Indochina, and a showpiece for French imperialism in the East.

In the meantime, Tu Duc would be succeeded by a series of emperors with micro-reigns. Some would occupy the throne for a number of years, others just a number of months; one – Tu Duc's immediate successor – was only emperor for three days! In the course of King Chulalongkorn's 42-year reign in Siam, seven Nguyen monarchs in total (including Tu Duc) sat on the Vietnamese throne.

Saigon is actually a twin city. Alongside Saigon itself, there was another predominantly Chinese commercial centre at Cholon. This other city had been established in the 18th century by Minh Huong loyalists of the Nguyen, fleeing south from Hoi An. Saigon-Cholon had been a canal city in the vein of Bangkok, Hoi An and Ayutthaya, with a dense network of waterways allowing for goods to be brought up the Saigon River deep into the heart of the city. When the French took over in 1862, they left Cholon largely untouched, but built

63. - SAIGON. - Le Théâtre Municipal

Early 20th century postcard of Saigon's Municipal Theatre, also known as the Saigon Opera House.

their colonial settlement at Saigon. Demolishing the earlier Nguyen-era architecture, they imposed an orderly, rational, Haussmann-ian grid system atop the pre-colonial canal-city.[23] In the late 19th century, many of the main canals in Saigon were filled in to become *grands boulevards* the likes of which had been laid out in Paris decades earlier.

The most visible sign of the French *mission civilisatrice* in Saigon was its thoroughly Gallic architecture. The city boasted a surfeit of impressive civic monuments designed in the elaborate Beaux-Arts style, the preferred architectural language of the French Empire. All the trappings of empire were, and still are, here. There was the impressive wedding-cake-like Hôtel des Postes (Central Post Office, built in 1891), not far from the Hôtel de Ville (City Hall, 1908). The neo-Gothic Notre Dame de Saïgon, the city's main cathedral (1880), channelled its namesake in Paris; and the Théâtre Municipale (Municipal Theatre, 1897) echoed its cousin, the Palais Garnier, designed in the ostentatious Second Empire style of Napoleon III.

Cutting a straight and unwavering line through the centre of the city to the banks of the river was Rue Catinat, the pulsing heart of *Saïgon ville*, its *l'avenue des Champs Élysées*. Most of Saigon's stupendous monuments were to be found on or not far from Rue Catinat, including the aforementioned, as well as the headquarters of the Banque de l'Indochine, the French colonial bank par excellence; the French Cercle Sportif, its equivalent to the British gentlemen's club; and the Governor's Palace, its centre of political power. The street was also a commercial thoroughfare, host to the city's foremost departmental stores and boutiques; and the city's most posh address, with luxurious residential apartments, grand colonial hotels, and high-end cafes and grocery stores. Two of the most famous hotels, the French-built-and-managed Hôtel Continental (1880) and the Chinese-built Hôtel Majestic (1925), were to be found within a stone's throw of each other, and seethed with diplomats, dignitaries and spies during the Vietnam War period. English novelist Graham Greene's best-selling 1955 work, *The Quiet American*, was set in Saigon and had many of its scenes play out in the Hôtel Continental.

Much later in the 1950s, immediately after the French left the city, Rue Catinat and other streets would become the birthplace of *banh mi*, Saigon's most iconic dish and culinary export. Essentially a Vietnamese-style meat sandwich, *banh mi* is a hybrid dish that had its origins in the French-style baguettes once only sold in the city's high-end delis. *Banh mi* refers to both "bread made with wheat" as well as the "sandwich" itself. It originated as street food, hastily put together along street intersections by enterprising and itinerant hawkers pushing humble food trucks. It is thus a far cry from the chic *baguettes* to be had in the city's former cafés; and its very existence is a form of popular resistance. While the French were still in town, they objected to the Vietnamese experimenting with Gallic cuisine, which they regarded as far superior to Vietnamese food. Once the French were gone, however, the Vietnamese democratised the baguette, making it far more affordable and much better suited to the complex and refined Vietnamese palate.

33. Penang & Pekalongan
Port Cities of the Peranakans

"Chinese born in Batavia, / Go to the city of Semarang to trade. / Who knows what befell you? / Your body feels so alone."

— Traditional *panton*.[24]

Kebaya is an iconic form of female dress in the port cities of Southeast Asia. The word "kebaya" refers to a tailored, long-sleeved blouse-top. This blouse-top is often worn with a *sarong* as skirt, and the ensemble thus referred to as *sarong kebaya*. There are many varieties of *kebaya* today, representing a rich diversity of cultural traditions and ethnic communities across the region.[25]

One of the most popular forms of *kebaya* consists of a sheer blouse made of lightweight material such as cotton voile or gauze, and adorned with elaborate patterns of lace and embroidery. It is tailored to fit, body-hugging and remarkably sensuous. Since it's sheer, it is typically worn with an undershirt or camisole. It doesn't have buttons, and as such, has to be held together down the front by a trio of brooches known as *kerongsang*.

The *sarong* is a long cloth (*kain panjang*) or stitched tube skirt that a woman wraps around her waist and secures by tying or folding the fabric. Modern-day *sarongs* can be fashioned from a variety of materials, but are most frequently made from elaborately-patterned and coloured batik cloth. The entire *sarong kebaya* ensemble is often completed with a *kasut manek*, or a pair of beaded ladies' slippers. Worn by women of all races, it holds a special place in the wardrobes and sartorial style of Nyonya, or Peranakan Chinese, women.

Peranakan communities are cross-cultural communities that emerged and have deep roots in the port cities of Southeast Asia. *Peranakan* is a Malay word, with the term *anak*, or "child", as its root. The original meaning of the word is simply "born in" or "locally-born".

The meaning of Peranakan expanded later to also refer to a non-Malay person born and bred in the larger Malay world. It was an inclusive sort of term: the Malays referred to locally-born foreigners as *peranakan*, in the sense of "being of the same womb". Peranakan, as understood today, refers to creole communities whose unifying trait is the melding of Malay culture with their own, and who have been in this part of the world since at least the 1500s. The Peranakans thus belong to the larger phenomenon of creole communities that emerged in the region's many port cities.

The most well-known of the Peranakan communities are the Peranakan Chinese – the term *Peranakan* is often used mistakenly to refer to them only. There are, however, other Peranakan communities such as the Chetty Melaka, who are Peranakan Indians, the Jawi Peranakan, who are Indian Muslim Peranakans, and the Arab Peranakans. Eurasians too, fall within the scope of *Peranakan*; a case in point being the Indo-Dutch communities in the former Dutch East Indies (today's Indonesia), who are sometimes referred to as Peranakan Belanda (*belanda* is Malay for "Dutch").

Of the Peranakan Chinese, the most commonly-known were the Baba-Nyonya, or Straits Chinese, in the Straits Settlements port cities of Penang, Melaka and Singapore. More recently, longstanding Chinese communities in the port cities of Indonesia, such as Jakarta (formerly Batavia), Surabaya and Semarang, have also identified themselves as *Peranakan Tionghoa*. There are also Peranakan Chinese communities resident in the port cities of Phuket in Thailand, and Yangon in Myanmar. These communities have traits very similar to that of the Baba-Nyonya, in that Chinese heritage is melded with local Malay or Indonesian (and some Thai or Burmese) elements, to give rise to an exuberant, never understated material culture.

Aside from the *sarong kebaya*, food is extremely important to the Peranakan Chinese. Peranakan cuisine owes a heavy debt to Malay cuisine and its dizzying array of spices, herbs and elaborate methods of preparation. In particular, the *rempah*, or base mélange of spices and herbs, is quintessentially Malay and also essential to Peranakan food; it is used to make spicy curries and *rendangs*. Other aspects of the cuisine borrow from Chinese tradition, such as the regular use of *babi*, or pork, as a main ingredient, something the Muslim Malays eschew.

And then there is the language, Baba Malay, a creole tongue which blends elements of Malay and Hokkien: two historic languages of trade and commerce in East and Southeast Asia. The best way to experience Baba Malay is by way of attending a *dondang sayang* performance during parties or social gatherings. At the core of the *dondang sayang* are *pantons* in Baba Malay, the equivalent to Malay *pantuns*, or traditional poems. These *pantons*, often ingeniously written and with layers of meaning, are set to music, sung in the style of a romantic ballad, and accompanied by dancing. A *dondang sayang* thus makes for a wonderful evening of wine, wit and song.

Penang is one of the cradles of Peranakan culture and civilisation, boasting a rich cultural heritage. All the trappings of Peranakan culture – the food, the dress, the architecture and interiors – are here.

The city was the first British colony in Southeast Asia, taken in 1786 by Captain Francis Light of the Honourable East India Company. For a good half-century, with its deep harbour and prime location on the Straits of Melaka, it enjoyed considerable prosperity as the British Empire's Far Eastern entrepôt, a convenient stopover between Calcutta and Canton. It would be superseded by Singapore from 1819.

In 1824, the Anglo-Dutch Treaty was signed, dividing the Malay Archipelago into British and Dutch colonial spheres of influence, a division which corresponds today to the nation-states of Indonesia to the south, and Malaysia, Brunei and Singapore to the north. Under the terms of the treaty, the Dutch colony of Melaka was ceded to the British in exchange for Bencoolen in Sumatra. Penang, Singapore and Melaka were then grouped and administered together as the Straits Settlements, with Singapore designated capital of the territory in 1932.

All three port cities were similar in profile, in that they were cosmopolitan melting pots. Melaka, in particular, had far older communities of resident Chinese, Indians, Arabs and Europeans – Peranakan communities who had lived and traded in the city since Portuguese times. With the city capitulating to the British, these Peranakan communities would move north and south to Penang and Singapore, introducing Peranakan cultures there.

In Penang, Peranakan heritage is concentrated in and around George Town. Located in the northeastern corner of the island of Pulau Pinang and one of the best-preserved British colonial cities in Southeast Asia, George Town, together with historic Melaka, was inscribed as a UNESCO World Heritage Site in 2008. Alongside monumental Palladian and neoclassical civic buildings erected by the British are thousands of so-called Nanyang-style shophouses: a hybrid form of vernacular architecture that emerged everywhere the overseas Chinese established a foothold, particularly in the Straits Settlements.

Nanyang shophouses are a blend of traditional Chinese courtyard house architecture and European-style townhouse architecture, sporting

Nanyang-style shophouses on Armenian Street, George Town, Penang.

neoclassical façades with ornamental motifs from Chinese tradition, such as lions, dragons, phoenixes and characters from Chinese folktales. They served both commercial and residential purposes. Émigré Chinese merchants operated small businesses on the ground floor, while maintaining apartments on the second where their families lived. Deceptively small from the outside, the shophouses extend deep within, and have air-wells and internal courtyards that provide air circulation and natural light. The distinctive form of the shophouse is believed to have been a result of a peculiar tax regime in Dutch-ruled Melaka, wherein these Chinese merchants were taxed based on the length of the street-front their physical establishments occupied. The result was narrow street-fronting façades, but interiors that extended way back.

Eventually, some of these shophouses evolved to become entirely residential townhouses; the most opulent and ornate of these were occupied by wealthy Baba-Nyonya families. One of the most visible attributes of a Peranakan townhouse was the presence of a *pintu pagar*, or traditional Malay-style fence-door fronting the main door, and allowing for fresh air to flow into the house when the main door was open – it looks just like saloon doors in Hollywood Westerns. Just in case you thought this was a Malay household, however, a wooden plaque embellished with Chinese calligraphy would be hung just over the main door. These wooden plaques spelt out the evocative names the

Chinese gave their private residences. Peranakan townhouses from the 1900s also often sported brightly-coloured glazed ceramic tiles on their façades. These were made in England or Belgium, often in art deco or art nouveau designs, and were known as majolica tiles, though they are conveniently referred to as "Peranakan tiles" today.

For a glimpse into the lives of the truly wealthy Peranakan Chinese in Penang, one must pay a visit to the Pinang Peranakan Mansion, an erstwhile private residence that has been immaculately restored, and is operated as a private museum and major tourist attraction in George Town. The house belonged to the *kapitan cina* Chung Keng Kwee, who was, as his title suggests, the "captain", or superintendent of the local Chinese community – many of the Straits Chinese families were leaders not just in commerce but also in society.

Known as the Hai Kee Chan, or the "Storehouse of Stories of the Sea", the house was built in the late 19th century and is a classic example of Straits eclectic, blending neoclassical and China Coast styles. It boasts a magnificent Victorian-style cast iron balcony on the exterior, made in and imported from Glasgow. Inside the mansion, there is a large Chinese-style courtyard ringed with cast iron pillars and upper-floor balustrades also made in Glasgow. Juxtaposed alongside these European-style elements are ornately carved Chinese-style wooden screens adorned with all manner of auspicious flora and fauna, decorated in gold leaf. These were made by master-carvers Kapitan Chung brought here from Canton, and are spectacular masterpieces of Chinese decorative art.

The house is furnished today with a dizzying array of antiques from the turn of the 20th century, further underscoring the hybridity of Straits Chinese taste. Alongside brightly-coloured *nyonya-ware*, or Chinese export porcelain made for the Baba-Nyonya market, one finds Victorian-era glass epergnes. There are exquisite pieces of Canton-style blackwood furniture inlaid with mother-of-pearl, as well as European-style furniture adapted for local taste. The Straits Chinese inherited their forefathers' practice of venerating their ancestors; and thus the large ancestor portraits on the walls of the dining room, accompanied by ritual accoutrements used in customary worship.

The historic atmosphere of the mansion is so reverentially maintained that one can almost imagine the *nyonya besar*, or matriarch, of the family sashaying into the grand reception hall of the mansion, welcoming guests to her humble abode. She is dressed in a light-pink, embroidered, lace *kebaya* (a *kebaya encim*) tailored locally, with a matching pink-and-lilac floral batik sarong undersigned by the most fashionable batik atelier at the turn of the century. Her enormous star-shaped, diamond-studded *kerongsang* glisten in the light and her custom-made *kasut manek* add a touch of fashionable whimsy, with the popular animated characters, Betty Boop and Mickey Mouse, rendered in exquisite beadwork.

"*Aiyoh*, so good to see you, *sayang!*" she exclaims, gesturing affectionately. "You look so *cantik* today ah! Come come! Make yourself at home *lah!*"

And won over by her warmth, you do.

In the early decades of the 20th century, fashionable Peranakan ladies looked to Pekalongan, located on the northern coast of Java, some 360 kilometres east of Batavia (Jakarta), for their *kain panjang*, or skirt cloth. Pekalongan too, was a cosmopolitan port city. Like Melaka and Batavia, the city had been home to resident Arabs and Chinese since at least the 14th century, with the Dutch arriving from the 17th century on. It thus had a significantly large community of *Peranakan Cina* as well as *Peranakan Belanda*, or Indo-Dutch Peranakans.

Pekalongan was a major production centre for batik, a traditional form of printed textile prevalent across the Malay Archipelago. Batik's origins lie in Central Java, in the royal courts of Solo and Yogyakarta, which splintered off from the ancient Kingdom of Mataram sometime in the 18th century. From thence it spread to other royal courts as well as coastal regions across the Nusantara.

Batik cloth is made by way of a wax-resist dyeing method. One of the earliest and most detailed Western accounts of batik-making occurs in Sir Stamford Raffles' 1817 *The History of Java*.[26] In Raffles' time, natural dyes would have been used in making batiks, resulting in a rather more limited repertoire of colours and motifs. By the turn of the 20th century, chemical dyes had arrived, allowing for a greater variety of colours. That, combined with aesthetic influences from the Arab, Chinese and European traditions, resulted in a burst of creativity in batik-making in the port cities of the northern Javanese coast: Cirebon, Lasem and Pekalongan, amongst others. This new form of batik was known as *batik pesisir*, or coastal batik. Heavily influenced by foreign cultures, it sported patterns, motifs and colour schemes entirely different from the courtly batiks of the Javanese interior.

Pekalongan, in particular, was known for its extremely fine and exuberantly-coloured hand-drawn batik. The work was so admired that it was sought after not just in Java but across the entire region, and also in the Netherlands. An 1890 Dutch colonial report on the state of batik studios in Java and Madura already notes that:

> "Batik in Pekalongan manufactured under the supervision of European and Indo-European ladies is eagerly bought for high prices and exported to all parts of Java and further afield. The art of batik is also practiced by many Chinese and Arab women [...] The market for Pekalongan batik goods is increasing."[27]

By the early 20th century, the market was booming. Many Chinese and Eurasian batik makers set up their own ateliers, employing craftsmen and craftswomen who applied age-old traditions to produce modern and innovative designs. Some of them began to undersign their own work – also an innovation, since traditional batiks were never signed by their makers. A few of these "branded" batik *kain* were highly sought after indeed.

One distinguishing feature of Peranakan Chinese-style batik was its use of bright and auspicious colours such as red, orange and yellow. Courtly batiks tended to brown, black or white colour palettes, none of which were particularly popular with the Chinese. Auspicious, symbolic motifs from Chinese tradition – birds, butterflies, dragons, phoenixes, kirins, bats, deer, lotuses, chrysanthemums, peonies and more – would appear alongside Buddhist or Taoist symbols and traditional Javanese motifs such as the *sawat, parang*, or *kawung*.[28] Later, Chinese-style batiks became more secular and purely decorative in nature, with new floral and figurative designs – such as orchids, grapes, peacocks and songbirds – catering to the taste of Peranakan ladies across the region.

Alongside Chinese batiks, *batik belanda*, or Indo-Dutch batik, was also greatly in demand. European taste tended towards colours that were less intense than those favoured by the Chinese, and so Indo-Dutch batik came to be distinguished by its delicate pastel shades – cyan, lilac, lime-green and such. *Batik belanda* was also far more figurative in nature. Motifs could be drawn

Kebaya. Manado, Indonesia, late 19th to early 20th century. Cotton with embroidered lacework. Gift of Father Robbie Wowor in memory of grandmother, Mrs Tan Tjien Sian née Tjoa Soan Tjoe Nio. *Lavender and pale pink sarong* by Eliza Van Zuylen. Java, Pekalongan, 1930s. Cotton, drawn batik. Collection of the Peranakan Museum.

from European fairytales and tradition (think angels and Cupids), or from historical events such as the Java War in 1825. Designs could be copied from prints, postcards, magazines and other media and used on the textiles. Floral batiks too were particularly popular, with European blooms such as roses and irises making frequent appearances.

A notable collection of Pekalongan batiks, made by the most important Chinese and Indo-Dutch batik-makers and ateliers in the city, is preserved today at the Peranakan Museum in Singapore. A selection of exceptional pieces is always on display, and may be admired alongside exquisite *kebaya*, eye-catching *kerongsang* and delicate *kasut manek*. This makes the museum one of the best places anywhere to encounter and experience the *sarong kebaya* in all its splendour as the garment of choice for ladies in the port cities of the Peranakans.

34. Shanghai
Fashion and the Fast Life in China's Modern Metropolis

"Lovely flowers do not blossom very often, a wonderful view does not exist very long. / Sorrow covers my smiling brow, missing you brings tears to my eyes. / [Chorus] After we have parted today, when will you come back again?"

— Lyrics by Bei Lin, music by Liu Xue'an, 1937.
"When will you come back again?", performed by Zhou Xuan.[29]

Shanghai (上海) is China's great metropolis on the Whampoa (or Huangpu) River. Its name is often translated as "on the sea"; though it could also mean "to the sea", since nothing stands between this city and the ocean. The city was one of the original five treaty ports forced open to foreign trade in the aftermath of the First Opium War, and by the terms of the Treaty of Nanking in 1842. It would be the greatest and most successful of all treaty ports in China by the turn of the 20th century, second to none in terms of trading volume and sheer size; outstripping even Hong Kong.

Shanghai in the 1840s initially consisted of British, American and French concessions. In 1863, the British and Americans decided to join forces, merging their concessions and redesignating the resulting territory an International Settlement open to merchants of all nationalities, and governed by a Municipal Council consisting of representatives from all major Western powers. The French declined to be part of this settlement, choosing to stand apart from the Anglo-Saxons and administer their French Concession independently. In the meantime, the old Walled City of Shanghai remained under Chinese jurisdiction. So Shanghai was effectively one city with three different city jurisdictions.

Originally, Shanghai's foreign concessions were foreigners-only; Chinese were not allowed to reside here. However, not long after Shanghai was opened to foreign trade, this policy was deemed impractical as the concessions found themselves having to cope with waves of Chinese refugees fleeing conflict and civil war on the Mainland. The first wave came in the aftermath of the Taiping Rebellion between the 1850s to the 1870s.[30] Another wave struck following the Boxer Rebellion.

Between the 1890s and 1910s, the great powers took advantage of China's instability to vastly expand the size of their concessions. In 1899, the International Settlement was expanded to over 5500 acres (more than five times its original size in the 1840s), taking in rural areas to the west and east along the Huangpu River. Subsequently in 1914, on the eve of World War I, the French, too, managed to secure a vast tract of land westwards towards Siccawei (today's Xujiahui). Shanghai in the late 1910s was some 1.5 times the size of all other treaty ports combined at the time, and it was fast gaining a reputation as one of the safest and most stable places on earth, seemingly impervious to the increasingly violent geopolitics elsewhere and right at its doorstep.[31]

By the 1920s and '30s, the city was a boomtown. World War I and revolution in China and Russia sent thousands of Chinese and White Russians fleeing and seeking sanctuary; amongst them, warlords and aristocrats who brought their prodigious wealth with them to the city. The late '20s saw the Great Depression hit Europe and America, but here, it was business as usual, as industrialists simply diverted their capital east, to this safe haven upon the sea. Indeed, Shanghai became one of the world's greatest metropolises during this time, establishing itself firmly as a global banking, fashion and entertainment capital, dazzling and beguiling its visitors in turn with soaring skyscrapers and modern architecture.

To the first-time visitor, the city was entirely Western in outlook. In its initial years, it was built as a showpiece for the British Empire, a London-upon-sea, complete with the usual trappings to be found elsewhere, particularly in British India. There were the headquarters of banks and merchant houses, the requisite amenities such as the Shanghai Club, the Shanghai Racecourse, the Shanghai Yacht Club and more. British "natives" of the city coined a term, "Shanghailanders", to describe and distinguish themselves from the local (Chinese) Shanghainese.

Life was good for these Shanghailanders, who, being of more modest middle-class stock in the home countries, found themselves squarely in the upper classes out here in the colonies; a target of snobbery before, they partook avidly in dispensing it forthwith. Globetrotting author, Somerset Maugham, offers a glimpse of this privileged Shanghailander lifestyle in "Dr MacAlister", contained in his 1922 collection of short stories set in China, *On a Chinese Screen*:

> "I often laugh when I think of my first impressions of China," he said. "I came out expecting to undergo hardships and privations. My first shock was the steamer with ten-course dinners and first-class accommodation. There wasn't

much hardship in that, but I said to myself: wait till you get to China. Well, at Shanghai [...] I stayed in a fine house and was waited on by fine servants and I ate fine food. [...] I thought I'd never eaten so much and so well in my life. You did nothing for yourself. If you wanted a glass of water you called a boy and he brought it to you. [...] I began to think I shouldn't have to put up with much privation after all."[32]

By all accounts, Shanghai was not a "hardship posting" for the young functionary; it was a stepping stone to something much greater, and for some, the culmination of a great career.

The crowning glory of the British phase of the city's development is the Shanghai Bund, that legendary sliver of waterfront real estate built to awe and impress turn-of-the-century tourists and businessmen, and which continues to induce gasps from contemporary visitors to the city. The 22 historic buildings standing right on the Huangpu waterfront housed the headquarters of some of the most important banks and merchant houses in the world – Jardine, Matheson & Co. had an address here; as did the Banque de l'Indochine, the Yokohama Specie Bank and the Hongkong and Shanghai Banking Corporation.

Most of the buildings on the Bund were built between the 1880s and 1920s, and were designed in the Beaux-Arts or neoclassical style typical of imperialist architecture. The most spectacular of these is the HSBC Headquarters at number 12. Capped by an enormous dome, the HSBC building was a cathedral to commerce; and it has remained the most impressive edifice on the Bund ever since it opened in 1923. The story went that the manager of the bank had directed his architects to "spare no expense, but dominate the Bund".[33] These architects were Hong Kong-based Palmer & Turner, the foremost architects of the British Empire, responsible for many of the most important buildings in Shanghai – nine of the buildings on the Bund were designed by them.

In the late 1920s, a visitor to the city would still regard it as a thoroughly British one. But from 1929, as the Great Depression hit and American capital poured into the city, the face of the city itself changed. Art deco would make its debut, indelibly shaping Shanghai's urban landscape.

Art deco and its late variation, streamline moderne, defined modernity in the post-war period, across all genres of visual and decorative art. Originating in France in the 1910s, it became a major international movement following a seminal 1925 *Exposition Internationale des Arts Décoratifs et Industriels Modernes* in Paris, from whence the abbreviated

近附灘浦黃（海上）
Near Koho (Cannel, Shanghai)

term "art deco". The movement itself was motivated by a desire for a clean break with the past, coloured, as it was, by the horrors of World War I. The art deco style thus embraced essentialist, geometrical forms and stylised figural and natural-world representations. It drew from the past, but adopted an aesthetic that was distinctly industrial and machine-made; and only possible by way of new technologies of production.

It was the architectural style of choice particularly in the major cities of America, which, in the aftermath of World War I, shone as beacons of hope, progress and modernity. New York, Chicago and Miami were crucibles for art deco. There, it became inextricable from the Roaring Twenties and the Jazz Age, an age of hedonism and excess, champagne and Cuban cigars, flapper girls and dapper boys jiving all night in racy dancehalls. It was used in the construction of skyscrapers (such as the Chrysler Building), cinemas and theatres, piers and airports.

Shanghai's architects took to the new and utterly modern architectural style with gusto, even as American-style glitz and glamour, exemplified by the advent of cinema and new forms of entertainment and leisure, took over the city, resulting in it taking on the character of a New York-on-the-Huangpu.

One of the most striking examples of art deco is the soaring Sassoon House, at number 20 on the Bund. Opened in 1929, the building represented a definitive pivot towards the modern – it, too, was designed by Palmer and Turner. It is topped by a magnificent green roof in the shape of an Egyptian pyramid, and its stark, geometric form occupies an entire city block. The building housed the iconic Cathay Hotel, one of the most luxurious and opulent establishments east of Suez. It played host to numerous heads of state and celebrities, including English playwright Noel Coward, who famously wrote his play, *Private Lives*, in one of the suites. Sassoon House also housed the offices and private apartments of Sir Victor Sassoon, one of the greatest *taipans* in Shanghai and among the wealthiest men in the world in his time. Of Baghdadi Jewish origins, the Sassoons had interests in their home city of Bombay, as well as in Hong Kong and Shanghai.

The other famous exemplar of art deco was the equally-luxurious Park Hotel on Nanjing Road in the International Settlement, arriving just five years later in 1934. It was the tallest skyscraper in the city when it was built and remained so till the 1980s. Looming ostentatiously over the former Shanghai Racecourse (today's People's Park), its distinctly Gothic art deco style channelled midtown Manhattan. It was designed by Hungarian architect, Ladislav Hudec, who was responsible for many of the city's art deco gems. Another of his creations, the Grand Theatre, is located just down the road. Opened in 1933, it was one of more than a dozen glitzy cinemas built in Shanghai during the '30s and almost inevitably designed in art deco.

Meanwhile, architects in the French Concession were busy transforming their piece of the pie into a latter-day Paris of the East. Unlike the International Settlement, the French Concession never did take off as a viable commercial proposition; instead, it took on the character of a premier residential enclave (like Tianjin's Italian Concession). Here, one could find a proliferation of villas, mansions, as well as luxury residential apartments, many built in the latest architectural styles. Here, too, were all the trappings of a chic French lifestyle – the French club, French departmental stores, French cinemas, French restaurants and cafés, French-style grand boulevards.

The French Concession housed more than a dozen striking examples of art deco residential apartments, as well as a few classics in streamline moderne. As the name suggests, the style emerged in the 1930s as a *streamlining* of the art deco aesthetic. Elaborate ornamentation was done away with, in favour of clean lines and a light, aerodynamic feel. Travel and transportation were the sources of inspiration, with decorative elements drawn from ocean-liners, automobiles and airplanes. Buildings designed in this style thus resembled airports, cruise-liners or cruise-terminals, with long, horizontal balconies and cruise-ship portholes used as ornamentation.

The most iconic apartment block of this genre was undersigned by Leonard, Veysseyre & Kruze and stood just off Avenue Joffre. The architects were at the peak of their careers, and the 13-storey Gascogne Apartments, opened in 1934, was their crowning glory. It was one of the most luxurious and modern apartments at the time. Certainly, it was a sight to behold, with its stark, geometrical façade achieved through replicating long balconies across its floors, giving it the appearance of an airport terminal.

The other iconic example of the style was situated in the International Settlement, just off Nanjing Road. Eddington House (today's Changde Apartments), built in 1935, offered nine different apartment layouts for its eighteen apartment units. Today, the building stands surrounded by towering skyscrapers. It is preserved as the erstwhile home to one of Shanghai's most important modern novelists, Eileen Chang, whose widely-read novels captured the spirit of the city in the 1940s, not long before it was taken over by the Communists.

Shanghai was modern in other ways than architecture. For the Chinese, it was the premier gateway between East and West. The city has always been seen as the one place in China most open to foreign cultures.

After the fall of the Qing dynasty in 1911, the West was seen to be ascendant, and Western culture to be modern and progressive. Though Shanghai was administered by foreign powers, the predominant residents in both the International Settlement as well as the French Concession were Chinese. In close proximity to all manner of new ideas, fashions and technologies imported from the West, the Shanghainese pursued and consumed Western culture zealously, experimenting with and inventing a new hybrid Chinese cultural identity. In so doing, they established Shanghai as China's new capital of culture. From Shanghai, Western and hybrid forms of living would spread inland to the rest of China.

A new term, *modeng*, was coined in relation to this dynamic, ever-shifting cultural identity. It was a transliteration of the word "modern", though it meant much more than that, pointing to all things fashionable and connoting constant re-invention. The *modeng* was expressed most visibly in entertainment, consumption and fashion.[34]

Nanjing Road in the International Settlement became a source of everything *modeng*, hosting numerous large departmental stores selling all the latest consumer goods from the West. The departmental store itself was a key marker of *modeng*; a phenomenon invented by the Americans, adapted by the Japanese, and now, embraced by Shanghai. The biggest departmental stores in the city, boasting the latest architectural styles and state-of-the-art comforts and amenities, were situated within a hair's breadth of each other on Nanjing Road. The message was clear: anything the West had and desired should also be available here for the discerning Shanghainese customer.

Print advertising boomed in the city, with advertisers falling over each other in their eagerness to entice affluent consumers to part with their money. All manner of advertising posters festooned the city streets. The most iconic of these featured pretty young women, impeccably coiffed and fashionably dressed in *qipao* and high heeled shoes, touting all manner of consumer goods from cosmetics and soap, to home appliances, to alcohol and cigarettes. Everywhere you looked in the city, the Shanghai Girl stared back at you, smiling and selling Shanghai's distinctive brand of aspirational living.

1930s Shanghai cosmetics advertisement featuring a modern lady dressed in *qipao* and impeccably coiffed.

Cinema furthered the pursuit of the *modeng*, helping to drive trends and shape tastes. Shanghai was the cinematic capital of the East from the 1920s and '30s, with a huge investor base, and a heady and thriving celebrity culture to boot. Cinema contributed to the glamorous, film noir-ish image of the city as a space of desire: brooding leading men, in their sharply-tailored European-style suits and bowler hats, dallied with beautiful ingénues in their flapper dresses and *qipao*; they smoked Cuban cigars as their vintage automobiles revved down the rain-drenched and glowing expanse of the Bund. A bevy of starlets defined this gilded but short-lived age of Chinese film: the tragic (and tragically short-lived) heroine, Ruan Lingyu; the patriotic songbird, Zhou Xuan; and queen of the movies, Butterfly Wu. They enraptured, entranced and inspired a generation of audiences in turn, always impeccably dressed in the latest Western threads, or more likely than not, in *qipao*.

The *qipao* itself is arguably Shanghai's greatest and most iconic invention. It emerged as a new style of dress in the 1910s, as Shanghai was at the cusp of its golden age and experimenting with its own cultural identity. The *qipao* represented the modern, emancipated woman. It was the equivalent of the flapper dress in the West. Its very form symbolised the liberation of the woman's body from the restrictions of traditional dress codes put in place by patriarchal societies. Refreshingly simple in structure, it was also lightweight, as opposed to traditional Chinese and Manchu dress, which was heavy and difficult to put on, and served to restrict a woman's free movement.

At first, only young, affluent and highly-educated women wore the *qipao*, as a means of distinguishing themselves from their foresisters and declaring that they were ready to take their place alongside the men. Eventually, it became de facto national dress, and was popularly worn by all women, rich or poor, society lady or of the working classes. A dizzying array of *qipao* from the very luxurious to the simple and quotidian catered to a wide diversity of needs.

Emancipation was the spirit of the day, and Shanghai was also a safe haven for Chinese intellectuals, who sought sanctuary as China descended into ever-accelerating cycles of chaos and instability in the course of the early 20th century. That much brainpower meant the city was also a petri dish fomenting new political ideas and emergent revolutionary movements.

In 1921, the Communist Party of China was founded here and had its first Congress in a historical building in the French Concession. By the late 1930s, the Party, led by one Mao Zedong, had built up a formidable presence across China, including in Shanghai, notwithstanding the city's capitalistic excess. Initially allied to the Kuomintang (or Nationalist Party) in their efforts to overthrow Japanese rule, the Communist Party would split from the Nationalist Party after World War II. In 1949, the People's Liberation Army of the Communist Party swept into Shanghai after having fought a series of battles against the Kuomintang.

The rest is history.

35. Tokyo
From the Meiji Restoration to World War II

> "I have heard that it did not take ten years for San Francisco to be a finer city than before the earthquake. Tokyo too would be rebuilt in ten years, into a solid expanse of splendid buildings like the Marunouchi Building and the Marine Insurance Building. I imagined the grandeur of the new metropolis, and all the changes that would come in customs and manners as well. An orderly pattern of streets, their bright new pavements gleaming. A flood of automobiles. The geometric beauty of block towering upon block, and elevated lines and subways and trolleys weaving among them, and the stir of a nightless city, and pleasure facilities to rival those of Paris and New York..."
>
> — Tanizaki Junichiro, 1935. "Tokyo Reminiscence". In *Osaka Essays (Setsuyo Zuihitsu)*. [35]

Tokyo Station appears, as if in a dream; a rare instance of a low-rise building in Central Tokyo, silhouetted against the towering glass-and-steel skyscrapers that make up the skyline. The station stands facing the Imperial Palace, ancient seat of the Tokugawa shoguns in the Edo period, and today, home to the Japanese Imperial Family. It also occupies a central place at the heart of the city's gargantuan transport network, as well as its sense of self.

The station was conceived in the Meiji era, but only opened in 1914. It was designed by architect Tatsuno Kingo, regarded as the foremost Japanese architect of the era. He was a student of British architect, Josiah Conder, so-called "father of modern Japanese architecture", who built the first hybrid, east-west-style buildings now considered characteristic of the Meiji period. Conder's most illustrious protégé, Tatsuno would continue in his mentor's footsteps, designing dozens of buildings in Tokyo and across Japan, and playing a critical role in shaping modern Japanese architectural and cultural identity. [36]

Designed in a British, Queen-Anne style, the station is built with red brick, is perfectly symmetrical in form, and has an exquisite, dollhouse-like look. Its main entrance is at centre and was formerly reserved for the Imperial Family's use. This middle portion of the building approximates the Second Empire style and resembles a French chateau. The station's two ends used to contain its passenger entrance and exit; they are each topped by large eye-catching domes cast in mahogany-hued bronze.

The station building was also home to the historic Tokyo Station Hotel, opened in 1915 to cater to the needs of discerning travellers.

To the Tokyo public, the station is known fondly as the Aka Renga Station, or "red brick station". It was originally commissioned to commemorate Japan's victory in the Russo-Japanese War, and thus has to be seen as a triumphal monument akin to the Arc de Triomphe in Paris. The brief to Tatsuno had been for a structure that would amaze the world; one befitting of a strong and modern nation able to defeat the great Russian Empire. When it was first opened, the station had three storeys and its main body was built over a frame of reinforced steel – an innovation imported from the West. This structure helped it survive the Great Kanto Earthquake of 1923; though the building would be severely damaged by air raids during World War II.

Much of the third floor was destroyed and had to be removed in the course of restoration efforts undertaken just after the war. In 2007, the station underwent a second, major restoration which returned it to its former glory. It reopened in late 2012 to popular and critical acclaim. Not long after, the Tokyo Station Hotel, too, reopened its doors as one of the most historic luxury hotels in the city.

The Meiji Emperor ascended Japan's Chrysanthemum Throne in 1867, at just 15 years of age. This was a time of great change and uncertainty. Barely a decade before, Commodore Matthew Perry's "black ships" had sailed into Edo Bay, and Japan had been forced to

Tokyo Station,
Marunouchi.

sign a series of unequal treaties with the Western powers. For over
250 years, the Land of the Rising Sun had been ruled by the powerful
Tokugawa shoguns from their ancestral seat in Edo. Rival *daimyo* clans
saw the Tokugawas' capitulation to the West as weakness, and a grave and
humiliating mistake. They feared that unless Japan reformed itself and
grew strong, it would be colonised by the Western powers.

In an extraordinary turn of events, leaders of the powerful, rival
Satsuma and Choshu clans came to a strategic alliance and orchestrated
a revolution. Whisking the young emperor out from seclusion in Kyoto,
they lobbied for the Japanese monarchy to be restored to power, and for
the end to the Tokugawa *bakufu*.

"*Sonno joi*!" – "Revere the Emperor! Expel the Barbarians!"
– became their rallying cry and slogan. Securing unprecedented
support from other powerful *daimyo* clans across the nation, they
succeeded in forcing the last Tokugawa shogun to abdicate and return
his governing power to the emperor. In 1868, a new era name was
proclaimed: Meiji, meaning "Enlightened Rule". Thus this seismic
shift in Japanese political history would be known as the *Meiji Ishin*,
or Meiji Restoration.

Since at least the 13th century, Japan had been ruled by shoguns,
with the emperor a mere figurehead, cloistered in the imperial palace at
Kyoto. Soon after the Meiji proclamation, the emperor would move his
seat of government from Kyoto to the harbour city of Edo, renaming
the city Tokyo (東京), or "Eastern Capital". A year later, as part of a

series of sweeping reforms, all *daimyo* were asked to relinquish their domains voluntarily to the emperor, thus allowing for a concentration of political power in the imperial court at Tokyo. Meanwhile, there was no settling down for the emperor as his court coined a new slogan to rally the masses.

"*Bunmei kaika*," was their new rallying cry – "Civilisation and Enlightenment"! This signalled a massive, concerted and prolonged drive to Westernise Japan at all costs. The intent was to have Japan stand confidently alongside the Western powers as a great power of its own. The imperial court seethed at the continuing existence of treaty ports in Japan. They knew that to abolish the unequal treaties, they had to persuade the Western powers that Japan was an equal.

Between 1871 and 1873, a formal imperial embassy – known as the Iwakura Mission – was sent abroad to America, Britain, France, Germany and other European countries, ostensibly for Japan to learn from the West. The outcome of this mission was wholesale borrowing of Western forms of governance, intellectual thought, technology and culture. The best bits of different Western traditions were selected and adapted to Japan's specific context. In politics, a constitutional monarchy was adopted, drawing upon Prussian and British models at the time. Japanese men started donning Western-style suits and bowler hats in public and at work. Japanese women experimented with corsets and bustles, even as they continued to wear the traditional kimono. The most visible change came in the field of architecture, where different architectural styles and traditions – French Beaux-Arts, Italian Renaissance, English neoclassical and Queen Anne – were mashed up to create the curious "Japanese-style Western architecture" that approximated the western tradition but was in reality a completely new hybrid genre tied to Japan's new imperial ambitions.

The Meiji Emperor played his role of symbolic figurehead perfectly. Wherever he appeared in public, he would be dressed in the style of a European monarch, riding a horse or ensconced in his thoroughly European horse carriage. Eschewing the traditional, shadowy and distant personage of the emperor, Meiji was a public figure, delivering speeches and addresses, attending opening ceremonies and events, visiting schools and factories, inspecting the battalions, and hosting international high-society balls in his state banqueting house. He played the role European constitutional monarchs were accustomed to and still play today.

The wholesale transformation of Japanese culture and society had its effect. In 1899, Japan succeeded in having the unequal treaties reversed; though in return, it would open itself up entirely to foreign trade, and actively engage in international affairs. The active Westernisation of Japanese culture and society would continue even after the Meiji Emperor passed away in 1912.

The Taisho Emperor's reign was brief but heralded a shift in popular culture. Cinema and art deco made their appearance during this time, alongside new socio-cultural phenomena such as the *moga* – an abbreviation of "modern girl". *Moga* were young, liberated and financially-independent Japanese women who pursued Western fashions (such as the flapper dress), lifestyles and sexual proclivities, and expressed their identities through material consumption. Their equivalent was the *mobo*, or "modern boy" – the uber-fashionable "it" boy who, like his counterpart, pooh-poohed society's traditional expectations of him. *Moga* and *mobo* were most frequently spotted in the newly-fashionable shopping and commercial district of Ginza, puffing away louchely on their cigarettes and spouting the latest slang.

The Great Kanto Earthquake in 1923 demolished vast tracts of Tokyo. Much of what had been Old Edo, including part of the former imperial palace, was flattened. What emerged from the ashes was a brand-new city far more confident in its identity, forward-looking and progressive, constantly re-inventing itself in a bid to stand alongside the great nations of the world. But there was a worrying dark cloud in all this joyful exuberance and excess.

Earlier in the 1870s, the Japanese had opted to reform their military after the Prussian example: anchored in authoritarianism and unquestioning loyalty bordering on fanaticism. This austere and extreme form of militarism resonated with Japan's feudal samurai culture. During the Meiji era, the government had coined (yet another) slogan speaking to the need to shore up the army as a means of showing Japan's strength. "*Fukoku kyohei*," it went – "Enrich the Nation, Strengthen the Army", as though one thing led to the other.

The turn of the 20th century thus corresponded with Japan's transition to a highly-militaristic, imperialist power. This was initially motivated by a Pan-Asian idealism; a sense that it was Japan's destiny as Asia's most advanced nation to rally its Asian neighbours against the

Western powers, as well as to save the ordinary peoples of East Asia from China's moribund East Asian Order of Things.

In 1879, the Ryukyu Islands, traditionally a Chinese vassal, were summarily annexed as a Japanese prefecture, despite China's objections. Next came Taiwan, seized and brutally suppressed in the aftermath of the First Sino-Japanese War in 1895. In 1910, the Japanese would extricate Korea from China's sphere of influence, annexing the entire peninsula as an inalienable province, and thus pulling the last block out from China's proverbial *tianxia*.

All this and more was achieved during the Meiji era alone. During the Taisho and Showa periods, Japan grew even more belligerent and nationalistic. It no longer pretended to be a benign saviour of its Eastern brethren. Instead, it regarded the Japanese people as the superior race, and saw imperialism as the means by which it would finally occupy a seat at the Great Power table.

An expansionist, militaristic foreign agenda meant Japan needed to colonise new territory in order to secure access to raw materials. In 1932, taking advantage of civil war in China, Japan annexed Manchuria, renaming it Manchukuo and inviting the last emperor of China, Pu Yi, to rule in name as a puppet monarch. This same ravenous hunger for raw materials and resources was the motivation behind the so-called Greater East Asian Co-Prosperity Sphere (大東亜共栄圏 – *dai to'a kyoeiken*), first conceptualised in the 1930s as a propagandistic means of justifying Japanese rule to the peoples of their colonised territories, and essentially a modern expression of the Japanese *tenka* (*tianxia*).

The Second Sino-Japanese War of 1937 escalated into World War II in the aftermath of Japanese war planes bombing Pearl Harbour in 1941. Japan joined the Axis powers, Nazi Germany and Italy, in declaring war against the Allies. In a matter of years, and in the name of the Greater East Asian Co-Prosperity Sphere, Japanese troops would conquer and occupy large parts of China and practically all of Southeast Asia. Japanese occupation of these territories would be characterised by horrific brutality, with the Japanese colonial record being just as bad or worse than that of the Europeans. World War II came to an end in 1945 when the Americans dropped atomic bombs on Hiroshima and on the port city of Nagasaki.

Central Tokyo, on the eve of the surrender, had been almost entirely laid waste by Allied bombings and air raids. Photographs of the time depict a city so completely devastated and devoid of feature as to be unrecognisable. On 15 August 1945, the day of the surrender, grieving Tokyo-ites turned on the radio and tuned in, disbelieving, as the Showa Emperor delivered his portentous declaration:

> "After pondering deeply the general trends of the world and the actual conditions obtaining in our Empire today, We have decided to effect a settlement of the present situation by resorting to an extraordinary measure.
>
> We have ordered our government to communicate to the governments of the United States, Great Britain, China and the Soviet Union that our Empire accepts the provisions of their joint declaration.
>
> [...]
>
> The hardships and sufferings to which our nation is to be subjected hereafter will be certainly great. We are keenly aware of the inmost feelings of all of you, our subjects. However, it is according to the dictates of time and fate that We have resolved to pave the way for a grand peace for all the generations to come by enduring the unendurable and suffering what is insufferable."

When it ended, there was a mix of confusion and silence as an entire nation contemplated the end of an era.

Old Edo persists today, just barely, in the bustling historic quarter of Asakusa. This was the heart of the Shitamachi, or Low City, where the common folk dwelled; its merchants and traders, in particular. Edo (江戸) was a harbour city and domestic centre for trade and commerce – its name meant "river estuary". Here on the banks of the Sumida River were the bazaars and markets, bars and teahouses, *kabuki* theatres and pleasure quarters of old, immortalised in "pictures of a floating world", the *ukiyo-e* of the 18th and early 19th centuries.

The Senso-ji Temple has stood here since 645, and it is dedicated to Kannon, or the goddess of mercy. Legend goes that a golden statue of the deity had been fortuitously found here along the banks of Sumida by two fishermen, and that Senso-ji Temple had been built to house it. The statue purportedly still exists within the temple precinct, though few have actually seen it.

Senso-ji Temple and Asakusa are among the most popular historic sites and tourist attractions in Tokyo today. On any given day, the temple precinct is thronged with thousands of tourists and worshippers, seeking blessings and posing for selfies in front of the iconic Kaminarimon, or Thunder Gate, with its large, eye-catching red lantern. The Nakamise-dori, a traditional bazaar street, leads from the gate to the temple proper. Delightfully evoking Old Edo, it is lined

with dozens of small shops selling various traditional Japanese crafts, sweets and snacks.

Once in the temple proper, one of the most popular activities is the drawing of an *o-mikuji*, or paper fortune. For a small donation, the visitor draws out a number by shaking a box full of numbered wooden sticks repeatedly until one falls out. The number on each stick corresponds to a specific fortune, written on a piece of paper which the fortune-seeker then retrieves from a drawer. If it is a good fortune, then all is well, and the visitor retains the slip of paper. If it is a bad fortune, however, the way to mitigate the bad luck is to tie the piece of paper onto one of many lines of metal wire left there for the purpose, and thus leave this bad fortune behind. From the looks of the many slips of paper left behind, bad fortunes are as frequent as good ones.

Though Senso-ji is Tokyo's oldest temple, the present temple building itself dates to 1958. When the bombs flattened Tokyo, Asakusa and the Senso-ji, too, were destroyed by the fires that swept through the city for days. But like the proverbial phoenix or *fushicho* ("bird which never dies"), the temple, and the city to which it offers protection, would rise again from the ashes, re-inventing itself one more time, just as it had done for centuries.

36. Semarang & Surabaya (Samarang & Soerabaja)
Tempo Doeloe and the Road to Merdeka

"The chief messenger, squatting with his glowing wick in his hand, peeped attentively at his master, as though thinking: 'How strange, those Hollanders!... What is he thinking now?... Why is he behaving like this?... Just at this time and on this spot?... The sea-spirits are about now... there are [crocodiles] under the water, and every [crocodile] is a spirit... Look, they have been sacrificing to them there: [...] What is the [master] doing here?... It is not good here, it is not good here, alas, alas!' [...] How strange, those Hollanders, how strange!..."

— Louis Couperus, 1900. *The Hidden Force.*[37]

In the faded photograph, the *njonja besar*, or matriarch, of the family sits off-centre. She is formally dressed in a long, white, lace-rimmed *kabaia*, and a *sarong* in the Pekalongan style, made at a fashionable Chinese atelier. She stares straight at the camera, her brown eyes and dark skin contrasting with the whiteness of her *kabaia*. Though of mixed race, she identifies as Dutch. Her husband stands behind her, dressed in a white planters' uniform that men wear for formal occasions during the day. Their four children pose beside them. The second son is the fairest of skin, with light blue eyes. He is all dapper in a suit like his father's, and, unlike everyone else, smiles at the camera, his eyes twinkling. Their youngest daughter also dons a *sarong kabaia*, and looks the spitting image of her mother.

The setting of the photograph is the commodious verandah of the family home, built in the Old Indies style, a hybrid of Dutch and local vernaculars. Single-storeyed, it is topped with a steep and hipped *joglo* roof designed for the heavy tropical rains, and borrowed from Javanese palace architecture. To stave off the tropical heat, the house has very high ceilings and large verandahs, allowing for improved air circulation. The verandah functions as an outdoor sitting room and resembles the Javanese *pendopo*, or pavilion; it is customary for families to entertain guests here, particularly in the evenings when it is cooler.

"Hold still everyone!" the matriarch hisses as the photographer attempts to capture the moment.

And then, with a brilliant flash of light, it is done.

Sixty years later, the youngest daughter, now a grandmother, rummaging through her mother's things at home in the Netherlands, chances upon this old photograph. She gasps as she remembers the very morning when it was taken: the surfeit of light … the *waringin* tree towering just beyond the garden… the suffocating heat… the birdsong and the scent of *melati*… She remembers her mother's anxiety that morning, her father's grumpiness. Her second brother, the handsome one in the family, had just been accepted into university in the Netherlands; he was leaving home in a matter of weeks, and he had been so happy.

"Ah, *tempo doeloe!*" she sighs wistfully as the floodgates of memory open. "Ah, those were the days."

More than anything, *tempo doeloe* is a feeling: a sense of loss for time past that may never return. As a sentiment and expression, it described the experience of the Dutch community in the Indies, who called themselves the Indische, or "Indies" people.

There were many cycles of *tempo doeloe*. At the turn of the century, the Indische community was already expressing *tempo doeloe* for the good old days before the Suez Canal opened. The canal brought Holland immeasurably closer to Java, and the new wave of settlers – *totok*, they called them, "new arrivals" – inadvertently brought new kinds of biases to this closed community. Where before, the races were less segregated and mixed-race families were commonplace, the post-Suez period brought a newfound obsession with "whiteness" and racial purity. Mixed marriages began to be frowned upon where they had been an established fact of life in colonial Indies society before.

Then there was the *tempo doeloe* of the 1950s, when the Dutch were expelled from a newly independent Indonesia, and some 300,000 of the Indische (and Indo) community repatriated en masse, with most settling in cold and grey Den Haag (The Hague). There, sitting in their new homes still furnished in the old style, rummaging through their old family portraits and photographs, putting on old phonograph records of *krontjong* standards, they would yearn for their past lives in their sundrenched Indies-style bungalows.[38]

Dutch East Indies literature is imbued with *tempo doeloe*. A small but influential group of turn-of-the-century authors is held up today as exemplars of the genre. Two of the most important were Louis Couperus and Robert Nieuwenhuys.

Former headquarters of the Nederlandsch-Indische Spoorweg Maatschappij, otherwise known as Lawang Sewu, in Semarang.

Couperus, a *totok*, was known for his masterpiece (and only novel set in the Indies), *The Hidden Force* (1900), in which he tells the tale of a colonial regent's family, plagued and finally destroyed by supernatural forces. It caused a scandal when it was released, particularly because of its depiction of the young Mrs Van Oudijck, wife to the regent, who has affairs with her stepson and her daughter's paramour. The book laid bare the social mores of Indies society and the hypocrisy of the entire colonial project.

Nieuwenhuys was Indische born and bred; his hometown was Samarang, though he spent his childhood in the legendary Hotel des Indes in Batavia, where his father was the director. While interned in a Japanese concentration camp during World War II, he authored an autobiographical novel – *Faded Portraits* (1954) – in which he tenderly and nostalgically recalled scenes from his childhood. He is also known for his *Mirror of the East Indies* (1972), a comprehensive survey of Dutch East Indies literature; and for his best-selling photo-book, *Tempo Doeloe: Photographic Documents from the Old Indies, 1870-1914* (1973), which includes cherished family photos of many Indies families from their time in the "Old Indies". This was the first book to prominently explore and sentimentalise *tempo doeloe*. More than any other author, Nieuwenhuys and his works defined *tempo doeloe* as acute post-colonial nostalgia for a generation of former colonials.

Tempo doeloe (or *tempo dulu* in contemporary Bahasa Indonesia) is nowadays also used in reference to old colonial architecture and streetscapes still existing in Indonesian cities. A good way to experience this historic architecture is to visit the port cities of Surabaya and Semarang, the second and third cities of the former Dutch East Indies. Though Batavia was the capital, very little of its historic architecture remains today. Post-independence, Batavia was renamed Jakarta, and remained the political and economic capital of the new republic. The concentration of wealth in the city meant swift and rampant development, resulting in many historic buildings being torn down. There was very little affection for them at the time, due to these buildings' indelible links to colonialism; and the Dutch had been unrelentingly brutal in their efforts to colonise the archipelago.

In Semarang, the former Oude Stad or Kota Lama – meaning "Old Town" – has been touted as the best-preserved Dutch colonial settlement in Indonesia. More than 100 buildings remain in this former city centre, and many have been painstakingly restored since the 2000s. Like its sister city, Batavia, Semarang began as a former VOC settlement, with a five-pointed *kasteel*, or fort, standing sentinel on the waterfront. The advent of the railroads post-1870 brought prosperity to the city as it was linked directly to Batavia as well as other major cities on the island. The decision by the Dutch colonial administration to locate the headquarters of the Nederlandsch-Indische Spoorweg Maatschappij, or Dutch East Indies Railway Company, here went a long way in raising the profile and visibility of the city.

By far the most outstanding structure in the Old Town – often held up as the symbol of Semarang *tempo doeloe* – is the former Immanuel Church, more popularly known as the Gereja Blenduk, or "Dome Church", on account of its huge and eye-catching reddish-bronze dome, and the fact that it dominates the old town's skyline even today. Established in 1753, it has the distinction of being the oldest church in Central Java, though the current building was built in 1787. The architecture of the church is unique: it is octagonal in shape and features two minaret-like towers at the front, each of which is capped by a smaller dome. The entrance to the church is marked by a Palladian-style *porte-cochère* with pediment and neoclassical columns: the church thus looks like a pagan Roman temple, and it closely resembles its cousin, the Wolvendaal Church in Colombo.

The city's other significant historic building – its crowning glory – is the so-called Lawang Sewu, or "Building of a Thousand Doors". This is the former headquarters of the Nederlandsch-Indische Spoorweg Maatschappij, located a quick ten-minute drive away from the Old Town. The building is monumental in size. It is one of the most spectacular examples of the New Indies style, which appeared at the turn of the 20th century and melded modern forms of architecture – such as art deco and Dutch rationalism – with local, Javanese elements attuned to the tropical climate. The building thus features wraparound verandahs to keep out the rain and the sun, as well as a proliferation of large shuttered doors opening onto the verandahs to draw in the breeze – these doors explain its popular name. Like many other bank and commercial buildings in the Dutch East Indies, Lawang Sewu boasts magnificent stained-glass windows in the Dutch symbolist style, featuring allegorical personifications of Venus and Fortuna, alongside the coats of arms of cities in the Netherlands and the Indies.

Surabaya, too, retains a large concentration of historic buildings, particularly in and around the Jembatan Merah, or "Red Bridge", which lies at the heart of the old town. The bridge spans the Kalimas, or "River of Gold", Surabaya's age-old river, which flows all the way to the mouth of its still operating *pinisi* harbour. West of the Red Bridge is the former Dutch Oude Stad proper. Here, lining the riverfront, stand the former premises of Dutch and other European merchant houses, many of which have been preserved. The most unforgettable of these is the former headquarters of the Maatschappij Tot Exploitatie van het Bureau Gebroeders Knaud. Built in 1916, it sports an eye-catching side tower crowned with a slim, reddish-bronze dome – it's quite impossible to miss. It is popularly known as the Cigar Building on account of the shape of its dome and tower; though to the untrained eye, dome and tower might look rather more like a bullet, piercing the sky.

Heading south from the Oude Stad, we come to the leafy and fashionable Tunjungan district, which houses a proliferation of art deco buildings and Old Indies-style bungalows, still standing amidst towering skyscrapers and gleaming new shopping malls. Here in Tunjungan stands another of the city's historic landmarks: the former Oranje Hotel, which goes by the name Hotel Majapahit today. The Oranje Hotel was the city's grand hotel, built in 1910 by Javanese relatives of the legendary Armenian hoteliers, the Sarkies Brothers. Originally designed in an Indo-Persian style, like its cousins in Malaya and Burma, the hotel was extended in 1930 and given a new art deco façade. Otherwise, the expansive grounds of the hotel itself remain largely unchanged and were immaculately restored in the early '90s. A stroll in its grounds – a rare oasis of calm – is essential, if only for a taste of Soerabaja *tempo doeloe*, as the Dutch would have experienced it.

Unlike in Semarang, major landmarks in Surabaya are also associated with another sentiment that speaks to the soul of contemporary Indonesia – *Merdeka*, or freedom. Surabaya itself, by a twist of fate, is indelibly linked to revolutionary activity and Indonesia's Independence Movement. To underscore Surabaya's heroic credentials, the city is home to two of Indonesia's most important thinkers and revolutionaries.

The first is Pramoedya Ananta Toer, one of Indonesia's most important novelists. Pramoedya began his career as a journalist in Surabaya, and wrote some of his earliest novels while being incarcerated by the Dutch for supporting the independence movement. His crowning achievement is *The Buru Quartet* – a series of four political novels set mainly in Surabaya. Published in the 1980s, in post-independence Indonesia, the world of the *Quartet* is that of the Dutch East Indies in its twilight years, at the turn of the 20th century. The lead character, Minke, is a Javanese aristocrat who admires European civilisation for its progressiveness but gradually sees through to the corruption and abject racism of the Dutch colonial administration. Initially choosing a literary career, he would eventually grow into the role of an independence fighter.

The other of Surabaya's native sons is Koesno Sosrodihardjo, better known as Soekarno (Sukarno in Bahasa Indonesia).[39] Born in Surabaya to a Javanese father and a Hindu Balinese mother, Sukarno was the charismatic leader, par excellence, of the Indonesian Independence movement, and he would become the first president of the Republic of Indonesia. Like Pramoedya Ananta Toer, he had been arrested and imprisoned by the Dutch for his political activities, and he became a popular hero in the 1930s, publishing various articles calling for independence.

His greatest achievement remains his founding of the Indonesian nation, based on the *Pancasila*, or five foundational principles, that he had played an instrumental role in expounding. These are: the unity of Indonesia in all its cultural diversity; a belief in a common, civilised and just humanity; representative and consultative democracy that favours consensus; social justice for all; as well as an acceptance of a transcendent Higher Divinity that provides for the inclusion of all faiths and enshrines religious harmony. Indonesia was thus conceived as a democratic, multicultural and multi-religious nation.

The end of World War II, and the expulsion of the Japanese from occupied territories in Asia, precipitated a wave of decolonisation and independence movements across the region. One of the first Asian nations to declare their independence was Indonesia.

In the early hours of 17 August 1945, two days after the Japanese surrender, a group of men from the Partai Nasional Indonesia (Indonesian National Party) gathered at Sukarno's private residence. A microphone had been set up so that Sukarno's Proclamation of Independence would be broadcast around the new nation. Uttering a prayer to God, Sukarno addressed his people, acknowledging how they had struggled for decades to secure their country's freedom, and declaring that the moment had come for them to take their nation's destiny into their own hands. Said he:

> "WE THE PEOPLE OF INDONESIA HEREBY
> DECLARE THE INDEPENDENCE OF INDONESIA.
> MATTERS WHICH CONCERN THE TRANSFER OF POWER
> AND OTHER THINGS WILL BE EXECUTED BY CAREFUL MEANS
> AND IN THE SHORTEST POSSIBLE TIME.
> DJAKARTA, 17 AUGUST 1945
> IN THE NAME OF THE PEOPLE OF INDONESIA
> SUKARNO—HATTA"[40]

Sukarno's Proclamation sparked a war. The Dutch weren't about to give up their former colony without a fight, and determined to re-establish colonial rule after the Japanese left. Many of them had been in the Indies all their lives, their families and entire livelihoods anchored here – this was, after all, their home.

The Battle for Surabaya initially began as a skirmish between the Javanese and the ordinary Dutch and Indo citizens of the city. On 19 September, a month after the Proclamation of Independence, members of the local Indies community, released from internment and ensconced in the Oranje Hotel, decided to hoist a Dutch flag above the building as an indication that the Dutch were back in control. This incensed local Javanese freedom fighters. One of them clambered up to the roof of the hotel in a fury, and, tearing off the blue portion of the Dutch flag, transformed it into the revolutionary red-and-white of Indonesia.

Hostilities ensued and violence escalated over the following weeks. There were hundreds of casualties. In late October, more than 6000

British troops were called in to keep the peace. The Netherlands hadn't had the resources to maintain a Far Eastern military presence during the Japanese Occupation. Britain, being allied to the Netherlands, stepped in to help; it, too, was concerned for the fate of its colonies and stood in solidarity with its European ally.

The Battle of Surabaya commenced proper on 27 October, with the most intense fighting taking place between 10 to 29 November. It was documented extensively in photographs by wartime journalists in and around the city. The epicentre of the fighting was at the Jembatan Merah, in the very heart of the city. Dozens of photographs depict British soldiers – many of them actually of Indian ethnicity – in the thick of battle, lying prone with their guns aimed to fire, or crouching behind armed vehicles. There are shots of tanks rolling down the ruined streets. The same wartime photographers also captured portraits of the Indonesian freedom fighters: young and defiant heroes who would lay down their lives in the days that came.

One of the most iconic photographs of the Battle of Surabaya features the burnt-out husk of a once-glamourous LaSalle 1940 Series 52 sedan, manufactured by General Motors. The car had belonged to one Brigadier Aubertin W. S. Mallaby, commander of the British troops on the ground. Approaching the epicentre of the conflict at Jembatan Merah in his car, Brigadier Mallaby had been shot to death in a gunfire skirmish, and his vehicle blown up by a grenade. To the left of the smouldering vehicle, standing tall in the distance, is the familiar bullet-shaped dome and tower of Surabaya's Cigar Building. To the right of the vehicle, and just behind it, is a billboard with the image of the Indonesian flag and these immortal words: "Once and Forever – The Indonesian Republic".

Merdeka! one almost hears the rallying cry. *Merdeka! Merdeka!*

The British would win the Battle of Surabaya, just barely; and the struggle for independence would take another four long years. But time and history were on Sukarno's side. The Dutch finally relinquished Indonesia in 1949 and the Republic would come into being on 17 August 1950, exactly five years after Sukarno's Proclamation. Indonesia's Independence Day would be set on 17 August, while 10 November was declared Hari Pahlawan, or National Heroes' Day, in commemoration of all who died in the Battle of Surabaya.

Between 1945 and 1965, almost all former colonies in Asia and around the Indian Ocean gained their independence. Some would manage to accomplish this transition peacefully; most would find themselves lapsing into the violent throes of civil war en route to nationhood. By the 1970s, only a few territories remained in the hands of the imperial powers, and a new dawn broke over the East.

[Afternote: In this chapter, the Dutch transliteration of Malay is used.]

OF CONTAINERS
AND
CONNECTIVITY

20th Century — Today

37. Singapore
The Raffles Brand and the Global City

"To keep Raffles' statue was easy. My colleagues and I had no desire
to rewrite the past and perpetuate ourselves by renaming streets or
buildings or putting our faces on postage stamps or currency notes.
Winsemius said we would need large-scale technical, managerial,
entrepreneurial and marketing knowhow from America and Europe.
Investors wanted to see what a new socialist government in Singapore
was going to do to the statue of Raffles. Letting it remain would be
a symbol of public acceptance of the British heritage and could have
a positive effect."

— Lee Kuan Yew, 2000. *From Third World to First –
The Singapore Story: 1965 – 2000.*[1]

Depictions of Singapore in travel-guides and postcards from the
colonial era largely still apply to Singapore today. Grand colonial
edifices continue to characterise the urban landscape in the city centre,
albeit interspersed with equally grand edifices of glass and steel. The
Botanic Gardens and the Raffles Hotel still welcome visitors from all
over the world, and a little further outside the city centre, one can still
find colonial-era black-and-white bungalows nestled in the city suburbs,
housing the city's resident elites.

A distinguishing feature of Singapore's post-colonial history lay in
how it was hardly postcolonial: its narratives of nationhood did not
emphasise notions of victimised Asian and oppressor White. Indeed,
Singapore's transition from colonial city to independent nation-state was
starkly different from that of its Southeast Asian neighbours, most of
which experienced some degree of violent self-reflection and were quick
to efface physical traces of the colonial past upon achieving nationhood.

Singapore's decision to preserve its colonial past was a function
of pragmatism. Post-1965, when Singapore became independent
from Britain *and* Malaysia, the national priority was overwhelmingly
economic; there was a need to lift a large proportion of its people out
of poverty and to reassure resident elites and foreign investors that the
country would not sink immediately into social and economic chaos.[2]
The Singapore government's approach to addressing its colonial legacy
was therefore to singularly divert it towards a new nationalistic ideology
of progress and prosperity at all costs. The nation capitalised on its
colonial heritage, exploited it strategically as a form of resource for

OVERLEAF: Marina,
Marine City, Busan.

OPPOSITE PAGE:
Changi Airport Control
Tower, Singapore.

The black statue of Raffles stands today in front of the Victoria Memorial Hall, at Empress Place, just around the corner from the Asian Civilisations Museum.

economic growth, and in so doing, performed a sort of symbolic effacement of the colonial: colonial built heritage and social practices remained, but the ghosts of the colonial past inherent in them were exorcised.

The first act of exorcism, of a ghost of rather significant stature, took place in 1961, two years after Singapore attained full internal self-government. A team from the United Nations Development Programme, led by Dutch economist, Dr Albert Winsemius, was dispatched to Singapore to advise the newly self-governing territory on strategies for industrialisation and economic development. Among the recommendations presented to Singapore's founding prime minister Lee Kuan Yew was the suggestion that Singapore not remove the bronze statue of Sir Thomas Stamford Raffles, the erstwhile "founder" of modern Singapore, from its place in the civic district, the heart of the former colonial administration.

The statue of Raffles, now a popular icon of Singapore, was first erected in 1887 and is currently located in front of the Victoria Memorial Hall, Singapore's oldest performing arts venue, named after Queen Victoria, and located in the Empress Place precinct (referring to Victoria as Empress of India). It originally stood on the Padang, a huge public square in the heart of the colonial city centre; but it was apparently often hit by flying footballs or used as a vantage point to catch cricket games. As such, it was moved to its current location in 1919, the hundredth anniversary of Singapore's "founding" by Raffles.

At the point of Singapore's independence, the statue became a symbol of the entire British imperialist enterprise in Singapore and thus occupied a precarious position. Lee Kuan Yew's eventual decision to retain the statue effectively stripped it of its (painful) historical meaning, relegating it to the role of a signpost pointing to Singapore's business-readiness; one with "Invest here!" writ large across it. With Raffles symbolically effaced, Singapore pragmatically shrugged off any lingering (latently violent) post-colonial sentiments it might have had and was reborn as "Singapore Inc." – a nation and city-state that was also a large corporation. Meanwhile, Raffles was touted by the fledgling state as the "Founder of

Modern Singapore", even as his statue continued to remain in a position of prominence at the heart of the colonial city centre.

1972 was a crucial year for Singapore Inc. on account of a timely and strategic conjunction of events. The first was the opening of the Tanjong Pagar Container Terminal, the very first port terminal in Southeast Asia to utilise container berths. In 1956, an American businessman, Malcolm McLean, invented the container – a standard-sized, pre-packed metal box for cargo – and sailed the world's first container vessel from the port city of Newark, New Jersey, to Houston, Texas.[3] This invention revolutionised the shipping industry. Within decades, containers became the basic storage unit for shipping all kinds of cargo, and container ships replaced the cargo tankers of before.

The greatest advantages of containerisation were speed, efficiency and safety. A container ship could be fully loaded or unloaded in a matter of hours, as opposed to older cargo ships, which might require days. Cargo now came in standard, pre-packed units, rather than in differently-sized packs and cartons – this allowed for maximisation of space on the ship deck since containers could be regularly stacked sideways and upwards. Containers were also industrially-sealed, and so the risk of cargo shifting or being stolen during the journey was greatly minimised.

The result was that shipping costs dropped tremendously, as did the time taken for cargo to reach its destination. The volume of world trade greatly expanded as a consequence. A new unit of trade, the Twenty-foot Equivalent Unit, or TEU, was developed based on the dimensions of a standard 20-foot-long container. The TEU became a measure of cargo capacity both for container vessels, as well as for container ports. So when one says a ship is able to carry 10,000 TEU, it means it is able to ship the equivalent of 10,000 20-foot-long containers of cargo. Likewise, a port able to handle two million TEU annually can process some two million of these 20-foot-long containers of cargo a year.

To accommodate container ships, existing port infrastructure needed to be massively upgraded across the world's major ports, and so the worldwide adoption of this new technology took the better part of the '70s and '80s. Singapore had shrewdly invested millions in upgrading its port facilities early to enjoy first-mover advantage. Its very first container ship arrived on 23 June 1972. By 1986 – just 14 years later – Singapore had become the busiest port in the world in terms of shipping tonnage. Today, it receives some 140,000 vessels a year from more than 600 ports in 120 countries. In keeping with its history as an entrepôt port par excellence, Singapore remains top in the world for transhipments – i.e. cargo imported to be exported elsewhere – handling some 37.3 million TEU of cargo in 2022.[4]

1972 also saw the incorporation of Singapore's legendary flagship carrier, Singapore Airlines, upon the dissolution of the former Malaysia-Singapore Airlines. Air transport had already reached Southeast Asia in the 1930s, with the first flights between the region and Europe departing from major colonial capitals like Batavia and Singapore. As air travel technologies advanced and airplanes became ever larger and more comfortable, travel by plane became not only much faster but also increasingly more affordable.

By the 1970s, air travel had overtaken sea travel for leisure and tourism; passenger steamliners had been relegated to history as expensive novelties and were no longer the norm for most tourists. Air travel greatly increased the connectivity between different countries. Where a journey from Singapore to London once took over three weeks by steamship, it could now be completed in less than a day by jumbo jet. Mass tourism took off around this time, fuelled by cheaper flights and all-inclusive packaged vacations. Ports continued to export and receive cargo; but they were no longer ports-of-call for people. Airports – the name a mere extension of the word "port" – took their place; and port cities such as Singapore also increasingly multitasked as airport cities, welcoming millions of visitors from around the world.

To capture a share of this "golden age" of mass tourism, Singapore invested in and opened its new Changi International Airport in 1981. Meanwhile, the Singapore Girl, with her figure-hugging batik *kebaya* designed by French fashion stalwart, Pierre Balmain, would "conquer" the skies. A fixture on all Singapore Airlines flights, where she played the role of flight stewardess, the Singapore Girl would go on to become one of the most iconic symbols of air travel, recognisable almost anywhere on earth. As a testament to its impeccable service and hospitality, Singapore Airlines was first voted the best airline in the world in the late 1980s, and has the distinction of being the most awarded airline in history. Changi Airport has also been repeatedly named best airport in the world since 2000.

These crucial infrastructural developments made sense in the context of an important speech delivered by Singapore's then deputy prime minister Sinnathamby Rajaratnam at a Singapore Press Club event on 6 February 1972, in which he declared, unequivocally, Singapore's ambitions to be an important node in a global network of trade, finance and communications. First addressing the obvious limitations Singapore faced as an independent island nation with no geographical hinterland, he suggested that these limitations were not crippling ones since Singapore's "hinterland" would, by necessity, be the entire world.

He continued as follows:

> "...times are changing and there will be less and less demand for the traditional type of entrepôt services Singapore has rendered for well over a century. Its role as the trading city of South-East Asia, the marketplace of the region, will become less and less important.
> This is because it is transforming itself into a new kind of city – the Global City. It is a new form of human organisation and settlement that has [...] no precedent in mankind's history. People have become aware of this new type of city only very recently. [...] It is the city that electronic communications, supersonic planes, giant tankers and modern economic and industrial organisation have made inevitable." [5]

Rajaratnam's speech remains a driving manifesto for Singapore Inc. even today, articulating three basic principles of its success: rapid investment in and adoption of new technologies; an export- and tourism-driven economy facilitated through excellent maritime and air travel connectivity; and the anchoring of multinational corporations and global financial services in order to drive employment and innovation. Singapore's success is rooted in and thrives on (to further quote Rajaratnam) "a relationship of interdependence in the rapidly expanding global economic system" – in other words, *globalisation*.

Globalisation and the global city as concepts would only be further expounded upon and popularised from the 1990s on. But Singapore had already caught on in the 1970s and positioned itself as a first-mover, hoping to reap the benefits, which would prove astronomical. Singapore's Gross Domestic Product (GDP) per capita today is about 150 times that at independence, and is one of the highest in the world.[6]

But what of Raffles in this surfeit of achievement?

Our tale of the events of 1972 would not be complete without a mention of the Singapore Tourism Board's unveiling, that same year, of a brand-new, white polymarble statue of Sir Stamford Raffles, placed within a stone's throw of the earlier bronze statue, and almost identical to it. The statue was erected on the banks of the Singapore River, to commemorate the spot where Raffles purportedly made landfall in 1819.

The erection of the second Raffles statue effectively made "Raffles" itself a brand, intimately associated with Singapore as Global City. Even during the colonial period, Raffles had already been strongly associated with all that was commercial and cosmopolitan about the colony. There was historic Raffles Place, just across the river, which housed the city's commercial and financial centre and was home to the Singapore headquarters of Jardine, Matheson & Co., the Hongkong and Shanghai Bank, the Chartered Bank of India, Australia and China (today's Standard Chartered Bank) and the like. Raffles Hotel, with its legendary Singapore Sling, was a destination in its own right, renowned far and wide as one of the greatest hotel establishments east of Suez. Just beside the hotel was the prestigious Raffles Institution, founded by Stamford Raffles himself, and alma mater to the colony's captains of industry and society.

Singapore Inc. built on this association and pushed it to its limits. By the 1980s, Raffles Place would become a landscape of towering skyscrapers that housed the city's global financial centre – today a top-tier affair, ranked alongside those in London, New York and Hong Kong. Up until the mid-2000s, Business Class on Singapore Airlines flights was known as "Raffles Class" in a nod to the Raffles-as-Founder myth. Raffles Hotel is now the flagship property of Raffles Hotels and Resorts Group, with properties in Asia, Europe and the Middle East. Across the street stands Raffles City, built in the 1980s and the city's tallest skyscraper at the time, housing a shopping mall and hotel that were both among the most luxurious in town. Meanwhile, the venerable Raffles Institution remains one of the nation's most prestigious educational institutions and is still churning out its technocratic leaders.

The Raffles brand by the 2000s was a premium brand which spoke to the values of heritage and tradition, luxury and quality, efficiency and reliability. All things that Singapore as Global City also represented. Thus, without Raffles, there would be no Singapore Inc.

2019 saw Singapore commemorating the 200th anniversary of Raffles' *arrival* in Singapore – considering it a "founding" was now, finally, seen as giving Raffles and the English too much credit. This milestone year catalysed a slew of celebratory and reflective activities organised by the state as well as by the public, and which explored the continuities of Singapore's port city heritage.

After all, Singapore is all that remains of the former cosmopolitan Asian port cities of the colonial era. The rest of these port cities,

Singapore's siblings – Batavia, Manila, Saigon, Bombay, Calcutta, Colombo, Shanghai, Hong Kong, Macau and more – have been absorbed, one after the other, into larger nation-states and hinterlands, in the process of which they have begun to lose their cosmopolitan outlook and turn increasingly landwards. By a twist of fate, Singapore endures both as a port city and an independent nation-state, and has thus been able to preserve the unique, cross-cultural, maritime heritage that had defined it for centuries. Openness, cosmopolitanism and cultural diversity have remained an integral part of the port-city-nation-state's economic as well as social development strategies since its founding years.

Alongside the white Raffles statue, the Singapore Tourist Promotion Board also unveiled Singapore's iconic statue of the Merlion in 1972. The Merlion was a nod to Singapore's pre-colonial heritage, referring to the legend of Sang Nila Utama and the lion.

In the lead-up to 2019, the public were encouraged to celebrate the fact that Singapore and Singaporeans' cultural diversity went beyond the orderly, state-ordained frame of Chinese, Malay, Indian and Other – or CMIO – that had been in place since the 1960s to describe and regulate the city's multiculturalism. What had been seen in the past as perhaps more than a little messy was now acknowledged and promoted as a form of cultural wealth and distinctiveness.

Museums, academics and communities researched and presented publications and exhibitions that delved deeper into the C, M, I and O – exposing the dizzying cultural diversity within each racial category. The Malays were not just Malays, for example; they were also Javanese, Bugis, Boyanese, Minangkabau and so on. Likewise, Indians as a meta-category included the Tamils, Malayalees, Gujaratis, Bengalis, and many more sub-ethnicities. The Chinese were Hokkiens, Cantonese, Teochews, Hakkas, Hainanese, et cetera. And the "O" was revealed to contain a plethora of other port city communities somewhat forgotten: the Eurasians (and Europeans), the Peranakans, the Jews, the Arabs, the Armenians and more. Finally, Singapore could revel in its full ethnic and cultural splendour.

2019 also saw a delving backwards in time to explore the ancient origins of Singapore's port city heritage. Since the 1980s, archaeological excavations around the historic Singapore River and Fort Canning Hill had unearthed a large quantity of porcelain shards and other valuable material, revealing the existence of a trading settlement dating back some 700 years. The archaeological evidence appeared to corroborate what the textual record already suggested: that some 700 years ago, there was an important Malay kingdom situated here on the island of Temasek. When Raffles arrived in 1819, he had, after all, remarked the existence of ancient fortifications on Fort Canning Hill, which the Malays called Bukit Larangan, or "Forbidden Hill", and revered as a royal precinct. These fortifications were unfortunately razed by the British, who proceeded to build their new Government House atop the foundations.

Official histories (and history textbooks) of Singapore were backdated some 500 years from 1819. Singapore's history would henceforth no longer commence with Raffles' arrival. Instead, the *Sulalat al-Salatin*, or the *Genealogy of Kings* – the great epic of the Malays – became an official reference point for the island nation's beginnings in antiquity. Thus were Singapore's historical roots traced back to Srivijaya and the great port city of Palembang; and thus too, our tale of port cities has come full circle from containers and connectivity to sailors and shipwrecks.

38. Bali
Island of the Gods, Resort to the World

"Today almost everybody has heard of Bali. To some it means a smart place to go, one of the many ports in a round-the-world cruise; to others it brings mental images of brown girls with beautiful breasts, palm trees, rolling waves and all the romantic notions that go to make a South Sea Island paradise. In general, the popular knowledge of Bali ends there. But only six years ago, when I sailed with Rose for the remote island, no one seemed even to have heard of the place; we had to point it out on the map, a tiny dot in the swarm of islands east of Java."

— Miguel Covarrubias, 1937. *Island of Bali.*[7]

I n the early hours of the morning, 20 September 1906, the raja of Badung, his wives and children, his courtly retinue, temple priests and military guards, dressed in white cremation garments, bedecked in jewellery, and wielding ceremonial *keris* and spears, emerged from the Pura Satria – the royal temple – in a silent procession. For days now, the city of Denpasar had been bombarded and besieged by the Dutch. Seeing no hope of recovery, the raja had called for the ritual *puputan*, or "fight to the very end", in order to defend the honour and dignity of the kingdom.

On the main street in Denpasar, the Dutch army was waiting for them, heavily armed with guns and artillery. They stared, disbelieving, at the surreal spectacle before them, unsure of what to do. At some hundred paces before the Dutch, the Balinese halted. There was tense silence. And then the raja motioned for the attack, and dozens of his retinue ran unheeding towards the Dutch, wielding their *keris*. Gunfire ensued and the Balinese were felled by the dozens. The raja himself – at the head of the procession – was amongst the first to be shot to death. As the body of the monarch fell, the Dutch watched in horror as his various queens and consorts, dressed in the manner of warriors, threw gold coins contemptuously to the Dutch as thanks for bestowing them death, and then stabbed themselves and each other with their *keris*, their bodies falling lifeless over the still corpse of their king. Unbeknownst to the Dutch, the gold coins had earlier been cursed such that whoever took them from the women as spoils of war would never find peace.

Dutch gunfire continued to mow down Balinese men and children, even as the women stabbed themselves in the heart, choosing ritual suicide

Legong dancers in Bali, c. 1930. Shelfmark: KITLV 180901. Collection of the Leiden University Libraries.

rather than humiliation. In less than an hour, it was all over, the street of Denpasar littered with the bodies of dead aristocrats and their retinue. Before the smoke had dissipated, the Dutch were crawling all over the corpses like cockroaches, relieving them of their gold and jewels. Then they had the Puri Denpasar – the magnificent royal palace of the Badung Kingdom – razed to the ground.

But the fight that day wasn't over; this was just Act One. Not far from Puri Denpasar stood Puri Pamecutan, where the co-raja of Badung held court. The Dutch military marched the short distance to the second *puri*, only to find a similar procession awaiting them, dressed all in white and prepared for the end. What ensued was the second *puputan* that day, in the capital city of the Kingdom of Badung.

Between 1906 and 1908, the other kingdoms of Bali would capitulate to the Dutch in turn, some rajas choosing ritual suicide and others deciding to surrender. In 1908, the raja of Klungkung, who was the nominal Dewa Agung, or Supreme Ruler of Bali, enacted the final *puputan*, meeting an honourable end, and thus terminating 1000 years of rule by local Balinese kings. From 1908, the entire island of Bali fell to the Dutch. Having held out for some 300 years, it would be the last island in the Indonesian archipelago to be incorporated into the Dutch East Indies. Ironically, the Dutch would only rule Bali fully for some 34 years until the Japanese Occupation in 1942 – it seems the cursed gold coins of the Balinese women would have prophetic effect.

The tragic and gruesome nature of the *puputans* captivated and horrified Europe in turn, and the Dutch came under fire for the massacres. They faced immense pressure to govern their colonies and colonial subjects more ethically. In a stroke of supreme irony, the Dutch refashioned themselves as custodians of Bali's heritage, and determined thus to preserve and further the island's culture, in place of its former kings. Propping up distant relatives of these erstwhile monarchs as puppet regents, they set about resuscitating, researching, and promoting Balinese culture, albeit of a kind that was stripped of its more war-like elements, and made it better suited for spectacle. Bali was administered as a "living museum" – a quaint, exotic relic of the past, in which the locals practiced their ancestral cultures and traditions with little regard for the modern world, while above and around them hovered the god-like figures of their white captors.

The Dutch also saw Bali's tourism potential, and were eager to refashion the image of the island in a manner that would sweep aside all memory of their bloody conquest. From the 1920s on, they would promote Bali as an exotic and untouched "Island of the Gods". Tourism campaigns featured Bali's breathtaking natural scenery and cultural heritage, its exotic forms of dance and drama, presented by way of stylised art deco posters that were all the rage at the time. Photography had become a mainstream artform by this time, and it was also used to promote Bali's singular attractions. In particular, images of slim, young Balinese men, and nubile, bare-breasted Balinese women became widely circulated. The idea was that Bali was a sort of "Garden of Eden" or "Paradise Lost", its "natives" unsullied by the modern values of the west and remaining in a state of primordial and child-like innocence.

In 1924, the first regular weekly steamship service, operated by the Koninklijke Paketvaart Maatschappij (KPM), began taking passengers between Batavia, Surabaya, Makassar and Bali, stopping at the port of Singaraja, to the north of the island. In 1928, in response to growing demand, the KPM built the iconic Bali Hotel in Denpasar atop the very site of the raja of Denpasar's *puputan*. By the late 1930s, tourist arrivals in Bali had grown from a few hundred to a few thousand.[8]

Aside from successful Dutch tourism promotional campaigns, a small group of influential foreign expatriates on the island would also contribute to spreading the word on Bali. Chief amongst these was the Russian-born German artist, Walter Spies, who arrived in Bali in 1927 and is still regarded by the Balinese today with a degree of reverence. Spies, who chose to reside in the village of Ubud, played a critical role in the growth of modern Balinese visual and performing arts. At his idyllic hillside residence situated at the confluence of two rivers, he received a steady, glittering, cosmopolitan set of visitors: celebrities such as Charlie Chaplin and Noel Coward, anthropologists such as the husband-and-wife team, Gregory Bateson and Margaret Mead, and fellow artists like Rudolf Bonnet and Miguel Covarrubias.

The latter and his wife, Rose, became particularly close to Spies. In 1937, he would publish *Island of Bali*, still considered the most authoritative tome on Bali today. The opening lines to this part-travelogue and part-ethnographic study summarise popular notions of Bali between the wars. By the late 1930s, Bali's image as a "South Sea Island paradise" featuring palm trees, magnificent surf and "brown girls with beautiful breasts" had been set in stone, and would endure until the eve of World War II.

Post-war, an independent Indonesia perpetuated and built on Dutch policies of positioning Bali as an exotic island paradise and tourist destination. Sukarno, who was himself part-Balinese – his mother hailed from the island – was determined to have Bali form the basis of a new Indonesian identity that harked back to and referenced the great Hindu-Buddhist civilisation of Majapahit in the 14th century. Building himself a presidential palace in Bali, he used the island as a tool of cultural diplomacy, frequently hosting foreign heads of state and dignitaries, and regaling them with performances of traditional Balinese dance.

During this time, the village of Ubud became Bali's cultural centre par excellence, on account of canny positioning on the part of a prince of the Royal House of Gianyar, Cokorda Agung Sukawati. A republican with political ambitions, Cokorda Agung would later find a loyal supporter in Sukarno. In fact, Ubud was often the preferred destination for Sukarno and his VIP guests, and Sukarno himself became a patron of the arts and heritage in the village. Building on a strong foundation earlier established by Walter Spies and his set, Cokorda Agung would shrewdly and successfully champion Ubud as the centre of artistic production, at the forefront of an efflorescence of modern Balinese culture.

Here in Ubud was where most visitors would encounter two of Bali's most iconic traditional performing artforms: the *legong* and the *kecak*. The *legong* originated as a secular dance typically performed outside temple grounds. It is performed by three young girls, bedecked in gold and dressed in exquisite woven textiles, executing a highly-choreographed dance to the lilting sounds of a *gamelan* orchestra. The dance likely came into existence in the late 19th century, but the format of the *legong* as it is performed today probably dates to the Dutch colonial period of the 1910s to 1930s. Today, it is performed regularly for tourists in the Pura Dalem Ubud (Ubud's main temple) in the heart of town.

Most visitors assume that the *kecak*, or "Monkey Dance", is a traditional artform, but it was actually invented by Walter Spies and Indonesian dancer Wayan Limbak in the 1930s, adapted from traditional Balinese exorcism rituals, and choreographed to be performed specifically for foreign audiences. *Kecak* is thus, at its core, a product of cultural tourism. It is performed entirely by men, clad simply in sarongs, chanting and waving their arms in a trance-like frenzy. Loosely based on events from the Hindu epic, *The Ramayana*, it typically takes place at night for full dramatic effect. The most spectacular performances are held in the grounds of Bali's iconic waterfront temples at Uluwatu and Tanah Lot.

Sukarno's successor, Suharto, did not deviate much from his predecessor with regard to Bali's positioning. During his time as president, a new cultural tourism policy was developed with help from the French, and with some limited Balinese input. The new policy saw the development of large-scale tourism-related infrastructure such as hotels and resorts. Bali was opened up fully to international tourism and in fact, there was a concerted effort to position Bali as the tourism gateway to Indonesia. A new I Gusti Ngurah Rai International Airport was opened at Denpasar in 1968 and increasingly, more tourists arrived by plane via this airport city in South Bali rather than the port city of Singaraja in the north. By the 1980s, visitor arrivals to the island had reached the hundreds of thousands.[9]

During this time, the village of Kuta rose to prominence, developing into a major gateway and the first stop for most visitors arriving in Bali. Blessed with a beautiful shoreline and magnificent surf, the village became a magnet for a new type of tourist: backpacking surfers, many of whom were Australian. They came, not for Bali's cultural heritage, but for "sun, sand and sea" – its beaches, waves and spectacular sunsets.

The first of these young, Western travellers had "discovered" Kuta in the late 1960s; their numbers grew steadily in the '70s and '80s. They weren't what the local government had hoped to attract since they were, essentially, budget travellers. The Balinese referred to them as "hippies", and they also introduced a counter-culture of promiscuity and drug use. As more of them came, however, an entire tourist economy emerged organically around them. Some enterprising locals rented rooms and other accommodations to these visitors; others set up *warungs* along the beach to offer drinks and food. Local transportation adapted to the needs of these transients, and shops selling surf and other merchandise sprang up in the village centre. Soon, the Balinese themselves began taking up surfing, having picked up the sport from foreign mentors. By the 1980s, there was already a generation of Balinese surfers making a living from their sport, with surfing becoming an integral part of local Kuta culture.

From a tiny fishing village, Kuta grew to become a cosmopolitan city. Alongside Western visitors and short-term residents, migrants from all over Indonesia moved in to take advantage of the boom in tourism. Javanese, Sundanese, Sasaks from Lombok, Minangkabau from Sumatra and many other Indonesians eked out a living alongside the Balinese. By 1994, visitor arrivals had crossed the million mark, and one quarter of visitors to Indonesia now came via Bali. At this time, Kuta had become notorious worldwide for being a paradise of free love, easy drugs, and exuberant nightlife. Kuta's main street, Jalan Legian, was now a throbbing, pulsing, 24/7 hub of leisure and entertainment, chock-full of bars, restaurants, nightclubs, boutiques, budget and mid-range hotels.

But along with this growth came other problems: overcrowding and over-development, particularly along Jalan Legian, plagued by rampant land speculation amongst private developers, and which grew to become a noisy, enervating concrete strip rife with touts and prostitutes (male and female). There were now huge traffic jams all throughout the city, and waves of crime required regular police patrolling of the downtown area. That many tourists and cars also meant pollution and environmental degradation. In particular, Kuta's white-sand beaches started to be strewn with rubbish, and the pristine surf its visitors once enjoyed was now sullied with plastic waste, Styrofoam and other forms of trash.[10]

There was a growing sense that tourism was becoming unsustainable, and that a reckoning was due to the inhabitants of this now-heaving, unbridled centre of licentiousness and hedonism. This reckoning came in the form of the Bali bombings in 2002, wherein terrorists set off bombs in two of the most crowded nightclubs on Kuta's main drag. More than 200 people were killed in one night, many of them Australian. The Balinese blamed themselves, believing that in allowing their island to go the way of Mammon, they had offended the island's original gods.

The negative impact of the Bali bombings softened with time, and tourism arrivals rebounded. By now, Bali was finally seeing the sort of high-end, high-spending tourist the local government had hoped to attract. North of Kuta, the village of Seminyak came into its own as an exclusive enclave of high-end restaurants, bars and spas, five-star beachfront hotel resorts, and luxurious private villas and residences. Joined to Kuta by the same main road, Jalan Legian, Seminyak had earlier been a sideshow to its more boisterous sibling down south. But as Kuta became overcrowded, visitors started craving slightly more sophisticated and upmarket experiences. The number of foreign expatriates deciding to make Seminyak their second or main home also began to increase significantly.

In the meantime, Bali was busy refashioning itself (once again) into a global centre for wellness, aided in no small part by *Eat Pray Love*, the hugely successful memoir by Elizabeth Gilbert (published in 2006) and a movie of the same name (released in 2010 and starring Hollywood megastar, Julia Roberts). In both novel and movie, the lead female protagonist travels to Ubud, Bali to find love and spirituality. Spas and spa resorts were already a fixture in the typical Bali tourist's itinerary. Post-*Eat Pray Love*, health, wellness and spirituality became the focus of a new form of tourism, attracting a brand new international crowd.

As of 2019, foreign tourist arrivals to Bali had grown to a whopping 6.3 million; and this did not include the tally of domestic tourists from elsewhere in Indonesia, which probably matched that number.[11] Bali had metamorphosed into one of the few premier resort islands on the globe. It was now well and truly a resort to the world: from cultural destination to surf mecca to wellness retreat, it had something for every tourist, discerning and budget alike.

The question remains as to whether the pace of development is sustainable for the island, in environmental as well as in cultural terms. Or in other words: between the concrete jungle and the hordes of foreign revellers, where, one might ask, may one still find traces of the gods?

For a closer encounter with the divine, one must travel east from Ubud to Karangasem Regency, where, at the foot of majestic Mount Agung – Bali's holy mountain – the Pura Besakih stands, as it has done since at least the 14th century.

Besakih is Bali's mother temple. It is the largest and most ancient religious structure on the island, consisting of more than 20 separate temples within a sprawling temple precinct, built on six levels, on painstakingly-terraced slopes. It used to be a sacred temple of ancient Gelgel, the kingdom that ruled over all of Bali in the 17th century before fragmenting and splintering into nine competing minor kingdoms (including Klungkung, Badung, Gianyar and others).

The architecture of the temple is quintessentially Majapahit. The main entrance to the complex is framed by a magnificent *candi bentar*, or "split gate" that is, in essence, a Hindu-Buddhist stupa that has been sliced down the middle, forced apart and made to function as an entrance gateway. Standing alongside the *candi bentar* are mythical

The main entrance of Pura Besakih, with Mount Agung in the background.

guardian figures, snarling protectively and wielding ceremonial *keris*. Further up the temple complex, one is confronted with a breathtaking sight – that of a veritable forest of *pelinggih meru*, or meru towers. These are multi-tiered, pagoda-like roofed pavilions that are meant, by way of their form, to evoke mythical Mount Meru – the sacred mountain of the gods in Hindu-Buddhist tradition. Interspersed with these *pelinggih meru* are dozens of *bale kulkul*, distinctive watchtowers topped with thatched roofs.

Standing up here near the top of Pura Besakih, one gets a sense of the splendour of Majapahit. 800 years ago, this Hindu-Buddhist maritime power succeeded Srivijaya as the main *mandala* in the lands below the winds. Its seat of power was in Java and its sphere of influence extended to encompass Sumatra, the Malay Peninsula, parts of Borneo and the islands east of Java, including Bali. It was ruled by powerful kings as well as queens.

When the Majapahit fell to the Muslim Demak Sultanate in the early 16th century, it is said that many of its aristocrats and high priests fled to Bali, along with artisans and dancers. They brought sacred texts and poetic epics with them to their new home. This would precipitate a flowering of Balinese culture. Certainly, Bali remained the last bastion of Majapahit, Hindu-Buddhist culture in the Muslim Nusantara, a role it would cherish and continue to hone to perfection in the course of its history, even till the present day. When we admire a *candi bentar*, or enjoy a performance of the *legong*, when we listen to a *gamelan* performance or a recitation of an epic in the lilting Balinese language – what we are witnessing is the physical manifestation of a culture that is at once eight centuries old, and yet still pulsing with life, able to absorb new influences and adapt itself to the vicissitudes of the 21st century. This timeless vitality and propensity for reinvention resides at the very heart of Bali's spirit.

39. Mumbai (Bombay)
British Raj, Bollywood and Bombay Duck

"They leaned over the rail looking at the city which had begun to appear out of the haze – the Taj Mahal Hotel, the Readymoney Building, the Yacht Club, the Gateway of India and the green eminence of Malabar Hill, dotted with bungalows and the palaces of the Maharajahs with the Towers of Silence at the foot of them all [...] Yes, Bombay was fantastic and romantic and extraordinary things happened there, if you didn't notice the coolies, the women and the children sleeping on sidewalks and in gutters as you drove home from a good party about sunrise."

— Louis Bromfield, 1940. *Night in Bombay.*[12]

It is a little-known fact, outside of India, that Mumbai (मुंबई) is home to the second-largest number of art deco buildings in the world, after Miami Beach. In fact, the city has its very own equivalent of Miami's Ocean Drive: a spectacular, arching waterfront thoroughfare extending to the horizon, and lined with dozens of art deco apartment buildings.

Marine Drive, Mumbai, runs for some three and a half kilometres along the glistening, azure waters of Back Bay, linking historic Bombay Old Town with legendary Malabar Hill, abode of the city's rich and famous. It is best experienced by car – preferably vintage convertible – in the early evening. As you turn the corner from Nariman Point, you inevitably gasp as you take in the vista, splendid in its scale and cohesiveness. When night falls, the buildings are lit up and gleam like jewels, accounting for Marine Drive's alternate moniker, "Queen's Necklace".[13] Along the endless embankment, you spot dozens of dating couples, hand in hand, whispering sweet nothings to each other, against one of the most romantic backdrops in the world.

Bombay's massive Backbay Reclamation Scheme in the 1920s was commissioned by the British colonial government in a bid to ease population congestion in the old town. Huge tracts of land reclaimed from the sea were freed up for development as new commercial and residential precincts. Bombay's wealthy merchant and business families swooped in on the opportunity, financing and erecting most of the buildings here. Indian princes from elsewhere in the British Raj too, got in on the act, commissioning opulent and thoroughly-modern pleasure palaces. A brand new extension to the city called for a brand new architectural vernacular

Fashionable 1930s art deco apartment block along Marine Drive, Mumbai.

that looked resolutely to the future. Art deco, already regarded as a symbol of modernity and luxury, became the vernacular of choice for this phase of the city's growth. Strict regulation ensured uniformity of height, style, colour palette and materials used, resulting in a remarkably coherent ensemble.

Bombay's glittering coterie of movie stars moved in. By the 1920s and '30s, Bombay stood alongside Calcutta as one of India's wealthiest cities; a truly modern and cosmopolitan metropolis in the vein of London, Paris, New York, Shanghai and Tokyo. Marine Drive was the city's glitziest and most fashionable address, associated with bright lights and big dreams.

The apartment blocks on Marine Drive were built in the 1930s and '40s, and are largely designed in the streamline moderne style. All the buildings here were built in reinforced concrete with little adornment, speaking to a self-consciously modern, minimalist, industrial aesthetic. Incredibly, many of these buildings were actually designed by Indian, rather than British or European, architects. While adhering to moderne principles, they also playfully incorporate Indian and tropical elements, such as depictions of local flora and fauna.

Marine Drive forms part of the larger Churchgate District created by way of the Backbay Reclamation Scheme, and located to the west of the city's Oval Maidan – its grand cricketing green and public park. Here in Churchgate are found not only apartment blocks, but also offices, hotels and cinemas in art deco style. The Eros Cinema, in particular, occupies a prominent location to the north of the Oval Maidan, its ziggurat-like tower dwarfing the buildings in its immediate vicinity even as it evokes Bombay's heritage as a city of film.

The Oval Maidan is remarkable for being flanked by two contrasting architectural styles that represent two major phases of Bombay's historic development. To the west: yet another delightfully uniform ensemble of art deco apartment blocks. To the east: stupendously monumental civic institutions designed in the Victorian Gothic Revival style that defined the city in the 1870s and '80s. In fact, east of the Oval Maidan stands the largest concentration of Victorian Gothic public buildings anywhere on earth.

Unlike in Calcutta and Madras, the Indo-Saracenic style did not take off in Bombay. Part of the reason was that Bombay saw itself as a European, rather than an Indian, city. It was west-facing, oriented towards Europe rather than Asia, and one of the first stops for any vessel coming through the Suez Canal. Certainly, the city itself was legitimately founded by the British, in that there was no local antecedent; only the seven islands once collectively called Bom Bahia (by the Portuguese), and thereafter, rechristened and conjoined through land reclamation by the East India Company. Additionally, many of the city's major civic monuments were funded by local Parsi and Jewish philanthropists, who hailed from minority communities. Anglophilic in outlook, they adopted English customs and championed European styles of architecture.

Bombay experienced spectacular economic growth between the 1860s and the end of the 19th century, which coincided with the heyday of the Victorian era and the British Raj. A rash of civic buildings was erected during this time, characterised as English Gothic by way of their imposing, mediaeval and ponderous aesthetic, channelling Wuthering Heights and trumpeting imperial might. Elements from Venetian and Florentine architecture were borrowed and incorporated into the design, as well as local building materials and some eastern elements, such as verandahs adapted to the tropical weather.

Among the most important of these Victorian Gothic buildings are the three which flank the Oval Maidan: the Old Secretariat (built in 1874), the High Court (1878, inspired by London's Law Courts), and the Convocation Hall of the University of Mumbai (1874), to which is affixed the iconic Rajabai Clock Tower (1878), modelled after Giotto's Campanile in Florence, and funded by a local Jain business magnate. Other important buildings in the vicinity include the Public Works Department (1872), the Central Telegraph Office (1872), the Royal Alfred Sailor's Home (1876), and the Municipal Corporation Building (1893).

By far the most impressive and awe-inspiring building of all – the crowning glory of Bombay Gothic – is Victoria Terminus, Bombay's main train station, completed in 1887 and commissioned to commemorate 50 years of Queen Victoria's rule. Modelled after St Pancras Station in London, it is a fusion of English as well as Italian Gothic styles; and was designed by British architect Frederick William Stevens. Its sheer size is simply astonishing, as is the detail and extensiveness of ornamentation: spires and arches abound, as do gargoyles and bas-reliefs, featuring Indian flora and fauna, as well as local castes and communities.

Sporting a central domed structure with two side wings, it is a mash-up of Buckingham Palace and Saint Peter's Basilica. Atop the central dome is an enormous allegorical statue representing Progress, while crowning its entrance pediments are statues representing Commerce, Agriculture and Civil Engineering. The forecourt to the structure is flanked by statues of the Lion of Britain and the Tiger of India, while the interior is adorned with magnificent stained glass windows featuring coats of arms of various cities, and stylised depictions of locomotive trains.

The Victoria Terminus, today renamed the Chhatrapati Shivaji Terminus (or CST, for short), was inscribed as a UNESCO World Heritage Site in its own right in 2004.[14] Mumbai's ensemble of art deco and Victorian Gothic architecture flanking the Oval Maidan and along Marine Drive, and consisting of more than 90 individual buildings, was collectively inscribed as a UNESCO World Heritage site later in 2018.

At the stroke of midnight, 15 August 1947, British India ceased to exist. The historic moment forms the heart of novelist Salman Rushdie's 1981 magnum opus, *Midnight's Children*. Mr Rushdie, himself a Bombay native, would recount the ensuing events post-independence, in particular, the partition of British India into the republics of India and Pakistan, in a magic realist style and from the perspective of his main character, Saleem Sinai, born at the stroke of midnight, exactly when the new India was born.

The Partition resulted in widespread violence, and the displacement of more than 10 million people across the India-Pakistan border. Its aftereffects still haunt India and Pakistan today, more than half a century later. Violence was particularly intense in the capital, New Delhi. But Bombay was spared and indeed, was the scene of jubilant celebrations rather than religious riots.

The British left India by way of their former imperial port city of Bombay. The final British regiments on Indian soil set sail from the iconic Gateway of India, at Apollo Bunder, on 28 February 1948. The monumental archway, a rare example of the Indo-Saracenic in the city, had been commissioned to commemorate the visit of King George V to Bombay in 1911, and was completed in 1924. It was frequently used as a literal gateway to India – the first port of embarkation for royalty and heads of state arriving in the city by sea. To the right of the Gateway stands the equally iconic Taj Mahal Palace Hotel, erected by Parsi magnate Jamsetji Tata in 1903, purportedly because he had been refused entry into the city's European grand hotel at the time. The Taj was also designed in the Indo-Saracenic style and thus recalls its namesake in Agra, even as it stands as a symbol of nationalist pride.

Post-colonial Bombay remained a multicultural melting pot of a metropolis. Though physically part of Maharashtra state, less than half of the city's denizens were Marathi-speaking. Many Bombay-ites were Indians from elsewhere in India – in particular, Hindustanis, Gujaratis and Goans – and from all over the world; they had come seeking fame and fortune in the city, which had accommodated their dreams in turn. The city was also multi-religious and multi-ethnic in nature, counting in its midst Hindus, Muslims, Buddhists, Jains, Parsis, Iranis, East Indians (Bombay Catholics), St Thomas Christians, Armenians, Jews, and even a thriving Chinese community. This many communities, all with their own languages, meant that Bombay-ites spoke a particular local dialect, known as Bambaiya. Mr Rushdie in his 1999 novel, *The Ground Beneath Her Feet*, memorably pokes fun at his polyglot heritage, noting that Bombayites spoke a sort of slang known as "Hug-me", an acronym for Hindi, Urdu, Gujarati, Marathi and English.[15]

Bombay was (and still is) also a phenomenally unequal city, home to the greatest number of billionaires in India. Southwest of the city, in the rarefied environs of Malabar Hill, live some of the richest and most powerful people in the world. Many of them are scions of the legendary Parsi business dynasties who built Bombay. Not far away towers Antilia, the 27-storey, regulation-defying private residence of Indian billionaire, Mukesh Ambani, born in Aden but bred in Bombay.

At the opposite extreme is Dharavi in Mumbai's Western suburbs, one of the largest slums in the world, home to almost a million residents eking out a humble existence amidst obscene wealth, and without proper public services like water and sanitation. Situated on prime land near Mumbai International Airport and the city's spanking new Bandra-Kurla Complex (the city's brand-new financial centre), Dharavi is at the centre of an ambitious redevelopment plan due to commence soon. It was most famously featured in the 2008 British blockbuster movie, *Slumdog Millionaire*, directed by Briton Danny Boyle and starring British actor Dev Patel as the titular "slumdog" from Dharavi, who, by a twist of fate, finds himself winning the local version of *Who Wants to Be a Millionaire?* The film, which borrows heavily from Indian cinema, played a pivotal role in catapulting Bollywood into the international spotlight, even if its reception amongst Indian audiences was lukewarm at best.

Bollywood would be Bombay's greatest export yet. The term, first coined in the 1960s or '70s, is a fusion of "Bombay" and "Hollywood", in reference to the city being the largest film production centre in India. These days, it is used to refer loosely to Hindi-language cinema in general, just as Hollywood generally refers to America's English-language film industry, regardless of where in America the film is made.

Even before independence, Bombay had stellar cinematic credentials. In 1896, the Lumiere Brothers screened the very first moving pictures in India right here in this city, at the former Watson's Hotel – the very same Europeans-only hotel that had denied Jamsetji Tata entry because of his race. India's first full feature film, *Raja Harishchandra*, based on the Hindu epic, *The Mahabharata*, and directed by the father of Indian cinema, Dadasaheb Phalke, was released less than 20 years later in 1913, a year before Hollywood's first feature film helmed by Cecil B. DeMille.

The general format of Bollywood movies was established early in the '30s and has been finessed to a formula today. Bollywood movies always feature singing and dancing, and extravagant, highly-choreographed musical numbers. They are lush productions featuring elaborate sets, and often running for more than three hours. There is always a central

Chhatrapati Shivaji Maharaj Terminus.

romantic couple trading innuendo and suggestive looks but having very little physical contact (on account of strict local censorship). Effect is as important as plot – characters may burst into song at any provocation! – and movies are generally G-rated, allowing for a very broad audience base. Movies also often bank on star actors and actresses to drive marketing. In the 1970s, the term *masala* was coined to refer to this formulaic "spice mix" of music, song, dance, drama, comedy and romance, thrown shrewdly together in a slick and lavish package.

Post-independence, Indian cinema played a key role in furthering the image of India as a progressive, multicultural nation. Bombay's film industry had multicultural roots, with prominent early protagonists – directors, actors, composers – hailing from the city's Indian Muslim and Parsi communities. The love songs that permeate its movies had their roots in poetry written in Urdu, widely regarded as the language of love. Movie dialogues featured Hindustani: a mix of Hindi and Urdu, rather than Hindi per se, in order to reach the broadest audiences. And up until the early 2000s, movie titles on billboards and onscreen were routinely written in both Hindi as well as Urdu.

The 1990s saw a major shift in the market for Bollywood, with Indian movies targeting not only locals but also NRIs (non-resident

Indians) – a global, affluent Indian diaspora community residing in the United Kingdom, the United States of America and elsewhere. *Masala* became *global masala* as settings moved from India to more "exotic" locations such as London, New York and Switzerland, and star actors and actresses also played NRI characters.[16] By the 1990s, Bollywood was also exporting its films to markets everywhere but in the West: its immediate neighbours, Pakistan and Bangladesh, for example; but also Turkey, Iran, the Arab Middle East, Africa and Southeast Asia. The universality and inoffensiveness of Bollywood movies probably account for their far-reaching impact.

Bollywood would become truly globe-spanning in the 2000s. In 2003, *Time Magazine* featured its very first Indian actor on the cover, with a title that read "The New Face of Film". That face belonged to Bollywood actress, Aishwarya Rai, who was already a force to be reckoned with in India. In 1994, she had become only the second Indian to win the Miss World beauty pageant, and for years, had been deemed "the most beautiful woman on earth" with her dark hair, queenly features and striking blue eyes.

The same year she covered *Time*, Rai had also been the first Indian actress ever to be invited on the jury for feature films at the Cannes Film Festival. In 2004, a by-now iconic photograph of Rai attending the festival, arm in arm with fellow jury members, Chinese actress Gong Li and French actress Laetitia Casta, took international media by storm. The message was clear. Bollywood's time on the world stage had come, and here was its Queen. When, in 2007, Rai married fellow actor Abhishek Bachchan, himself the son of legendary Bollywood actor, Amitabh Bachchan, she became well and truly Bollywood royalty.

Meanwhile, her frequent co-star and erstwhile paramour Shah Rukh Khan would take up the mantle of King. In 2009, Shah Rukh famously appeared at the Golden Globe Awards to introduce *Slumdog Millionaire* in the category of Best Picture – he would be the first Indian actor ever invited to present at a Hollywood film award ceremony. Accompanied by Frieda Pinto, lead actress in the movie and Bombay-ite born and bred, he walked on stage to thunderous applause even as the evening's host introduced him as "King of Bollywood." *Slumdog Millionaire* would go on to win four Golden Globes that evening. It would do even better at the Academy Awards, sweeping up eight Oscars, including for Best Picture, Best Director, Best Original Score and Best Original Song for Bollywood film composer, A. R. Rahman. The award-winning theme song for the movie, "Jai Ho", meaning "Let There Be Victory", became a huge hit worldwide.

Bombay's name was officially changed to Mumbai in 1995. The name-change anchored Bombay firmly in Maharashtra State, though some felt the new Marathi name for the city played down its historic cosmopolitanism. The old moniker still clings on formally in some quarters, most notably in the names of a few venerable institutions such as the Royal Bombay Yacht Club and the High Court of Bombay. Many locals, particularly those of the older generation, also continue to refer affectionately to their beloved city as Bombay, rather than Mumbai.

"Bombay" stubbornly remains in a local dish that Mumbai-kers of all creeds, races and ages enjoy: Bombay duck, which is not a species of poultry, but actually a fearsome-looking, foul-smelling, bottom-dwelling fish native to Mumbai's coasts, and normally eaten during the monsoons. The fish (*Harpadon nehereus*) is also known as lizardfish, because of its appearance. It is the colour of human flesh, has slimy, reptilian skin and a huge jaw adorned with razor-sharp teeth. Its hideousness has to be seen to be believed.

It is unclear how the fish got its English name. Some believe it's derived from the Marathi name, *bombil* – fishmongers in the market would traditionally call out "*bombiltak, bombiltak*", meaning "*bombil* for sale here". British colonials could have anglicised that to "Bombay duck". Another source for the name might be the Bombay mail trains, known locally as *Bombay dak*, that would take cartloads of the smelly, dried fish from the coast to the interior.

Whatever the origins of the name, Bombay duck is prepared in a variety of ways unique to each of Mumbai's many ethnic and faith communities. One of the oldest preparation methods is to salt and dry the fish out in the sun – something fishing communities here have been doing for centuries. The dried fish is later rehydrated and eaten deep-fried or in curries and stews. The Parsi method of cooking Bombay duck is to batter and deep-fry it whole such that the fish is crispy and fluffy on the outside, but soft, warm and creamy on the inside. The soft flesh has an indescribably umami flavour that tastes of the sea, the timeless monsoon, as well as the muddy coastal waters of Mumbai. It is an acquired taste, for sure. For those who love it, though, it is simply delectable.

40. Kaohsiung & Busan
Asian Tigers, Industrial Cities and Urban Revitalisation

> "Without our native soil, how can there be literature?"
> — Yeh Shih-Tao, 1985. This oft-quoted line is the title of
> one of his essay collections, and is inscribed next to
> a statue of Yeh at the Kaohsiung Literary Museum.[17]

The 1980s and '90s saw the emergence of so-called newly industrialised economies, or NIEs, in the East Asian region. These were regions which had experienced swift, sustained economic growth in the post-war period, and had attained levels of prosperity very close to that of first-world nations in the West. Four NIEs, in particular, stood out for their spectacular growth and emergence on the world stage, and were given the collective moniker "Asian Tigers" or, occasionally, "Little Dragons" (in reference to China as the "big dragon"). These were South Korea, Taiwan, Hong Kong and Singapore.

The four Asian Tigers followed closely on the coat-tails of Japan, which had experienced phenomenal economic growth from the 1950s to 1970s based on a manufacturing and export-driven industrialisation strategy. Japan became the second-largest economy in the world in 1968, after the United States of America, a position it would hold until 2010 when it was overtaken by China. During this time, Japanese consumer goods and Japanese brands such as Sony, Canon, Toyota and Mitsubishi became household names across the globe, outcompeting American and European equivalents based on price, quality and dependability.

South Korea and Taiwan were the two larger economies amongst the Asian Tigers. They began their industrialisation early on, in the 1960s. Both economies were "estranged region-states", so to speak; the product of geopolitics and civil wars that had divided their respective motherlands.

The Korean Peninsula had been split into two nation-states in 1948 as a result of the Cold War and ongoing enmity between the United States, which backed South Korea, and the Soviet Union, which backed North Korea. In 1950, the North attacked the South, precipitating a three-year Korean War which ended in a stalemate and the creation of the infamous Demilitarised Zone, or DMZ, between North and South. Till today, the North and South are still technically at war and furthermore, are divided by ideology, with the South being proudly and aggressively capitalistic, and the North remaining staunchly Communist.

Taiwan is an anomaly in contemporary geopolitics: an autonomous political entity that is not a nation-state. Its specific circumstance was a result of the Chinese Communist Revolution between 1945 and 1949, which

The Busan Modern History Museum is located at the former Busan branch building of the Oriental Development Company (*Toyo Takushoku Kabushiki Gaisha*), built in the 1920s. This was the representative organisation for Imperial Japanese economic exploitation of Korea.

saw the Kuomintang (KMT), or Republican government of China, led by Generalissimo Chiang Kai-Shek, flee to the island of Taiwan in 1949, even as the Chinese Communist Party, led by Comrade Mao Zedong, declared victory on the mainland. Since then, the People's Republic of China (PRC) and Taiwan have co-existed uneasily. Though hostilities ended in 1979, no formal peace treaty was signed and China continues to claim Taiwan as a breakaway province.

Between 1965 and 1994, economic growth for South Korea and Taiwan was astonishingly high, hovering at 9.9 per cent per annum in the '60s and '70s to around 7 per cent in the '90s. In just ten years between 1983 and 1993, the Gross National Product (GNP) per capita of South Korea more than tripled from around US$2000 to US$7600, and that of Taiwan quadrupled from around US$2600 to US$10,000.[18] South Korea joined the Organisation for Economic Co-operation and Development (OECD), essentially the "club" of industrialised first-world nations, in 1996, only the second Asian nation to do so after Japan. Following the Asian Financial Crisis of 1997, both South Korea and Taiwan recuperated at record speed, and today, their GNPs per capita have pushed past US$30,000, making them amongst some of the richest places on earth.[19]

Numerous theories abound as to why the Asian Tigers alone – out of other developing countries and regions in the world – managed to pull themselves out of poverty, and at such a phenomenal speed. One of the key reasons is post-war US aid and the opening of US consumer markets to cheaper East Asian, particularly Korean and Taiwanese, goods – textiles and clothing initially, and subsequently, electronics. Having both been Japanese colonies in the early 20th century, Korea and Taiwan also benefited from significant colonial investment in infrastructure, and would later adapt Japanese approaches to economic development, particularly the decision to pursue an export-oriented economic policy. In addition, both regions saw a form of authoritarian capitalism imposed upon them in the early decades of growth, wherein a technocratic government took an active, interventionist role in championing economic development even as it suppressed political freedom. For these two Asian Tigers, it was thus economic growth at all costs, with the understanding that sacrifices had to be made for the common good.

Cultural theorists would argue that the success of the Asian Tigers was also in no small part due to their specific, East Asian, Confucian heritage: unwavering loyalty and obedience to a just, paternalistic (possibly authoritarian) ruler; the propensity to endure hardship today in order to reap rewards tomorrow – thus an understanding of thrift and the importance of saving for the future; a drive to compete and a willingness to adapt; and the notion of group (i.e. family and community) benefit rather than individual reward.

While culture might have played a role in attitudes to work and thrift at the individual and familial level (and certainly, all four Tigers had a highly-disciplined, adaptable and productive labour force), at the macro-economic level, conditions were vastly different in Korea and Taiwan, let alone in Hong Kong and Singapore. South Korea's success depended on the role of its *chaebols*, or large and powerful family-owned conglomerates – think Samsung, LG and Hyundai – with whom the government actively partnered to drive economic growth top-down. In contrast, Taiwan's growth was driven by its thriving small-and-medium enterprise (SME) sector and a grassroots spirit of entrepreneurship.

Perhaps one concession to a common culture would be that of a deep-seated sense of vulnerability to invasion, and an understanding that growth and prosperity were necessary means of defence. With wealth comes the ability to equip oneself adequately with advanced military technologies and networks of international allies that can serve as deterrence and insurance in the event of war.[20]

Kaohsiung and Busan have remarkably similar profiles and histories as Taiwan's and South Korea's busiest ports respectively. Both were major ports during the Japanese colonial period, and both are the second largest metropolitan areas in their respective jurisdictions today. As of 2022,

Busan was the 7th largest port in the world in terms of volume, able to process more than 22 million TEU of cargo annually. Kaohsiung ranked 17th, with its capacity of some 9.5 million TEU annually.[21]

For much of the Ming period, Kaohsiung was better known as Dagou, which literally meant "beating the dog". It was home to pirates, or *wokou*, at least until 1624, when the Dutch VOC established a fortified settlement, Fort Zeelandia, in nearby Tainan; and Formosa (as the island was then called by the Portuguese) became largely a Dutch colony. The Dutch were later chased off by Ming loyalist, Zheng Chenggong. Better known in the West as Koxinga, he established his independent Kingdom of Tungning on the island, with its capital also at Tainan. Between 1662 and 1683, the Kingdom of Tungning would attempt to oust the Qing and re-establish Ming China from their Formosan base, prefiguring the KMT in Taiwan some three centuries later. At this time, Kaohsiung retained its original name, and was known to the West as Takau.

The Qing retook Formosa in 1683 and ruled their province of Taiwan at arm's length. In 1895, Taiwan was ceded to Japan as part of the terms of the Treaty of Shimonoseki, which ended the First Sino-Japanese War. Takau attained city status in 1924, and was bestowed new, more elegant Kanji characters (高雄) – meaning "Great and Majestic". The new Kanji were still pronounced *ta-kao* in Japanese, but in Mandarin, they were read *gao-xiong*, anglicised as Kaohsiung.

From the 1960s on, Kaohsiung was the location for post-colonial Taiwan's Export Processing Zones (EPZs), known as *jiagong chukou qu* (加工出口区) in Chinese. These were special, fenced-off customs areas wherein businesses were allowed to import all manner of equipment and raw materials for the manufacture of goods for export, without paying duties or taxes to the state. These EPZs took the form of industrial or business parks, and were critical to an export-oriented economic development strategy. They attracted local manufacturing companies as well as foreign multinational corporations (MNCs) looking for a regional base to expand their Asian operations. It was by way of these EPZs and foreign MNCs that new technologies and approaches to business were imported into the region-state. These EPZs would also provide a template for the PRC's Special Economic Zones (SEZs) later in the 1980s.

Busan's maritime history is closely linked to that of Japan, given its proximity to the Japanese islands. For centuries, trade had taken place between Japan and Korea by way of the city. In fact, Busan still retains traces of samurai castles built towards the end of the 16th century when an ebullient Toyotomi Hideyoshi invaded Korea and attempted to take on Ming China. Toyotomi failed in his attempt and the Japanese were henceforth summarily kicked off the East Asian Order of Things. The castles, however, remained in Busan.

By the terms of the Treaty of Ganghwa in 1876, signed between the Japanese Empire and the Joseon Kingdom, Busan was forced open (by gunboat) to trade with Japan, and subsequently to trade with other nations in 1883. The Busan area, known as Fuzan (釜山 – meaning "cauldron mountain") in Japanese, played host to major Japanese and Chinese concessions. Isabella Bird, travelling to the treaty port of Busan, remarks in her 1897 travel journal, *Korea and Her Neighbours*:

> "It is not Korea but Japan which meets one on anchoring. The lighters are Japanese. An official of the Nippon Yusen Kaisha (Japan Mail Steamship Co.), to which the *Higo Maru* belongs, comes off with orders. […] The foreign settlement of Fusan is dominated by a steep bluff with a Buddhist temple on the top, concealed by a number of fine cryptomeria [Japanese cedar], planted during the Japanese occupation in 1592. It is a fairly good-looking Japanese town, somewhat packed between the hills and the sea, with wide streets of Japanese shops and various Anglo-Japanese buildings, among which the Consulate and a Bank are the most important. It has substantial retaining and sea walls, and draining, lighting, and roadmaking have been carried out at the expense of the municipality."[22]

Japan would eventually annex all of the Korean Peninsula by the terms of the Japan-Korea Treaty of 1910. At this time, Fuzan became a city and formally adopted its name; the Kanji – or Hanja, rather – are pronounced *bu-san* (부산) in Korean.

The Korean War obliterated most of the northern part of South Korea, leaving Busan and the south largely unscathed. Busan thus featured prominently in South Korea's post-war economic and trade development from the 1960s. In particular, it was the major port driving the nation's export-oriented industrialisation. The city also benefited from significant investment in research and development, and is the centre for more than twenty institutions of higher education.

As primarily port- and heavy industry-oriented cities for much of the post-war period, both Kaohsiung and Busan faced inevitable economic decline as the economies of Taiwan and South Korea diversified from manufacturing production to services, and the centre of national economic growth and activity became increasingly concentrated in the capital cities of Taipei and Seoul. From the 1990s on, both cities faced shrinking populations as residents left to find better jobs and economic opportunities elsewhere.

The decline of the port-and-industrial city wasn't a particularly Asian phenomenon. Historic port cities in the West also experienced this. A notable example is that of Liverpool in Britain, which declined dramatically in the 1960s and '70s. The city government began to rethink its approach to urban development in the 1980s, adopting a strategy of culture-led regeneration in order to attract domestic and foreign tourists, as well as new sources of investment, into the city. The city's historic docks were restored, refurbished and re-positioned as residential, lifestyle and cultural quarters. In 1988, Liverpool became the first city to host a prestigious branch of the Tate Gallery outside of London, at the heart of Albert Dock. 1998 saw the launch of the Liverpool Biennial, which would grow to become the largest contemporary art festival in the United Kingdom. In 2008, the city was named European Capital of Culture, capping some 20 years of cultural development.

In a similar fashion, the former port city of Bilbao in Spain was catapulted into the global spotlight in the aftermath of the opening of the Guggenheim Bilbao in 1997, with its startlingly contemporary architecture by Canadian-American "starchitect" Frank Gehry. The Guggenheim Bilbao would become one of the most successful cases of urban regeneration in recent history, giving rise to the term "Bilbao Effect": a phenomenon whereby cultural institutions boasting spectacular, eye-catching architecture are used in high-profile urban rejuvenation projects.

With Liverpool, Bilbao and other port cities having set a precedent, Kaohsiung and Busan too embarked on their own strategies of culture-led city regeneration around the turn of the 21st century.

Busan started first, playing host in 1996 to the inaugural Busan International Film Festival (BIFF), the very first international film festival in South Korea. In the course of the 2000s, the BIFF would play a significant role in catapulting the Korean film industry into the global spotlight. In 2011, the BIFF moved into the purpose-built Busan Cinema Centre, located in the spanking new Centum City, a large-scale, mixed-use commercial and residential development in Busan's Haeundae district, which – with its epic seaside setting and historic beach – had become one of the most popular filming locations in Korean film and television. Three years later, Busan was designated UNESCO's Creative

City of Film, acknowledging its contribution to film and media. Today's BIFF Square is one of the city's most popular tourist destinations, housing a cluster of first-run cinemas specialising in hosting high-profile film premieres; while the BIFF itself now ranks as Asia's largest, and one of its most important, film festivals.

Alongside its reputation as movie capital, Busan is popularly known as the "summer capital of South Korea", thanks to its natural landscape, no less than six beautiful beaches, glamorous marina and boardwalk, and impossibly quaint and picture-perfect historic villages perched on hillsides. It is home to hundreds of hot springs and spas and prides itself on being a centre for wellness and back-to-nature retreats.

It also promotes itself as a "City of Festivals", and organises a year-round calendar of events, aside from the iconic BIFF. There are festivals celebrating cultural heritage, such as the Jagalchi Festival (spotlighting Busan's food and maritime heritage) and the Joseon Tongsinsa Festival (a re-enactment of historical embassies sent by Joseon Korea to Japan); and there are festivals celebrating contemporary arts and culture, such as the Busan Rock Festival, the Busan Biennale and the Busan International Fireworks Festival (inaugurated in 2000, 2002 and 2005 respectively). In 2016, Busan jumped onto the K-pop bandwagon, launching the Busan One Asia Festival, a massive event that brought the country's biggest and most important K-pop acts to the city to perform for hundreds of thousands of screaming young fans from across the country.

In its most recent incarnation, Busan has thus reinvented itself as Korea's cultural capital, using festivals, events and its natural advantages to boost its tourism economy, while contributing to furthering South Korea's soft power and the global impact of the so-called *hallyu* or "Korean Wave".

Meanwhile, Kaohsiung's efforts at city revitalisation began in earnest in the 2000s, with an ambitious, architecture- and infrastructure-led strategy that is classic "Bilbao effect". Successfully bidding for and hosting the World Games in 2009, the city took the opportunity to build a brand-new National Stadium, designed by Japanese starchitect, Toyo Ito. The stadium pioneered "green" architecture far ahead of its time – it was one of the first stadiums in the world to be entirely powered by solar energy, by way of thousands of solar panels built into its façade. Viewed from a distance, this shimmering façade recalls the sinuous, scaly form of an Asian dragon.

Kaohsiung Music Center, seen from the harbour. It was designed by Spanish architect, Manuel A. Monteserín Lahoz, and features a geometrical design that simulates organic aquatic forms like waves, seaweed, coral and whales. It sits at the mouth of Kaohsiung's historic Love River, or Aihe, at the point where it flows into Kaohsiung Harbour.

In 2018, the National Kaohsiung Center for the Arts opened to great fanfare in what had been a disused military training base. After having been in the works for 12 long years, it finally opened its doors as the "largest performing arts centre under one roof", hosting an opera house (with 2236 seats), a concert hall (1981 seats), a playhouse (1210 seats), a recital hall (434 seats) and an outdoor amphitheatre. Designed by Dutch architectural firm, Mecanoo, it sits within a beautifully landscaped metropolitan park, and its startlingly contemporary architecture is inspired by the sprawling crowns of banyan trees, local to Taiwan.

Alongside these high-profile developments, the centrepiece of the city's urban rejuvenation plan was slowly taking shape. Since 2011, the city's Old Harbour district had been in the throes of a massive redevelopment project, with the intent to transform some 600 hectares of former port and industrial space into a new cultural and entertainment precinct called the Asia New Bay Area. A string of spanking-new cultural facilities opened in the course of the 2010s and 2020s: the Kaohsiung Exhibition Center in 2014, the Kaohsiung Main Public Library (also in 2014, and touted as the "world's first column-suspended 'green' building"), and the eye-catching Kaohsiung Music Center in 2021. They stand alongside other facilities like a hi-tech park (the 5G AIoT Innovation Park), a passenger cruise terminal, a massive "Dream Mall" (the largest shopping mall in Taiwan), and high-end hotels and residential properties.

Situated at the heart of the harbour district is the Pier-2 Art Center, located in what was formerly a cluster of abandoned warehouses, and – thanks to concerted lobbying by the local arts community – run as an arts space since 2001. From the Center, a leisurely twenty-minute bus ride takes one to the Kaohsiung Literary Museum, a former public library repositioned in 2003 as a community space celebrating pioneering Taiwanese authors and poets. Situated in verdant Central Park, it is the perfect spot for a moment of quiet contemplation, after a whirlwind tour of the city's new cultural infrastructure.

The jury is still out as to the full impact of these developments on Kaohsiung's economy; though certainly the city is sparing no effort in ensuring that Kaohsiung's image is transformed from that of a former industrial town and "cultural desert", to that of a culturally-vibrant, livable and sustainable metropolis.

41. Dubai
Palm Fronds in the Persian Gulf

"I said goodbye to my companions at Sharja, hoping to be with them again in four months' time. I then went to Dibai and stayed [...by] the creek which divided the town, the largest on the Trucial Coast with about twenty-five thousand inhabitants. Many native craft were anchored in the creek or were careened on the mud along the waterfront. There were booms from Kuwait, sambuks from Sur, jaulbauts, and even a large, stately baghla [...] To the English all these vessels were dhows, a name no longer remembered by the Arabs."

— Wilfred Thesiger, 1959. *Arabian Sands*.[23]

Extending some five kilometres from the coast of Dubai (دبي) and into the sparkling blue waters of the Persian Gulf, the Palm Jumeirah is a man-made wonder. It is the largest artificial island in the world; so large, it can be seen from space. And indeed, it is best taken in from above. A bird's eye view reveals the elegance of its form: that of a desert palm, or *nakhl*, evocative of the oasis towns of Arabia.

The island-palm has seventeen stylised fronds, each one densely packed with row-upon-row of private residential villas and mansions. There are only exclusive, high-end properties here; the Fronds are designed such that every single villa has its own beachfront, and a spectacular ocean view. These luxury estates house many of Dubai's wealthiest foreign expatriates, who snapped them up long before they had been built, fuelling fierce speculation and sparking a real estate boom in the city in the early 2000s.

The Fronds are connected to the mainland by a kilometre-and-a-half-long Trunk that houses luxury apartments, hotels, parks and a shopping mall. A public monorail system links the mainland to the Trunk and its Fronds, while roads form the spine of the entire island. Encircling the Palm is the Crescent, which functions as a breakwater, preventing the sandy Fronds from being swept away by the sea. Two breaks in the Crescent provide for adequate flow, ensuring that seawater on the island does not stagnate. Occupying a prominent spot at the northwestern tip of the Crescent is the enormous, five-star Atlantis Hotel, rising like a mirage on the edge of the horizon, and housing a bottlenose dolphin lagoon and underwater hotel rooms, amongst other novelties. The rest of the Crescent hosts local branches of other five-star luxury hotel and resort chains.

The Palm Jumeirah and The World, seen from space.

The plural of *nakhl* is *nakheel*. It is thus no coincidence that the state-owned real estate development company responsible for the artificial island is called Nakheel ("The Palms"). A brainchild of Dubai's CEO-Sheikh, Mohammed bin Rashid al Maktoum, Nakheel created the Palm Jumeirah by way of massive land reclamation. Desert sand being too fine for the purposes of creating new land from water, the sand used in the Palm Jumeirah had to be obtained offshore, unceremoniously dredged from the bottom of the Persian Gulf.

Land reclamation works were undertaken in record time – just a few years between 2001 and 2007, so much so that the repeated dredging and depositing of sand affected the fragile ecosystem of the Gulf. The Palm itself also irrevocably altered currents in the Gulf, and thus the pattern of sedimentation and erosion along the coast. Instead of allowing the sand to settle, villas were built not long after land was reclaimed, and these villas were made available for occupation soon after. Yet, despite worrisome concerns about unsustainability, Palm Jumeirah has attracted tens of thousands of residents from around the world thus far, and millions of tourists a year.

By the time of Palm Jumeirah's opening, Nakheel had completed land reclamations for a second "palm" – Palm Jebel Ali – to the west of Palm Jumeirah, and about fifty percent larger. Four kilometres from the coast of Dubai, Nakheel had also reclaimed "The World": a sprawling, artificial archipelago of some 300 islands that, as the name suggests, resembles a map of the world. These were destined to be sold off as private island resort-homes for the rich and famous. A third "palm" – Palm Deira – had been planned. This would have been a few times the size of Palm Jumeirah.

But then a global economic crisis hit and by 2009, Dubai was in trouble. Nakheel found itself mired in a debt crisis. Today, Palm Jebel Ali and The World remain largely undeveloped, awaiting their time in the sun. In the meantime, Palm Deira has been repositioned as just "Dubai Islands", with the "palm" sent back to the recesses of the drawing board.

Dubai itself is a mirage made real; an oasis town on steroids and a hallucinatory spectacle of skyscrapers mushrooming in the middle of the Arabian desert. The city today is inextricably associated with brash vision, unbridled wealth and hedonistic excess. It is a city of superlatives: world's tallest building, world's largest airport terminal, world's largest man-made archipelago. And yet it is also a city of dreams, attracting millions of foreigners from all over the world, keen to pursue (uncertain) opportunity and build new lives in this landscape of shifting sands. Some ninety per cent of the city's population is foreign, with a significant proportion being of South Asian extraction. This means a highly cosmopolitan society found nowhere else in the Gulf, or in the Middle East, for that matter.

Certainly, this cosmopolitanism isn't a new thing at all for the historic port cities of the Gulf. The port cities here were always hybrid in outlook, hosting a heady residential mix of merchants from across the Gulf and Indian Ocean worlds: Arabs and Persians, of course; but also *bohras* and *baniyas* from India, East Africans from the Swahili Coast and later on, Europeans. The term, *khaleeji* (خليجي) – peoples of the Gulf – emerged to describe this distinctive community which moved easily between multiple languages, chief of all Arabic and Farsi. Till today, Arabs and Iranians do not agree on the proper name for the Gulf: "Persian Gulf" is the more popular name, though it is "Arabian Gulf" for the Arabs.

At the turn of the 20th century, the most important economic sector in al-Khaleej, or the Gulf region, was pearling. The coasts along Qatar, Bahrain and the former Trucial States (today's United Arab Emirates) were a mecca for pearl fishing, and whole economies depended on the seasonal dive for natural pearls. A 1915 account notes that:

> "Pearl fishing is the premier industry of the Persian Gulf; it is, besides being the occupation most peculiar to that region, the principal or only source of wealth among the residents of the Arabian side. Were the supply of pearls to fail, the trade of Kuwait would be severely crippled, while that of Bahrain might—it is estimated—be reduced to about one-fifth of its present dimensions and the ports of Trucial Oman, which have no other resources, would practically cease to exist."[24]

The Great Depression in the late 1920s, and the invention of cultured pearls by the Japanese, devastated the local pearling industry, wreaking economic havoc along the Gulf's coastal communities. The discovery of oil in the early 20th century changed all that. From being host to some of the poorest communities on earth, the Gulf States suddenly found themselves becoming some of the world's richest nations.

Oil had a lasting impact on Gulf society, especially in the wake of the pearling industry's collapse. Pre-oil, the nobility and merchant class had enjoyed a symbiotic relationship: the ruling classes depended on important merchant families for financial and political support, and thus ruled in a more consultative manner. After oil was discovered, revenues from the sale and export of oil went straight to the coffers of major regional royal families, such that they no longer relied quite so heavily on trade in other commodities, and on merchants who facilitated that trade. Oil transformed erstwhile petty sheikhdoms into powerful absolute monarchies. The 1960s and '70s saw the emergence of nation-states in the Gulf, notably Kuwait in 1961, followed by Qatar, Bahrain and the United Arab Emirates ten years later. The latter was a coalition of seven sheikhdoms rebranded as "emirates", chief of all being oil-rich Abu Dhabi and Dubai.[25]

From the beginning, Dubai knew it would have to go its own way. Relative to those of its neighbours, Abu Dhabi and Saudi Arabia, Dubai's oil reserves have always been minuscule. Diversification of the economy was thus seen as something inevitable, and so the ruling al-Maktoum family shrewdly began to invest oil revenues into the city's infrastructure very early on.

The first major infrastructural developments were helmed by the late Sheikh Rashid bin Saeed al-Maktoum. Chief of these was an overhaul in port and trading facilities. In the late 1950s, Sheikh Rashid called for the large-scale dredging of Dubai Creek, the historic waterway that for centuries had welcomed traders in their dhows. Silting in the waterway had severely threatened the city's trading lifeline, and it was a question of dredge or die. Port Rashid was opened in 1972 and was followed, in 1979, by Port Jebel Ali, the largest man-made harbour in the world, then and today. Dubai's ports – managed by DP World (formerly Dubai Ports World) – would prove instrumental to the city becoming the Middle East's foremost entrepôt by the turn of the millennium.

Meanwhile, on land, Sheikh Rashid would oversee the construction of Sheikh Zayed Road, the epic highway named after the UAE's founding president, Sheikh Zayed bin Sultan Al Nahyan of Abu Dhabi, and connecting Dubai to Abu Dhabi. Completed in 1980, it ran past the tallest buildings in Dubai at the time: the World Trade Centre, Dubai's first real skyscraper (completed in 1979), and the Emirates Towers (built in 1999). In the late 1980s and early 1990s, photographs of Dubai pictured Sheikh Zayed Road, surrounded by a desert stark and startling in its emptiness. Nothing prepared the world for what was to come.

The 1990s and 2000s saw the swift ascent to power of Sheikh Mohammed, Rashid's third son. Like his father, Mohammed knew the importance of mega-infrastructural projects to the city's development; unlike his father, he had an uncanny understanding of the importance of iconic architecture to city branding. He pursued major infrastructural projects with a zeal and imagination far exceeding that of his father, with the goal of transforming Dubai into the premier tourism destination in the Middle East and one of the world's top-tier cities. In his capacity as crown prince and minister of defence, Mohammed oversaw the massive expansion of Dubai's international airport (established by his father in 1960), turning it into the behemoth it is today: the busiest airport in the world in terms of international passenger volume. He also set up Dubai's flagship airline, Emirates: today it is among the most profitable airlines globally, owning one of the world's largest fleets of planes and connecting the city to a dizzying number of destinations.

1999 saw a turning point in Dubai's fortunes with the opening of the breathtaking Burj al-Arab, again a brainchild of Sheikh Mohammed's. The world's "only seven-star hotel" (as it is commonly described), the Burj al-Arab is a vision in white perched on its own artificial island at the edge of the Persian Gulf, along Dubai's posh Jumeirah coast. It is designed to evoke the billowing sail of a yacht and famously boasts a helipad on its roof. Fiendishly expensive to build, it transformed Dubai's image and brand in one fell swoop, becoming one of the world's most recognisable architectural symbols. After the Burj al-Arab came the deluge of mega-infrastructural projects that would place Dubai firmly on the world map.

First came the slew of free economic zones, so-called "cities within the city" that facilitated the agglomeration of specific industries. The late '90s and 2000s saw the creation of Dubai Internet City, Dubai Media City, Dubai International Financial Centre and Dubai Science Park, to name a few. A flurry of high-profile residential mega-developments were built to attract the sort of well-heeled western professionals Dubai hoped would work in these Free Zones. Developments such as Dubai Marina, Emirates Hills and Dubai Hills culminated in the city's ultimate gated residential community: the Palm Jumeirah.

To spur tourism and consumption, Dubai also became a city of grandiose shopping malls which, given the lack of public cultural and community amenities, doubled up as civic and cultural spaces for the city's denizens. Some of these malls are icons in and of themselves: the Ibn Battuta Mall, for example, named after the globetrotting Moroccan adventurer, and featuring whole sections themed after regions of the world. The Mall of the Emirates houses Dubai's notorious indoor ski-jump, with real snow fabricated in the midst of the desert, even in the fifty-degree heat of summer. And then there is the colossal Dubai Mall which, until recently, held the distinction of being the biggest shopping mall in the entire world.

Naturally, there was a dark side to all this development. Living in the shadow of excess and privilege was a massive and growing community of migrant workers: millions of mostly South Asian men who worked in the hundreds of building sites in the city. For much of the 2000s, Dubai came under international scrutiny for the appalling conditions under which its labourers were housed and the often life-threatening conditions under which they worked. Dubai's commitment to laissez-faire commerce also meant turning a blind eye to more insalubrious aspects of trade, such as smuggling and prostitution.

The September 11 terrorist attacks and their aftermath saw America and the West becoming increasingly suspicious of Muslims and the Middle East. Things came to a head in 2006, when the United States government blocked the acquisition of a few American ports by Dubai's DP World, on account of national security. The suggestion was that Dubai had dangerous links to global terrorist networks; the reality was more likely that a first-world, Caucasian power would not conceive of themselves being neo-colonised by the erstwhile third-world subaltern.

In any case, America would soon export a crisis of its own. The Lehman Brothers mortgage crisis in 2008 led to a global economic recession. Dubai was hit hard and much of the mega-development here – funded by large-scale borrowing – came to a grinding halt. Dubai was only saved, at the very last minute, by massive emergency bailouts from big brother, Abu Dhabi.

In 2010, Dubai inaugurated its latest, brashest architectural icon yet: the 828-metre tall Burj Dubai, twice the height of the Empire State Building and (still) the tallest building and structure in the world. On the eve of the Burj's opening, Sheikh Mohammed announced that the tower would be renamed the Burj Khalifa, in honour of Sheikh Khalifa bin Zayed bin Sultan al-Nahyan, then-ruler of Abu Dhabi. The gesture was read as expressing both gratitude as well as deference to Abu Dhabi; and a much-chastened Dubai would mellow tremendously in the course of the 2010s, even as it fought to restructure its debt and rebuild its battered economy.

Meanwhile, amidst the towering skyscrapers of would-be global-city Dubai, Old Dubai persists, just barely, on the banks of the historic Dubai Creek, known locally as *Khor Dubai*. Even today, the creek is a bustling centre for the dhow trade, with the modest vessels transporting all manner of goods – legal and illegal – from spices, to consumer goods and electronics, to gold. *Abras* (عبرة), or traditional water taxis, ferry passengers from one bank to the other, and up and down the creek, much like they have done for decades.

The banks of the creek pulse with life and are a delightful and authentic experience. For centuries now, long-distance dhows from all over the region have plied this humble waterway. The ones we see today are successors to the legendary *marakib al-Sin* we first encountered in our

Historic al-Bastakiya in Dubai, with its distinctive *barjeel*, or wind-towers.

Basra chapter, and that once sailed from the Persian Gulf to China in the 9th century. Granted, most of these contemporary vessels are much smaller in size, and almost all of them are no longer dhows in the traditional sense, driven by diesel engines instead of sails and the monsoon winds.

Much of the cargo that is brought here to the banks of the creek makes its way to the historic warehouse district of Deira, where Dubai's traditional souks, or bazaars, are found. In the narrow, busy alleyways here, one just about gets a sense of how the city may have looked a hundred years ago. Here too, in spice and gold souks recalling the sights and smells of yesteryear, one feels the ancient pulse of the *dar al-Islam*: a hint of Sindbad in this futuristic equivalent of mediaeval Basra.

Across the creek from Deira is another heritage district, al-Bastakiya, so-called on account of its historic ties to the Bastak district in Iran. In 1900, following the abolition of free trade on the Iranian side of the Gulf, hundreds of Iranian merchants moved their lives and their livelihoods here. The then-Sheikh of Dubai, Maktoum bin Hasher al-Maktoum – Rashid's grandfather – welcomed them with open arms, offering them land along the banks of the creek. Many became naturalised citizens in the 1920s and '30s.

The *ajami* (عجمي – "foreigners"), as the Iranian communities of the Arab Gulf are called, brought with them their own distinctive vernacular architecture, notably in the form of wind towers that rise from the roofs of local residences. These function as traditional forms of air conditioning, catching and funnelling air through to the sheltered interiors of the home. Any hot air that travels down the towers is inevitably cooled.

Once, al-Bastakiya had innumerable wind towers – known locally as *barjeel*, from the Persian *badgir* – adorning its coral-and-mud houses. But many of these houses and their wind towers were demolished in Dubai's haste to modernise in the late 20th century. Those that remained were painstakingly restored in the 2000s, though they no longer serve their original function as residences, and have instead been repositioned as fashionable cafés, restaurants and galleries. The entire district has also been renamed the Al-Fahidi Historical Neighbourhood, in line with a broader trend of Arab Gulf nations effacing their own Iranian heritage in a bid to bolster Arab identity.

This effacement is merely symbolic in Dubai, however. The city's links with Iran and Iranian merchants run deep and it has refused to cut these historic ties, even in the face of regional and international pressure. Successive regime changes in Iran during the 20th century, and tax policies that remained stubbornly unfavourable to trade and commerce, sent droves of Iranian merchants to Dubai. They are still coming. Today, as in the past, trade with Iran forms a major part of the city's economy, and billions of dollars in Iranian capital flow constantly into the city. Dubai is Iran's economic gateway to the rest of the world, and one of the Islamic Republic's most important trading partners. One is just as likely to hear Farsi spoken downtown; and the Persian food here is unparalleled. All this harks back to the historic cosmopolitanism of the region, when it was neither Persian nor Arab, but simply al-Khaleej – the Gulf.

42. Shenzhen & Wuhan
Digital Economies, New Silk Roads and a Global Pandemic

"Recently I told a foreign guest that the Shenzhen Special Economic Zone was an experiment. That made some people abroad wonder if China was going to change its policies again and if I had reversed my previous judgement about special economic zones. So I want to confirm two things here and now. First, the policy of establishing special economic zones is correct; and second, the special economic zones are an experiment. There is no contradiction here. Our entire policy of opening to the outside is an experiment too, and a big one from the world point of view. In short, China's open policy will remain unchanged, but in pursuing it we must proceed with caution. We have achieved some successes, but we must stay modest."

— Deng Xiaoping, 1985. "Special Economic Zones should Shift their Economy from a Domestic Orientation to an External Orientation."[26]

U p until very recently, "Ali Baba" was generally known as the fictional lead in the tale, "Ali Baba and the Forty Thieves", contained within that epic work of Arab literature, *The Thousand and One Nights*. These days, people are more likely to associate "Ali Baba" with alibaba.com, perhaps the most successful e-commerce platform ever invented; and with Chinese entrepreneur and billionaire, Jack Ma, its charismatic and outspoken founder. Established in 1999, Alibaba was initially modelled after American e-commerce platform, eBay. But it quickly morphed into an entire retail ecosystem online, including a retail portal, Taobao ("trawling for treasure") and an electronic payment platform, AliPay, which, with more than a billion users, is the largest e-payment platform in the world today.

Alibaba's contemporary and rival, Tencent (*tengxun* in Chinese, meaning "galloping signal"), is less well-known outside of China, even though it is a tech behemoth in its own right. Tencent is best known for its WeChat (*weixin* in Chinese, meaning "micro-message") service. Introduced in 2011, it too serves more than a billion users around the world today, though most of this user base is in mainland China.[27] Initially modelled after Facebook and Whatsapp, WeChat evolved into a "super-app". Not only does it offer instant messaging, voice and video calls, it also allows for social networking and micro-blogging. In the

The futuristic Tencent Seafront Towers exemplifies Shenzhen's skyscraping ambitions.

course of the 2010s, it would add online gaming, music and video streaming, food-delivery and ride-hailing services to its offerings, and introduce its own wildly successful payment system, which had built-in bill payment and wealth management functionalities. One could thus spend an entire day on the WeChat super-app, accomplishing all sorts of errands, making all sorts of payments (such as for monthly utilities bills or housing loan instalments), buying all sorts of things, and consuming all forms of entertainment.

Tencent is headquartered in the southern Chinese city of Shenzhen (深圳, meaning "deep ditch"), which, by the 2010s, had grown into China's high-tech metropolis. Its headquarters – two gleaming, futuristic towers of glass and steel – stand at the heart of the city's Nanshan ("Southern Hills") district, just off its central business district and financial centre. They command a stunning view of Shenzhen Harbour, and are testament to how far China has come in its economic development.

In this city, too, stand the headquarters of China's other great technology corporations – Tencent's peers. Chief of these is Huawei Technologies, one of the largest manufacturers of smartphones in the world, along with Apple and Samsung. Huawei's other achievements lie in the introduction of extra-rapid 5G wireless mobile networks in China and the manufacture of a full range of smart devices and appliances that can link to the Internet, and process and share personal data. The name, Huawei, innocuous in English, means "great achievement of the Chinese people" in Chinese, and is thus an ultimate expression of cultural pride and patriotism. Huawei's large and sprawling campus to the north of the city features buildings that replicate old-world European landmarks and are erected amidst beautifully landscaped, impossibly verdant gardens.

The city is also home to China's foremost financial institution, Ping An Insurance, a major conglomerate with interests in not only insurance, but also banking, wealth and asset management, and healthcare services. Its expertise is in fintech: the use of new digital technologies, rather than traditional pen, paper and in-person methods, to deliver financial services. Notably, Ping An revolutionised China's insurance sector in the 2010s by offering micro-insurance and wealth management services to the bulk of China's population, who were otherwise too poor to qualify for conventional insurance and banking services by its competitors. The Ping An Financial Centre, at 115 storeys and 599 metres tall, is to date the tallest skyscraper in Shenzhen, the second tallest building in China (after the Shanghai Tower) and the fifth tallest building in the world.

Shenzhen is China's economic miracle. From a humble accumulation of villages in the 1970s, it has grown to become China's third-largest megacity, ranking just behind Beijing and Shanghai in terms of its GDP (more than 3 trillion *yuan*), overtaking Guangzhou and far surpassing Hong Kong. In terms of total population, it ranks fourth nationally with some 17.6 million residents, after Beijing, Shanghai and Guangzhou.[28] The city was famously designated the first Special Economic Zone (SEZ) in 1979 by the late Paramount Leader Deng Xiaoping, who used Shenzhen as the showpiece city for the "Reform and Opening Up" (改革开放 - *gaige kaifang*) movement that would transform China into the economic powerhouse it is today.

Economic reforms were deemed imperative in the aftermath of Mao Zedong's death in 1976. By that time, China had witnessed two devastating nationwide movements – the Great Leap Forward from 1958 to 1962, which caused a nation-wide famine, and the Cultural Revolution from 1966 to Mao's death. These had left an entire nation on the verge of bankruptcy, its populace demoralised and crippled by poverty. Deng Xiaoping rightly believed that the key to uplifting the nation and maintaining the legitimacy of the Chinese Communist Party was to modernise, open China up to economic growth, and – in his own words – "let some people get wealthy first".

The term "special economic zone" (经济特区 - *jingji tequ*) had been used to differentiate the SEZs from Taiwan's "export processing zones". However, the basic operating principle in Shenzhen was essentially a form of export-oriented industrialisation modelled upon that of the Asian Tigers, especially Taiwan and Singapore. The choice of Shenzhen as an SEZ had also been due to its strategic location just north of Hong Kong: the city was initially seen as a means of complementing and tapping into Hong Kong's wealth and business acumen.

Shenzhen's growth began with its port, newly developed at Shekou ("mouth of the serpent") in the 1980s, and expanded over time to include port and harbour facilities elsewhere in Shenzhen Harbour. As of 2022, the Port of Shenzhen was the third-largest by trade volume in China, and the fourth-largest in the world.[29] The city's economic growth strategy initially targeted Hong Kong manufacturing companies; great effort was undertaken to position the city as a low-cost option across the border for the outsourcing of industrial production.

In 2001, the People's Republic of China joined the World Trade Organisation, to great fanfare. Efforts were made to diversify and upstream Shenzhen's economy, and to open it up to foreign direct investment. Manufacturing gave way to higher-value-added services, in particular, banking and finance, as well as the knowledge, innovation, and R&D sectors. The Futian ("prosperous paddy-fields") district was developed as the city's central business district, anchoring local and international banks and financial institutions. Today, it is an ultra-modern financial district that wouldn't look out of place in London, Hong Kong or New York.

Indeed, the first impression a visitor might have of Shenzhen is how tall the buildings are; how its skyline is a breathtaking, aspirational, unrelenting forest of skyscrapers. Shenzhen has been described as an "instant city", in reference to the speed at which it has grown from low-rise rural region to towering metropolis in just four decades. Its very first skyscraper was its International Foreign Trade Centre (*Guomao Dasha* in Chinese). Construction on the 50-floor building commenced in late 1982 and was finished just over three years later in 1985. Completed at a record speed of one floor every three days, it was the tallest building in the city at the time, and exemplified what became known as "Shenzhen Speed".[30] Later building projects would break the one-floor-in-three-days record.

Shenzhen's phenomenal growth meant massive migration from all parts of China. The city today is both multi-ethnic and multi-lingual, a cosmopolitan place with Chinese migrants arriving here from all over the nation. Although they live in Cantonese-speaking Guangdong province, the city's denizens are polyglot, speaking a variety of tongues and consuming a wide variety of regional Chinese cuisines. The saying goes that "once you've arrived, you are a Shenzhen-er!"

Shenzhen is thus a radical form of port city: port, airport, and smart-port – a central node of worldwide digital connectivity – all at once. It is simultaneously global – due to its international footprint and the benchmarks used in its various hi-tech knowledge, financial and service-sector economies – and very much local, in terms of its cosmopolitan but majority-Chinese populace.

2013 saw China introduce a sweeping, next-generation economic and geopolitical strategy calculated to build on Deng Xiaoping's earlier "Reform and Opening Up" movement, and to secure China's prominence on the world stage. It heralded a confident and outward-looking Middle Kingdom in place of a China which, Deng had advised, should bide its time patiently like a slumbering dragon as it grew strong. Promulgated by Xi Jinping, the new paramount leader who took office in 2012, the Belt and Road Initiative, or BRI for short, was a stark departure from earlier policy, designed to show the world that the dragon had awakened and was now a force to be reckoned with. It was anchored in the historic silk roads of antiquity, and evoked China's pre-eminence on the overland and maritime silk roads as a producer of luxury objects desired by the known world at the time.

The BRI called for the establishment of a network of grand, transcontinental economic trade corridors – "new silk roads" for the 21st century. The "Silk Road Economic Belt" referred to multiple terrestrial freight and transport corridors that would link China by high-speed rail across Eurasia to Europe. The "21st Century Maritime Silk Road" was a multi-corridor maritime equivalent linking China by sea to Southeast Asia, Africa and the Middle East. Belt and Road would require massive and strategic financial investment in trade and transport infrastructure on the part of China: railway tracks overland, and seaports in friendly nations on the "maritime silk road". Nations who signed up would receive significant funding and aid from China in developing

Former Bank of Indochina building on the Hankow Bund, Wuhan.

new infrastructure that would benefit them in turn. All would profit together, harmoniously and "(in) the spirit of peace and cooperation, openness and inclusiveness, mutual learning and mutual benefit" – so went the Chinese pitch.[31]

The manner in which the nations of the world swiftly lined up to partake of BRI inevitably echoed yet another

historic and universal Chinese template for trade: that of the East Asian Order of Things – the proverbial *tianxia* ("all under heaven"), under which the "barbarian nations of the world" (*zhu fanguo*) were suffered to offer tribute to, rather than trade with, the Middle Kingdom. The mid-2010s saw China developing the BRI in earnest, negotiating free trade agreements with countries along BRI trade corridors, championing common rail standards across Eurasia, and investing in a number of high-profile new port development projects in Sri Lanka, Kenya, Tanzania, Malaysia – familiar places the Ming admiral Zheng He had stopped at with his treasure fleets half a millennium ago. And indeed, the admiral himself was trotted out as an unofficial mascot of the BRI, representing the peaceful and harmonious manner in which China had historically engaged with nations of the sea in order to reap common prosperity.

Naturally, the BRI had its critics, including some beneficiary countries in the global south. Even before the BRI, China had been extending substantial loans to Africa for infrastructural development, and there were fears that the Middle Kingdom was entangling African nations in a "debt trap". The BRI also emerged at a time when relations between China and the USA, under the auspices of the Trump administration, were at their chilliest yet; and the USA objected to the BRI on the basis of national security.

Meanwhile, China muscled on for what remained of the 2010s, and it seemed as though it would achieve its herculean goal of implementing Phase One of the BRI by 2025. Not once did it imagine that its unprecedentedly globe-spanning, mega-infrastructural uber-project would be laid low by the smallest of things: a microscopic organism that would cause a worldwide pandemic, the greatest-ever disruption to the global economic order.

Not that this was anything new, of course. The historic silk roads, too, were harbingers of death and disease. Open trade routes and large-scale movement of peoples have always facilitated the concurrent spread of far less salubrious things like pests and viral outbreaks. The bubonic plague in the 14th century was spread by rats that travelled alongside humans on caravans and ships across the Eurasian continent. Likewise, the Spanish Flu pandemic of the late 1910s saw the influenza virus spread rapidly worldwide by way of advances in long-distance travel infrastructure, and the unprecedentedly large number of people moving across the globe in the aftermath of World War I. More recently from 2002 to 2004, the SARS virus, transmitted from civet cats to humans, spread rapidly worldwide by plane, though it was also rapidly vanquished within six months.

By late 2019, it was clear that the world was about to come face-to-face with a new and lethal coronavirus. The ostensible origin of the virus was the Chinese metropolis of Wuhan (武汉); though how exactly the virus came to be is the subject of various conspiracy theories. One of the earliest first-hand accounts of the pandemic was written in 2020, in the form of a serial micro-blog on China's popular smartphone app, Sina Weibo. These accounts were published that same year in English as *Wuhan Diary: Dispatches from a Quarantine City*.

The global pandemic that broke out in 2020 and 2021 was far more severe than the SARS outbreak, and hit closer in scale and impact to the Spanish Flu pandemic. COVID-19, as the virus came to be known, caused an almost-total shutdown in the global movement of peoples, as travel was curtailed, airports were shut down and fleets of planes were left idle on tarmacs.

For the first time in history, large parts of the world went into lockdown, or self-imposed quarantine, to prevent the spread of the virus. China was the first to do so – the great city of Wuhan, with its population of 11 million, was the very first city in the world to be totally locked down, in January 2020. As China emerged from its first wave of lockdowns in mid-2020, other countries would commence their own, falling like dominoes in the face of ever-rising infection rates.

There would be successive variants of COVID-19 – Delta, followed by Omicron – precipitating recurring waves of infection and virus prevention regimes that would swing temperamentally between loosening and tightening restrictions. As the rest of the world re-emerged from lockdown in late 2021, China locked itself back in the face of an Omicron wave. In the meantime, a flurry of new vaccines would be developed in record time, and inoculations dispensed on an epic scale to millions of individuals worldwide. By 2022, most nations in the world, reassured by domestic vaccination rates, would opt for the approach of living with the virus. China, which continued to pursue a policy of "Zero Covid" and imposed draconian lockdowns on its major cities at any hint of a new wave of infections, eventually moderated this policy and opened up to the world again in 2023.

While travel was severely curtailed, global trade networks and supply chains resumed after a brief period of disruption. What Covid-19 did instead was to bring about a significant shift in trade and consumption behaviour, with much of the world migrating onto digital platforms for work, play and for securing basic needs like food and clothing. Food delivery apps became essential rather than simply convenient, as did online retail and e-commerce platforms, as millions of consumers found themselves trapped at home for weeks or months on end, their only source of contact with the outside world, their computers or mobile phones. Mobile or e-payments became commonplace – the virus spread by way of contact, and thus contactless forms of payment were encouraged and hastily implemented. "Zoom" calls – virtual voice and video calls – became the only way by which people could meet, whether in professional or social settings. Business meetings, social gatherings, even classes in school, went completely online for many countries while in lockdown, or emerging from it.

Even as the world re-emerges from Covid-19 and retraces its development trajectory in the physical realm, the digital layer is unlikely to be displaced. Rather, a new "hybrid" form of living, working, playing and learning – wherein we toggle between the physical and the digital, sometimes simultaneously straddling both – is likely to be the norm. Thus anyone, anywhere on earth, and at any time, whether at home, at play or in the office, can be a "port" in their own right, plugging digitally into a global network of peoples, projects, locations, goods, ideas and cultures; and gaining access to an unprecedented volume of knowledge, social capital and consumer goods once only available to whole cities.

We end our epic journey in China's great metropolis of Wuhan, which, unbeknownst to most contemporary visitors, was once also a historic port city. Wuhan is actually three cities in one, comprising the ancient capital city of Wuchang, the European treaty port of Hankou, and the industrial heartland of Hanyang. The megacity's name is an amalgamation of the names of its three constituent parts – Wu + Han + Han.

In considering the major treaty ports of China, Hankou (or Hankow, as it was once transliterated) is often forgotten. Understandably so, as it simply isn't as famous today as the likes of Shanghai, Tianjin and Xiamen; and it sits some 750 kilometres away from the sea. In its time, however, Hankou was a very important treaty port indeed, by virtue of its location along the banks of the Yangzi River, the major artery for trade in tea, porcelain and silk. It was China's most important inland riverine port –

by securing Hankou, the Western powers secured direct access to markets and production centres in China's vast interior. Along with Tianjin and nine other cities, Hankou was part of the second wave of treaty ports established in 1860 in the aftermath of the Second Opium War, and by way of the Convention of Peking.

Hankou was also one of the largest treaty ports, housing five foreign concessions – British (the largest), Russian, French, German and Japanese – all of which had waterfront access. Unlike in Shanghai, the concessions proper were concentrated along a relatively narrow strip of land along the river. The historic Hankow Bund, at some four kilometres in length, was – and still is – double the length of the Shanghai Bund. Unlike its Shanghainese cousin, the Hankow Bund hasn't survived in its entirety, but enough concession-era buildings remain here to make a walk down the Bund entirely worthwhile.

By the 1920s, almost all the foreign concessions had been returned to the Chinese: the German towards the end of World War I in 1917, the Russian in 1920 after the Bolsheviks took control of Russia, the British in 1929, when the Kuomintang's revolutionary forces occupied the territory. This left only the Japanese and French concessions, which were returned after World War II, in 1945 and 1946 respectively. Early relinquishing of the concessions by the British, Russians and Germans, and the ensuing isolation of the French Concession, is probably one reason why Hankou remains somewhat obscure today, except for history aficionados.

Across the river from Hankou is its much-older sibling, Wuchang – a must-visit for newcomers to Wuhan. Wuchang dates back to 221 CE, during the Three Kingdoms period, and is one of the oldest cities in China. The region Wuchang is situated in also once formed part of the ancient Chu Kingdom in the Warring States period; and the surreal, eye-opening and distinctly un-(Han)-Chinese Chu culture is reverently displayed in the city's excellent Hubei Provincial Museum. A highlight of any visit here is a set of spectacular bronze bells and other astonishing treasures unearthed from the tomb of the Marquis Yi of Zeng, a small state existing at the periphery of the Chu Kingdom.

Wuchang was also the epicentre of the Chinese revolution of 1911. The Wuchang Uprising was the precursor to the Xinhai Revolution that ultimately toppled the Qing dynasty and made an exile of the last Qing emperor, Pu Yi. In fact, one of the most significant landmarks related to the revolution stands here: this is the former Hubei Military Government building, where the government of the revolutionary army was founded

Yellow Crane Tower. An Zhengwen. China, Ming dynasty. Hanging scroll; ink and colours on silk, 162.5 x 105.5 cm. Collection of the Shanghai Museum.

on 10 October 1911, heralding the end of the Qing.

The building is designed in the nationalist style, mixing Anglo-Indian and Chinese architectural vernaculars. A two-storey building constructed in red brick, it features China Coast, or Compradoric, architectural elements such as sheltered walkways and covered verandahs on the second floor; a Palladian façade complete with pediment; and an angular, four-sided dome that probably draws from Chinese temple architecture. A statue of Sun Yat Sen stands in front of the building's compound, which today houses the Wuchang Uprising Museum.

Elsewhere, the most famous attraction in the city – famous since the Tang dynasty, no less – is the historic Yellow Crane Pagoda. The present structure dates to 1985, though a Yellow Crane Pagoda has stood more or less in this same spot since 223 CE; and has been successively rebuilt in the course of China's long history. The Chinese, like the Japanese, make a practice of rebuilding historical monuments, particularly in the event of destruction by natural or human disasters. The Yellow Crane Pagoda has the dubious distinction of having been destroyed by war or natural disaster 12 times in its illustrious history.

The pagoda is an imposing sight, built on a hill in the heart of the city, and rising some five storeys up. A short climb to the very top is essential, if only for the stunning views extending to the horizon everywhere you look; and just visible in the distance, the timeless arc of the Yangzi winding eastwards to the sea. Though a contemporary structure constructed with contemporary materials, the building is designed in the traditional Chinese fashion, with hipped roofs marked by dramatically upturned eaves. The present form of the pagoda approximates how it used to look in the late 1800s, before it was destroyed (again) by war.

The pagoda's long history has ensured its depiction in Chinese art, folklore and literature through the ages. Most notably, Yellow Crane

Pagoda is the very same pagoda that served as a lookout for the great Tang poet Li Bai some 1300 years ago, as he strained to catch a glimpse of the humble vessel taking his old friend, Meng Haoran, down the Yangzi River to the city of Yangzhou. As boat and friend disappeared into the misty horizon, Li Bai would capture and immortalise the moment in a quietly poignant poem of parting.

Acknowledgements

My port city journey began by chance when, in 2012, I was invited to attend a good friend's wedding in Penang, and ended up exploring and photographing Penang's historic architecture instead. What I thought would be a singular experience became an epic *rihlah*, as once a month, I jetted off to a major port city in Southeast Asia for the weekend, to wander, shoot the city and imbibe its historical atmosphere. When I was done with Southeast Asia, I went on to port cities in East and South Asia, expanding my scope to include imperial capitals that sat inland. Between 2012 and 2019, I travelled to and photographed more than 40 cities. A stint at each city would be accompanied by extensive reading on each city's history, architecture and culture, before or after I returned from the shoot. Quite a few of the cities I've shot feature in these pages, though there are many others in the book that I have not yet visited.

In 2016, my career took a turn when I was appointed Director of the Asian Civilisations Museum and Peranakan Museum in Singapore. My personal and professional interests were aligned as I brought my travels quite literally into the museum's galleries: acquiring pieces related to Asian port cities, and overseeing the curation of gallery displays and special exhibitions on maritime trade. As Director, I've also had the opportunity to work with and learn from curators, collectors, archaeologists, academics and experts in a wide number of domains; as well as a full range of communities of ethnicity, culture, faith and creative practice. The museum has thus, inevitably, impressed itself upon these pages.

I wish to thank the hundreds of writers and thinkers whose scholarly and non-academic works I've had the joy and privilege of reading and referencing, and most of whose names are honoured in the bibliography. This book was made possible by their research, creativity and labour. I'd like to thank Dr Kwok Kian-Woon, Dr John Miksic, Mr Kwa Chong Guan, Dr Peter Borschberg and my former colleague, Dr Stephen A. Murphy, for their invaluable advice in the initial stages on how to approach this book; on essential reading and academics whose works I had to consult; and on which port cities to include, and why. Special thanks go to Stephen, whose paper on the Bujang Valley informs the first chapter of the book and inspired this entire tome in the first place.

Big thanks go to the Board, patrons and my colleagues at the ACM and Peranakan Museum, and at the Singapore National Heritage Board, for their patience as I juggled writing this book and leading the museum as its Director. It has not been easy, and I am grateful for their support. Thanks go in particular to Jessie Woon, Clement Onn, Ng Wan Gui, Ian Liu, Jackie Yoong, Nor Wang, Lum Jia Yi, Melissa Viswani and Angeline Tan. My gratitude goes also to Ian Pringle, Janice Ng and the entire team at Talisman for the opportunity to work on this book – massive thanks to Stephy Chee for the amazing design and layout! My heartfelt thanks to Malcolm Jack for penning the foreword and being a dear friend and mentor. Big thanks to my editor, Zhang Ruihe, for taking a leap of faith on this project, factchecking the manuscript, and making it read beautifully. Finally, I have to thank friends and family – thank you, dearest Ben! – for being so understanding and unstinting of your love and care, as I hid myself away socially for months on end to agonise and beaver away at this foolishly epic endeavour.

A Note on References, Languages, Transliteration and Dates

This journey through the port cities of Asia and the Indian Ocean draws from a massive amount of secondary research across many fields, in different languages, and in the form of books, published journal articles, news articles and online media. Since this book is non-scholarly in nature and intended for the lay reader, I have chosen to list all works referenced in the bibliography, and refrained, as much as possible, from inserting references as notes in the text. Some exceptions to this rule are in the case of quotations or statistics cited, or where ideas, arguments or expositions draw on work done by specific academics. The book is only possible because of the many historians, art historians, sociologists, political economists, thinkers and academics who have put their minds to the subject of Asian port cities – and I thank them all for being sources of knowledge and inspiration.

Many languages feature in the narrative; this is a reflection of the cross-cultural, multi-lingual nature of trade across Asia and the Indian Ocean. I would have wished to include non-Latin-scripted languages in their original script, each time I introduce a name, a place-name or a word from another language. But this Babel of tongues would have been distracting for the reader. Instead, I have opted to have Latin script transliterations of Asian names and words, with Asian scripts appearing only where I introduce the name of the port city featured in each chapter, or terminology related to cities and maritime trade. There are also a few instances where I include Chinese characters for clarity, because these characters are meant to be read in Mandarin and another Chinese dialect (such as Hokkien or Cantonese). Note also that for quotes culled from a primary source written in a language other than English, the translation in these pages is mine.

Because so many texts and sources have been used in this book, it is impossible to have one standard system of transliteration. I have chosen to go for the simplest approach, which involves minimising accents and diacritical marks for ease of print and reading. This applies to all Asian languages, including Vietnamese, formally written in a Latin script with accents and diacritical marks, which I have opted to leave out (with sincerest apologies). Where the transliteration of a place-name or word in a cited quotation differs from mine, I have retained the form used in the source text, though without accents and diacritical marks, for consistency.

Finally, this being a history book, conventional practice calls for including dates in parentheses for important time periods, dynasties, kingdoms and empires, e.g. Song dynasty (960 – 1279); or whenever an important personage or character is introduced, e.g. Ibn Battutah (1304 – 1369). But as the scope of the book takes in almost two millennia and more than an entire continent, a great many dynasties, empires and personalities appear in these pages. To avoid overwhelming the reader, I've chosen to list all important dynasties, kingdoms, sultanates, empires and accompanying dates in a separate appendix. For personalities, I invoke hypertextuality, counting on the reader being able to do a simple online search to find out more. Except for a general mention of the broad time period within which the person lived, I've avoided listing birth and death dates in parentheses. Note that as a general principle, all dates mentioned in the text are in the Common Era (CE), unless otherwise indicated.

Appendix – Empires, Kingdoms and Historical Periods

This is a non-exhaustive list of the great empires, kingdoms, sultanates, dynasties and political periods mentioned in the pages of this book. All dates are in the Common Era (CE) unless otherwise indicated.

IN EAST ASIA

China

Han dynasty, 206 BCE – 220 CE
Three Kingdoms (Wei, Shu & Wu), 220 – 280
Sui dynasty, 581 – 618
Tang dynasty, 618 – 907
Song dynasty, 960 – 1279
Yuan dynasty, 1279 – 1368
Ming dynasty, 1368 – 1644
Qing dynasty, 1644 – 1911
Republican period, 1912 – 1949
People's Republic of China, 1949 –
Taiwan, 1949 –

Japan

Nara period, 710 – 784
Heian period, 794 – 1185
Kamakura period, 1185 – 1333
Edo period (Tokugawa Shogunate), 1603 – 1867
Meiji period, 1868 – 1912
Taisho period, 1912 – 1926
Showa period, 1926 – 1989
Heisei period, 1989 – 2019

Korea

Joseon dynasty, 1392 – 1897
Korean Empire, 1897 – 1910
Republic of Korea (South Korea), 1948 –

IN SOUTHEAST ASIA

Malay Peninsula

Kedah, possibly 2nd – 11th century
Melaka Sultanate, 1400 – 1511
Johor-Riau-Lingga Sultanate, 1528 – 1824
Malaysia, 1963 –
Republic of Singapore, 1965 –

Indonesian Archipelago (and beyond)

Srivijaya, possibly 7th – 12th century
Majapahit, late 13th to early 16th century
Mataram Sultanate, late 16th to early 18th century
Republic of Indonesia, proclaimed 1945 –

Cambodia

Funan, possibly 1st – 6th century
Khmer Empire, 9th – 15th century
Kingdom of Cambodia, 1953 –

Thailand

Ayutthaya Kingdom, 1351 – 1767
Rattanakosin Kingdom, 1782 – 1932
Kingdom of Siam, 1932 – 1939
Kingdom of Thailand, 1939 –

Vietnam

Le dynasty, 1428 – 1527 and 1533 – 1789
Nguyen dynasty, 1802 – 1945
Socialist Republic of Vietnam, 1976 –

IN SOUTH ASIA

Northern India

Gupta Empire, 4th – 6th century
Vaghela dynasty, 1244 – 1304
Delhi Sultanate, 1206 – 1526

Southern India

Sangam age (the Cheras, the early Cholas and the Pandyas), 3rd century BCE – 3rd century CE
Pallava dynasty, 4th – 9th century
Chola Empire, 9th – 13th century
Vijayanagara Empire, 1336 – 1646

Indian Subcontinent

Mughal Empire, 1526 – 1857
Republic of India, 1950 –

Sri Lanka

Kingdom of Kotte, 1412 – 1597
Kandyan Period, 1597 – 1815
Dominion of Ceylon, 1948 – 1972
Democratic Socialist Republic of Sri Lanka, 1972 –

IN THE MIDDLE EAST AND EAST AFRICA

Abbasid Caliphate, 8th – 13th century

Buyid dynasty (based in Iran), 10th – 11th century
Fatimid Caliphate (based in Egypt), 909 – 1171
Mamluk Sultanate (based in Egypt), 1250 – 1517
Safavid Empire (based in Iran), 1501 – 1736
Omani Empire, 1696 – 1856
Ottoman Empire, c. 1299 – 1922
Kingdom of Saudi Arabia, 1932 –
United Republic of Tanzania, 1964 –
Sultanate of Oman (contemporary), 1970 –
United Arab Emirates, 1971 –

EUROPEANS IN ASIA

East India Companies

Vereenigde Oost-Indische Compagnie (VOC), 1602 – 1799
East India Company (EIC), 1600 – 1874
French East India Company, 1664 – 1794
Danish East India and Asiatic Companies, 1616 – 1772

Empires, Territories and Eras

Estado da Índia (Portuguese India), 1505 – 1961
Portuguese Macau, 1557 – 1999
The Philippines (under Spanish rule), 1565 – 1898
Dutch East Indies, 1800 – 1949
Danish India, 1620 – 1869
French Indochina, 1887 – 1954
Company Rule in India, 1773 – 1858
British Raj (British India), 1858 – 1947
Straits Settlements, 1826 – 1946
British Malaya, 1826 – 1957
Canton System era, 1757 – 1842
Treaty Port era, 1842 – 1997 (ending with the handover of Hong Kong)

Endnotes

INTRODUCTION

1   Valmiki, *The Rámáyan*, translated by Ralph T. H. Griffith, Book IV, Canto XL, lines 39–62.

2   Wu, *Xiyouji*, chapter 24, 188.

PART I: OF SAILORS AND SHIPWRECKS

1   Quoted in Ray, *Coastal Shrines*, 98.

2   This is one of the theories. It's not exactly clear what the Chinese were referring to when they used the term "Chitu", particularly since most of the Malay Peninsula has reddish earth. Chitu could also have been a reference to another civilisation contemporaneous with Kedah: this was Langkasuka, located along the northeastern coast of the Malay Peninsula, near the Kra Isthmus.

3   The Hokkien dialect, also known as the Minnan dialect, is spoken in the southern Chinese province of Hokkien (also known as Fujian or Fukien). Hokkien is a far older Chinese dialect than Mandarin. The ancient Han Chinese were believed to have spoken a version of the Hokkien dialect. The fall of the Northern and Southern Song dynasties from the 12th to 13th centuries forced millions of proto-Hokkien speaking Han Chinese south of the Yangzi River, where they remain to this very day.

4   Quoted in Bowring, *Empire of the Winds*, 38.

5   See Miksic and Goh, *Ancient Southeast Asia*, 162.

6   Haddawy, *Sindbad*, 39.

7   Borrowing a line from George F. Hourani's *Arab Seafaring*, 61.

8   The Hijrah (الهجرة – also Hegira) was the Prophet Muhammad's landmark move from Mecca to Medina, which he made his capital city. This event marks the beginning of the Islamic Calendar.

9   Zoroastrianism is an ancient, monotheistic religion that emerged in Persia and was also widespread in Central Asia. It is based on the teachings of the prophet Zoroaster, hence the name. Zoroastrians worship a divine being known as Ahura Mazda. Fire is sacred to them, representing purity.

10   The central place of cities in Islamic society can be explained by the particular meaning ascribed to the word *madinah* (مدينة), the Arabic word most often used to translate "city". The root of *madinah* is *din* (دين), a highly-nuanced concept that simultaneously means (as noun) "law", "religion", "social obligations" and (as verb) "to rule", "to submit to (a higher authority)" and "to be indebted". Commerce and trade take pride of place in a *madinah* in the sense that they are grounded in debt, credit and contractual obligations. A *madinah* is thus a sum total of political, social, religious and commercial life; a concrete and idealised expression of the state of being urban in Islamic thought. At the heart of the city and public life, often inextricable from each other, are the mosque and the souk (bazaar) – faith and trade.

11   Quoted in Van Gelder, "Kufa vs Basra", 342.

12   Though it bears explaining that Sindbad never makes it to China in his voyages; and thus none of the ships he sails in are likely to be *marakib al-Sin* proper.

13   Chinese has different words for different kinds of cities. A *cheng* (城) is a walled city, such as Chang'an. A *shi* (市) is a merchant city, and literally translates to "bazaar", or "marketplace". A *zhou* (州) is a walled city that sits by a river. A *fu* (府) is a city overseen by a governor appointed by the imperial court; the word means "official residence". A *jing* (京) is an imperial capital, as in Beijing ("Northern Capital"). A *du*

(都) is also a kind of capital, but smaller than a *jing*; it refers to a metropolitan centre of a particular region. Yangzhou's full name is *Yangzhou-fu*, which means "walled city by the Yangzi River, which is also official residence of a governor. Yangzhou was also called "Jiangdu" because it was the metropolitan centre of the Yangzi River region.

14   Ennin, *Ennin's Diary*, translated by Reischauer, 1.

15   Quoted in Mo, "Jibei Zhenbei", para. 5.

16   Quoted in Munoz, *Early Kingdoms*, 123.

17   Pallava originated in the southern Indian Pallava Kingdom, and spread to Southeast Asia in the early centuries of the first millennium. Variants of the script are still used today to write contemporary Thai, Khmer, Burmese, Javanese and Balinese.

18   Quoted in Miksic and Goh, *Ancient Southeast Asia*, 292–293.

19   "Nusantara" originally refers to the islands within Majapahit's sphere of influence. I use it here to refer broadly to the vast Malay-Indonesian archipelago, or the Malay-speaking world. "Nusantara" has more recently been used by Indonesia to refer only to the islands that form part of the contemporary nation-state. I have opted for a more inclusive definition, which sees the term refer to all the islands and peninsulas that constitute the whole or parts of today's nation-states of Indonesia, Malaysia, Singapore, Brunei, Thailand and the Philippines.

20   Quoted in Kulke, Kesavapany and Sakhuja, *Nagapattinam to Suvarnadwipa*, 170.

21   *Naga* possibly derives from *naagu*, or conch, in a nod to the local trade. It could also be a reference to *nagar*, an ancient word for the peoples of Sri Lanka, suggesting long-standing trading links and resident merchant communities. The rest of the name is a Tamil suffix, *-pattinam* (பட்டினம்), which means "port city", or literally "a town on the seashore". It is distinguished from the Sanskrit *-puram*, which refers to a capital city blessed by the gods.

22   A *lingam*, meaning "sign", is an abstract, symbolic representation of Shiva that also represents the masculine principle in Hindu tradition.

23   The *puranam* recounts how fisherman, Atthipatthar, devoted to Lord Shiva, would set a fish free every day in the name of his Lord, even if he should net only one fish that day. The Lord Shiva decides to test him, first by sending him only one fish a day for multiple days. These fish Atthipatthar would return to the sea without fail each day, even as his body begins to weaken from hunger. As an ultimate test, the Lord Shiva sends Atthipatthar a golden fish studded with gems, which the latter also decides to toss back into the sea. Satisfied, Shiva thus appears before the fisherman in his full glory.

24   Ramachandran, "Athipattha Nayanar", translated from the Tamil, verses 3992 – 3995.

25   The Five Hundred Lords (*Swamis*) of Ayyavole have origins in the Deccan. They rose to prominence in the ancient city of Aihole, in Karnataka, and were at their most powerful and influential during the time of the mediaeval Cholas.

26   See Sen, "Military Campaigns of Rajendra Chola", in Kulke, Kesavapany and Sakhuja, *Nagapattinam to Suvarnadwipa*, 67–74.

27   Where exactly in the Tamilakam Rajendra Chola's warships departed from on their conquest of Srivijaya is unclear. I can only assume it would have been from a great port such as Nagapattinam, though there were also other ports along India's southeastern coast.

PART II: OF MONSOONS AND MERCHANTS

1   *Zaitun* means "olive" in Arabic, and thus there is a mistaken notion that Quanzhou is named after the olive tree, which does

not, in fact, exist in the city. It is much more likely that Zaitun is simply a transliteration of the city's other, popular name.

2   China's traditional system of social order, laid out along Confucianist principles grounded in the pursuit of order and harmony, saw the populace categorised into four occupational classes: *shi*, referring to the aristocracy or scholar-literati class; *nong*, or the farmer / agricultural class; *gong*, or artisans and craftspeople; and *shang*, or merchants. Merchants sat at the very bottom of the pecking order in Chinese society and there was a deep mistrust of them. They were regarded as a threat to social harmony due to their pursuit of profit rather than social good. They were also seen to be exploitative of the other classes, and to have a destabilising effect on society due to their accumulation of vast wealth, affording them power and status akin to the *shi* class. The status of merchants in China varied between dynasties, with early dynasties up to the Tang disdaining merchants and trade. During the Song and Yuan dynasties, commerce – and thus merchants – was more positively regarded. The Ming and Qing emperors were again suspicious of commerce on the whole, preferring to control and circumscribe trade.

3   In 1973, a Song-era ship was discovered wrecked off the coast of Quanzhou. Found on board the ship were some 95 wooden tags with characters written on them, including the words *nanjia* ("Southern Family"). Archaeologists believe this a reference to the *nanwai zongzi*, and so this ship likely carried cargo that belonged to a member of the royal family.

4   Zhuang Mishao writes about Quanzhou in his 1302 *Luo Cheng Wai Hao Ji*, or *Account of the City's Defensive Fortifications*. Quoted in Zhuang, *Quanzhou gang*, 103.

5   Polo, *Travels*, 204.

6   Battutah, *Rehlah*, 1976 English translation, 172.

7   Burgess, *Archaeological Survey of Western India*, 28.

8   Resist-dyeing involves the application of hot wax as a "resist" to the dye: where the wax is applied, the colour does not take; instead, parts of the fabric around the dye are stained. The alternating of dyed and undyed portions of the fabric results in the creation of a specific pattern or design. Mordant-dyeing, on the other hand, refers to the application of a chemical to the dyeing process to ensure that the dye itself better adheres to the fabric. The mordant ultimately ensures that colour remains fast even if the textile is washed repeatedly later on.

9   Pires, *Suma Oriental*, vol. 1, 39–42.

10   Quoted in Margariti, *Aden*, 27 and in Vallet, *L'Arabie marchande*, 22.

11   See Reese, *Imperial Muslims*, 22.

12   A *geniza* is a "cemetery" for books and papers, typically located in the grounds of a synagogue. Jewish tradition has it that any writing containing the name of God may not be burnt or destroyed, but should instead be "buried" like a human body. This practice extended not only to religious or liturgical texts, but also included documents and personal letters, which often commenced with an invocation of God's name and an appeal for blessing. In 1897, American scholar and rabbi, Solomon Schechter, travelled to Old Fustat to retrieve and preserve the contents of the historic *geniza* at Cairo's ancient Ben Ezra Synagogue. He retrieved a trove of more than 400,000 documents. Today, these documents are scattered across museum collections in Russia, America, Britain and Egypt.

13   Quoted in Goitein, "From Aden to India", 53.

14   Batoutah, *Voyages*, vol. 1, 191–192.

15   Polo, *Travels*, 241.

16   Christian tradition has it that in the 1st century, the apostle Saint Thomas travelled to Muziris, bringing the faith to India. He would be pursued by disbelievers across the Subcontinent, before finally settling down along the Coromandel Coast. His sacred remains are housed today in the Basilica of Santhome, in the town of Mylapore, a suburb of the great port city of Chennai (formerly Madras). Saint Thomas Christians are also known as Syrian Christians as they originate from ancient Syria and their liturgy is conducted in Syriac. Communities of Saint Thomas Christians emigrated to southern India from the 3rd to 9th century onwards.

17   While "Mappila" commonly means Malabari Muslim communities today, the term actually referred to Middle Eastern communities in general: Saint Thomas Christians were known as Nasrani (from "Nazarene") Mappila and Jews as Juda Mappila.

18   Battutah, *Rehlah*, 1976 English translation, 192.

19   In the course of the 16th to the early 20th centuries, Chettiar communities would settle permanently in Southeast Asian port cities like Saigon, Melaka and Singapore. There, they diversified their trade, becoming bankers and moneylenders.

20   Li, *Longjiang Chuanchang*, vol. 3, para. 47.

21   Zhang, "Mazu Worship in Late Imperial China", 13.

22   Tun Seri Lenang, *Sulalat al-Salatin*, 2020 translation, 60–61.

23   See Wang, "The First Three Rulers of Melaka", 16. The tale of Melaka's early rulers and initial decades, told in these pages, draws heavily from this seminal paper.

24   Tun Seri Lenang, *Sulalat al-Salatin*, 2020 translation, 70.

25   Pires, *Suma Oriental*, vol. 2, 269 – 287.

PART III: OF SPICES AND COMPANIES

1   Camões, *Lusiad*, 1776 English translation by Mickle, 309.

2   The Goa Inquisition lasted from 1560 to 1812. Its intent was to stamp out all other faiths and impose a strictly orthodox form of Catholicism. Hindus were particularly targeted – temples were destroyed, feasts and festivals banned, and scores of Hindus forced to convert, or tried and persecuted for resisting. Jews and Muslims were also targets, as were Saint Thomas Christians. Harsh punishments were meted out to New Christians: those who had converted to Catholicism, but still held onto some syncretic practices from their erstwhile Hindu faith. Punishments ranged from imprisonment to whipping to being burnt at the stake. Burnings and executions would be meted out during one of the many horrifying *auto-da-fé*, or public religious spectacles carried out by the Inquisition, and which took place at the city's main square.

3   Quoted in Shetty, *Goa Travels*, 27-28.

4   Quoted in Shetty, *Goa Travels*, 28.

5   Coates, *A Macao Narrative*, 52.

6   The Columbian Exchange is the large-scale to-ing and fro-ing of flora and fauna between the two hemispheres that has been taking place since Christopher Columbus (hence the name) made contact with the American continent in 1492. The chilli and potato (including varietals such as the sweet potato), arrived in Africa and Asia by sea, through maritime trade networks established by the Portuguese, and later the Spanish. The earliest Chinese name for chilli was *fan jiao* ("barbarian pepper") while *fan shu* ("barbarian tuber") was the name for the sweet potato – because they were brought to the Middle Kingdom by *fan*, or foreign barbarians of the sea.

7   The Shimabara Rebellion of 1637 – 38 took place when peasants in the Shimabara Domain rose up in protest against exorbitant taxes imposed upon them by their *daimyo*, even as they were facing a famine. Many of the peasants who rebelled were Catholics, and Portuguese traders were suspected to have aided in the rebellion. In the aftermath of the rebellion, the Tokugawa shogun expelled all Portuguese from Japan, prohibited Christianity and went into *sakoku*, or seclusion.

8   Quoted in Angara and Madrid, *Manila-Acapulco Galleons*, 67.

9   Quoted in Schurz, *The Manila Galleon*, 63–64.

10 In *The Boxer Codex*, a late 16th century Spanish manuscript that depicts various groups of people living and trading in the Philippines, a local "sangley" couple is pictured with the characters for "arriving frequently".

11 Rafudeen, *Aqidah*, 8.

12 The Dutch referred to the Mardijkers as "black Portuguese". These were freed former slaves from Malacca and other Portuguese settlements fallen to the Dutch; they had Portuguese names, but nary any Portuguese blood, and were Catholics, as opposed to the Dutch, who were Protestant.

13 Quoted in Bown, *Merchant Kings*, 38.

14 Quoted in van der Cruysse, *Siam & the West*, 27.

15 Quoted in Lockard, "'The Sea Common to All'", 236.

16 Doeff, *Recollections*, xl.

17 *Byobu*, or Japanese folding screens, were quintessential elements of the Japanese home, akin to moveable walls and used to separate different areas of one's living space, often to afford greater privacy. Many traditional Japanese *byobu* were works of art, depicting classical scenes such as cherry blossoms in spring or cypress trees in the snow, cranes in flight or dragons swirling in the clouds, panoramic views of the city and its denizens, or episodes from the Japanese epic, *The Tale of Genji*.

18 Quoted in Vaporis, *Early Modern Japan*, 101.

19 Quoted in Sweetser, "History of Coffee", 48.

20 *Fatwas* are "points of legal clarification on Islamic law issued by a *mufti*, or recognised authority in Islam". In this case, the *fatwas* related to the prohibition of drinking coffee. Muftis would continue to issue these fatwas on coffee well into the 18th century.

21 Quoted in Subrahmanyam, "Rise of Surat", 25–26. Sultan Mahmud delegated the task of building the castle to a close confidante, Khudawand Khan, who was bestowed the royal title "Khwaja Safar". Khudawand Khan was an Ottoman expatriate.

22 Delamare, *Désordres à Pondichéry*, 1997 Kailash Éditions, 14.

23 Quoted in Narasiah, *Madras*, 88–89.

24 French-ruled Chandernagore, in Bengal, had earlier been absorbed into West Bengal state in 1954.

PART IV: OF TREATIES AND EMPIRE

1 Quoted in Khan, "The Sultanahs of Aceh", 13.

2 Pasai had been a major port city since the 12th century, the first stop for Islam as it spread to the region; here it was that the oldest Islamic tombstones in Southeast Asia have been found. Some of these were elaborate, expensive Cambay headstones imported from Gujarat. By the 15th century, it had also become the world's second-most important producer of black pepper, after the Malabar Coast in India.

3 See Khan, "The Sultanahs of Aceh", 18–22. The tale of the Sultanahs of Aceh, told in these pages, draws from this paper, as well as Khan's book, *Sovereign Women in a Muslim Kingdom*.

4 Cummings, *Makassar Annals*, 107.

5 Quoted in Koolhof, "The 'La Galigo'", 368–369.

6 Quoted in Wang and Su, "Kangxidi haijiang zhengce", 166.

7 The word "factory" derived from the term "factor", an old-fashioned English word used to refer to a commercial agent. A factory was thus essentially a merchant house or trading company. The Chinese word for "factor" is pronounced *hong* in Cantonese.

8 Leland, *Pidgin-English Sing-Song*, 29–30.

9 Pepys, *Diary*, entry on Tuesday, 25 September 1660.

10 Burckhardt, *Travels in Arabia*, 9–11.

11 The Kaaba (meaning "cube") is a black, cube-like sacred structure venerated by Muslims as the House of God. It stands in a grand square at the heart of the Masjid al-Haram, or the Grand Mosque. It is the holiest place on earth for Muslims, who observe their daily prayers facing in its direction – this is known as the *qibla*.

12 Niebuhr, *Travels through Arabia*, 1:235.

13 Quoted in Freitag, *History of Jeddah*, 1.

14 The smaller-scale, primarily commercial outlook of the city probably explains why Old Jeddah is referred to as *balad* (بلد), rather than *madinah*. In Arabic, *balad* refers to an urban or built-up area without the fullest trappings of human culture and civilisation; more akin to "town" than "city". *Madinah* means "city" proper, and refers to not only an urban area, but also the urban life within it; the sum total of its religious, commercial and social life – *balad*-plus-plus, so to speak. And then there is *qaryah* (قرية), which means village, or literally "a place where humans gather and settle". It is a basic unit or building block of urbanisation. The plural of *qaryah* is *qura*, from whence Mecca's name *Umm al-Qura* (أم القرى): "mother of all human settlements" derives. All of this is admittedly an oversimplification of the differences between the concepts of *balad*, *madinah* and *qaryah* as treated in the Qur'an.

15 "The White Man's Burden", published in 1899, was actually about the Philippine-American War, but the sentiments expressed were in line with that of pro-imperialists in Britain.

16 An allusion to the Black Hole of Calcutta, a notorious incident in 1756, wherein the Nawab of Bengal had some 60-odd officers of the EIC imprisoned overnight in a "black hole" of a prison dungeon. More than half of them perished in the cramped conditions. This would form the excuse for the subsequent Battle of Plassey and the Nawab of Bengal's deposing.

17 Tagore, *Gitanjali*, Verse 35.

18 Han, *Many-Splendoured Thing*, 37.

19 This component was actually included in a subsequent Supplementary Treaty of the Bogue, signed in 1843 between China and Britain. Soon after this, the other great powers also imposed on the Qing government to extend extraterritoriality to their subjects: French citizens subject to French law, Americans to American law, and so on. Extraterritoriality would become a defining aspect of China's treaty ports, allowing the great powers to administer these ports like colonies in all but name.

20 These unequal treaties negotiated between the Western Powers and China were collectively referred to as the Treaty of Tientsin because they were signed in Tianjin (Tientsin) in 1858. The treaties were formally ratified by the Qing emperor, Xianfeng, at the 1860 Convention of Peking, which took place in Beijing (Peking).

21 Bird, *Golden Chersonese*, Letter 1, para. 4.

22 Welsh, *History of Hong Kong*, 1 and Crisswell, *The Taipans*, 60.

23 Dennys, *Treaty Ports*, 250.

24 The term Nanhai, used from the Tang to the Ming dynasties, meant "Southern Seas" and referred to Southeast Asia. From the Qing dynasty on, the term Nanyang was preferred, though in the aftermath of the Opium War, this term also referred to the parts of South China and the South China Sea occupied by "Xiyangren", or Westerners. The use of Nanyang could possibly also be in reference to the term Xiyang, or "Western Ocean", which the Manchu court later agreed to use as a broad term for Westerners, instead of the earlier *yi* (夷), which the Chinese explained, meant "strangers". The British, however, interpreted *yi* as "foreign barbarians".

25 The word "coolie" came from Hindi and was first used to describe low-wage Indian labourers. Later, it became much more strongly associated with Hokkien labourers. In Chinese, the word is transliterated as *ku-li*, which literally means "hard labour".

26 Tan Kah Kee Hall, at the University of California, Berkeley, was

opened in 1997 and funded significantly by Overseas Chinese in Southeast Asia.

27 From Sir Robert Hamilton Bruce Lockhart's *Return to Malaya* (1936). Lockhart was a British diplomat, journalist and spy. He began his career in the rubber plantations of Malaya. This excerpt is quoted in Brown, *Old Xiamen*, 68.

28 Quoted in Munson, "Curiosities of the Five Nations", 28.

29 See Yonemura, *Yokohama: Prints*, 31–34. *Ukiyo-e*, meaning "pictures of a floating world", emerged as a popular mass artform in the Edo period, particularly during the 17th century. The name derives from the courtesan quarters of the city of Edo (today's Tokyo), which were also its leisure and entertainment quarters. Woodblock prints were the equivalent of playbills and posters, and the geishas and stage actors they depicted, the celebrities of their time. Later, *ukiyo-e* would take over the travel industry, with landscape series such as *36 Views of Mount Fuji* by the legendary Hokusai and *53 Stations of the Tokaido* by the equally legendary Hiroshige becoming commercially popular works, selling out in the thousands.

30 Bird, *Unbeaten Tracks*, 2:215.

PART V: OF STEAMSHIPS AND MODERNITY

1   Cave, *Book of Ceylon*, 54.

2   See Penfield, *East of Suez*, 17 and Cave, *Book of Ceylon*, 29.

3   Penfield, *East of Suez*, 32–33.

4   Ruete, *Memoirs*, 1.

5   The Portuguese took the Persian Gulf port cities of Hormuz and Muscat in 1507, and ruled over Oman for some 150 years. For much of the 16th century, they would attempt to establish a permanent presence on the East African coast. In 1592, they finally conquered Mombasa, from whence they ruled over Zanzibar and other parts of the coast.

6   *Seyyid*, also spelled *Sayid* or *Said*, is an honorific used to indicate persons who are descended from the Prophet Muhammad, and broadly translates to "Lord" in English.

7   Clove trees, or *Syzygium aromaticum*, are native to the Moluccas in Indonesia. They are large, tropical, evergreen trees that grow to more than ten metres in height. What we know as cloves are the buds of the tree, harvested before they blossom and then dried in the sun. The dried cloves are used to spice food and beverages, and also to enhance fragrances and spike cigarettes.

8   The Shirazis were noble Swahili families in Zanzibar who could trace their ancestry to ancient Persian Gulf settlers on the East African coast: see the Mombasa chapter for more details. The Omani land grab would have long-term implications, resulting in a new landowning Arab gentry or upper-class, and brewing resentment amongst disenfranchised Shirazis and other local Africans. If anything, the presence of an Arab ruling class accentuated Shirazi identity amongst the Zanzibari, who strived to distinguish themselves from former slaves and other Africans from the mainland.

9   Burton, *Zanzibar*, 462–463.

10 Statistics from Bennett, *History of the Arab State of Zanzibar*, 28.

11 See Folkers, "Early Modern African Architecture", 25–29.

12 Bundesarchiv (German Federal Archives), *Tsingtao-Lied*.

13 See Marinelli, "Genesis of the Italian Concession", "Internal and External Spaces" and "Triumph of the Uncanny" for a fuller story of the Italian Concession in Tianjin.

14 In 1899, Chinese villagers and townsfolk in the north rose up in armed protest against what they saw was increasing foreign influence in China in the face of a weak Qing government. Calling themselves the Yihequan, or "Righteous and Harmonious Fists", they were referred to by the Western powers as Boxers due to their being skilled martial arts practitioners. The Boxers swept across Northern China, targeting foreign property and Christians. Things came to a head when they lay siege to the Legation Quarter in Beijing and the foreign concessions in Tianjin. At this time, the Qing court also decided to throw their support behind the Boxers. In 1900, an Eight Nation Alliance moved into China and subdued the Boxers at Beijing and Tianjin. The Qing government was then forced to sign the 1901 Boxer Protocol, which saw China give up further territorial concessions to the Western powers.

15 Quoted in Marinelli, "Internal and External Spaces", 64.

16 Groeneveld explores the construction of a second "Deutsche Heimat" in Qingdao in "Far Away at Home".

17 The Garden City principles of planning were first proposed by Englishman Sir Ebenezer Howard in 1898. As the name suggests, these principles involved housing people in a utopian setting that combined the best of both city and countryside. The concept proved popular around the world and was adopted in the United Kingdom, the United States, across Europe and in colonial cities in Asia and Africa.

18 Incidentally, in the aftermath of the First Sino-Japanese War in 1895, the Japanese had already succeeded in wresting the Kwantung Leased Territory from China. They were prevented from occupying it by the so-called "Triple Intervention" wherein France, Germany and Russia intervened to persuade the Japanese to relinquish their claim. The Japanese acceded, but seethed with resentment thereafter. When the Russians themselves took Kwantung, it was only a matter of time before the Japanese would take what they felt was theirs in the first place.

19 Rajanubhab, "Western Culture", 96.

20 The city's full and formal name is Krung Thep Maha Nakhon Amon Rattanakosin Mahinthara Ayuthaya Mahadilok Phop Noppharat Ratchathani Burirom Udomratchaniwet Mahasathan Amon Piman Awatan Sathit Sakkathattiya Witsanukam Prasit, which means something to the effect of "City of Angels, Great City of Immortals, Magnificent City of the Nine Gems, Seat of the King, City of Royal Palaces, Home of Gods Incarnate, erected by Vishvakarma at Indra's behest."

21 Quoted in Goscha, *Penguin History of Modern Vietnam*, 65. The ultimatum was issued by French official, Jules Harmand, to the Nguyen emperor in the aftermath of the Battle of Thuan An and leading up to the Treaty of Hue in August 1883.

22 See Nguyen, "A King's Seal".

23 Saigon's settlement as a French colony coincided with the transformation of Paris from a mediaeval city to a thoroughly modern one by Baron Georges-Eugène Haussmann. Haussmann imposed an orderly, Cartesian grid system upon Paris, complete with grand avenues and boulevards, and magnificent Beaux-Arts architecture. Huge tracts of the old city were demolished and rebuilt from scratch. Haussmann's Paris would be largely constructed from the 1850s to 1870, with further plans carried out till 1927.

24 *Panton Dondang Sayang Baba Baba Pranakan*, Vol. 5. Published 1916 in Singapore by Koh & Co.

25 *Kebaya* as vestment likely has roots in the Arab world, where a long, loose-fitting coat or outer garment has been known as a *qaba* since the 7th century. This form of dress spread eastward across the centuries by way of trade, through Persia, Turkey and India, to Southeast Asia.

26 Hot wax is applied by hand to create patterns on a plain, white woven textile, before the textile is then dipped into a dye. Where the wax is applied, the dye does not take to the cloth. Sometimes the cloth is double-dipped to deepen the colour. The wax is then melted away, leaving areas of white where the wax had been. If the batik is multi-coloured, the waxing and dyeing has to be repeated for each colour. The process is laborious and can take weeks to complete for more elaborately patterned and coloured batik.

27 From Angelino, *Rapport betreffende*. Quoted in Lee, *Sarong*

Kebaya, 193.

28 The *sawat* is a stylised representation of Garuda, the half-bird, half-man deity in Hindu-Buddhist tradition; the *parang* is a stylised "knife" motif borrowed from courtly batik tradition; likewise the *kawung*, which is a sort of stylised four-lobed flower.

29 Steen, "Zhou Xuan", 131.

30 The Taiping Rebellion took place between 1850 and 1864. It was a movement led by Han Chinese nationalists who practised a form of Christianity that blended traditional Chinese elements. The intent was to overthrow the Manchu Qing government. Though referred to as a rebellion, it was a full-scale civil war which cost the lives of millions.

31 See Denison and Guang, *Building Shanghai*, 82 and Ma, "Rise of a Financial Revolution", 7.

32 Maugham, *Chinese Screen*, 83–84.

33 Warr, *Shanghai Architecture*, 34.

34 See Han, "Qipao and Female Fashion", 7–9.

35 Quoted in Seidensticker, *A History of Tokyo*, 34.

36 Tatsuno also designed the Bank of Japan's Old Building just a few minutes' walk away from Tokyo Station. The bank is classic Meiji with a neo-baroque edifice and green dome, and was purportedly modelled after a bank in Belgium. Opening its doors in 1896, it was the city's first important Western-style building to be designed by a Japanese architect. Tokyo Station and the Bank of Japan Old Building are two of only a handful of historic buildings that still stand today in Central Tokyo.

37 Couperus, *The Hidden Force*, 17.

38 *Krontjong*, also spelled *keroncong*, is a traditional form of musical performance that has Portuguese origins. *Keroncong* pieces are typically lilting, nostalgic ballads, mainly accompanied by Western instruments such as the guitar, violin, flute and double bass.

39 Sukarno frequently signed his name as "Soekarno" as he said he was too used to the earlier Dutch-style spelling and couldn't change his ways.

40 Quoted in Kahin, "Sukarno's Proclamation", 2. Mohammad Hatta was the first vice president of the Republic of Indonesia. Together with Sukarno, he had played an instrumental role in Indonesia's Independence Movement and was at Sukarno's side when the latter made the Proclamation of Independence. They jointly signed off the Proclamation of Independence.

PART VI: OF CONTAINERS AND CONNECTIVITY

1 Lee, *From Third World to First*, 67.

2 In 1959, Singapore gained full internal self-government as part of a gradual loosening of British colonial control in the region. It would join the Federation of Malaya and attain independence in 1963 as part of Malaysia. In 1965, it was expelled from the Federation and became its own independent nation.

3 On 26 April 1956, the first container ship, a retrofitted World War II era tanker, sailed from the Port of Newark to Houston. *Ideal-X*, as this first container ship was named, carried only 58 containers. McLean called his new transportation service Sea-Land Service because of how containers could be transported overland in trucks and simply rolled on or off the new retrofitted ships.

4 Statistics drawn from the Maritime Port Authority of Singapore's website, www.mpa.gov.sg.

5 Rajaratnam, "Global City", 5.

6 GDP per capita was US$517 in 1965, and US$77,710 in 2021. Source: https://www.macrotrends.net/countries/SGP/singapore/gdp-per-capita.

7 Covarrubias, *Island of Bali*, xxv.

8 On Bali as a "living museum" and "Island of the Gods", see

Picard, "Cultural Heritage and Tourist Capital", 47–48.

9 Statistic from Hussey, "Tourism in a Balinese Village", 374.

10 See Hussey, "Tourism in a Balinese Village", 379–383 and Leonard, "Learning to Surf in Kuta", 1–2. These two papers provide a fuller tale of Kuta's development as a surf paradise. Statistic on 1994 visitor arrivals from Pickel-Chevalier and Ketut, "Towards Sustainable Tourism in Bali", 5.

11 Statistic from the Badan Pusat Statistik Provinsi Bali (Statistics of Bali Province) website: https://bali.bps.go.id/statictable/2018/02/09/28/banyaknya-wisatawan-mancanegara-ke-bali-dan-indonesia-1969-2022.html.

12 Bromfield, *Night in Bombay*, 13.

13 Marine Drive's official name today is Netaji Subhash Chandra Bose Road, though Mumbai-kers often still use the earlier name. Netaji ("Respected Leader") Subhash Chandra Bose (1897 – 1945) was an Indian politician who played a critical role in Indian Independence.

14 Chhatrapati Shivaji Maharaj was a 17th century Marathi king who fought against Mughal domination, and is regarded as an early Indian nationalist. Many monuments in Bombay were renamed after him in the 1990s, chief of these being Victoria Terminus, the Prince of Wales Museum (now Chhatrapati Shivaji Maharaj Vastu Sangrahalaya, or CSMVS, for short) and Mumbai's Chhatrapati Shivaji Maharaj International Airport.

15 Rushdie, *Ground Beneath Her Feet*, 7.

16 I borrow the term *global masala* from Lorenzen, "Go West", 22.

17 Yeh was a pioneer Taiwanese writer who began his career writing in Japanese during Taiwan's Japanese colonial period. Switching to Chinese later on, he would pen his most important work, *History of Taiwanese Literature*, in 1987. He was born in Tainan but passed away in Kaohsiung.

18 Statistics from Numazaki, "Export-Oriented Industrialization", 63.

19 The Asian Financial Crisis began in Thailand, when the Thai *baht* crashed spectacularly, precipitating currency flight. Due to interconnectivity of the region's economies, the crisis spread quickly to other Asian countries. South Korea was hit particularly hard, with the *won* going into a free-fall. The International Monetary Fund had to step in with a huge bailout package to stabilise the *won*. Korea was forced to undertake further economic reform limiting the power of its family-owned *chaebols*.

20 See Shin, "Political Economy", 3–31.

21 Data from Lloyd's List website: https://lloydslist.com/one-hundred-container-ports-2022.

22 Bird, *Korea*, 23–24.

23 Thesiger, *Arabian Sands*, 256–257, quoted in Fromherz, *The Gulf in World History*, 6–7.

24 John Gordon Lorimer, *Gazetteer of the Persian Gulf, Oman and Central Arabia, Volume 1: Historical*. Quoted in Carter, "Pearling in the Persian Gulf", 139–140.

25 See Potter, "Society in the Persian Gulf", 21–22. Note that the Kingdom of Saudi Arabia had earlier been formed in 1932; Iraq gained independence from the British that same year, while Oman gained independence from the British in 1951. The seven emirates are Abu Dhabi, Dubai, Sharjah, Fujairah, Ajman, Umm Al Quwain and Ras Al Khaimah. The capital of the UAE is at Abu Dhabi, though Dubai is the nation's largest city and economic capital. The ruler of Abu Dhabi, the largest constituent emirate, traditionally occupies the position of president, while the ruler of Dubai, its second-largest emirate, is vice president and prime minister.

26 Deng, "Special Economic Zones", para. 2.

27 WeChat's success was made possible by the advent of the smartphone on the mainland. China, at the time, lagged behind the rest of the developed world in terms of physical telecommunications, internet and information technology infrastructure. But the smartphone allowed its populace

to leapfrog over their counterparts in the West and in East Asia. China went straight to mobile and wireless technology, sidestepping the personal computer and broadband internet altogether.

28 Based on 2022 figures at http://www.sz.gov.cn/en_szgov/news/ latest/content/post_10397851.html for GDP and https://www. chinadaily.com.cn/a/202305/10/WS645b514ba310b6054 fad2310.html for population.

29 See Lloyd's List website: https://lloydslist.com/one-hundred- container-ports-2022.

30 See Du, *The Shenzhen Experiment*, 80–81. To be fair, this only applied to the thirtieth floor onwards. Prior to the thirtieth floor, the construction company struggled to acquire proper equipment to complete the building and were operating at a speed of one floor every fifteen days for the lower floors, and one floor every six days from the twentieth floor onwards.

31 Xi, "Silk Road Economic Belt", para. 3.

Bibliography

The histories of cosmopolitan Asian port cities are invariably interconnected, so references may pertain to more than one chapter. I have placed each reference in the chapter to which it best relates. References that pertain to multiple chapters across time and/or space are in the section, "Introduction & General Reference".

INTRODUCTION & GENERAL REFERENCE

Alpers, Edward A. *The Indian Ocean in World History*. Oxford: Oxford University Press, 2014.

Armitage, David, Alison Bashford, and Aujit Sivasundaram, eds. *Oceanic Histories*. Cambridge and New York: Cambridge University Press, 2018.

Asian Civilisations Museum. *ACM Treasures: Collection Highlights*. Singapore: Asian Civilisations Museum, 2017.

Broeze, Frank, ed. *Gateways of Asia: Port Cities of Asia in the 13th–20th Centuries*. Paperback ed. London and New York: Routledge, 2016.

Cengage. "Colonial Port Cities and Towns, South and Southeast Asia". Encyclopaedia.com. https://www.encyclopedia.com/history/encyclopedias-almanacs-transcripts-and-maps/colonial-port-cities-and-towns-south-and-southeast-asia.

Frankopan, Peter. *The Silk Roads: A New History of the World*. London: Bloomsbury, 2015.

Gipouloux, François. *La Méditerranée asiatique, XVIe–XXIe siècle* [The Asian Mediterranean, 16th–21st centuries]. Paris: CNRS Éditions, 2009.

Gordon, Stewart. *When Asia was the World*. New Haven and London: Yale University Press, 2008.

Hall, Richard. *Empires of the Monsoon: A History of the Indian Ocean and its Invaders*. London: Harper Collins Publishers, 1996.

Haneda, Masashi, ed. *Asian Port Cities, 1600–1800: Local and Foreign Cultural Interactions*. Singapore: NUS Press and Japan: Kyoto University Press, 2009.

Hansen, Valerie, and Kenneth R. Curtis. *Voyages in World History*. 3rd ed. USA: Cengage, 2017.

Hunt, Tristram. *Ten Cities that Made an Empire*. UK: Penguin Books, 2015.

Jackson, Anna, and Amin Jaffer. *Encounters: The Meeting of Asia and Europe, 1500–1800*. UK: V&A Publications, 2004.

Keay, John. *The Spice Route: A History*. Berkeley and Los Angeles: University of California Press, 2006.

Khanna, Parag. *Connectography: Mapping the Future of Global Civilization*. New York: Random House, 2016.

Kwa, Chong Guan. "The Maritime Silk Road: History of an Idea". 2016. Nalanda-Sriwijaya Centre Working Paper No. 23. Nalanda-Sriwijaya Centre, Singapore. https://www.iseas.edu.sg/images/pdf/nscwps23.pdf.

Kwa, Chong Guan, Derek Heng, Peter Borschberg, and Tan Tai Yong. *Seven Hundred Years: A History of Singapore*. Singapore: National Library Board, 2019.

Lee, Koon Choy. *Golden Dragon and Purple Phoenix: The Chinese and their Multi-Ethnic Descendants in Southeast Asia*. Singapore: World Scientific Publishing Co. Pte. Ltd, 2013.

Lee, Peter, Gael Newton, Barbara Watson Andaya, Leonard A. Andaya, and Alan Chong. *Port Cities: Multicultural Emporiums of Asia 1500–1900*. Singapore: Asian Civilisations Museum, 2016.

Li, Qingxin 李庆新. *Haishang sichou zhilu* 海上丝绸之路 [The Maritime Silk Roads]. Hong Kong: Joint Publishing (HK) Co. Ltd., 2017.

Marozzi, Justin. *Islamic Empires: Fifteen Cities that Define a Civilization*. UK: Penguin Books, 2019.

Masselos, Jim, ed. *The Great Empires of Asia*. Paperback ed. London: Thames & Hudson, 2018.

Paine, Lincoln. *The Sea & Civilization: A Maritime History of the World*. New York: Vintage Books, 2013.

Pearson, Michael. *The Indian Ocean*. London: Routledge, 2003.

Tagliacozzo, Eric. *In Asian Waters: Oceanic Worlds from Yemen to Yokohama*. USA: Princeton University Press, 2022.

Tagliacozzo, Eric, ed. *Southeast Asia and the Middle East: Islam, Movement and the Longue Durée*. Singapore: NUS Press, 2009.

Ting, Kennie. *Asian Civilisations Museum. Director's Choice*. London: Scala Arts & Heritage Publishers Ltd, 2021.

Valmiki. *The Rámáyan of Válmíki. Translated into English Verse*. 5th to 1st century BCE. Translated by Ralph T. H. Griffith. London and Benares: Trübner & Co. and E. J. Lazarus and Co., 1870–1874. Project Gutenberg Ebook, 2008. https://www.gutenberg.org/files/24869/24869-pdf.pdf.

Wang, Gungwu. "The Nanhai Trade: A Study of the Early History of Chinese Trade in the South China Sea". *Journal of the Malayan Branch of the Royal Asiatic Society* 31, no. 2 (182) (1958): 1–135. http://www.jstor.org/stable/41503138.

Wu, Cheng'en 吴承恩. *Xiyouji* 西游记 [Journey to the West]. 16th century. Shanghai: Shanghai Guji Chubanshe, 1994.

OF SAILORS AND SHIPWRECKS

The Bujang Valley & Oc Eo

Andaya, Leonard Y. *Leaves of the Same Tree: Trade and Ethnicity in the Straits of Melaka*. Singapore: NUS Press, 2010.

Bowring, Philip. *Empire of the Winds: The Global Role of Asia's Great Archipelago*. London: I.B. Taurus, 2019.

Guy, John, ed. *Lost Kingdoms: Hindu-Buddhist Sculpture of Early Southeast Asia*. New York: The Metropolitan Museum of Art, 2014.

Jacq-Hergoualc'h, Michel. *The Malay Peninsula: Crossroads of the Maritime Silk Road (100 BC–1300 AD)*. Translated by Victoria Hobson. Leiden: Brill, 2002.

Kang, Heejung. "Kunlun and Kunlun Slaves as Buddhists in the Eyes of the Tang Chinese". *KEMANUSIAAN* 22, no. 1 (2015): 27–52. http://web.usm.my/kajh/vol22_1_2015/KAJH%2022(1)%20Art%202%20(27-52)%20(1).pdf.

Kang, Tai 康泰. *Wushi waiguo zhuan* 吴时外国传 [Accounts of foreign states in Wu times]. 240. https://ctext.org/taiping-yulan/zh?searchu=%E5%90%B3%E6%99%82%E5%A4%96%E5%9C%8B%E5%82%B3.

Kaur, Marganjeet, and Mariana Isa. *Between the Bay of Bengal and the Java Sea*. Singapore: Marshall Cavendish, 2020.

McCullough, Theresa, Stephen Murphy, Pierre Baptiste, and Thierry Zephir, eds. *Angkor: Exploring Cambodia's Sacred City*. Singapore: Asian Civilisations Museum, 2018.

Miksic, John N., and Goh Geok Yian. *Ancient Southeast Asia*. UK: Routledge, 2017.

Murphy, Stephen A. "Revisiting the Bujang Valley: A Southeast Asian Entrepôt Complex on the Maritime Trade Route". *Journal of the Royal Asiatic Society* 28, no. 2 (2017): 355–389. https://www.researchgate.net/publication/320933268_Revisiting_the_Bujang_Valley_A_Southeast_Asian_entrepot_complex_on_the_maritime_trade_route.

Ray, Himanshu Prabha. *Coastal Shrines and Transnational Maritime Networks Across India and Southeast Asia*. London: Routledge, 2021.

Tarling, Nicholas, ed. *The Cambridge History of Southeast Asia, Volume One: From Early Times to c. 1500*. UK: Cambridge University Press, 1992.

Wei, Cheng et al 魏徵等. "Juan 82 liezhuan di 47: Nanman". 卷八十二列传第四十七：南蛮 [Folio 82, Account 47: Southern barbarians].

Sui Shu 隋书 [History of the Sui dynasty], 636. Zhongguo zhexueshu dianzihua jihua. https://ctext.org/wiki.pl?if=gb&chapter=329994&remap=gb.

Wheatley, Paul. *Nāgara and Commandery: Origins of the Southeast Asian Urban Traditions.* The University of Chicago Department of Geography Research Paper Nos. 207–208. Chicago: University of Chicago, 1983.

Wheatley, Paul. *The Golden Khersonese: Studies in the Historical Geography of the Malay Peninsula before A.D. 1500.* Kuala Lumpur: University of Malaya Press, 1961.

Basra

Abu-Lughod, Janet L. "The Islamic City: Historic Myth, Islamic Essence, and Contemporary Relevance". *International Journal of Middle East Studies* 19, no. 2 (1987): 155–76. http://www.jstor.org/stable/163352.

Al-Hariri. *Impostures: Fifty Rogues' Tales Translated Fifty Ways.* Translated by Michael Cooperson. New York: NYU Press, 2020.

Chong, Alan, and Stephen A. Murphy, eds. *The Tang Shipwreck: Art and Exchange in the 9th Century.* Singapore: Asian Civilisations Museum, 2017.

El-Hibri, Tayeb. *The Abbasid Caliphate: A History.* Cambridge: Cambridge University Press, 2021.

Fromherz, Allen James, ed. *The Gulf in World History: Arabia at the Global Crossroads.* Edinburgh: Edinburgh University Press, 2020.

Haddawy, Husain, trans. *Sindbad and Other Stories from the Arabian Nights.* New York: W. W. Norton & Company, 2008.

Haddawy, Husain, trans. *The Arabian Nights.* New York: W. W. Norton & Company, 2008.

Hourani, George F. *Arab Seafaring.* Expanded ed. New Jersey: Princeton University Press, 1995.

Institut du monde arabe and MUCEM. *Aventuriers des mers, VIIe–XVIIe siècle* [Adventurers of the seas, 7th–17th centuries]. Paris: Hazan, IMA and MUCEM, 2017.

Khosravi, Hamed. "Medina". *The City as a Project – A Research Collective,* 4 June 2012. http://thecityasaproject.org/2012/06/medina/

Kraal, Regina, John Guy, J. Keith Wilson, and Julian Raby, eds. *Shipwrecked: Tang Treasures and Monsoon Winds.* Singapore: Smithsonian Institution, National Heritage Board and Singapore Tourism Board, 2010.

Smith, Margaret. *Rabi'a the Mystic and her Fellow-Saints in Islam.* 1928. Reprinted ed. Cambridge: Cambridge University Press, 2010.

Van Gelder, Geert Jan. "Kufa vs Basra: The Literary Debate". *Asiatische Studien - Études Asiatiques. Zeitschrift der Schweizerischen Asiengesellschaft – Revue de la Société Suisse-Asie* 50 (1996): 339–362. https://doi.org/10.5169/seals-147256.

Yangzhou

Bai, Juyi 白居易. *Bailianjing – ban huangwang jianye* 百炼镜－辨皇王鉴也 [Mirror of Perfection – authenticating the real object for the emperor]. 9th century. https://m.gdwxcn.com/article/9549.html.

Chen, Yexuan 陈烨轩. "Heishihao shang de 'gongtingciqi' – zhonggu chenchuan beihou de zhengzhijingjishi" 黑石号上的 '宫廷瓷器'：中古沉船背后的政治经济史 ['Imperial ceramics' onboard the Belitung Wreck: political and economic history behind a shipwreck from the Middle Ages]. *Beijingdaxue xuebao (zhexue shehui kexue ban)* 北京大学学报(哲学社会科学版) 57, no. 1 (2020): 119–129. http://journal.pku.edu.cn/CN/abstract/abstract750.shtml#

Gong, Shuduo, and Liu Delin 龚书铎, 刘德麟, eds. *Tushuo tianxia: Sui Tang Wudai* 图说天下：隋唐五代 [Picturing the Chinese Empire (Tianxia): the Sui and Tang dynasties and the Five Dynasties]. Changchun: Jilin chubanjituan youxian zeren gongsi, 2006.

Kim, Sang-bum 金相范. "Tangdai houqi Yangzhou de fazhan he waiguoren shehui" 唐代后期扬州的发展和外国人社会 [Prosperity of Yangzhou and its foreign community in the late Tang dynasty]. *Taiwan Shida lishi xuebao* 台湾师大历史学报 44 (2010-12): 37–66. https://doi.org/10.6243/BHR.2010.044.037.

Lewis, Mark Edward. *China's Cosmopolitan Empire: The Tang Dynasty.* Cambridge, MA: The Belknap Press of Harvard University Press, 2009.

Li, Bai 李白. "Huanghe lou song Meng Haoran zhi Guangling" 黄鹤楼送孟浩然之广陵 [Saying farewell to Meng Haoran at Yellow Crane Pagoda, as he travels to Guangling]. 730 CE. https://www.guwenxuexi.com/classical/6030.html.

Li, Dehui 李德辉. "Tangdai Changan, Lingnan, Yangzhou jiaotong: wenxuesanjiao de xingcheng yu yiyi" 唐代长安，岭南，扬州交通：文学三角的形成与意义 [Chang'an, Lingnan and Yangzhou connectivity during the Tang dynasty: formation and symbolism of the literary triumvirate]. *Zhongzhou Xuekan* 中州学刊, no. 282 (2020): 146–153. https://www.zzxk1979.com/Uploads/PdfFile/2020-07-27/5f1eb031bdd8b.pdf.

Li, Yanxian 李延先. *Tangdai Yangzhou shikao* 唐代扬州史考 [A history and analysis of Yangzhou during the Tang dynasty]. Jiangsu: Jiangsu guji chubanshe, 2002.

Wang, Jian 王健. "Ye kan Yangzhou shi" 夜看扬州市 [Yangzhou Bazaar at night]. 8th century. https://m.gushici.com/t_664927.

Hakata

Batten, Bruce L. *Gateway to Japan: Hakata in War and Peace, 500–1300.* Honolulu: University of Hawaii Press, 2006.

Cobbing, Andrew, ed. *Hakata: The Cultural Worlds of Northern Kyushu.* Leiden & Boston: Brill, 2013.

Cross, Tim. "Locating Hakata: History, Self and Masculine Mythology". *Fukuoka University Review of Literature & Humanities* 39, no. 4 (2008):985–1037. https://www.academia.edu/24098432/Locating_Hakata_History_Self_and_Masculine_Mythology.

Ennin. *Ennin's Diary: The Record of a Pilgrimage to China in Search of the Law.* Translated by Reischauer, Edwin O. New York: Angelico Press, 1955.

Fukuoka City Museum, 2017. *Classic City Fukuoka.* Fukuoka: Fukuoka City Museum. http://museum.city.fukuoka.jp/en/ccf.html.

Fuqua, Douglas Sherwin. "The Japanese Missions to Tang China and Maritime Exchange in East Asia, 7th–9th Centuries". PhD diss., University of Hawaii, 2004. https://scholarspace.manoa.hawaii.edu/items/9f0726cc-f7ad-4316-aee8-c39b5e6c8d9e.

Mo, Wenqin 莫文沁. "Jibei Zhenbei yu *Si Jiao Lei Ju*" 吉备真备与《私教类聚》 [Kibi no Makibi and the *Shikyo Ruiju (A private education)*]. *Guangming Ribao* 光明日报, 15 February 2020. https://news.gmw.cn/2020-02/15/content_33557014.htm.

Reischauer, Edwin O. *Ennin's Travels in T'ang China.* Reprint ed. New York: Angelico Press, 2020.

Xing, Yong-feng 邢永凤. "Jibei Zhenbei yu Tangdai yixue dongzhuan" 吉备真备与唐代易学东传 [Research on the relation between Kibi no Makibi and the spread of the Yi in Japan in the Tang dynasty]. *Zhouyi yanjiu* 周易研究, no. 104 (2010): 61–65. https://tcsc.sdu.edu.cn/PDF/jibeizhenbeiyutangdaiyixuedongchuan_xingyongfeng.pdf.

Palembang

Dellios, R., and R. J. Ferguson. "Thinking through Srivijaya: Polycentric Networks in Traditional Southeast Asia". In *Proceedings of the 2nd Global South International Studies Conference (GSCIS), Singapore,*

8–10 January 2015, 1–21. USA: ISA Services Inc. http://web.isanet.org/Web/Conferences/GSCIS%20Singapore%202015/Archive/23e81aa1-2e38-42a5-86f5-d95c45e4d9ce.pdf.

Hall, Kenneth R., and John K. Whitmore, eds. *Explorations in Early Southeast Asian History: The Origins of Southeast Asian Statecraft*. Ann Arbor: The University of Michigan Center for South and Southeast Asian Studies, 1976.

I-Tsing. *A Record of the Buddhist Religion as Practices in India and the Malay Archipelago (A.D. 671–695)*. 7th century. Translated by J. Takakusu. Oxford: Clarendon Press, 1896.

Kulke, Hermann. "Śrīvijaya Revisited: Reflections on State Formation of a Southeast Asian Thalassocracy". *Bulletin de l'École française d'Extrême-Orient* 102 (2016): 45–95. https://doi.org/10.3406/befeo.2016.6231.

Manguin, Pierre-Yves. "Palembang and Sriwijaya: An Early Malay Harbour-City Rediscovered". *Journal of the Malaysian Branch of the Royal Asiatic Society* 66, no. 1 (264) (1993): 23–46. http://www.jstor.org/stable/41486188.

Manguin, Pierre-Yves. "The Amorphous Nature of Coastal Polities in Insular Southeast Asia: Restricted Centres, Extended Peripheries". *Moussons* 5 (2002): 73–99. https://doi.org/10.4000/moussons.2699.

Manguin, Pierre-Yves, A. Mani, and Geoff Wade, eds. *Early Interactions between South and Southeast Asia: Reflections on Cross-Cultural Exchange*. Singapore & New Delhi: Institute of Southeast Asian Studies & Manohar, 2011.

Miksic, John N. *Singapore & the Silk Road of the Sea: 1300–1800*. Singapore: NUS Press, 2013.

Munoz, Paul Michel. *Early Kingdoms of the Indonesian Archipelago and the Malay Peninsula*. Singapore: Editions Didier Millet, 2006.

Sastri, K. A. Nilakanta. "Sri Vijaya". *Bulletin de l'École française d'Extrême-Orient* 40, no. 2 (1940): 239–313. https://www.persee.fr/doc/befeo_0336-1519_1940_num_40_2_4796.

Sen, Tansen. "Yijing and the Buddhist Cosmopolis of the Seventh Century". In *Texts and Transformations: Essays in Honor of the 75th Birthday of Victor H. Mair*. Edited by Haun Saussy, 345–368. Amherst: Cambria Press, 2018. https://www.academia.edu/36271818/Yijing_and_the_Buddhist_Cosmopolis_of_the_Seventh_Century.

Wolters, O. W. *Early Indonesian Commerce: A Study of the Origins of Srivijaya*. Ithaca & London: Cornell University Press, 1967.

Nagapattinam

Chelliah, J. V., trans. 1946. *Pattupattu: Ten Tamil Idylls. Tamil Verses with English Translation*. Reprint ed. Thanjavur: Tamil University, 1985. https://archive.org/details/pattupattutentamilidyllschelliahj.v._108_Q/page/38/mode/2up.

Coomaraswamy, Ananda K. *The Dance of Shiva: Fourteen Indian Essays*. Revised ed. New York: The Noonday Press, 1957.

Dehejia, Vidya. *The Sensuous and the Sacred: Chola Bronzes from South India*. New York: American Federation of Arts, 2002.

Guy, John. "The Lost Temples of Nagapattinam and Quanzhou: A Study in Sino-Indian Relations". *Silk Road Art and Archaeology* 3 (1993/94): 291–310. https://www.academia.edu/37943421/_The_lost_temples_of_Nagapattinam_and_Quanzhou_a_study_in_Sino_Indian_relations_.

Kanisetti, Anirudh. *Lords of the Deccan: Southern India from the Chalukyas to the Cholas*. New Delhi: Juggernaut Books, 2022.

Kulke, Hermann, K. Kesavapany, and Vijay Sakhuja, eds. *Nagapattinam to Suvarnadwipa: Reflections on the Chola Naval Expeditions to Southeast Asia*. Singapore: Institute of Southeast Asian Studies, 2009.

Mahizhnan, Arun, and Nalina Gopal, eds. *Sojourners to Settlers: Tamils in Southeast Asia and Singapore*. Singapore: Indian Heritage Centre and Institute of Policy Studies, 2019.

Rajan, K. Mavali, and Palas Kumar Saha. "Early Buddhist Sites in the East Coast of Tamil Nadu". *Heritage: Journal of Multidisciplinary Studies in Archaeology* 8, no. 2 (2020): 175–192. http://www.heritageuniversityofkerala.com/JournalPDF/Volume8.2/9.pdf.

Rajavelu, S. "Nagapattinam – A Medieval Port of South India". Paper presented at Asia Pacific Conference on Underwater Cultural Heritage, Honolulu, 12–16 May 2014. http://www.themua.org/collections/files/original/d17afdb7c37f492e6c286329778f9b71.pdf

Ramachandran, T. N., trans. 1990. "The Puranam of Athipattha Nayanar". In *Periyapuranam of Sekkizhar*. Online ed. https://shaivam.org/devotees/the-puranam-of-athipattha-nayanar.

Sastri, K. A. Nilakanta. *The Colas*. Chennai: University of Madras, 1935.

Sen, Tansen. "The Military Campaigns of Rajendra Chola and the Chola-Srivijaya-China Triangle". In *Nagapattinam to Suvarnadwipa: Reflections on the Chola Naval Expeditions to Southeast Asia*, edited by Herman Kulke, K. Kesavapany and Vijay Sakhuja, 61–75. Singapore: Institute of Southeast Asian Studies, 2009.

OF MONSOONS AND MERCHANTS

Quanzhou (Zaitun)

Chen, Tao 陈陶. "Quanzhou citonghua yong qiancheng zhao shijun" 泉州刺桐花咏兼呈赵使君 [An ode to Quanzhou's zaitun flowers, presented to Envoy Zhao]. Tang dynasty, 9th century. http://m.shangshiwen.com/27177.html.

Hansen, Valerie. *The Open Empire: A History of China to 1800*. 2nd ed. New York and London: W. W. Norton & Company, 2015.

Hansen, Valerie. *The Year 1000: When Explorers Connected the World and Globalization Began*. UK: Penguin Books, 2020.

Lee, Risha. "Constructing Community: Tamil Merchant Temples in India and China, 850–1291". PhD diss., Columbia University, 2012. https://doi.org/10.7916/D8W95H8W.

Li, Yukun 李玉昆. *Quanzhou haiwai jiaotong shilue* 泉州海外交通史略 [A brief history of Quanzhou's connections with the world]. Quanzhou: Xiamen Daxue Chubanshe, 1995.

Polo, Marco. *The Travels of Marco Polo*. 14th century. Edited by Milton Rugoff. New York: Signet Classics, 2004.

Schottenhammer, Angela. "The 'China Seas' in World History: A General Outline of the Role of Chinese and East Asian Maritime Space from its Origins to c. 1800". *Journal of Marine and Island Cultures* 1, no. 2 (2012): 63–86. https://core.ac.uk/download/pdf/45439063.pdf.

Wang, Dayuan 汪大渊. *Daoyi Zhilue* 岛夷志略 [A brief description of islands and barbarian peoples]. 14th century. https://zh.m.wikisource.org/zh-hans/島夷誌略.

Wu, Sylvia. "The Ashab Mosque in Quanzhou: A Coastal Mosque in South China". *Khamseen: Islamic Art History Online*, published 8 September 2022. https://sites.lsa.umich.edu/khamseen/short-form-videos/2022/the-ashab-mosque-in-quanzhou/.

Zhuang, Jinghui 庄景辉. *Quanzhou gang kaogu yu haiwai jiaotongshi yanjiu* 泉州港考古与海外交通史研究 [Research into the archaeology and international networks of Quanzhou port]. Changsha: Yuelu Shushe, 2006.

Khambhat (Cambay)

Akhtar, Jawaid. "The Culture of Mercantile Communities of Gujarat in Mughal Times". *Proceedings of the Indian History Congress* 71 (2010): 409–416. www.jstor.org/stable/44147508.

Alpers, Edward A., and Chhaya Goswami, eds. *Transregional Trade and Traders: Situating Gujarat in the Indian Ocean from Early Times to 1900*. New Delhi: Oxford University Press, 2019.

Battutah, Ibn. *The Rehlah of Ibn Battuta (India, Maldive Islands and Ceylon)*. 14th century. Translated by Mahdi Husain. Baroda: Oriental Institute, 1976.

Burgess, JAS. *Archaeological Survey of Western India, Vol. VI. On The Muhammadan Architecture of Bharoch, Cambay, Dholkar, Champanir and Mahmudabad In Gujarat*. London: W. M. Griggs & Sons Ltd, 1896. https://rarebooksocietyofindia.org/book_archive/196174216674_10151367082326675.pdf.

Fatima, Sadaf. "The Gulf of Cambay: Port Towns in the Sixteenth and the Seventeenth Century". *Proceedings of the Indian History Congress* 70 (2009): 354–362. www.jstor.org/stable/44147682.

Habib, Irfan. "The Mercantile Classes of India During the Period of the Delhi Sultanate". *Proceedings of the Indian History Congress* 69 (2008): 297–308. www.jstor.org/stable/44147193.

Ho, Engseng. "The Two Arms of Cambay: Diasporic Texts of Ecumenical Islam in the Indian Ocean". *Journal of the Economic and Social History of the Orient* 50, no. 2/3 (2007): 347–361. www.jstor.org/stable/25165199.

Lambourn, Elizabeth. "'A Collection of Merits…': Architectural Influences in the Friday Mosque and Kazaruni Tomb Complex at Cambay, Gujarat". *South Asian Studies* 17 (2001): 117–149. https://doi.org/10.1080/02666030.2001.9628596.

Lambourn, Elizabeth. "Carving and Communities: Marble Carving for Muslim Patrons at Khambat and around the Indian Ocean Rim, Late Thirteenth – Mid-Fifteenth Centuries". *Ars Orientalis* 34 (2004): 99–133. www.jstor.org/stable/4629610.

Maloni, Ruby. "Gujarat's Trade with South East Asia, 16th & 17th Centuries". *Proceedings of the Indian History Congress* 75 (2014): 336–340. www.jstor.org/stable/44158400.

McCullough, Theresa, and Ruth Barnes, eds. *Patterns of Trade: Indian Textiles for Export in the Asian Civilisations Museum*. Singapore: Asian Civilisations Museum, 2023.

Pires, Tomé. *The Suma Oriental of Tomé Pires – An Account of the East, from the Red Sea to Japan, Written in Malacca and India in 1512–1515*. Translated by Armando Cortesão. 2 vols. London: Hakluyt Society, 1944.

Prakash, Om. "The Indian Maritime Merchant, 1500–1800". *Journal of the Economic and Social History of the Orient* 47, no. 3 (2004): 435–457. www.jstor.org/stable/25165056.

Ray, Himanshu Prabha, ed. *The Archaeology of Knowledge Traditions of the Indian Ocean World*. London: Routledge, 2021.

Singh, Pradyuman Kumar. "Cambay—Trade and Commerce (A.D. 900 to 1300)". *Proceedings of the Indian History Congress* 48 (1987): 116–124. www.jstor.org/stable/44141658.

Aden

Al-Muqaddasi. *The Best Divisions for Knowledge of the Regions*. 10th century. Translated by Basil Anthony Collins. Reading: Garnet Publishing, 1994.

Batoutah, Ibn. *Voyages d'Ibn Batoutah*. 14th century. Translated by Charles Defrémery & Beniamino Raffaello Sanguinetti. 1853. Digital ed. https://archive.org/details/voyagesdibnbato00batugoog/page/n274/mode/2up.

Chakravarti, Ranabir. "Maritime Trade Between Malabar and Aden: Gleanings from a Jewish Business Letter (1139)". *Proceedings of the Indian History Congress* 55 (1994): 132–141. www.jstor.org/stable/44143340.

Goitein, S. D. "From Aden to India: Specimens of the Correspondence of India Traders of the Twelfth Century". *Journal of the Economic and Social History of the Orient* 23, no. 1/2 (1980): 43–66. https://doi.org/10.2307/3632233.

Goitein, S. D. "From the Mediterranean to India: Documents on the Trade to India, South Arabia, and East Africa from the Eleventh and Twelfth Centuries". *Speculum* 29, no. 2 (1954): 181–197. https://doi.org/10.2307/2849328.

Margariti, Roxani Eleni. *Aden & the Indian Ocean Trade: 150 Years in the Life of a Medieval Arabian Port*. USA: The University of North Carolina Press, 2007.

Margariti, Roxani Eleni. "Mercantile Networks, Port Cities, and 'Pirate' States: Conflict and Competition in the Indian Ocean World of Trade before the Sixteenth Century". *Journal of the Economic and Social History of the Orient* 51, no. 4 (2008): 543–577. www.jstor.org/stable/25165268.

Reese, Scott S. *Imperial Muslims: Islam, Community and Authority in the Indian Ocean, 1839–1937*. Edinburgh: Edinburgh University Press, 2019.

Vallet, Éric. *L'Arabie marchande: État et commerce sous les sultans rasūlides du Yémen (626–858 / 1229–1454)* [Mercantile Arabia: state and commerce during the reign of the Rasulid sultans of Yemen (626–858/1229–1454)]. Paris: Éditions de la Sorbonne, 2010. https://books.openedition.org/psorbonne/2441?lang=en.

Mombasa

Allen, James De Vere. "Swahili Culture and the Nature of East Coast Settlement". *The International Journal of African Historical Studies* 14, no. 2 (1981): 306–334. https://www.jstor.org/stable/218047.

Berg, F. J. "The Swahili Community of Mombasa, 1500–1900". *The Journal of African History* 9, no. 1 (1968): 35–56. https://doi.org/10.1017/S0021853700008343.

De Silva, Chandra Richard. "Indian Ocean but not African Sea: The Erasure of East African Commerce from History". *Journal of Black Studies* 29, no. 5 (1999): 684–694. www.jstor.org/stable/2645859.

Hoogervorst, Tom. "Sailors, Tailors, Cooks, and Crooks: On Loanwords and Neglected Lives in Indian Ocean Ports". *Itinerario* 42, no. 3 (2018): 516–548. https://doi.org/10.1017/S0165115318000645.

Noble, D. S. "The Coastal Dhow Trade of Kenya". *The Geographical Journal* 129, no. 4 (1963): 498–501. https://doi.org/10.2307/1794664.

Pouwels, Randall L. "Eastern Africa and the Indian Ocean to 1800: Reviewing Relations in Historical Perspective". *The International Journal of African Historical Studies* 35, no. 2/3 (2002): 385–425. https://doi.org/10.2307/3097619.

Prins, A. H. J. "The Mtepe of Lamu, Mombasa and the Zanzibar Sea". *Paideuma* 28 (1982): 85–100. www.jstor.org/stable/41409876.

Shen, Du 沈度. *Ruiying qilin songxu* 瑞应麒麟颂序 [Prelude and ode to the auspicious qilin]. 15th century. https://zh.wikisource.org/zh-hans/瑞應麒麟頌序.

Shepherd, Gill. "The Making of the Swahili: A View from the Southern End of the East African Coast". *Paideuma* 28 (1982): 129–147. www.jstor.org/stable/41409879.

Spear, Thomas. "Early Swahili History Reconsidered". *The International Journal of African Historical Studies* 33, no. 2 (2000): 257–290. https://doi.org/10.2307/220649.

Walsh, Martin. "Sewn boats of the Swahili Coast: The *Mtepe* and the *Dau* Reconsidered". *Kenya Past & Present* 47 (2020): 23–32. https://www.academia.edu/51346567/Sewn_boats_of_the_Swahili_coast_the_mtepe_and_the_dau_reconsidered.

Watt, James C. Y. "The Giraffe as the Mythical Qilin in Chinese Art: A Painting and a Rank Badge in the Metropolitan Museum". *Metropolitan Museum Journal* 43 (2008): 111–115. www.jstor.org/stable/25699088.

Kollam, Kozhikode & Kochi (Quilon, Calicut & Cochin)

Chaudhuri, K. N. *Trade and Civilisation in the Indian Ocean: An Economic History from the Rise of Islam to 1750.* Cambridge: Cambridge University Press, 1985.

Kamalakaran, Ajay. "Mishkal Mosque in Calicut, Kerala". *Paper Planes* (online), 25 June 2022. https://www.joinpaperplanes.com/mishkal-mosque-in-calicut/.

Koya, S.M. Mohamad. "Muslims of the Malabar Coast as Descendants of the Arabs". *Proceedings of the Indian History Congress* 37 (1976): 195–200. http://www.jstor.org/stable/44138933.

Kumar, Ajit, Vinuraj B., S. V. Rajesh, Abhayan Gs, and H. Sasaki. "Allusions and Artifacts of Chinese Trade from Kollam, South Kerala, India". *Journal of Indian Ocean Archaeology*, no. 12 (2016): 136–153. https://www.researchgate.net/publication/333602953_Allusions_and_Artifacts_of_Chinese_Trade_from_Kollam_South_Kerala_India.

Prange, Sebastian R. *Monsoon Islam: Trade and Faith on the Medieval Malabar Coast.* Cambridge: Cambridge University Press, 2018.

Rosa, Fernando. "The Malabar Coast (Kerala) and Cosmopolitanism". In *The Portuguese in the Creole Indian Ocean.* Palgrave Series in Indian Ocean World Studies. New York: Palgrave Macmillan, 2015. https://doi.org/10.1007/978-1-137-56626-3_3.

Sen, Tansen. "Maritime Interactions between China and India: Coastal India and the Ascendancy of Chinese Maritime Power in the Indian Ocean". *Journal of Central Eurasian Studies* 2 (2011): 41–82. http://cces.snu.ac.kr/data/publications/jces2_3sen.pdf.

Sheriff, Abdul. *Dhow Cultures of the Indian Ocean: Cosmopolitanism, Commerce and Islam.* London: Hurst & Company, 2010.

Varghese, V. J. "Malabar and its Economic Niche". In *The Hindu,* 2 February 2012. https://www.researchgate.net/publication/258884998_Malabar_and_its_economic_niche.

Woodcock, George. *Kerala: A Portrait of the Malabar Coast.* London: Faber and Faber, 1967.

Nanjing

Church, Sally K. "Nanjing Municipal Museum (Nanjing shi bowu guan), Ming Dynasty Baochuanchang Shipyard in Nanjing". *Archipel* 74 (2007): 261–265. http://www.persee.fr/doc/arch_00448613_2007_num_74_1_3922_t11_0261_0000_1.

Church, Sally K. "Two Ming Dynasty Shipyards in Nanjing and their Infrastructure". In *Shipwreck Asia: Thematic Studies in East Asian Maritime Archaeology.* Edited by Jun Kimura. Adelaide: Maritime Archaeology Programme, Flinders University, 2010. http://www.shipwreckasia.org/wp-content/uploads/Chapter3.pdf.

Hvistendahl, Mara. "Rebuilding a Treasure Ship". *Archaeology* 61, no. 2 (2008): 40–45. www.jstor.org/stable/41780343.

Levathes, Louise. *When China Ruled the Seas: The Treasure Fleet of the Dragon Throne, 1405–1433.* New York and Oxford: Oxford University Press, 1996.

Li, Shaoxiang 李昭祥. *Longjiang chuanchang zhi* 龙江船厂志 [Longjiang Shipyards Treatise]. 1553. https://ctext.org/wiki.pl?if=en&res=860978.

Ma, Huan 马欢. *Yingya Shenglan* 瀛涯胜览 [A triumphant survey of the farthest corners of the ocean]. 1451. https://ctext.org/wiki.pl?if=en&chapter=566144.

Peterson, Barbara Bennett. "The Ming Voyages of Cheng Ho (Zheng He), 1371–1433". *The Great Circle* 16, no. 1 (1994): 43–51. www.jstor.org/stable/41562881.

Wade, Geoff. "The Zheng He Voyages: A Reassessment". *Journal of the Malaysian Branch of the Royal Asiatic Society* 78, no. 1 (288) (2005): 37–58. http://www.jstor.org/stable/41493537.

Ward, Sarah. "Chinese Whispers: Zheng He's Treasure Ships in the Context of Chinese Maritime Policy in the Ming Dynasty". MA diss., University of Southampton, 2006. https://doi.org/10.13140/RG.2.1.1666.5201.

Zhang, Fu 张辅, ed. *Ming taizong shilu* 明太宗实录 [Imperial annals of the Ming emperors – Taizong]. 14th–17th century. https://ctext.org/wiki.pl?if=gb&res=279435&remap=gb.

Zhang, Tingyu 张延玉, ed. "Zheng He Zhuan" 郑和传 [An account of Zheng He]. In *Mingshi* 明史 [History of the Ming dynasty]. 17th–18th century. http://wyw.5156edu.com/html/z5062m8590j2595.html.

Zhang, Yanchao. "Mazu Worship in Late Imperial China: Gender, Politics, Religion, and Identity Construction". PhD diss., University of Florida, 2018. https://ufdcimages.uflib.ufl.edu/UF/E0/05/28/82/00001/ZHANG_Y.pdf.

Zhang, Yanchao. "The State Canonization of Mazu: Bringing the Notion of Imperial Metaphor into Conversation with the Personal Model". *Religions* 10, 151 (2019). https://doi.org/10.3390/rel10030151.

Melaka

Borschberg, Peter. "The Melaka Sultanate, c.1400–1528". *Journal of the Economic and Social History of the Orient* 65, no. 3 (2022): 344–377. https://doi.org/10.1163/15685209-12341570.

Borschberg, Peter. "The Singapore Straits in the Latter Middle Ages and Early Modern Period (c. 13th to 17th Centuries) Facts, Fancy and Historiographical Challenges". *Journal of Asian History* 46, no. 2 (2012): 193–224. http://www.jstor.org/stable/41933621.

Borschberg, Peter. "Urban Impermanence on the Southern Malay Peninsula: The Case of Batu Sawar Johor (1587–c.1615)". *Journal of East-Asian Urban History* 3, no. 1 (2021): 57–82. https://doi.org/10.22769/JEUH.2021.3.1.57.

Chambert-Loir, Henri. "The Sulalat Al-Salatin as a Political Myth". *Indonesia,* no. 79 (2005): 131–160. http://www.jstor.org/stable/3351336.

Cheah, Boon Kheng. "Ming China's Support for Sultan Mahmud of Melaka and its Hostility towards the Portuguese after the Fall of Melaka in 1511". *Journal of the Malaysian Branch of the Royal Asiatic Society* 85, no. 2 (303) (2012): 55–77. http://www.jstor.org/stable/24894191.

Cheah, Boon Kheng. "The Rise and Fall of the Great Melakan Empire: Moral Judgement in Tun Bambang's 'Sejarah Melayu'". *Journal of the Malaysian Branch of the Royal Asiatic Society* 71, no. 2 (275) (1998): 104–121. http://www.jstor.org/stable/41493366.

Kathirithamby-Wells, J. "The Islamic City: Melaka to Jogjakarta, c. 1500–1800". *Modern Asian Studies* 20, no. 2 (1986): 333–351. http://www.jstor.org/stable/312579.

McRoberts, Robert W. "A Study in Growth: An Economic History of Melaka 1400–1510". *Journal of the Malaysian Branch of the Royal Asiatic Society* 64, no. 2 (261) (1991): 47–78. http://www.jstor.org/stable/41493186.

Tun Seri Lenang. *Sulalat al-Salatin. The Genealogy of Kings.* 1612–1614. Translated by Prof Muhammad Haji Salleh. Singapore: Penguin Random House SEA, 2020.

Wake, Christopher H. "Malacca's Early Kings and the Reception of Islam". *Journal of Southeast Asian History* 5, no. 2 (1964): 104–128. http://www.jstor.org/stable/20067505.

Wang, Gungwu. "The First Three Rulers of Malacca". *Journal of the Malaysian Branch of the Royal Asiatic Society* 41, no. 1 (213) (1968): 11–22. http://www.jstor.org/stable/41491931.

Winstedt, R. O. "Muslim Tombstones in Raffles Museum". *Journal of the Malayan Branch of the Royal Asiatic Society* 10, no. 1 (113) (1932): 6–8. www.jstor.org/stable/41587425.

Wolters, O. W. *The Fall of Srivijaya in Malay History*. Kuala Lumpur and Singapore: Oxford University Press, 1975.

Woodley, Kate. "Towards a Re-interpretation of Early Islamisation Processes in Southeast Asia". *ANU Undergraduate Research Journal* 2 (2010): 115–124. https://doi.org/10.22459/AURJ.02.2010.07.

OF SPICES AND COMPANIES

Goa

Camões, Luíz Vaz de. *The Lusiad, or The Discovery of India*. 1572. Translated by William Julius Mickle in 1776. Fifth ed. London: George Bell and Sons, 1877. www.gutenberg.org/files/32528/32528-h/32 528-h.htm.

Coleridge, Henry James. *The Life and Letters of St. Francis Xavier. 2 Vols.* New ed. London: Burns and Oates, 1881. www.hoyletutoring.com/ books/Coleridge-St_Francis_Xavier-1.pdf and www.hoyletutoring. com/books/Coleridge-St_Francis_Xavier-2.pdf.

Disney, A. R. *A History of Portugal and the Portuguese Empire. Volume Two: The Portuguese Empire*. USA: Cambridge University Press, 2009.

Hall, Maurice. *Window on Goa: A History and Guide*. 2nd ed. London: Quiller Press, 1992.

Mormando, Franco, and Jill G. Thomas, eds. *Francis Xavier and the Jesuit Missions in the Far East. An Anniversary Exhibition of Early Printed Works from the Jesuitana Collection of the John J. Burns Library, Boston College*. Chestnut Hill, MA: The Jesuit Institute of Boston College, 2006. www.bc.edu/content/dam/files/libraries/pdf/ frances-xavier-catalog.pdf.

Rajagopalan, S. *Old Goa: World Heritage Series*. New Delhi: Archaeological Survey of India, 2004.

Shetty, Manohar, ed. *Goa Travels: Being the Accounts of Travellers from the 16th to the 21st Century*. New Delhi: Rupa Publications India, 2014.

Van Linschoten, Jan Huygen. *Itinerario*. 1596. Translated as *His Discours of Voyages into ye Easte and West Indies*. Translated by William Philip. London: John Wolfe, 1598. Ann Arbor: Text Creation Partnership, 2011. https://quod.lib.umich.edu/cgi/t/text/text-idx?c =eebo;idno=A05569.0001.001.

Macau

Coates, Austin. *A Macao Narrative*. 1978. Echoes: Classics in Hong Kong Culture and History ed. Hong Kong: Hong Kong University Press, 2009.

Crosby, Alfred W., Jr. *The Columbian Exchange: Biological and Cultural Consequences of 1492*. 1972. 30th Anniversary ed. London: Praeger, 2003.

Ferreira, José dos Santos. "Macau sâm assi". 1968. Translated by Anerneq (Joshua). https://lyricstranslate.com/en/macau-s%C3%A2m-assi-macau.html.

Hao, Zhidong. *Macau: History and Society*. 2nd ed. Hong Kong: Hong Kong University Press, 2020.

Jackson, Annabel. *The Making of Macau's Fusion Cuisine: From Family Table to World Stage*. Hong Kong: Hong Kong University Press, 2020.

Pons, Philippe. *Macao*. English ed. Translated by Sarah Adams. London:

Reaktion Books, 2002.

Porter, Jonathan. *Macau: The Imaginary City*. Oxford and USA: Routledge, 1999.

Sá Cunha, Luís, ed. *The Macanese: Anthropology, History, Ethnology. Review of Culture* 20. English ed. Macau: Instituto Cultural de Macau, 1994.

Wong, Kevin Martens. "Kodrah Kristang: The Initiative to Revitalize the Kristang Language in Singapore". In *Documentation and Maintenance of Contact Languages from South Asia to East Asia*, edited by Mário Pinharanda-Nunes and Hugo C. Cardoso, 35–121. Honolulu: University of Hawai'i Press, 2019. https://nflrc.hawaii. edu/ldc/sp19/.

Wordie, Jason. *Macao: People and Places, Past and Present*. Hong Kong: Angsana, 2013.

Manila

Angara, Edgardo J., and Carlos Madrid. *The World of the Manila-Acapulco Galleons: The Global and Human Context*. Quezon City: Vibal Foundation, 2017.

Anonymous. *The Boxer Codex*. c. 1590. http://webapp1.dlib.indiana.edu/ metsnav3/general/index.html#mets=http%3A%2F%2Fpurl.dlib. indiana.edu%2Fiudl%2Fgeneral%2Fmets%2FVAB8326&page=5.

De Castro, Eloísa Parco, ed. *Carlos L. Quirino's Old Manila*. 2nd ed. With "The Families of Old Manila" by Augusto M.R. González III. Quezon City: Vibal Foundation, 2016.

Giraldez, Arturo. *The Age of Trade: The Manila Galleons and the Dawn of the Global Economy*. London: Rowman & Littlefield, 2015.

Gordon, Peter, and Juan José Morales. *The Silver Way: China, Spanish America and the Birth of Globalisation, 1565–1815*. UK: Penguin Books, 2017.

Museo Internacional del Barroco, Puebla, Mexico and Museo Franz Mayer, Mexico City. *Return Voyage: The China Galleon and the Baroque in Mexico, 1565–1815*. Mexico: Government of the State of Puebla, 2016.

Pierce, Donna, and Ronald Otsuka, eds. *Asia & Spanish America: Trans-Pacific Artistic & Cultural Exchange, 1500–1850. Papers from the 2006 Mayer Center for Pre-Columbian & Spanish Colonial Art Symposium at the Denver Art Museum*. USA: Denver Art Museum, 2009.

Schurz, William Lytle. *The Manila Galleon: The Romantic History of the Spanish Galleons Trading Between Manila and Acapulco*. New York: E. P. Dutton & Co, Inc, 1939.

Jakarta (Batavia) & Cape Town (Kaapstad)

Baderoon, Gabeba. "The African Oceans—Tracing the Sea as Memory of Slavery in South African Literature and Culture". *Research in African Literatures* 40, no. 4 (2009): 89–107. http://www.jstor.org/ stable/40468163.

Bown, Stephen R. *Merchant Kings: When Companies Ruled the World, 1600–1900*. New York: Thomas Dunne Books, St. Martin's Press, 2009.

Bruijn, Jaap R. "Between Batavia and the Cape: Shipping Patterns of the Dutch East India Company". *Journal of Southeast Asian Studies* 11, no. 2 (1980): 251–65. http://www.jstor.org/ stable/20070358.

Burnet, Ian. *East Indies: The 200 Year Struggle between the Portuguese Crown, the Dutch East India Company and the English East India Company for Supremacy in the Eastern Seas*. Australia: Rosenberg Publishing, 2013.

Gosselink, Martine, Maria Holtrop, and Robert Ross, eds. *Good Hope: South Africa and the Netherlands from 1600*. The Netherlands:

Rijksmuseum and Uitgeverij Vantilt, 2017.

Heuken, Adolf, SJ. *Historical Sites of Jakarta*. 7th ed. Jakarta: Cipta Loka Caraka, 2007.

Jack, Malcolm. *To the Fairest Cape: European Encounters in the Cape of Good Hope*. Lewisburg, Pennsylvania: Bucknell University Press, 2019.

Rafudeen, Auwis, trans. *The 'Aqīdah of Tuan Guru by 'Abdullah ibn Qadi 'Abd al-Salam*. Cape Town: Samander Publications, 2004. https://www.academia.edu/1489273/The_Aqidah_of_Tuan_Guru.

Snyman, Lannice. "South Africa's Rainbow Cuisine". *Gastronomica* 4, no. 1 (2004): 91–93. https://doi.org/10.1525/gfc.2004.4.1.91.

Van de Geijn-Verhoeven, Monique, et al. *Domestic Interiors at the Cape and in Batavia, 1602–1795*. The Netherlands: Wanders Uitgevers, Zwolle and Gemeentemuseum Den Haag, 2002.

Van der Linde, Herald. *Jakarta: History of a Misunderstood City*. Singapore: Marshall Cavendish Editions, 2020.

Worden, Nigel. "Space and Identity in VOC Cape Town". *Kronos* 25 (1998): 72–87. http://www.jstor.org/stable/41056428.

Ayutthaya & Hoi An

Baker, Chris. "Ayutthaya Rising: From Land or Sea?". *Journal of Southeast Asian Studies* 34, no. 1 (2003): 41–62. www.jstor.org/stable/20072474.

Baker, Chris, and Pasuk Phongpaichit. *A History of Ayutthaya: Siam in the Early Modern World*. Cambridge: Cambridge University Press, 2017.

Borschberg, Peter. "Jacques de Coutre on Trade and Violence in Monsoon Asia (Early 17th century)". *Jahrbuch für Europäische Überseegeschichte* 17 (2017): 43–74. https://www.academia.edu/34603227/Jacques_de_Coutre_on_Trade_and_Violence_in_Monsoon_Asia_early_17th_Century.

Chiung, Wi-Vun 蔣為文. "Yuenan Hui'an gucheng dangdai mingxiangren, huaren, ji yuenanren zhi hudong guanxi yu wenhua jiechu" 越南会安古城当代明乡人、华人及越南人之互动关系与文化接触 [Contemporary interactions and cultural contacts among Minh Huong people, ethnic Chinese and Vietnamese in Hoi An ancient town of Vietnam]. *Yatai yanjiu luntan* 亚太研究论坛 [Asia-Pacific Research Forum], no. 61 (2015-12): 131–155. Taiwan: Zhongyang yanjiuyuan renwenshehuikexue yanjiuzhongxin yataiquyu yanjiuzhuantizhongxin. https://www.rchss.sinica.edu.tw/files_news/1260_d8b5ce0e.pdf.

Chularatana, Julispong. "Indo-Persian Influence on Late Ayutthaya Art, Architecture, and Design". *Journal of the Siam Society* 105 (2017): 43-72. https://so06.tci-thaijo.org/index.php/pub_jss/article/view/158009.

Garnier, Derick. *Ayutthaya: Venice of the East*. Thailand: River Books, 2004.

Howland, Carol. *Secrets of Hoi An: Vietnam's Historic Port*. Hanoi: The Gioi Publishers, 2011.

Ibrahim, Muhammad Rabi Ibn Muhammad. *The Ship of Sulaiman*. 1685–1688. Translated by John O'Kane. London: Routledge & Kegan Paul, 1972.

Lockard, Craig A. "'The Sea Common to All': Maritime Frontiers, Port Cities, and Chinese Traders in the Southeast Asian Age of Commerce, ca. 1400–1750". *Journal of World History* 21, no. 2 (2010): 219–247. http://www.jstor.org/stable/20752948.

Marcinkowski, Christoph. "Persians and Shi'ites in Thailand: From the Ayutthaya Period to the Present". Nalanda-Sriwijaya Centre Working Paper Series No. 15 (2014). Nalanda-Sriwijaya Centre, Institute of Southeast Asian Studies, Singapore. https://www.iseas.edu.sg/images/pdf/nsc_working_paper_series_15.pdf.

Van der Cruysse, Dirk. *Siam & the West, 1500–1700*. Translated by

Michael Smithies. Thailand: Silkworm Books, 2002.

Nagasaki

Cho, Hung-Guk. "The Trade between China, Japan, Korea and Southeast Asia in the 14th Century through the 17th Century Period". *International Area Studies Review* 3, no. 2 (2000). https://doi.org/10.1177/223386590000300205.

Doeff, Hendrik. *Recollections of Japan*. 1833. Translated by Annick M. Doeff. Canada: Trafford Publishing, 2003.

Haggard, Stephan, and David C. Kang, eds. *East Asia in the World: Twelve Events That Shaped the Modern International Order*. Cambridge: Cambridge University Press, 2000.

Haneda Masashi 羽田正. *Tou indo kaisha to ajia no umi* 東インド会社とアジアの海. [East India Companies and the oceans of Asia]. Tokyo: Kabushiki-gaisha Kodansha, 2018.

Mizuno, Norihito. "China in Tokugawa Foreign Relations: The Tokugawa Bakufu's Perception of and Attitudes towards Ming-Qing China". *Sino-Japanese Studies Journal* 15 (2003): 108–144. https://chinajapan.org/articles/15/mizuno15.108-144.pdf.

Nagasaki shi kyoiku iinkai 長崎市教育委員會. *Nagasaki shi no bunkazai* 長崎市の文化財 [Cultural properties of Nagasaki City]. Nagasaki: Nagasaki shi kyoiku iinkai, 1994.

Vaporis, Constantine Nomikos. *Voices of Early Modern Japan: Contemporary Accounts of Daily Life during the Age of the Shoguns*. USA: Westview Press, 2012.

Mocha & Surat

Casale, Giancarlo. "The Ottoman Administration of the Spice Trade in the Sixteenth-Century Red Sea and Persian Gulf". *Journal of the Economic and Social History of the Orient* 49, no. 2 (2006): 170–198. http://www.jstor.org/stable/25165138.

Chaiklin, Martha. "Surat: City of Ivory". In *Transregional Trade and Traders: Situating Gujarat in the Indian Ocean from Early Times to 1900*, edited by Edward A. Alpers and Chhaya Goswami, 218–238. New Delhi: Oxford University Press, 2019.

Dames, M. Longworth. "The Portuguese and Turks in the Indian Ocean in the Sixteenth Century". *Journal of the Royal Asiatic Society of Great Britain and Ireland*, no. 1 (1921): 1–28. http://www.jstor.org/stable/25209694.

Eschner, Kat. "Your Mocha is Named After the Birthplace of the Coffee Trade". *Smithsonian Magazine*, 29 September 2017. https://www.smithsonianmag.com/smart-news/your-mocha-named-after-birthplace-coffee-trade-180965016/.

Gilbert, David. "The History of Mocha Coffee and Yemeni Coffee Culture". *Perfect Daily Grind*, 20 September 2017. https://perfectdailygrind.com/2017/09/the-history-of-mocha-coffee-yemeni-coffee-culture/.

Goswami, Chhaya. "Coffee Mocha: From the Highlands of Yemen to Surat, Muscat and Mandvi". In *Transregional Trade and Traders: Situating Gujarat in the Indian Ocean from Early Times to 1900*, edited by Edward A. Alpers and Chhaya Goswami, 239–268. New Delhi: Oxford University Press, 2019.

Hathaway, Jane. "The Ottomans and the Yemeni Coffee Trade". *Oriente Moderno* 25 (86), no. 1 (2006): 161–171. http://www.jstor.org/stable/25818052.

Khan, Iftikar A. "Coffee Trade of the Red Sea in 17th and 18th Century". *Proceedings of the Indian History Congress* 57 (1996): 304–315. http://www.jstor.org/stable/44133322.

Kinariwala, Denish Yasvin. *Walled City of Surat: History, Settlement and Architecture*. Germany: LAP Lambert Academic Publishing, 2012.

Parveen, Sagufta. "Surat: As a Major Port-Town of Gujarat and its Trade

History". *IOSR Journal of Humanities and Social Science (IOSR-JHSS)* 19, no. 5 (VI) (2014): 69–73. https://www.iosrjournals.org/iosr-jhss/papers/Vol19-issue5/Version-6/K019566973.pdf.

Pendergrast, Mark. *Uncommon Grounds: The History of Coffee and How it Transformed our World*. New ed. New York: Basic Books, 2019.

Subrahmanyam, Sanjay. "A Note on the Rise of Surat in the Sixteenth Century". *Journal of the Economic and Social History of the Orient* 43, no. 1 (2000): 23–33. http://www.jstor.org/stable/3632771.

Sweetser, Heather Marie. "A Chapter in the History of Coffee: A Critical Edition and Translation of Murtada az-Zabidi's Epistle on Coffee". MA diss., Ohio State University, 2012. http://rave.ohiolink.edu/etdc/view?acc_num=osu1339184075.

Um, Nancy. *The Merchant Houses of Mocha: Trade & Architecture in an Indian Ocean Port*. USA: University of Washington Press, 2009.

Chennai, Puducherry & Tharangambadi (Madras, Pondicherry & Tranquebar)

Belle, Carl Vadivella. *Thaipusam in Malaysia: A Hindu Festival in the Tamil Diaspora*. Singapore: ISEAS-Yusof Ishak Institute, 2017.

Brimnes, Niels. *Indien: Tranquebar, Serampore og Nicobarerne*. Denmark: Gads Forlag, 2017.

Delamare, Georges. *Désordres à Pondichéry* [Disorder in Pondicherry]. 1938. Pondicherry: Kailash Éditions, 1997.

Helles, Knud. *Danish Trade Companies in South and East Asia*. Tranquebar: Tranquebar Maritime Museum and The Tranquebar Association, 2011.

Indian National Trust for Art and Cultural Heritage (INTACH) Pondicherry Chapter. *Architectural Heritage of Pondicherry: Tamil and French Precincts*. Pondicherry: INTACH, 2010.

Kalpana, K., and Frank Schiller. *Madras: The Architectural Heritage. An INTACH Guide*. Chennai: INTACH, 2003.

Keay, John. *The Honourable Company: A History of the English East India Company*. New York: Macmillan Publishing Company, 1991.

Lazar, P. Maria. *Tales of Tranquebar*. Karaikal: Vizhichudar Pathipagam, 2010.

Malleson, George Bruce. *Histoire des Français dans l'Inde, depuis la fondation de Pondichéry jusqu'à la prise de cette ville (1674–1761)*. Translated by Mme S. Le Page. Paris: Librairie de la Société Bibliographique, 1874.

Metcalf, Thomas R. *An Imperial Vision: Indian Architecture and Britain's Raj*. London: Faber and Faber, 1989.

Moxham, Roy. *The Theft of India: The European Conquests of India 1498–1765*. India: HarperCollins Publishers India, 2016.

Muthiah, S. *Madras Rediscovered: A Historical Guide to Looking Around, Supplemented with Tales of Once Upon a City*. Revised and expanded ed. Mumbai: East West, 2014.

Narasiah, K. R. A. *Madras: Tracing the Growth of the City since 1639*. Chennai: Oxygen Books, 2008.

Sriram, Aditi. *Beyond the Boulevards: A Short Biography of Pondicherry*. New Delhi: Aleph Book Company, 2019.

Subramaniam, Lakshmi, ed. *Ports, Towns, Cities: A Historical Tour of the Indian Littoral*. Mumbai: Marg Publications, 2008.

OF TREATIES AND EMPIRE

Aceh & Makassar

Acciaioli, Greg. "From Economic Actor to Moral Agent: Knowledge, Fate and Hierarchy among the Bugis of Sulawesi". *Indonesia*, no. 78 (2004): 147–179. http://www.jstor.org/stable/3351291.

Ammarell, Gene. "Bugis Migration and Modes of Adaptation to Local Situations". *Ethnology* 41, no. 1 (2002): 51–67. https://doi.org/10.2307/4153020.

Ammarell, Gene. "Knowing When to Set Sail: Practical Knowledge and Simple Heuristics in Bugis Navigational Strategies". *Bijdragen tot de Taal-, Land- En Volkenkunde* 158, no. 2 (2002): 191–223. http://www.jstor.org/stable/24026052.

Andaya, Leonard Y. "The Bugis-Makassar Diasporas". *Journal of the Malaysian Branch of the Royal Asiatic Society* 68, no. 1 (268) (1995): 119–138. http://www.jstor.org/stable/41493268.

Andaya, Leonard Y. *The Heritage of Arung Palakka: A History of South Sulawesi (Celebes) in the Seventeenth Century*. The Hague: Martinus Nijhof, 1981. http://www.jstor.org/stable/10.1163/j.ctvbnm4wp.

Cummings, William, ed. and trans. *The Makassar Annals*. Leiden: KITLV Press, 2010.

Hägerdal, Hans. "The Bugis-Makassar Seafarers: Pirates or Entrepreneurs?" In *Piracy in World History*, edited by Stefan Amirell, Hans Hägerdal, and Bruce Buchan, 109–128. Amsterdam: Amsterdam University Press, 2021. https://doi.org/10.2307/j.ctv21r3j8m.8.

Khan, Sher Banu A. L. *Sovereign Women in a Muslim Kingdom: The Sultanahs of Aceh, 1641–1699*. Singapore: NUS Press, 2017.

Khan, Sher Banu A. L. "The Sultanahs of Aceh, 1641–99". In *Aceh: History, Politics and Culture*, edited by Arndt Graf, Susanne Schröter, and Edwin Wieringa, 3–25. Singapore: ISEAS Publishing, 2010.

Koolhof, Sirtjo. "The 'La Galigo': A Bugis Encyclopedia and Its Growth". *Bijdragen tot de Taal-, Land- En Volkenkunde* 155, no. 3 (1999): 362–387. http://www.jstor.org/stable/27865543.

Noorduyn, J. "The Bugis Genealogy of the Raja Muda Family of Riau-Johor". *Journal of the Malaysian Branch of the Royal Asiatic Society* 61, no. 2 (255) (1988): 63–92. http://www.jstor.org/stable/41493103.

Pelras, Christian. *The Bugis*. Oxford and Cambridge, Massachusetts: Wiley-Blackwell Publications, 1996.

Reid, Anthony. "Aceh and the Turkish Connection". In *Aceh: History, Politics and Culture*, edited by Arndt Graf, Susanne Schröter and Edwin Wieringa, 26–38. Singapore: ISEAS Publishing, 2010.

Reid, Anthony. "Turkey as Aceh's Alternative Imperium". *Archipel* 87 (2014): 81–102. https://doi.org/10.3406/arch.2014.4458.

Rivers, P. J. "Negeri Below and Above the Wind: Malacca and Cathay". *Journal of the Malaysian Branch of the Royal Asiatic Society* 78, no. 2 (289) (2005): 1–32. http://www.jstor.org/stable/41493547.

Guangzhou (Canton)

Chan, Libby Lai-Pik, ed., with Nina Lai-Na Wan. *The Dragon and the Eagle: American Traders in China. A Century of Trade from 1784 to 1900*. Hong Kong: Hong Kong Maritime Museum, 2018.

Conner, Patrick. *The Hongs of Canton: Western Merchants in South China 1700–1900, as Seen in Chinese Export Paintings*. London: English Art Books, 2009.

Garrett, Valery M. *Heaven is High and the Emperor Far Away: Merchants and Mandarins in Old Canton*. Oxford: Oxford University Press, 2009.

Ghosh, Amitav. *River of Smoke*. London: John Murray, 2011.

Hunter, William C. *The 'Fan Kwae' at Canton Before Treaty Days, 1825–1844*. London: Kegan Paul, Trench, & Co., 1882. Project Gutenberg EBook, 2013. https://www.gutenberg.org/files/42685/42685-h/42685-h.htm.

Leland, Charles G. *Pidgin-English Sing-Song, or Songs and Stories in the China-English Dialect. With a Vocabulary*. London: Trübner & Co, 1876. https://ia800307.us.archive.org/25/items/pidginenglishsin00lelaiala/pidginenglishsin00lelaiala.pdf.

Martin, Laura C. *A History of Tea: The Life and Times of the World's Favorite Beverage*. Singapore: Tuttle Publishing, 2018.

Pepys, Samuel. *The Diary of Samuel Pepys, Complete*. London: George Bell & Sons, 1893. Project Gutenberg E-book, 2003. https://www.gutenberg.org/files/4200/4200-h/4200-h.htm.

Perdue, Peter C. "Rise & Fall of the Canton Trade System I, III and IV". *MIT Visualizing Cultures*, 2009. https://visualizingcultures.mit.edu/rise_fall_canton_01/index.html.

Perdue, Peter C. "The First Opium War: The Anglo-Chinese War of 1839–1842". *MIT Visualizing Cultures*, 2011. https://visualizingcultures.mit.edu/opium_wars_01/index.html.

Van Dyke, Paul A. *The Canton Trade: Life and Enterprise on the China Coast, 1700–1845*. Hong Kong: Hong Kong University Press, 2007.

Wang, Rigen, and Su Huiping 王日根, 苏惠苹. "Kangxidi haijiang zhengce fanfu bianyi xilun" 康熙帝海疆政策反复变易析论 [An analysis of the Kangxi Emperor's changing maritime and terrestrial border policies]. *Jianghai Xuekan* 江海学刊, no. 2 (2010): 161–168. https://core.ac.uk/download/pdf/41358683.pdf.

Zhao, Tiefeng 赵轶峰. "Qing qianqi de youxian kaifang – yi maoyi guanxi wei zhongxin" 清前期的有限开放 —以贸易关系为中心 [China's limited opening to the outside world during the early Qing period – trade as the focus]. *Gugong Bowuyuan Yuankan* 故宫博物院院刊 no. 6 (182) (2015): 99–115. https://www.dpm.org.cn/Uploads/File/2018/06/04/u5b1523084c845.pdf.

Jeddah

Abbas, H. M. "A Tale of Two Rushans: Architecture Through Oral History". *International Journal of Heritage Architecture* 1, no. 3 (2017): 365–378. https://www.academia.edu/28117940/A_TALE_OF_TWO_RUSHANS_ARCHITECTURE_THROUGH_ORAL_HISTORY.

Al-Lyaly, Sameer Mahmoud Z. "The Traditional House of Jeddah: A Study of the Interaction Between Climate, Form and Living Patterns". PhD diss., University of Edinburgh, 1990. https://www.era.lib.ed.ac.uk/bitstream/1842/7276/1/536548.pdf.

Autiero, Serena. "The Red Sea Style in Saudi Arabia: A Reassessment of the Evidence and New Insights". *Research & Heritage* 5 (2015): 81–100. https://www.academia.edu/22187788/The_Red_Sea_Style_in_Saudi_Arabia_A_Reassessment_of_the_Evidence_and_New_Insights_2015.

Burckhardt, John Lewis. *Travels In Arabia: An Account of those Territories in Hedjaz which the Mohammedans Regard as Sacred*. London: Henry Colburn, 1829. Project Gutenberg Ebook, 2005. http://public-library.uk/pdfs/2/463.pdf.

Freitag, Ulrike. *A History of Jeddah: The Gate to Mecca in the Nineteenth and Twentieth Centuries*. United Kingdom: Cambridge University Press, 2020.

Matthews, Derek H. "The Red Sea Style". *Kush: Journal of the Sudan Antiquities Service* 1, no. 1 (1953): 60–87.

Niebuhr, Carsten. *Travels through Arabia and Other Countries in the East*. 2 vols. Translated by Robert Heron. Edinburgh: R. Morrison and Son, 1792. https://ia902604.us.archive.org/34/items/travelsthrougha00conggoog/travelsthrougha00conggoog.pdf.

Nyazi, Ghayda, and Özlem Sağıroğlu. "The Traditional Coral Stone Buildings of the Red Sea Coast: Case Study of Historic Jeddah". *Gazi University Journal of Science* 6, no. 4 (2018): 159–165. https://dergipark.org.tr/tr/download/article-file/624547.

Ochsenwald, William. "Ottoman Arabia and the Holy Hijaz, 1516–1918". *Journal of Global Initiatives* 10, no. 1 (2016): 22–34. https://digitalcommons.kennesaw.edu/cgi/viewcontent.cgi?article=1184&context=jgi.

Omer, Spahic. "Historic Jeddah as a Unique Islamic City". *IIUM Journal of Religion and Civilisational Studies* 4, no. 1 (2021): 60–81. https://journals.iium.edu.my/irkh/index.php/ijrcs/article/view/186/77.

Omer, Spahic. "Meanings of Balad, Madinah & Qaryah in the Quran". *About Islam*, 24 June 2020. https://aboutislam.net/reading-islam/research-studies/meaning-of-balad-madinah-qaryah-in-the-quran/#:~:text=Balad%20or%20baldah%20means%20any,their%20physical%20aspects%20and%20features.

Sardar, Ziauddin. *Mecca: The Sacred City*. London: Bloomsbury, 2014.

Saudi Commission for Tourism and Antiquities. *Historic Jeddah, the Gate to Makkah: Nomination Document for the Inscription on the World Heritage List*. Executive Summary. Saudi Arabia: Saudi Commission for Tourism and Antiquities, 2013. https://whc.unesco.org/en/list/1361/documents/.

Um, Nancy. "Reflections on the Red Sea Style: Beyond the Surface of Coastal Architecture". *Northeast African Studies* 12, no. 1 (2012): 243–271. https://www.jstor.org/stable/41960564.

Wynbrandt, James. *A Brief History of Saudi Arabia*. USA: Facts on File, 2004.

Kolkata (Calcutta)

Bach, Brian Paul. *Calcutta's Edifice: The Buildings of a Great City*. New Delhi: Rupa & Co., 2006.

Banerjea, Dhrubajyoti. *European Calcutta: Images and Recollections of a Bygone Era*. New Delhi: UBS Publishers Distributors Pvt. Ltd, 2005.

Choudhury, Kushanava. *The Epic City: The World on the Streets of Calcutta*. London: Bloomsbury Publishing, 2017.

Chowdhury, Ahsan. "The Sahib in Late Eighteenth-Century Mughal India". *Lumen* 32 (2013): 109–125. https://doi.org/10.7202/1015487ar.

Deb Lal, Nilina. *Calcutta: Built Heritage Today. An INTACH Guide*. Kolkata: INTACH Calcutta Regional Chapter, 2006.

Dutta, Krishna. *Calcutta: A Cultural and Literary History*. 2003. 2nd revised ed. Oxford: Signal Books, 2009.

Hazra, Indrajit. *Grand Delusions: A Short Biography of Kolkata*. New Delhi: Aleph Book Company, 2013.

Ivermee, Robert. *Hooghly: The Global History of a River*. London: Hurst & Company, 2020.

Kipling, Rudyard. "A Tale of Two Cities". In *Verse: 1885–1918. Inclusive Edition*. New York: Doubleday, 1922.

Kipling, Rudyard. "The White Man's Burden". 1899. https://www.kiplingsociety.co.uk/poem/poems_burden.htm.

Lawson, Philip, and Jim Phillips. "'Our Execrable Banditti': Perceptions of Nabobs in Mid-Eighteenth Century Britain". *Albion* 16, no. 3 (1984): 225–241. https://doi.org/10.2307/4048755.

Metcalf, Thomas R. *Ideologies of the Raj*. Cambridge: Cambridge University Press, 1995.

Moorhouse, Geoffrey. *Calcutta: The City Revealed*. 1971. New Delhi: Penguin Books India, 1994.

Tagore, Rabindranath. *Gitanjali: Song Offerings*. 1912. Translated by the author. Project Gutenberg Ebook, 2004. https://www.gutenberg.org/cache/epub/7164/pg7164-images.html.

Taylor, Joanne. *The Forgotten Palaces of Calcutta*. New Delhi: Niyogi Books, 2006.

Hong Kong

Bird, Isabella L. *The Golden Chersonese and the Way Thither*. New York: G. P. Putnam's Sons, 1883. Project Gutenberg Ebook, 2002. https://www.gutenberg.org/cache/epub/3412/pg3412.html.

Cassan, Benjamin. "William Jardine: Architect of the First Opium War". *Historia* 14, (2005): 106–117. https://www.eiu.edu/historia/Cassan.pdf.

Chan, Ming K. "Hong Kong: Colonial Legacy, Transformation, and

Challenge". *The Annals of the American Academy of Political and Social Science*, vol. 547 (1996): 11–23. http://www.jstor.org/stable/1048360.

Cooke, Ariel. "Hong Kong and Shanghai Bank". In *Architecture + City Form: A Compilation of Essays by Students of PLX599 The Human World at Ryerson University*, edited by Rémi Carreiro et al, 299–304. Toronto: Ryerson University, 2013. https://issuu.com/remicarreiro/docs/architecture___city_form_plx599_201.

Crisswell, Colin N. *The Taipans: Hong Kong's Merchant Princes*. Oxford University Press, 1981.

Han, Suyin. *A Many-Splendoured Thing*. London: The Reprint Society, 1954. https://archive.org/details/manysplendouredt0000unse/page/n7/mode/2up.

Jack, Malcolm. *My Hong Kong*. London: Austin Macauley, 2022.

Lee, Leo Ou-fan. *City Between Worlds: My Hong Kong*. Cambridge, MA: The Belknap Press of Harvard University Press, 2008.

Lin, Zexu. "Letter to the Queen of England, from the High Imperial Commissioner Lin, and his Colleagues". In *The Chinese Repository: Vol. VIII. From May, 1839, to April, 1840*, 9–12. Canton: Canton, 1840. https://babel.hathitrust.org/cgi/pt?id=hvd.32044005277884&view=1up&seq=509.

Lovell, Julia. *The Opium War: Drugs, Dreams and the Making of China*. London: Picador, 2011.

Sandhaus, Derek. *Tales of Old Hong Kong*. Hong Kong: Earnshaw Books, 2010.

Waters, Dan. "Hong Kong Hongs with Long Histories and British Connections". *Journal of the Hong Kong Branch of the Royal Asiatic Society* 30 (1990): 219–256. http://www.jstor.org/stable/23889755.

Welsh, Frank. *A History of Hong Kong*. London: HarperCollins Publishers, 1993.

Xiamen (Amoy)

Air fufu 夫妇. *Mishi. Gulangyu*. 迷失。鼓浪屿。 [Lost in Gulangyu]. Beijing: Cheers Publishing, 2011.

Brown, Bill. *Old Xiamen (Formerly Amoy): Cradle of Modern Chinese Business & Chinese Business Education*. Bilingual ed. Xiamen: Xiamen University Press, 2012.

Dennys, N. B., ed. *The Treaty Ports of China and Japan: A Complete Guide to the Open Ports of those Countries, Together with Peking, Yedo, Hongkong and Macao*. London: Trübner and Co. and Hongkong: A. Shortrede and Co., 1867; USA: Cambridge University Press, 2012.

Gacek, Łukasz. "Confucian Way of Tan Kah Kee: Pursue Excellence, Strive for Perfection". *Politeja* 44 (2016): 171–182. http://www.jstor.org/stable/24920300.

Godley, Michael R. "The Treaty Port Connection: An Essay". *Journal of Southeast Asian Studies* 12, no. 1 (1981): 248–259. http://www.jstor.org/stable/20070424.

Han, Shufang 韩淑芳, ed. *Lao Xiamen / Laochengji – Minguo Qudu* 老厦门/老城记 – 民国趣谈 [Old Xiamen / Records of old cities – trivia from the Republican Era]. Beijing: Zhongguo Wenshi Chubanshe, 2019.

Jia, Ruixue. "The Legacies of Forced Freedom: China's Treaty Ports". *The Review of Economics and Statistics* 96, no. 4 (2014): 596–608. http://www.jstor.org/stable/43554942.

Ng, Chin-keong. *Boundaries and Beyond: China's Maritime Southeast in Late Imperial Times*. Singapore: NUS Press, 2017. http://www.jstor.org/stable/j.ctv3wdbw4.

Nield, Robert. "Treaty Ports and Other Foreign Stations in China". *Journal of the Royal Asiatic Society Hong Kong Branch* 50 (2010): 123–39. http://www.jstor.org/stable/23891203.

Ong, Soon Keong. *Coming Home to a Foreign Country: Xiamen and Returned Overseas Chinese, 1843–1938*. Ithaca and London: Cornell East Asia Series, an imprint of Cornell University Press, 2021.

Pan, Maoyuan 潘懋元. "Jiaoyu shiyejia Chen Jiageng jiaoyu sixiang xintan" 教育事业家陈嘉庚教育思想新探 [The exploration of education thoughts from educationist Chen Jiageng]. *Private Education Research* 民办教育研究 6, no. 5 (2007): 1–2. https://core.ac.uk/download/pdf/41344228.pdf.

Yokohama & Kobe

Bird, Isabella L. *Unbeaten Tracks in Japan: An Account of Travels in the Interior including Visits to the Aborigines of Yezo and the Shrine of Nikkô*. 2 vols. London: John Murray, 1880.

Cortazzi, Hugh. *Victorians in Japan: In and Around the Treaty Ports*. London: The Athlone Press, 1987.

Dower, John W. "Black Ships & Samurai: Commodore Perry and the Opening of Japan (1853–1854)". *MIT Visualizing Cultures*, 2008. https://visualizingcultures.mit.edu/black_ships_and_samurai/pdf/bss_essay.pdf.

Dower, John W. "Yokohama Boomtown: Foreigners in Treaty-Port Japan (1859–1872)". *MIT Visualizing Cultures*, 2008. https://visualizingcultures.mit.edu/yokohama/pdf/yb_essay.pdf.

Ennals, Peter. *Opening a Window to the West: The Foreign Concession at Kōbe, Japan, 1868–1899*. Toronto: University of Toronto Press, 2014.

Hamashita, Takeshi. "Tribute and Treaties: East Asian Treaty Ports Networks in the Era of Negotiation, 1834–1894". *European Journal of East Asian Studies* 1, no. 1 (2001): 59–87. https://www.jstor.org/stable/23615532.

Munson, Todd S. "Curiosities of the Five Nations: Nansoan Shohaku's Yokohama Tales". *Japanese Studies Review* 12 (2008): 23–36. https://asian.fiu.edu/jsr/munson-curiosities-of-the-five-nations-p23.pdf.

Sabin, Burritt. *A Historical Guide to Yokohama: Sketches of the Twice-Risen Phoenix*. Yokohama: Yurindo, 2002.

Shirahara, Yukiko, ed. *Japan Envisions the West: 16th–19th Century Japanese Art from Kobe City Museum*. Seattle: Seattle Art Museum, 2007.

Takano, Yayori. "Foreign Influence and the Transformation of Early Modern Japan". *Emory Endeavors Journal* 3 (2011): 82–93. https://www.semanticscholar.org/paper/Foreign-Influence-and-the-Transformation-of-Early-Takano/0e91ab3c86b26b89ff6d53f2ec3d82ae0c61ebfd.

Yonemura, Ann. *Yokohama: Prints from Nineteenth-Century Japan*. USA: Smithsonian Institution, 1990.

OF STEAMSHIPS AND MODERNITY

Colombo

Biedermann, Zoltán, and Alan Strathern, eds. *Sri Lanka at the Crossroads of History*. London: UCL Press, 2017.

Cave, Henry W. *The Book of Ceylon: Being A Guide to its Railway System and an Account of its Varied Attractions for the Visitor and Tourist*. London: Cassell and Company, Limited, 1908.

Darwin, John. *Unlocking the World: Port Cities and Globalization in the Age of Steam 1830–1930*. UK: Allen Lane, 2020.

Edirisinghe, Janakie. "Revitalizing the Built Heritage for Urban Development: A Case Study on City of Colombo, Sri Lanka". *European Academic Research* 2, no. 5 (2014): 6365–6397. https://www.researchgate.net/publication/283571520_Revitalizing_the_

Built_Heritage_for_Urban_Development_A_Case_Study_on_City_of_Colombo_Sri_Lanka.

Fonseka, Manel. "Old Colombo, Sri Lanka". *Monumentum* 25, no. 2 (1982): 109–128. https://www.icomos.org/monumentum/vol25-2/vol25-2_2.pdf.

Institut du monde arabe. *L'Épopée du Canal de Suez* [The era of the Suez Canal]. Paris: Gallimard, Institut du monde arabe and Musée d'histoire de Marseille, 2018.

Karabell, Zachary. *Parting the Desert: The Creation of the Suez Canal*. New York: Vintage Books, 2003.

Mendis, Chryshane. "The Fortress of Colombo: from the Portuguese and Dutch to the British". *Fort* 45 (2017): 56–69. https://www.researchgate.net/publication/333264382_The_Fortress_of_Colombo_from_the_Portuguese_and_Dutch_to_the_British.

Peleggi, Maurizio. "Consuming Colonial Nostalgia: The Monumentalism of Historic Hotels in Urban South-East Asia". *Asia Pacific Viewpoint* 46, No. 3 (2005): 255–265. https://doi.org/10.1111/j.1467-8373.2005.00289.x.

Peleggi, Maurizio. "The Social and Material Life of Colonial Hotels: Comfort Zones as Contact Zones in British Colombo and Singapore, ca. 1870–1930". *Journal of Social History* 46, no. 1 (2012): 124–153. https://www.researchgate.net/publication/262084462_The_Social_and_Material_Life_of_Colonial_Hotels_Comfort_Zones_as_Contact_Zones_in_British_Colombo_and_Singapore_ca_1870-1930.

Penfield, Frederic Courtland. *East of Suez: Ceylon, India, China and Japan*. New York: The Century Co., 1907.

Sally, Razeen. *Return to Sri Lanka: Travels in a Paradoxical Island*. New Delhi: Juggernaut Books, 2019.

Muscat & Zanzibar

Agius, Dionisius A. *Seafaring in the Arabian Gulf and Oman: The People of the Dhow*. New York and London: Routledge, 2005.

Alavi, Seema. *Sovereigns of the Sea: Omani Ambition in the Age of Empire*. Gurugram: Penguin Random House India.

Bennett, Norman R. *A History of the Arab State of Zanzibar*. London: Methuen, 1978.

Bhacker, M. Reda. "Family Strife and Foreign Intervention: Causes in the Separation of Zanzibar from Oman: A Reappraisal". *Bulletin of the School of Oriental and African Studies, University of London* 54, no. 2 (1991): 269–280. http://www.jstor.org/stable/619135.

Burton, Richard F. *Zanzibar; Island, City and Coast*. 2 vols. London: Tinsley Brothers, 1872.

Folkers, A. "Early Modern African Architecture. The House of Wonders Revisited". *Docomomo Journal* 48 (2013): 20–29. https://doi.org/10.52200/48.A.FKXY01XV.

Ghazal, Amal N. "The Other 'Andalus': The Omani Elite in Zanzibar and the Making of an Identity, 1880s–1930s". *MIT Electronic Journal of Middle East Studies* 5 (2005): 43–58. https://www.academia.edu/3055902/_The_Other_Andalus_The_Omani_Elite_in_Zanzibar_and_the_Making_of_an_Identity_1880s-1930s._MIT-Electronic_Journal_of_Middle_East_Studies_5_Fall_2005_43-58.

Gordon, Murray. *Slavery in the Arab World*. USA: New Amsterdam Books, 1989.

Ingrams, W. H. *Zanzibar: Its History and Its People*. London: Frank Cass & Co., 1967.

Meier, Prita. *Swahili Port Cities: The Architecture of Elsewhere*. USA: Indiana University Press, 2016.

Ntui, Daniel Okorn, James A. Aboh, and Patrick O. Odey. "The Omani Empire and the Development of East Africa". *International Journal of Arts and Humanities* 4, no. 6 (2020): 163–172. https://doi.org/10.46609/IJAH.2020.v04i06.002.

Prestholdt, Jeremy. "Mirroring Modernity: On Consumerism in Cosmopolitan Zanzibar". *Transforming Cultures eJournal* 4, no. 2 (2009). https://doi.org/10.5130/tfc.v4i2.1383.

Ruete, Emily née Princess of Oman and Zanzibar. *Memoirs of an Arabian Princess: An Autobiography*. New York: D. Appleton and Company, 1888.

Sheriff, Abdul. *Slaves, Spices & Ivory in Zanzibar*. Oxford: James Currey, 1987.

Steyn, Gerald, and Dieter Holm. "An Analysis of an Omani house in Stone Town, Zanzibar". *South African Journal of Art History* 16 (2001): 110–131. https://www.researchgate.net/publication/265889781_An_analysis_of_an_Omani_house_in_Stone_Town_Zanzibar.

Tianjin, Qingdao & Dalian (Tientsin, Tsingtao & Dalniy / Dairen)

Bickers, Robert. *The Scramble for China: Foreign Devils in the Qing Empire, 1832–1914*. London: Penguin Books, 2012.

Bundesarchiv [German Federal Archives]. *Tsingtao-Lied*, 16 October 1912. BArch N224/65. Scanned image of a Tsingtao-lied typed on paper, with handwritten notes. From the documents / estate of "Troupel, Oskar von (Admiral)". https://artsandculture.google.com/asset/tsingtao-lied/3gFpW0hKyzTkhw.

Coco, Orazio. "Italian Colonialism in China: The Concession of Tianjin (1901–1947)". *Giornale di storia* 23 (2017): 1–12. https://www.giornaledistoria.net/saggi/articoli/the-concession-of-tianjin-1901-1947/?ss=1_164_.

Cookson Smith, Peter. *The Urban Design of Concession: Tradition and Transformation in the Chinese Treaty Ports*. Hong Kong: MCCM Creations, 2011.

Groeneveld, Sabina. "'A Hotbed of Sins' or 'Just Like Home'? Drinking Cultures in Colonial Qingdao (1897–1914)". In *Alcohol Flows Across Cultures: Drinking Cultures in Transnational and Comparative Perspective*, edited by Waltraud Ernst. London: Routledge, 2020. https://www.taylorfrancis.com/chapters/edit/10.4324/9780203732038-7/hotbed-sins-like-home-sabina-groeneveld.

Groeneveld, Sabina. "Far Away at Home in Qingdao (1897–1914)". *German Studies Review* 39, no. 1 (2016): 65–79. http://www.jstor.org/stable/24809058.

Hess, Christian A. "From Colonial Jewel to Socialist Metropolis: Dalian 1895–1955". PhD diss., University of California, San Diego, 2006. https://escholarship.org/content/qt2zb7n2x9/qt2zb7n2x9_noSplash_2d4c3a6f03aa0e79db014b637229378a.pdf.

Johnston, Tess, and Deke Erh. *Far From Home: Western Architecture in China's Northern Treaty Ports*. Hong Kong: Old China Hand Press, 1996.

Marinelli, Maurizio. "Internal and External Spaces: The Emotional Capital of Tianjin's Italian Concession". *Emotion, Space and Society* 3, no.1 (2010): 62–70. https://doi.org/10.1016/j.emospa.2010.01.009.

Marinelli, Maurizio. "The Genesis of the Italian Concession in Tianjin: A Combination of Wishful Thinking and Realpolitik". *Journal of Modern Italian Studies* 15, no. 4 (2010): 536–556. https://doi.org/10.1080/1354571X.2010.501975.

Marinelli, Maurizio. "The Triumph of the Uncanny: Italians and Italian Architecture in Tianjin". *Cultural Studies Review* 19, no. 2 (2013): 70–98. https://doi.org/10.5130/csr.v19i2.2846.

Nuzzo, Luigi. "The Birth of an Imperial Location: Comparative Perspectives on Western Colonialism in China". *Leiden Journal of International Law* 31, no. 3 (2018): 569–596. https://doi.org/10.1017/S0922156518000274.

Perrins, Robert John. "'Great Connections': The Creation of a City, Dalian. 1905-1931. China and Japan on the Liaodong Peninsula". PhD diss., York University, North York, Ontario, Canada, 1997. https://www.collectionscanada.gc.ca/obj/s4/f2/dsk2/tape17/PQDD_

0020/NQ27316.pdf.

Van Dijk, Kees. *Pacific Strife*. Amsterdam: Amsterdam University Press, 2015. http://www.jstor.org/stable/j.ctt15nmjw8.

Zatsepine, Victor. *Beyond the Amur: Frontier Encounters between China and Russia, 1850–1930*. Vancouver: UBC Press, 2017.

Bangkok & Ho Chi Minh City (Saigon)

Brennan, Julia M., and Yaowalak Bunnag. "Thai Official Rank Robes (*Sua Khrui*): History, Fabrication and the Conservation of the Admiral de Richelieu's 19th Century Robe". *Arts of Asia* 44, no. 3 (2014): 99–113.

Goscha, Christopher E. *Going Indochinese: Contesting Concepts of Space and Place in French Indochina*. Revised ed. Copenhagen: NIAS (Nordic Institute of Asian Studies) Press, 2012.

Goscha, Christopher. *The Penguin History of Modern Vietnam*. UK: Penguin, 2017.

Joyaux, François. *Nouvelle histoire de l'Indochine française* [A new history of French Indochina]. Paris: Perrin, 2022.

Lien, Vu-Hong. *Royal Hue: Heritage of the Nguyen Dynasty of Vietnam*. Photography by Paisarn Piemmettawat. Bangkok: River Books, 2015.

McGrath, Brian. "Bangkok: The Architecture of Three Ecologies". *Perspecta, The Yale Architectural Journal* 39 (2007): 17–29. https://www.academia.edu/852222/Bangkok_The_Architecture_of_Three_Ecologies.

Meyers, Dean. "Siam Under Siege (1893–1902): Modern Thailand's Decisive Decade, from the 'Paknam Incident' to the First Flowering of the 'Chakri Reformation'". *Journal of the Siam Society* 82, no. 2 (1994): 120–133. https://thesiamsociety.org/wp-content/uploads/1994/03/JSS_082_0k_Meyers_SiamUnderSiege1893to1902.pdf.

Nguyen, Dac Xuan. "A King's Seal and a Turning Point in History". *Vietnam Heritage Magazine* 11, no. 2 (November 2012). http://vietnamheritage.com.vn/a-king-s-seal-and-a-turning-point-in-history/.

Norindr, Panivong. *Phantasmatic Indochina: French Colonial Ideology in Architecture, Film, and Literature*. Durham and London: Duke University Press, 1996.

O'Neil, Maryvelma. *Bangkok: A Cultural and Literary History*. Oxford: Signal Books, 2008.

Rajanubhab, H. R. H. Prince Damrong. "'The Introduction of Western Culture in Siam'. A paper read by H. R. H. Prince Damrong Rajanubhab at the Rotarian dinner of the United Club, on August 7th, 1925." https://thesiamsociety.org/wp-content/uploads/2020/02/JSS_020_2b_PrinceDamrong_IntroductionOfWesternCultureInSiam.pdf.

Penang & Pekalongan

Angelino, P. De Kat. *Rapport betreffende eene gehouden enquête naar de arbeidstoestanden in de batikkerijen op Java en Madoera* [Report on a survey of working conditions in the batik factories on Java and Madura]. 3 vols. Weltevreden (Jakarta): Landsdrukkerij, 1930–31.

Asian Civilisations Museum. *Peranakan Museum Guide*. Singapore: Asian Civilisations Museum, 2008.

Barber, Andrew. *Colonial Penang 1786–1957*. Kuala Lumpur: Karamoja Press, 2017.

Davison, Julian. *Singapore Shophouse*. Singapore: Talisman, 2010.

Ishwara, Helen, L. R. Supriyapto Yahya, and Xenia Moeis. *Batik Pesisir: An Indonesian Heritage. Collection of Hartono Sumarsono*. 2nd ed. Jakarta: KPG (Kepustakaan Populer Gramedia), 2016.

Lee, Peter. *Sarong Kebaya: Peranakan Fashion in an Interconnected*

World, 1500–1950. Singapore: Asian Civilisations Museum, 2014.

Lewis, Su Lin. "Print Culture and the New Maritime Frontier in Rangoon and Penang". *Moussons* 17 (2011): 127–144. https://doi.org/10.4000/moussons.583.

Neo, David HJ, Ngo Sheau-Shi, and Jenny Gek Koon Heng. "Popular Imaginary and Cultural Constructions of the Nonya in Peranakan Chinese Culture of the Straits Settlements". *Ethnicities* 20, no. 1 (2019): 1–25. https://doi.org/10.1177/1468796819867399.

Panton Dondang Sayang Baba Baba Pranakan (Vol. 5). Singapore: Koh & Company, 1916.

Raffles, Thomas Stamford. *A History of Java*. 2 vols. London: John Murray, 1817.

Salleh, Muhammad Haji. "Sailing the Archipelago in a Boat of Rhymes – Pantun in the Malay World". *Wacana, Journal of the Humanities of Indonesia* 13, no. 1 (2011): 78–104. https://doi.org/10.17510/wjhi.v13i1.10.

Veldhuisen, Harmen C. *Batik Belanda 1840–1940: Dutch Influence in Batik from Java – History and Stories*. 1993. Jakarta: Gaya Favorit Press, 2007.

Shanghai

Benton, Charlotte, Tim Benton, and Ghislaine Wood, eds. *Art Deco 1910–1939*. 2003. London: V&A Publishing, 2015.

Denison, Edward, and Guang Yu Ren. *Building Shanghai: The Story of China's Gateway*. UK: John Wiley & Sons, 2006.

Han, Qingxuan. "Qipao and Female Fashion in Republican China and Shanghai (1912–1937): The Discovery and Expression of Individuality". *Senior Projects Fall 2019*, 37. https://digitalcommons.bard.edu/senproj_f2019/37.

Hibbard, Peter. *Peace at the Cathay*. Hong Kong: Earnshaw Books, 2013.

Huters, Theodore. *Bringing the World Home: Appropriating the West in Late Qing and Early Republican China*. Hawai'i: University of Hawai'i Press, 2005.

Johnston, Tess, and Deke Erh. *The Last Colonies: Western Architecture in China's Southern Treaty Ports*. Hong Kong: Old China Hand Press, 1997.

Kuo, Jason C., ed. *Visual Culture in Shanghai 1850s–1930s*. Washington D.C.: New Academia Publishing, 2007.

Ma, Debin. "The Rise of a Financial Revolution in Republican China in 1900–1937: an Institutional Narrative". 2016. Economic History Working Papers No. 235. London School of Economics and Political Science. https://www.econhistdbm.com/uploads/8/1/9/7/81977286/the_rise_of_a_financial_revolution_in_republican_china_in_1900-1937.pdf.

Maugham, W. Somerset. *On a Chinese Screen*. London: Heinemann, 1922.

Steen, Andrew. "Zhou Xuan: 'When Will the Gentleman Come Back Again?'" *Chime* 14, no. 15 (1999/2000): 124–153. https://pure.au.dk/portal/files/71555987/Steen_2000_Zhou_Xuan_orig_.pdf.

Warr, Anne. *Shanghai Architecture*. Sydney: The Watermark Press, 2007.

Xie, Bingjie. "Becoming a Shanghailander: A Foreign City on Chinese Soil". *The Trinity Papers* (2011–present). Hartford, CT: Trinity College Digital Repository, 2017. https://digitalrepository.trincoll.edu/trinitypapers/49.

Tokyo

Clements, Jonathan. *Japan at War in the Pacific: The Rise and Fall of the Japanese Empire in Asia 1868–1945*. Tokyo: Tuttle, 2022.

Hirohito (Emperor). "Text of Hirohito's Radio Rescript". *The New York Times*. 15 August 1945, 3.

Kawaguchi, Akiko. "The Dawn of Modern Japanese Architecture". *Highlighting Japan* 125 (2018): 12–13. https://www.gov-online.go.jp/pdf/hlj/20181001/12-13.pdf.

Mansfield, Stephen. *Tokyo: A Biography. Disasters, Destruction and Renewal: The Story of an Indomitable City.* Tokyo: Tuttle, 2016.

Nakai, Masahiko. "Preservation and Restoration of Tokyo Station Marunouchi Building". *Japan Railway & Transport Review* No. 61 (2013): 6–15. https://www.ejrcf.or.jp/jrtr/jrtr61/pdf/6-15_web.pdf.

Ravina, Mark. *To Stand with the Nations of the World: Japan's Meiji Restoration in World History.* New York: Oxford University Press, 2017.

Seidensticker, Edward. *A History of Tokyo, 1867–1989. From EDO to SHOWA: The Emergence of the World's Greatest City.* Tokyo: Tuttle Publishing, 2019.

Visita, Christine Manzano. "Japanese Cultural Transition: Meiji Architecture and the Effect of Cross-Cultural Exchange with the West". *The Forum Journal of History* 1 (2009): 33–53. https://digitalcommons.calpoly.edu/cgi/viewcontent.cgi?article=1086&context=forum.

Semarang & Surabaya (Samarang & Soerabaja)

Achdian, Andi. "Colonial Modernity, Indonesian Nationalism, and Urban Governance: The Making of a Colonial City, Surabaya (ca. 1890–1942)". In *Cultural Dynamics in a Globalized World*, edited by Melani Budianta, Manneke Budiman, Abidin Kusno, and Mikihiro Moriyama, 749–754. London: Taylor & Francis Group, 2018.

Beekman, E. M. "Dutch Colonial Literature: Romanticism in the Tropics". *Indonesia*, no. 34 (1982): 17–39. https://doi.org/10.2307/3350946.

Bosma, Ulbe, and Remco Raben. *Being "Dutch" in the Indies: A History of Creolisation and Empire, 1500–1920.* Singapore: NUS Press, 2007.

Couperus, Louis. *The Hidden Force.* Translated by Alexander Teixeira de Mattos. Great Britain: Turnbull & Spears, 1922. Originally published as *De stille kracht* (Amsterdam: L.J. Veen, 1900).

De Mul, Sarah. "Nostalgia for Empire : 'Tempo Doeloe' in Contemporary Dutch Literature". *Memory Studies* 3, no. 4 (2010): 413–428. https://doi.org/10.1177/1750698010374928.

Kahin, George McT. "Sukarno's Proclamation of Indonesian Independence". *Indonesia*, no. 69 (2000): 1–3. https://doi.org/10.2307/3351273.

Louie, James. "How Life is Returning to the Old Town of Semarang". *DestinAsian*, 1 June 2021. https://destinasian.com/editorial/restoring-the-old-town-of-semarang.

Morfit, Michael. "Pancasila: The Indonesia State Ideology According to the New Order Government". *Far Eastern Survey* 21, no. 8 (1952): 838–851. https://doi.org/10.2307/2643886.

Nieuwenhuys, Robert (E. Breton de Nijs). *Faded Portraits.* Translated by Donald Sturtevant and Elsje Sturtevant. Singapore: Periplus Editions, 1999. Originally published as *Vergeelde portretten uit een Indisch familiealbum* (Amsterdam: Em. Querido, 1954).

Nieuwenhuys, Robert. *Mirror of the Indies.* Translated by Frans van Rosevelt. Singapore: Periplus Editions, 1999. Originally published as *Oost-Indische spiegel* (Amsterdam: Em. Querido, 1972).

Permanent Delegation of the Republic of Indonesia to UNESCO. "Semarang Old Town". *UNESCO World Heritage Tentative List*, 2015. https://whc.unesco.org/en/tentativelists/6011/.

Sukarno. *Sukarno: An Autobiography. As Told to Cindy Adams.* Indianapolis: Bobbs-Merrill, 1965.

Tajudeen, Imran bin. "Colonial-Vernacular Houses of Java, Malaya, and Singapore in the Nineteenth and Early Twentieth Centuries: Architectural Translations in the *Rumah Limas*, Compound House, and *Indische Woonhuis*". *Architecture Beyond Europe Journal* 11 (2017). https://doi.org/10.4000/abe.11008.

Ting, Kennie. *The Romance of the Grand Tour: 100 years of Travel in South East Asia.* Singapore: Talisman, 2015.

Toer, Pramoedya Ananta. *House of Glass.* 1988. Translated by Max Lane. New York: Penguin Books, 1992.

OF CONTAINERS AND CONNECTIVITY

Singapore

Clifford, Mark Lambert, Michael Shari, and B. Einhorn. "Remaking Singapore Inc." *Business Week* International Edition (Asia), 5 April 1999.

Cudahy, Brian J. *Box Boats: How Container Ships Changed the World.* New York: Fordham University Press, 2006.

Kipling, Rudyard. *From Sea to Sea and Other Sketches: Letters of Travel.* New York: Doubleday, 1889.

King, Anthony. D. "Actually Existing Postcolonialisms: Colonial Urbanism and Architecture after the Postcolonial Turn". In *Postcolonial Urbanism: Southeast Asian Cities and Global Processes*, edited by Ryan Bishop, John Philips and Wei-Wei Yeo, 167–186. New York: Routledge, 2003.

Koh, Buck Song. *Brand Singapore: Nation Branding After Lee Kuan Yew, in a Divisive World.* 2nd ed. Singapore: Marshall Cavendish Business, 2017.

Lee, Kuan Yew. *From Third World to First – The Singapore Story: 1965–2000.* London: Harper, 2000.

Lee, Pamelia. *Singapore, Tourism & Me.* Singapore: Pamelia Lee Pte Ltd, 2004.

Rajaratnam, S. "Singapore: Global City". Text of address to the Singapore Press Club on February 6, 1972. https://www.nas.gov.sg/archivesonline/data/pdfdoc/PressR19720206a.pdf.

Siddique, Sharon. *Asian Port Cities: Uniting Land and Water Worlds.* Singapore: Lee Kuan Yew Centre for Innovative Cities, 2016.

Tan, Tai Yong. *The Idea of Singapore: Smallness Unconstrained.* Singapore: World Scientific Publishing, 2020.

Ting, Kennie. *Singapore Chronicles: Heritage.* Singapore: Institute of Policy Studies and Straits Times Press, 2015.

Ting, Kennie. *Singapore 1819: A Living Legacy.* Singapore: Talisman Publishing, 2019.

Yeoh, Brenda S. A., Tan Ern Ser, Jennifer Wang, and Theresa Wong. "Tourism in Singapore: An Overview of Policies and Issues". In *Tourism Management and Policy: Perspectives from Singapore*, edited by Tan Ern Ser, Brenda S. A. Yeoh and Jennifer Wang, 3–15. Singapore: World Scientific Publishing, 2002.

Bali

Barnard, Bryn. "Packaged for Export". Institute of Current World Affairs. Letter dated 21 February 1984. http://www.icwa.org/wp-content/uploads/2015/09/BEB-24.pdf.

Covarrubias, Miguel. *Island of Bali.* 1937. Singapore: Periplus Editions, 2008.

Davies, Stephen. "The Beautiful in Bali". In *Artistic Visions and the Promise of Beauty: Cross-Cultural Perspectives*, edited by K. M. Higgins, S. Maira, and S. Sikka, 225–236. Dordrecht: Springer, 2017.

Davies, Stephen. "The Origins of Balinese Legong". *Bijdragen tot de Taal-, Land- En Volkenkunde* 164, no. 2/3 (2008): 194–211. http://www.jstor.org/stable/27868481.

Hanna, William A. *A Brief History of Bali: Piracy, Slavery, Opium and Guns: The Story of an Island Paradise.* 1976. Singapore: Tuttle Publishing. 2016.

Hussey, Antonia. "Tourism in a Balinese Village". *Geographical Review*

79, no. 3 (1989): 311–325. https://doi.org/10.2307/215575.

Idedhyana, Ida Bagus, Ngakan Putu Sueca, Ngakan Ketut Acwin Dwijendra, and Ida Bagus Wirawibawa. "Architecture of Padmasana Tiga in Besakih Temple, Bali Indonesia: Interpreted from the Concept of Shiva Siddhanta". *International Journal of Advanced Science and Technology* 29, no. 11s (2020): 13–26. https://www.researchgate.net/publication/341991004.

Leonard, Alex. "Learning to Surf in Kuta, Bali". *Review of Indonesian and Malaysian Affairs* 41, no. 1 (2007): 3–32. https://www.academia.edu/4656753/Learning_to_surf_in_Kuta_Bali.

Picard, Michel. "Bali: The Discourse of Cultural Tourism". In *EspacesTemps.net*, 2010. https://www.espacestemps.net/en/articles/bali-the-discourse-of-cultural-tourism/?output=pdf.

Picard, Michel. "Cultural Heritage and Tourist Capital: Cultural Tourism in Bali". In *International Tourism: Identity and Change*, edited by Marie Francois Lanfant, John B. Allcock & Edward M. Bruner, 44–66. London: Sage Publications, 1995.

Pickel-Chevalier, Sylvine, and Budarma Ketut. "Towards Sustainable Tourism in Bali". *Mondes du Tourisme Online* Hors-série (2016). https://doi.org/10.4000/tourisme.1187.

Pringle, Robert. *A Short History of Bali: Indonesia's Hindu Realm*. Australia: Allen & Unwin, 2004.

Vickers, Adrian. *Bali: A Paradise Created*. Singapore: Tuttle, 2012.

Vickers, Adrian. "Creating Heritage in Ubud, Bali". *Wacana* 20, no. 2 (2019): 250–265. https://doi.org/10.17510/wacana.v20i2.747.

Mumbai (Bombay)

Bhutto, Fatima. *New Kings of the World: Dispatches from Bollywood, Dizi and K-Pop*. New York: Columbia Global Reports, 2019.

Bromfield, Louis. *Night in Bombay*. 1940. New York: Bantam Books, 1946.

Çelikel, Mehmet Ali. "Heteroglossia and Multicultural Uniformity in Rushdie's Novels". *Journal of Narrative and Language Studies* 7, no. 12 (2019), 9–15. https://gcris.pau.edu.tr/bitstream/11499/28321/1/Heteroglossia%20and%20Multicultural%20Uniformity.pdf.

Iyer, Nityaa Lakshmi, and Atul Kumar. "Art Deco in Mumbai: Oval & Marine Drive". *Art Deco New York Journal* 3, no. 2 (2018): 19–21. https://www.artdeco.org/mumbai-art-deco-architecture.

Kavoori, Anandam P., and Aswin Punathambekar, eds. *Global Bollywood*. New York and London: New York University Press, 2008.

Lorenzen, Mark. "Go West: The Growth of Bollywood". Creative Encounters Working Paper no. 26. Frederiksberg: imagine... CBS, 2009. https://research.cbs.dk/en/publications/go-west-the-growth-of-bollywood.

Mehta, Rini Battacharya, and Rajeshwari V. Pandharipande, eds. *Bollywood and Globalization: Indian Popular Cinema, Nation, and Diaspora*. London: Anthem Press, 2011.

Mehta, Suketu. *Maximum City: Bombay Lost and Found*. New York: Vintage Books, 2004.

Mirza, Meher. "India's Brilliant Bombay Duck". *BBC Travel Online*, 21 January 2020. https://www.bbc.com/travel/article/20200120-indias-brilliant-bombay-duck.

Perry, Alex. "Queen of Bollywood". *Time*, Asia ed. 162, no. 16, 27 October 2003. https://content.time.com/time/subscriber/article/0,33009,524507,00.html.

Prakash, Gyan. *Mumbai Fables: A History of an Enchanted City*. Princeton: Princeton University Press, 2010.

Ramani, Navin. *Bombay Art Deco Architecture: A Visual Journey (1930–1953)*. 2nd ed. New Delhi: Roli Books, 2016.

Rushdie, Salman. *The Ground Beneath Her Feet*. 1999. London: Vintage, 2000.

Tharoor, Shashi. *India: From Midnight to the Millennium and Beyond*. 1997. New York: Arcade Publishing, 2012.

UNESCO World Heritage Committee. "Victorian Gothic and Art Deco Ensembles of Mumbai". *Executive Summary and Nomination Text*, 2018. https://whc.unesco.org/en/list/1480/documents/.

Kaohsiung & Busan

Ahn, SooJeong. *The Pusan International Film Festival, South Korean Cinema and Globalization*. Hong Kong: Hong Kong University Press, 2012.

Architectuul. "Kaohsiung Stadium". https://architectuul.com/architecture/kaohsiung-stadium.

Bird, Isabella L. *Korea and Her Neighbours*. New York: Fleming H. Revell Company, 1897. Project Gutenberg Ebook, 2022. https://www.gutenberg.org/cache/epub/69300/pg69300-images.html.

Busan Metropolitan City. "Come and Enjoy the City of Festivals, Busan". 13 September 2010. https://www.busan.go.kr/eng/bsnews01/795863.

Couch, Chris, and Sarah-Jane Farr. "Museums, Galleries, Tourism and Regeneration: Some Experiences from Liverpool". *Built Environment (1978–)* 26, no. 2 (2000): 152–163. http://www.jstor.org/stable/23288855.

Hung, Kun-Yao, Ming-Hung Lin, and Sung-Lin Hsueh. "A Study on Tourism Development Strategy of Kaohsiung City in Taiwan after Urban Style Regeneration". In *The 2018 International Conference of Organizational Innovation, KnE Social Sciences*, 1617–1629. https://doi.org/10.18502/kss.v3i10.3497.

Kaohsiung City Government. *Kaohsiung City Voluntary Local Review*, 2021. https://www.iges.or.jp/en/vlr/kaohsiung.

Kim, Eun Mee, ed. *The Four Asian Tigers: Economic Development and the Global Political Economy*. United Kingdom: Emerald Group Publishing Limited, 1998.

Lus Arana, Koldo. "Behind the Bilbao Effect: An Overnight Success in 20 Years". *MAS Context* 30–31 (2017): 27–33. https://mascontext.com/issues/bilbao/behind-the-bilbao-effect-an-overnight-success-in-20-years.

Mecanoo. "National Kaohsiung Center for the Arts". 2018. https://www.mecanoo.nl/Projects/project/54/National-Kaohsiung-Centre-for-the-Arts.

Numazaki, Ichiro. "The Export-Oriented Industrialization of Pacific Rim Nations and Their Presence in the Global Market". In *The Four Asian Tigers: Economic Development and the Global Political Economy*, edited by Kim Eun Mee, 61–89. United Kingdom: Emerald Group Publishing Limited, 1998.

Roy, Denny. *Taiwan: A Political History*. Ithaca, NY: Cornell University Press, 2003.

Shin, Kwang Yeong. "The Political Economy of Economic Growth in East Asia: South Korea and Taiwan". In *The Four Asian Tigers: Economic Development and the Global Political Economy*, edited by Kim Eun Mee, 3–31. United Kingdom: Emerald Group Publishing Limited, 1998.

Staff Writer, with CNA. "Kaohsiung Library is the World's First Column-Suspended 'Green' Building". *Taipei Times*, 29 August 2017. https://www.taipeitimes.com/News/taiwan/archives/2017/08/29/2003677381.

Vogel, Ezra F. *The Four Little Dragons: The Spread of Industrialization in East Asia*. Cambridge, MA: Harvard University Press, 1991.

Dubai

Ali, Syed. *Dubai: Gilded Cage*. New Haven and London: Yale University Press, 2010.

Boodrookas, Alex, and Arang Keshavarzian. "The Forever Frontier of Urbanism: Historicizing Persian Gulf Cities". *International Journal of Urban and Regional Research* 43, no. 1 (2019): 14–29. https://doi.org/10.1111/1468-2427.12664.

Carter, Robert. "The History and Prehistory of Pearling in the Persian Gulf". *Journal of the Economic and Social History of the Orient* 48, no. 2 (2005): 139–209. http://www.jstor.org/stable/25165089.

Davidson, Christopher M. *Dubai: The Vulnerability of Success*. London: Hurst & Company, 2008.

K., Aqil. "Pearl Industry in the UAE Region in 1869–1938: Its Construction, Reproduction, and Decline". *RUDN Journal of Sociology* 18, no. 3 (2018): 452–469. https://doi.org/10.22363/2313-2272-2018-18-3-452-469.

Kamrava, Mehran, ed. *Gateways to the World: Port Cities in the Persian Gulf*. London: Hurst & Company, 2016.

Kanna, Ahmed, ed. *The Superlative City: Dubai and the Urban Condition in the Early Twenty-First Century*. Cambridge, MA: Harvard University Graduate School of Design, 2013.

Kennedy, T. "Encoded Visions of Place at Dubai Creek". *Sustainable Development and Planning IV* 1 (2009): 401–408. https://doi.org/10.2495/SDP090381.

Krane, Jim. *City of Gold: Dubai and the Dream of Capitalism*. New York: Picador, 2010.

McCabe, Ciaran, and Susan Roaf. "The Wind Towers of Bastakiya: Assessing the Role of the Towers in the Whole House Ventilation System Using Dynamic Thermal Modelling". *Architectural Science Review* 56, no. 2 (2013): 183–194. https://doi.org/10.1080/00038628.2012.723398.

Mounajjed, Nadia. *Visual Culture(s) in the Gulf: An Anthology*. Cambridge: Gulf Research Centre, 2016.

Onley, James. "Britain and the Gulf Sheikdoms, 1820–1971: The Politics of Protection". Center for International and Regional Studies. *Occasional Paper No. 4*. Qatar: Georgetown University School of Foreign Service, 2009. https://repository.library.georgetown.edu/bitstream/handle/10822/558294/CIRSOccasionalPaper4JamesOnley2009.pdf.

Potter, Lawrence G. "Society in the Persian Gulf: Before and After Oil". Center for Regional and International Studies. *Occasional Paper No. 18*. Qatar: Georgetown University School of Foreign Service, 2017. https://repository.library.georgetown.edu/bitstream/handle/10822/1045467/CIRSOccasionalPaper18LawrencePotter2017.pdf

Shahin, Jasmine. "Dubai: City Branding or Place Making?" Paper presented at EURAU 2014: "Composite Cities", European Symposium on Research in Architecture and Urban Design, Istanbul, 12–14 November 2014. https://www.academia.edu/9757037/Dubai_City_Branding_or_Place_Making.

Thesiger, William. *Arabian Sands*. London: Longmans, 1959.

Shenzhen & Wuhan

Chen, Guoli, and Li Jianggan. *Seeing the Unseen: Behind Chinese Tech Giants' Global Venturing*. New Jersey: John Wiley & Sons, 2022.

Chen, Lulu Yilun. *Influence Empire: The Story of Tencent & China's Tech Ambition*. London: Hodder & Stoughton, 2022.

Deng, Xiaoping. 1 August 1985. "Special Economic Zones Should Shift their Economy from a Domestic Orientation to an External Orientation". In *The Selected Works of Deng Xiaoping*, Vol. 3 (1982–1992). Beijing: Foreign Languages Press, 1994. Online ed. https://dengxiaopingworks.wordpress.com/2013/03/18/special-economic-zones-should-shift-their-economy-from-a-domestic-orientation-to-an-external-orientation/.

Du, Juan. *The Shenzhen Experiment: The Story of China's Instant City*. Cambridge, MA: Harvard University Press, 2020.

Fang, Fang. *Wuhan Diary: Dispatches from a Quarantined City*. Translated by Michael Berry. USA: HarperVia, 2020.

Freymann, Eyck. *One Belt One Road: Chinese Power Meets the World*. Cambridge, MA: Harvard University Asia Centre, 2021.

Gervasi, Marco. *East Commerce: A Journey Through China E-Commerce and the Internet of Things*. United Kingdom: John Wiley & Sons, 2016.

Hu, Richard. *The Shenzhen Phenomenon: From Fishing Village to Global Knowledge City*. London: Routledge, 2021.

Ma, Winston. *China's Mobile Economy: Opportunities in the Largest and Fastest Information Consumption Boom*. United Kingdom: John Wiley & Sons, 2017.

United Nations Conference on Trade and Development (UNCTAD). "Special Economic Zones". *World Investment Report* (2019): 127–206. https://unctad.org/system/files/official-document/WIR2019_CH4.pdf.

Winter, Tim. "Geocultural Power: China's Belt and Road Initiative". *Geopolitics* 26, no. 5 (2021): 1376–1399. https://doi.org/10.1080/14650045.2020.1718656.

Winter, Tim. "Silk Road Diplomacy: Geopolitics and Histories of Connectivity". *International Journal of Cultural Policy* 26, no. 7 (2020): 898–912. https://doi.org/10.1080/10286632.2020.1765164.

Wuchangqu difangzhi bangongshi 武昌区地方志办公室. *Wuchang jiucheng* 武昌旧城 [The old city of Wuchang]. Wuhan: Wuhan Chubanshe, 2017.

Xi, Jinping. "Work Together to Build the Silk Road Economic Belt and the 21st Century Maritime Silk Road". Speech by H.E. Xi Jinping, President of the People's Republic of China, at the Opening Ceremony of The Belt and Road Forum for International Cooperation, 14 May 2017. https://www.fmprc.gov.cn/mfa_eng/wjdt_665385/zyjh_665391/201705/t20170527_678618.html.

Zhao, Jianying et al 赵剑英等. *Shenzhen jingyan yu Zhongguo tese shehui zhuyi daolu* 深圳经验与中国特色社会主义道路 [The experience of Shenzhen and the path of socialism with Chinese characteristics]. Beijing: Zhongguo Shehui Kexue Chubanshe, 2020.

Image Credits

All photographs and archival images are the author's except where listed below. A handful of maps in the book were created by the author for illustrative purposes, by way of adapting existing map resources also incorporated in the list below.

Collection of Asian Civilisations Museum and Peranakan Museum, National Heritage Board. Pages x, 11, 17, 55, 109, 139, 156, 168, 175, 193, 242, 255.

Collection of Asian Civilisations Museum and Peranakan Museum, National Heritage Board. Photograph by the author. Pages 4, 85, 158.

Collection of National Museum of Singapore, National Heritage Board. Photograph by the author. Page 88.

Images in the Public Domain. Pages vi, ix, xii, xv, xix, xxii, 13, 26, 29, 35, 38, 40, 60, 66, 75, 82, 90, 92, 94 – 95, 102, 113, 125, 134 – 135, 145, 160, 170, 226, 263, 272, 291, 320, 336.

Images from Creative Commons.

Page xvii, "Dhows" by Rod Waddington, CC BY-SA 2.0, https://www.flickr.com/photos/rod_waddington/7899247776/in/photolist-ai5MfN-d32Hab-9md12o-2ntX5cc-d7qwEU-9pgeEK-bR397n-4v5ChJ-fKYQjs-26MioLf-4ppzTx-2hYp1jv-pjETKz-UxvjsT-7gijSB-926agd-39aqZ-9232MF-7yAwts-2hZ8rhr-aA5hF3-bZFn41-6N276u-5qqZSS-kLj7A.

Pages xx – xxi, "Equirectangular-projection-topographic-world.jpg" By Gundan - Own work, CC BY-SA 4.0, https://commons.wikimedia.org/w/index.php?curid=92974338. [Cropped, recoloured and adapted.]

Page 2, "Borobudur 25" by Gryffindor - Own work, CC BY-SA 3.0, https://commons.wikimedia.org/w/index.php?curid=15718507.[Cropped.]

Page 6, "Topographic30deg N0E90.png" By Koba-chan, CC BY-SA 3.0, https://commons.wikimedia.org/w/index.php?curid=166887. [Cropped, recoloured and adapted.]

Page 18, "Five Pavilion Bridge and White Pagoda 2017.jpg" by Amarespeco - Own work, CC BY-SA 4.0, https://commons.wikimedia.org/w/index.php?curid=60981150. [Cropped.]

Page 33, "Telaga Batu inscription" by Gunawan Kartapranata - Own work, CC BY-SA 3.0, https://commons.wikimedia.org/w/index.php?curid=12121980.

Page 42, "Twin pagodas of Kaiyuan Temple" by Windmemories - Own work, CC BY-SA 4.0, https://commons.wikimedia.org/w/index.php?curid=128340161. [Cropped.]

Page 44, "Chinese history large - 51E146W, 14N52N-color topography.png" By Hugo Lopez – Wikimedia Commons user: Yug - Own work, CC BY-SA 3.0, https://commons.wikimedia.org/w/index.php?curid=15907354. [Cropped, recoloured and adapted.]

Page 47, "Quanzhou Qingjing Si 20120229-03.jpg" by Zhangzhugang - Own work, CC BY-SA 4.0, https://commons.wikimedia.org/w/index.php?curid=19159883. [Cropped.]

Page 51, "Entrance corridor area of Jami mosque from the eastern wall" by Mufaddal abdul Hussain - Own work, CC BY-SA 3.0, https://commons.wikimedia.org/w/index.php?curid=21046347.

Page 58, "Africa topography map.png" By Bamse - self-made, using GMT, CC BY-SA 3.0, https://commons.wikimedia.org/w/index.php?curid=3248552. [Cropped, recoloured and adapted.]

Page 64, "Dhow01" by SajjadF - Own work, CC BY-SA 3.0, https://commons.wikimedia.org/w/index.php?curid=29421820. [Cropped.]

Page 71, "Mishkal Mosque" by Axel Drainville, CC BY-SA 3.0, https://www.joinpaperplanes.com/mishkal-mosque-in-calicut/. [Cropped.]

Page 77, "夏天的明故宫午朝门" by 徐然宽 - Own work, CC BY-SA 3.0, https://commons.wikimedia.org/w/index.php?curid=28097508. [Cropped and recoloured.]

Page 131, "Hội An, Chùa Cầu, 2020-01 CN-02.jpg" by © Steffen Schmitz (Carschten), CC BY-SA 4.0, https://commons.wikimedia.org/w/index.php?curid=89105001.

Page 143, "West Asia non political with water system." By DEMIS Mapserver, CC BY-SA 3.0, https://commons.wikimedia.org/w/index.php?curid=92163731. [Cropped, recoloured, and adapted.]

Page 150, "Chepauk Palace – Minar" by Williamsatish25 - Own work, CC BY-SA 3.0, https://commons.wikimedia.org/w/index.php?curid=21642371. [Recoloured.]

Page 165, "Phinisi at Paotere, Makassar - 1.jpg" by S.Sarafian - Own work, CC BY-SA 4.0, https://commons.wikimedia.org/w/index.php?curid=61377441.

Page 184, "Victoria Memorial Hall, Kolkata.jpg" by Samitkumarsinha - Own work, CC BY-SA 3.0, https://commons.wikimedia.org/w/index.php?curid=20996677. [Cropped.]

Page 231, "Beit al Ajaib, 2010.jpg" by Willem van der Horst - https://www.flickr.com/photos/willemvdh/5335717482/, CC BY 2.0, https://commons.wikimedia.org/w/index.php?curid=41950148.

Page 233, "Karte der Konzessionsgebiete in Tientsin.jpg" by Maximilian Dörrbecker (Chumwa) - Own work, CC BY-SA 2.0, https://commons.wikimedia.org/w/index.php?curid=29301826. [Recoloured and adapted: German text translated into English.]

Pages 266 – 267, "Tokyo Station Marunouchi Building.jpg" by Kakidai - Own work, CC BY-SA 4.0, https://commons.wikimedia.org/w/index.php?curid=71070115. [Cropped.]

Page 275, "Lawang sewu semarang" by Galuhranitiara - Own work, CC BY-SA 4.0, https://commons.wikimedia.org/w/index.php?curid=112161218. [Cropped.]

Page 284, "Changi Airport Control Tower – panoramio" by AudaCity3371, CC BY-SA 3.0, https://commons.wikimedia.org/w/index.php?curid=56317849. [Cropped.]

Page 294, "Legong danseressen op Bali, KITLV 180901" by Anonymous - http://hdl.handle.net/1887.1/item:840821, CC BY 4.0, https://commons.wikimedia.org/w/index.php?curid=104903876.

Page 317, "Kaohsiung Music Center" by Hanyu Hsieh - Own work, CC BY-SA 4.0, https://commons.wikimedia.org/w/index.php?curid=91218719.

Page 325, "Al Bastakiya of Dubai" by Phil6007 - Own work, CC BY-SA 4.0, https://commons.wikimedia.org/w/index.php?curid=68459351. [Cropped.]

Page 328, "Tencent Seafront Tower in Dec2020" by Charlie fong - Own work, CC BY-SA 4.0, https://commons.wikimedia.org/w/index.php?curid=115342476. [Cropped.]

Index

rihlah, 33, 50, 52, 58

S

Safavid,126, 142–143, 160, 228
sakoku, 130, 132, 136–138, 245
Sang Nila Utama, 80, 291
Sanskrit, 3, 5, 8, 25, 29, 32, 36, 55, 82, 221, 223
Sassanian, 7
Sayyid, Seyyid, 116, 166, 226–229
shahbandar, 64, 86
Shiraz, 11, 50
shuinsen ("red-seal ships"), 126, 134–135
Silk Road, 327, 331–332
slave, 10, 13, 15, 32, 64, 66, 100–101, 114, 118, 120, 122, 132, 138, 226–228, 231
Song dynasty, 27, 33, 44, 47, 74, 78
South China Sea, 5, 107
spices, 45, 54, 62, 66, 68, 72, 91, 95, 101, 112, 119–120, 122, 132, 141–142, 144, 146, 149, 180, 250, 325
Srivijaya, 6, 8, 28–33, 35–39, 45, 51, 80, 82, 84, 86, 159, 292, 300
steamship,208, 215, 218–220, 234–235, 288, 295, 314
stone town, 66, 225–226, 229–231
streamline moderne, 259, 261, 302
Suez Canal, 62, 121, 178, 217–218, 220, 229–230, 274, 303
Sulalat al-Salatin, 80–81, 83, 86, 292
Swahili, 10, 45, 51–52, 58, 61, 63–66, 68, 76, 94, 145, 178, 200, 225–226, 228–230, 321

T

taipan, 191, 196–197, 261
Tang dynasty, 4–5, 10, 17–18, 20, 23, 35, 43, 78, 172, 336
Tang Shipwreck / Belitung Wreck, 11, 16
tianxia (tenka, thien ha), 76–77, 133–134, 245, 270, 332
Tokugawa, 104–105, 126, 132–135, 211, 240, 265, 267
treaty, 138, 157, 167, 171, 191, 193–194, 196, 199, 202, 207–213, 226, 233–234, 236, 238, 241, 243, 251, 257–258, 267–269, 311, 313–314, 334–335

U

UNESCO, 47, 67, 97, 105, 113, 127, 166, 179, 202, 229, 251, 304, 315

V

Vereenigde Oost-Indische Compagnie (VOC), 104, 117–123, 127, 137–139, 142, 148–150, 161–162, 170, 172, 200, 221, 276, 313

W

Western powers, 194, 209, 233–234, 242–243, 245, 257, 267–268, 270, 335
World War I, 181, 237, 258, 260, 332, 335
World War II, 4, 238, 240, 264–266, 270, 275, 279, 296, 335

X

Xiyang ("Western Ocean"), 67, 74, 76, 78
Xuanzong Emperor, 17–18, 24

Y

Yangzi River, 16, 19–20, 74, 234, 334, 337
Yongle Emperor, 67, 74, 77, 233
Yuan dynasty, 45, 49, 75

Z

Zanj, 13, 15, 63, 66–67, 228
Zheng He, 67, 72, 74–79, 84, 223, 332